THE CURIOUS

BARTENDER'S

AGAVE SAFARI

THE CURIOUS

BARTENDER'S
AGAVE SAFARI
DISCOVERING AND APPRECIATING MEXICO'S
TEQUILAS, MEZCALS & MORE

TRISTAN STEPHENSON

LONDON · NEW YORK

Designer: Geoff Borin
Editor: Nathan Joyce
Editorial director: Julia Charles
Head of production: Patricia Harrington
Creative director: Leslie Harrington
Indexer: Hilary Bird
Photographer: Addie Chinn

Published in 2025 by
Ryland Peters & Small
20–21 Jockey's Fields
London WC1R 4BW
and
1452 Davis Bugg Road
Warrenton, NC 27589

www.rylandpeters.com

10 9 8 7 6 5 4 3 2 1

ISBN: 978-1-78879-679-8

A CIP record for this book is available from the
British Library.

US Library of Congress CIP data has been applied for.

Printed in China

CONTENTS

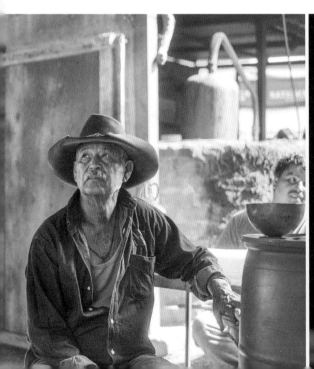

INTRODUCTION

The passenger footwell of our trusty VW Jetta has in it two legs (mine), a laptop and a few books, a collection of empty beer bottles, plus half a dozen bottles of partially consumed mezcal, tequila and raicilla. There are many more bottles clinking together in the boot and more that didn't make it this far. Over the past few weeks we have travelled through six Mexican states, discovering the spirit of Mexico in every sense of the term. Addie is in the back, camera in each hand as usual. He gasps at something beautiful out of the window – an impressive giant cardon cactus on this occasion – and the camera shutter clicks. Addie remarks for the thousandth time that there won't be enough pages in this book to fit all of his photos.

In the driver's seat is Pancho, whose ringing falsetto impressively matches Javier Solís' "Esclave y Amo" even as we suddenly swerve to avoid a pot hole in the road. Pancho is ostensibly our driver and translator, but to describe him that way would dramatically undersell his capability and character. Yes, he's the tequila industry's go-to guy for taxis and interpretation, but, with 16 years' experience of shuttling tequila nerds across Mexico, he has also built a vast knowledge of agave spirits matched only by his passion for sharing it. He also happens to own the best agave spirits bar in Guadalajara: Farmacia Rita Pérez.

Then there is me. Over the past 20 years, I have travelled to 100 countries and over 500 distilleries, seeking out spirit makers and attempting to understand how they make alcohol and why they make it. One thing that I have consistently found is that spirits have a deep connection to the environmental and cultural history of a place. The nature of a spirit captures the history and politics of a region in its methods of production as well as its legislative control. It speaks of tradition handed down between generations, of community and survival. Our spirits inspire songs and stories, mark rites of

passage and toasts to the dead, not to mention the fact that they capture the flavours of the plants with which we share the land.

In this last week I sampled a mezcal made by a teenager in rural Michoacán. He's the sixth generation of his family to produce agave spirits. The drink had been distilled from wild agave harvested on nearby mountain slopes along with the body of a coyote.

The week before that we shared a meal with four generations of the same family who were making the agave spirit raicilla on a small ranch in the mountains of western Jalisco. Numerous types of agave were growing all around us. The children played around the fermentation vats while the mothers made salsa and cooked tortillas on an open fire and the men packed a paste of agave fibres around the edge of a tiny copper still to seal it shut. All while the sweet, vegetal smell of cooked agave filled the air and the pungent, green, smack of raicilla coated our mouths. A few days before that we experienced a drug-like "high" from mezcal that cannot legally be called a mezcal made on the foothills of the Colima volcano, which may be where agave spirits first originated.

We have shared beers and mezcal with *jimadores* (agave farmers) cutting razor-sharp agaves on dusty hills in Michoacán, and sipped $300 (£230) tequilas with the grandest families in Jalisco, the culturally rich and economically vital Mexican state which, besides being the home of tequila, is also the birthplace of mariachi music. We have mixed mezcal and tequila in every conceivable way, visited and tasted hundreds of products ranging from those produced by multinational-owned mega-distilleries to the painstakingly small outputs from some of the most humble and hard-to-get-to distilleries in the world. We have witnessed a culture built around agave spirits and a respect for a plant that may be unparalleled in its depth and significance. Hardly surprising, as the indigenous

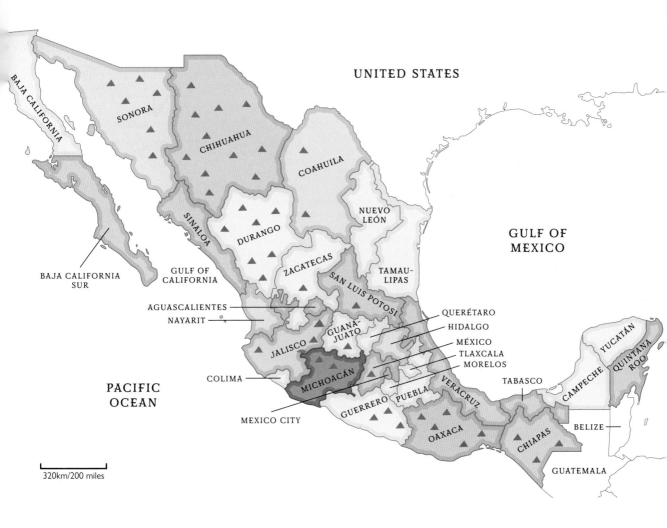

UNITED STATES

BAJA CALIFORNIA

SONORA

CHIHUAHUA

COAHUILA

NUEVO LEÓN

GULF OF MEXICO

BAJA CALIFORNIA SUR

GULF OF CALIFORNIA

SINALOA

DURANGO

ZACATECAS

SAN LUIS POTOSI

TAMAU-LIPAS

AGUASCALIENTES

NAYARIT

QUERÉTARO

HIDALGO

MÉXICO

TLAXCALA

MORELOS

GUANA-JUATO

JALISCO

COLIMA

PACIFIC OCEAN

MICHOACÁN

MEXICO CITY

GUERRERO

PUEBLA

VERACRUZ

TABASCO

CAMPECHE

YUCATÁN

QUINTANA ROO

BELIZE

OAXACA

CHIAPAS

GUATEMALA

320km/200 miles

Nahuatl of western Mexico literally worshipped the agave, in the form of the 100-breasted god Mayahuel. It's a bold statement, but I do not think anywhere in the world has a deeper connection with their native spirit than Mexico.

You're reading this book so you probably already have a good idea of what tequila and mezcal taste like. Hopefully you have already overcome the challenging circumstances of first contact that many of us experience, which tends to take place in a dingy nightclub or at the back of your friend's parents liquor cabinet, always with a bad-quality product and usually followed by sickness and a hangover. Hopefully you have enjoyed your first sip of authentically produced tequila or mezcal that opens up a new world of flavour for exploration.

For me that happened many years ago, but my journey through Mexico has challenged my preconceptions and broadened my appreciation much further than I thought possible. The diversity of agaves, production styles, culture and scale mean that the agave spirits' category is impossibly big to explore in its entirety and that new interpretations or revivals of old practices are occurring constantly.

This book is a journey through some of the heartlands of agave spirits production. It is a physical, geographical journey, but also a historical, cultural and spiritual one. On the way we will explore different producers, and their stories and philosophies, as well as the story of Mexican spirit: its food, cocktails, music, geography and politics. By the end I hope to have provided you with a strong taste of what makes this country so special and what makes agave spirits one of the most exciting of all the world's spirits. Above all I hope that it makes you curious to embark on your own journey through the flavour of Mexico.

7

THE TEQUILA VALLEY

On the approach to the town of Tequila, the landscape transforms into vast fields of blue agave plants, stretching out like a spiky sea under the warm Mexican sun. The town itself exudes a charming, rustic vibe, with cobbled streets and colonial buildings painted in vibrant colours. The air is often filled with the sweet, treacle aroma of cooking agave such is the number of distilleries in the area. This means that the drive into Tequila is not just scenic, but a gateway to a rich, cultural heritage centered around Mexico's most famous spirit.

ZACATECAS

NAYARIT

TEQUILA

1   4
2   AMATITÁN
3
5   EL ARENAL

VOLCÁN DE
TEQUILA

GUADALAJARA

LAGO DE CHAPALA

JALISCO

1   JOSE CUERVO

2   ARETTE

3   FORTALEZA

4   DON ABRAHAM

5   CASCAHUÍN

COLIMA

80km/50 miles

JOSE CUERVO

La Primera

Tequila is one of countless regional agave spirits produced in Mexico that have in the past been known collectively as *vino de mezcal* or mezcals. Vino de mezcal from in and around the town of Tequila began to prosper and garner recognition around the mid-19th century through a combination of factors, including a ready supply of fermentable material (agaves), wealthy land owners looking to capitalise on local demand for alcohol, and a favourable trading network to transport it into the US. In time, vino de mezcal de Tequila was shortened, first to mezcal de Tequila and eventually to just "tequila".

On my first trip to Jalisco 15 years ago, I was hosted by Jose Cuervo as part of a small crew of bartenders from the UK. We spent the better part of a week in Guadalajara (the Jaliscan capital), the town of Tequila itself and other parts of the Tequila-Amatitán Valley. Located an hour west of Guadalajara, the valley is the historical birthplace of tequila, and it gets its name from the Volcán de Tequila, a 2,920m (9,500ft) dormant volcano, named for the Hispanicised *tequitlan,* which means "place of work" in the Nahua language. To the north of the volcano, we find the three main hubs of tequila production in the area: Tequila, Amatitán and El Arenal.

Santiago de Tequila (as Tequila town was originally known) was founded in 1530 by Franciscan friars in an attempt to culturally assimilate the indigenous populace. The locals fiercely resisted Spanish encroachment, engaging in guerrilla warfare and using their knowledge of the rugged volcano and canyons as natural fortifications. Resistance was futile, however, and many were forced into *encomiendas* (a system of forced labour) or *repartimientos* (distributions of indigenous workers to Spanish landowners). The indigenous populations were slowly subjugated but their knowledge and cultural recognition of the agave was never lost.

During our stay we learned that tequila is made from the blue Weber agave, a variety native to Mexico that belongs to one of almost 300 identified agave species. Contrary to popular opinion, agaves are succulents, not cactuses. Comprising a rosette of barbed, fibrous, spear-like leaves known as *pencas*, the blue Weber agave takes five to seven years to reach full maturity, by which point it is around two metres (6ft) high and about the same in width. Proper maturation is usually indicated by the sudden protrusion of a *quiote* – a central stem that extends upwards of four metres. This stem, which looks like a supersized asparagus (agave is a relative of asparagus) quickly flowers for pollination, produces some seeds, and then the whole plant dies. One of the jobs of the agave farmer, or *jimador*, is to *capón* (castrate) the quiote before it flowers. This redirects the energy the plant had intended to use for reproduction to amass in the base of the plant. The jimador then cuts away the outer leaves and roots, leaving behind a large egg-shaped mass called a *piña*, named for its visual similarity to a pineapple. The piña is the heart of the agave plant and the basic material from which all agave spirits, including tequila, are made.

The rest of the process is fairly straightforward in its premise but, as we will see, can be achieved in a multitude of ways, each of which affects the outcome and thus the taste and quality of the spirit. Generally speaking though, the piña is cooked to convert its starches into sugars and then milled or mashed up to release its juices. These juices are fermented to create a kind of agave wine called *mosto*, which is then distilled through a process of evaporation followed by concentration to make a spirit. This spirit is put in oak barrels and aged for two to 12 months and bottled as *reposado* (rested) or for one to three years when it becomes *añejo* (aged). For more than three years, it's *extra-añejo*. Un-aged tequila is a *blanco*, and if you blend blanco with an aged tequila it's known as *joven* (young). All tequila must be bottled between 35 and 55% ABV for the Mexican market and over 40% for the US market.

We drive deeper into the belly of Tequila and our passage slows. The streets are alive with barrel-shaped tequila tour buses, taco stands, hat sellers and, of course, tequila bars. What was 150 years ago a quiet rural village with a handful of vino de mezcal producers has become something of a tequila theme park. The tequila market is growing at around 5% a year, fuelled by the revival of cocktail culture, celebrity endorsements and brand ownership, a rising number of super-premium tequilas, and increased interest in authentically produced spirits and in Mexican culture.

The tequila market is expected to grow from roughly $12bn (£9bn) in 2024 to $19bn (£14.5bn) by 2032. Mexico and the US are responsible for around 95% of the global market, with the US spending $7bn (£5.5bn) on it in 2024. Tequila and agave spirits are set to become the biggest spirit category in the US, having eclipsed American whiskey in 2022 and very likely toppling vodka – America's favourite spirit for over half a century – by the time you read this.

To that end, the small town of Tequila earned the title of a *pueblo mágico* or "magic city" by the Mexican government, denoting its importance for tourism-related development. Partnering with the National Geographic Society and Mondo Cuervo, the government plans to turn Tequila into a cutting-edge, interactive tourist hotspot.

To our left we pass the office of the Consejo Regulador del Tequila (CRT). Established in 1994, the CRT is a private non-profit company certified by the Mexican government to oversee the production, labelling and marketing of tequila in accordance with the Norma Oficial Mexicana (NOM), which lays out the rules as to how products should be made.

The NOM states that tequila must be made from a minimum of 51% blue agave with the remaining balance coming from non-agave sources such as cane sugar or molasses. To be called 100% blue agave tequila, it must be made from 100% blue agave with no other sugars added during fermentation. Additives such as colourings, sweeteners and glycerin (used to improve texture) are permitted up to 1% of the total volume. In addition to the NOM, there is the Denominación de Origen (DO), which sets out where tequila can be made, currently including 181 municipalities across five Mexican states comprising all of Jalisco and certain municipalities in the states of Guanajuato, Michoacán, Nayarit and Tamaulipas. We'll delve deeper into these often controversial economic, political and geocultural topics later in our journey.

The CRT office in Tequila is actually quite small, with the main office located in the urban sprawl of Guadalajara. I got the chance to have a quick look around on a previous trip, where I saw the four statues of the "Founding Families" of tequila in the office courtyard: Cuervo, Sauza, Peña (of the Herradura brand) and Orendain.

Cuervo is of course the most recognisable name in tequila history. The family story traces back to 1758 when José Antonio Cuervo Valdés acquired land in Tequila, complete with a distillery. He made vino de mezcal at this distillery for some years but his ambitions were thwarted in 1785 when King Charles III of Spain imposed a ban on alcohol production to boost revenue from wines and brandies imported from Spain. It's possible, if not likely, that Cuervo kept producing spirit illegally, because when Charles IV lifted the ban in 1795, he immediately granted José Antonio's son, José María Guadalupe de Cuervo y Montaño, a permit to cultivate and distil agave at the apparently ready-to-go Taberna de Cuervo.

When José Guadalupe died, the company passed to his children and then son-in-law, José Vicente Albino Rojas. Vicente changed the name of the distillery to *La Rojeña* (The Red Place) and spearheaded modernisation efforts, ramping up production in the process. By 1823 La Rojeña was turning over 400 barrels of vino mezcal de tequila a week. That's 10,000 bottles, though bottles were not used until 1880 when, under the control of the seasoned distiller Jesus Flores, La Rojeña tequila became the first tequila to be packaged in glass.

Following Jesus Flores' passing, his widow Ana González-Rubio inherited La Rojeña. In 1900 she married one of the distillery's trusted administrators, José Cuervo Labastida, the great-grandson of the distillery's founder. Shortly after, the company rebranded its tequila as the now-iconic Jose Cuervo. (Take note: if you want your spirit brand to go stratospheric be sure to give it a man's name beginning with 'J'. Johnnie Walker and Jack Daniel's can testify to this.)

While many of their competitors went bust or fled the country during the Mexican Revolution (1910–1920), Ana and José profited enormously, buying up huge swathes of land securing agave supply for decades to come. Later on in the 20th century, the company passed down through a further two generations, into the control of the Beckmann family who oversaw massive global expansion. Since 2007 Jose Cuervo has traded as a public company but the Beckmanns remain the largest shareholders, and are among the richest families in Mexico.

Today, Jose Cuervo stands as the oldest continuously operating tequila company with verifiable records and is the biggest tequila brand in the world. In 2023, the company sold 9.2 million cases of tequila – just under 20% of the entire category and roughly the same as the next three biggest brands (Patrón, Don Julio and Casamigos) put together. The fifth-biggest brand, 1800, is also a Jose Cuervo brand, as is another of the top-ten sellers, Centenario.

As we continue our drive into Tequila, we near the end of the road. Spanish cedars with their trunks painted white traverse the street and lush potted plants adorn the pavements. Seemingly everyone is wearing a sombrero as the sun beats down on the cobbled street. Dead ahead of us is Jose Cuervo's mustard-coloured fortress, La Rojeña, taking up a massive block of land on the western edge of the town. Big as it may be, it is entirely proportionate to the brand's economic and touristic clout in the region. With its ornate stone paving, manicured gardens and bronze statues of its founders, La Rojeña is one of the most beautiful distilleries in Mexico. But visitors may get the sense that they are missing something. That "something" is Jose Cuervo's closed-gated Los Camichines distillery, 100km (60 miles) away to the east of Guadalajara. That's the real Cuervo workhorse, and the largest distillery in Mexico. There's another distillery in pipeline too, to help process the 15 million agave plants that they own across something like 400 sq. km (150 sq. miles) of land.

Jose Cuervo has produced some great tequilas over the years, with its Reserva De La Familia Extra Añejo blend remaining one of the finest looking and tasting aged tequilas on the market in my opinion. But the vast majority of the portfolio is produced at a scale that sacrifices authenticity and quality. And that doesn't even begin to get into the murky waters of agriculture, sustainability and transparency – but brace yourself, because we will get there. First though, it's time for a drink.

Heading south through Tequila town on Calle Hidalgo we pull up outside one of the most famous tequila bars in the world: La Capilla. *Capilla* is Spanish for "chapel", which is fitting as this bar commands a near holy reverence among tequila pilgrims. There's scaffolding on the walls and two artists are standing high above the doors, working on a huge mural depicting the smiling face of the bar's late owner, Don Javier Delgado, who died in 2020.

Javier was born in Tequila and born *into* tequila, being surrounded by it from an early age. When Javier was still quite young, his father acquired a billiards hall in Tequila town and Javier worked behind the bar, cleaning glasses and wiping tables. Though the exact opening date of the billiards hall isn't clear, it's said that Javier spent at least 70 of his 96 years behind the bar, if not more.

Following his father's passing, Javier didn't have enough money to keep the billiards hall going, so it closed down and Javier transformed his father's old house at 33 Calle Hidalgo into a humble cantina bar, which he named affectionately La Capilla. Javier was a religious man and La Capilla's name reflected that. But for tequila lovers, it took on a different meaning. La Capilla, with its simple yet inviting ambience, was Javier's sanctuary. Decorated with mismatched furniture, sporting trophies, a modest selection of tequilas, one risqué 1970s glamour poster and, in later years, a gallery of framed photographs of the bar industry's fallen friends, it was a haven for locals and visitors alike. In 2011, it was rightfully crowned the 16th best bar in the world – a testament to Don Javier's enduring legacy.

I was fortunate enough to visit La Capilla a couple of times while Don Javier was alive. On the first occasion our group spent around two hours drinking tequila and talking to the locals, culminating in a chilli-eating contest with Javier's friends who were sat at the bar. That ended with me hiccuping/convulsing outside on the street, but not before I paid our tab and requested a receipt for our drinks from Javier. As far as I'm aware, La Capilla didn't have a till system back then and therefore no way of producing receipts, so Javier, apparently having never been asked for one before, hand-wrote our check on a piece of A4 paper. It read "16 batangas, 5 coronas: 600 pesos". I still have that piece of paper and it's a treasured possession.

On this visit, it's early in the day and the bar is quiet as we take our seats around a flimsy white plastic picnic table and order three Batangas. La Capilla became famous in part as the home of this cocktail, a simple mixture of tequila, coke and fresh lime stirred with a knife and served with a salt rim. Don Javier is credited with inventing the Batanga, though Mexicans have been enjoying tequila and coke with a splash of lime for longer even than Javier was around. Pancho tells us that another, even simpler, way of mixing coke and tequila is La Coquitas, where you buy a bottle of coke, take a swig and then top the bottle up with tequila.

Sugared, caffeinated, a little hydrated, and very much adulterated, we pay our bill and leave La Capilla. The car had turned into an oven while we cooled down, but fortunately our next stop is just a short walk to the home of Tequila Arette.

ARETTE

◇◇◇

la Familia

A couple of blocks' walk from La Capilla is El Llano distillery, where Tequila Arette is made. El Llano inhabits a beauty of a building, modelled in the colonial style and painted in sage-green and white with coordinating telegraph poles, and green wooden gates big enough to fit a truck full of agave through. It is owned, as it always has been, by the Orendain family, who are counted as one of the four Founding Families of tequila that I mentioned in the last chapter. Today, the Orendains stand as the only 100% independent, family-owned tequila makers of those original four.

The Orendain tequila history goes back to 1900 when Don Eduardo Orendain combined two smaller distilleries, El Llanito and La Conceptcion, into a new operation called El Llano. His tequila sold well, and in 1926 he expanded his operation, renovating a run-down distillery called *La Mexicana* on the western edge of town. In time most of the production moved there and it's still operational today, as Destilería Orendain, producing a bunch of brands including Batanga, Flecha Azul and Gran Orendain. El Llano closed its doors in the 1960s and remained silent for some 25 years until the next generation, Jaime and Eduardo Orendain, took it over and launched Tequila Arette in 1987.

In the early years the brand was very small – built almost exclusively to supply a single Hong Kong importer. After a couple of years that relationship fizzled out, so the brothers started selling Tequila Arette in Mexico. It was around that time, in the early 1990s, that the Arette brand was shifting from producing *mixto* tequila (where sugar is added to the agave juice before fermentation) to making 100% agave tequila. The distillery continued to produce mixto tequila until 1999, making bulk tequila for US brands as well as supplying Jose Cuervo, Sauza, and Jaime's father and grandfather at the Destilería Orendain. The new millennium marked a

new start for the brothers, as from then on they produced only 100% agave with a renewed focus on their own brands. The Arette family is now headed by Jaime and Eduardo, as well as Eduardo's son, Eduardo Jr.

Don Jaime Orendain appears, as if by magic, as we walk through the distillery gate. He is of middle age and has a quick smile and mischievous spirit. Pancho explains that we're interested in learning more about the Orendain family history but Jaime pulls him in for a tight embrace and corrects him, "It's the *Arette* family!"

Arette is the brand of tequila made at this distillery not a family name, but Jaime explains that everyone who works on the brand is part of Arette family, and as we tour the operation it is clear to see that he means it. He knows the first name of every employee and chats easily with them as we wander through the bottling room. This is the only part of the distillery in operation right now as production has been paused for essential maintenance.

"It takes 20 litres of water to produce one litre of tequila," says Jaime.

The water used in tequila production is drawn from wells that tap into underground aquifers. These aquifers are replenished by rainfall and river systems originating from the nearby Tequila volcano. The volcanic soil in the region is rich in minerals, which contributes to the unique flavour profile of Tequila's spirit. This explains why there are so many old tequila brands packed together in this town as close as bottles on a backbar, "Sauza is behind me," says Jaime. "Cuervo this side, D'Reyes that side, Fortaleza is two blocks from here, Tequileño is a block that way, Don Fulano another block."

Jaime explains that all of the agaves used to make Arette are owned by the family and grown in fields in the Tequila Valley across 500 acres (200 hectares) of land. Agaves mature at slightly different speeds even if they are planted together and there can be a big variance in size between two mature plants. Maturity is important as the quantity of starches in the agave increases over time along with flavour-giving compounds that will bring complexity to the product. Being selective in harvesting, as we will see, is common among producers who strive to make a quality product. However, some of the big brands have got into the habit of harvesting entire fields irrespective of maturity for speed and efficiency and to make way for the next crop.

The piñas of the agave are sometimes halved or quartered in the fields to make them a more manageable size for transportation. But sometimes they arrive at the distillery whole, and can weigh in excess of 70kg (150lbs). Larger piñas are broken down with an axe into smaller pieces before cooking so that everything in the oven is roughly the same size and therefore cooks uniformly.

There are three main ways to cook agave in tequila production. Ranging from traditional to modern they are: by brick oven, by autoclave, and by diffuser. El Llano uses both of the first two. The third (diffuser) is a modern innovation that is both highly efficient and highly controversial – we'll visit them later on in our journey.

Brick ovens are about the size of a small garage and made from brick or stone. In the case of the one here, at El Llano, it was built using a combination of bricks and volcanic rocks all sealed together with a cement made from agave fibres. The agave piñas are loaded in by hand, the steel door is shut, and steam is pumped into the oven for a day or two. Once the steam is turned off, a further day of cooling is allowed, then the doors are opened and the cooked agave revealed.

Cooking the agave makes the water inside the plant heat up and breaks down the fibrous structure that holds the plant together – just like cooking any other vegetable. So it goes that the volume of agave inside the brick oven shrinks as the cook progresses and the water boils out of the plant. The weight of the softening agave plants also squeeze juices out of the ones in the base of the oven. Pipes in the base allow these juices to run off during the cook. The first of these juices are known as *miels amargas* ("bitter honeys") and are usually discarded – they are the first dirty, sappy extracts, which are deemed counter-beneficial to the flavour of tequila. Then come the *miels dulces* ("sweet honeys"), which are rich in sugars with no off notes. These are collected, soon to be mixed back into the milled agave at the point of fermentation.

The other common method, an autoclave, is a cylindrical steel oven that looks a bit like the fuselage of an aircraft, with doors at each end. Autoclaves are typically bigger than brick ovens but come in a variety of sizes. The cooking process uses steam (like the brick oven) but an autoclave can operate under pressure (like a pressure cooker) typically ranging from 1.2 to 1.5 atmospheres. This pressure range raises the boiling point of water inside the autoclave up to about 120°C (248°F), which doesn't

BELOW LEFT The bottling line at Arette is a slick operation, and it's all done by hand (and with hair nets on).

BELOW RIGHT Two cooking methods at Destilería El Llano: the green autoclave and the brick oven behind it. Both turn starches into sugar but each has a subtly different effect on the final spirit.

sound like much, but it can cut the cooking time down to as little as eight hours or less.

As well as being faster, autoclaves are cheaper to operate, easier to install and simpler to repair. It's for these reasons that they've become synonymous with higher volume distilleries. But it's important to stress that autoclave tequila does not automatically mean poor-quality tequila, just as brick-oven cooking shouldn't be assumed to create great tequila. An autoclave is better viewed through a lens of flexibility: indeed it is entirely possible to run an autoclave at low pressure and come very close to imitating the conditions in a brick oven.

"We cook in the autoclave for 18 hours," says Jaime. "We could go faster, but if we go faster... the flavours change." At very high temperatures (and fast cooks) an autoclave can burn the outer skin of the agave and produce some off notes in the finished product.

Here at El Llano, Jaime uses both brick ovens and autoclaves, and they mark the beginning of the delineation between the two ranges of Arette products: Classic (a blend of autoclave and brick oven) and Artesanal (brick oven only).

Each range is also treated slightly differently in the fermentation stage, where the classic is fermented in 18,000-litre (4,750-gallon) stainless-steel fermenters, and Artesanal is fermented in 16,000-litre (4,350-gallon) concrete fermenters. Both of these materials are inert and do not directly impact the flavour of the ferment. But concrete has better insulating properties and thus creates a more stable fermentation environment that warms and cools more gently. This, in turn, produces a different array of flavourful compounds. Then, in distillation, those compounds can be boiled off and selected as the spirit runs off the still.

Classic and Artesanal are distilled using the same equipment but a far smaller "heart cut" – the part of the spirit that is collected for bottling – is taken for the Artesanal line. "It's less volume, but a more concentrated flavour," says Jaime.

For aged tequila, Arette stores most of its casks in a large warehouse a few blocks away, but around 1,000 barrels are held in a building directly across the road from the distillery. Jaime leads us over the road and unlocks the door. As we step inside it's like entering a mausoleum. My eyes take a moment to adjust to the dimness of the light after the brightness of the sun-drenched street, and it's at least 10 degrees cooler in here too. Looking left and right, the long hallway contains stacks of barrels behind huge iron gates that keep them secure. The smell is musty and slightly fruity.

Jaime explains that the Classic and Artesanal ranges also get treated differently in cask, with the Artesanal tending to be nearer the maximum age for reposado and añejo and Classic being a bit younger. Nearly all of the barrels here are ex-bourbon but there are other types being used for experiments and special releases, including some ex-wine casks.

Once outside again, which feels like when you exit a cinema during the daytime, we head next door through an unexceptional looking entrance on the corner of the block. Jaime leads us in to reveal a small tasting room styled like a colonial-era bar with wood panels, a ceiling fan and soft lighting. He takes his position behind the bar and pours us some tequila: Arette Artesanal Blanco (40%). *It's incredibly fresh in the glass; crisp, light and citrusy. These flavours carry through into the taste, along with a slight salinity and grapefruit zest. There's just a touch of bitterness on the finish with a restrained spice and heat.*

My glass is empty so Jaime pours some Arette Artesanal Reposado (40% ABV). *It's pale straw in colour. There's a slight mushroom note on the aroma, along with ginger and brown sugar. On the taste there's a slight tightness*

LEFT Jaime Orendain is like a preacher, baptising true believers with delicious tequila and delivering sermons from the scripture of tequila history.

from the oak. Subtle vanilla and butterscotch form the finish. Next is the Artesanal Añejo (40% ABV). *The vegetal agave note of the blanco has returned a little here, alongside wood and bung-cloth aromas. On the taste there's (bell) pepper, chocolate and coffee.*

"My brother and I are horse lovers," says Jaime. "I get on a horse nearly every day. In fact I rode a horse before I could walk." He points to the bottle of Arette in front of him and the horse's head on the label. "This is Arette," he says. Then he tells us one of the most incredible rags to riches stories I have ever heard.

Lieutenant-Colonel Humberto Mariles was a prize-winning equestrian and perhaps the most ambitious Mexican athlete of his generation. He first met the horse called Arete (one "t") in January 1948 when he was invited by the French Club in Mexico City to inspect a 10-year-old castrated one-eyed stallion that the club wanted to sell. In his younger years Arete had a fall that damaged his eye and took a chunk out of his right ear (his name means "earring"). The club president, also an equestrian, knew that despite his injuries, Arete was a skilled jumper, so he asked Mariles to ride him for a trial. Mariles was astounded by Arete and later recalled that after just two minutes on its back, the horse was the smoothest and most obedient he had ever ridden.

However, when Mariles told the nation that he would take Arete to the 1948 Olympic Games, Miguel Alemán Valdés, the Mexican president, stepped in citing reservations about a one-eyed horse's capability in competition and so its potential to embarrass Mexico. Undeterred, Mariles stole a convoy of army trucks and crossed the border into Texas with Arete and the rest of his entourage before catching a ship to Europe. When the president found out, he was furious and issued an arrest warrant for Mariles. He charged the Mexican ambassador to Italy with the unenviable task of capturing both a senior soldier and prize-winning horse and detaining them. Arete and Mariles arrived in Italy and managed not only to evade the ambassador but also to enter and win a clutch of tournaments. Next it was on to the Olympic Games in London where, in the final run of the day, Mariles and Arete emerged triumphant, clinching two gold medals in equestrian jumping. The pair bagged another bronze medal in eventing and in the wake of their success, the Mexican president phoned Mariles, congratulated him and promoted him to General. To this day, Mariles (and Arete) remain the only Mexicans to win two Olympic golds.

ABOVE Arette Gran Clase Extra Añejo is one of the best extra añejo tequilas on the market, and tastes all the better when served directly by Jaime Orendain.

Jaime pours another tequila, this time the Gran Clase Extra Añejo (40% ABV), which is a $250 (£190) bottle in the US. We toast Arete, "Salut!" *The aroma is very potent, with strong caramels, sweet agave nectar, banana and barbecued pineapple. The extra maturation has somehow returned a great deal of the agave character. It's incredible. The taste is round and polished, buttery and delicious – it's Olympic medal-winning quality!*

Jaime sips his tequila. Addie and I sip ours. Then a shadow passes over Jaime's face. "The story of General Mariles does not have a happy ending," he says.

On 14th August 1964, Mariles was driving home from a party in Mexico City when he was forced off the road. At the next traffic light, Mariles pulled out a pistol and shot the other driver. He was handed a 25-year prison sentence but released after five with a presidential pardon. His troubles persisted however, and in 1972 he faced arrest in Paris for drug smuggling and ultimately died in prison before trial – some say under suspicious circumstances.

Rather then end on a sour note, Jaime pops the cap off a bottle of Arette Fuerte Artesanal 101 Blanco (50.5% ABV), which lightens up the mood no end. *The aroma is brine, minerality, cinnamon, black pepper, citrus, herbs (thyme, sage) and a little ethanol. The taste is intense cooked agave, pepper, earthiness, citrus (particularly orange peel), baking spices, herbs (rosemary, mint), pineapple, and jalapeño heat.*

With an almost equestrian spring in our step we leave the bar and bid Jaime farewell. We don't have far to go...

FORTALEZA

◇◇

El Renacimiento

Directly next-door to El Llano is the white-washed complex of properties that make up the Sauza distillery, Known as La Perseverancia (The Perserverance), this sprawling facility occupies both sides and ends of the street and is spread across many buildings, some of which are connected by overhead pipes. Indeed, on a casual stroll down Francisco Javier Sauza Street, you could easily believe you have stumbled into the distillery itself, as huge trucks move in and around the gated complex and high-vis, hard-hatted, clipboard-wielding distillery workers pass between the buildings.

There's a good reason Sauza owns a big chunk of Tequila town. For nearly all of the latter half of the 20th century, Sauza was the biggest tequila brand in the world – bigger even than Jose Cuervo with which Sauza has been locked in a fierce rivalry for some 150 years.

The story begins with Cenobio Sauza, who came to work in Tequila at the young age of 16. For a while he worked as an administrator for Cuervo, but being both smart and fiercely ambitious, he saved enough money to buy his own operation. In 1873 he remodelled the La Antigua Cruz distillery in Tequila and renamed it La Perseverancia. That same year he exported 13 barrels and six demijohns across the border to El Paso, Texas. This marks the first documented occasion that tequila was exported to the US.

Sauza was an innovator in a time when industrial innovation came thick and fast and new technologies were sprouting up. When he began using steam boilers instead of wood-fired stills to cook agave, and stainless-steel tanks to ferment the mixture, it must have appeared to his contemporaries that a man from the future had arrived in Tequila. He would later be the first to install modern column-stills, to make production more efficient. He also championed the use of blue agave, which may have been valued for its flavour but was also prized for its high sugar content (which meant more alcohol) and relatively fast maturation time of just five to seven years. Sauza was a smart and ruthless man. Legend has it that during the Mexican Revolution, when bandits threatened to raid his distillery, Don Cenobio cunningly painted the word "agua" on his barrels of tequila, fooling the assailants into sparing his precious liquor.

This was at the dawn of a significant period of growth for the nascent tequila industry and it coincided with rising quantities of mineral exports travelling from Mexico to the US. As trains laden with precious metals trundled northwards, they carried an increasingly precious liquid cargo: bottles of agave spirit. The town of Tequila became a crucial stopover in this burgeoning trade network.

American consumers, particularly in the frontier states, developed a taste for this exotic Mexican liquor. Its popularity was bolstered by romantic – albeit often inaccurate – tales of its origins. The expansion of rail networks, notably E. H. Harriman's Southern Pacific line, facilitated tequila's spread across the west of the US on the eve of the Mexican Revolution.

Political turmoil on both sides of the border created a ready market for strong drink. To soldiers, adventurers and fortune-seekers, tequila was not a sacred indigenous elixir, but rather a powerful intoxicant with aristocratic associations thanks to the involvement of the powerful Cuervo and Sauza families. By the turn of the century, Mexican distilleries produced a staggering 10 million litres a year, much of it for export. This massive output meant over 70 million agave plants were processed each year.

The Sauza legacy continued to flourish under Don Cenobio's son, Eladio Sauza. Known for his charismatic charm and entrepreneurial spirit, Eladio expanded the family business, acquiring more agave fields and further modernising production techniques. Eladio hated the

Cuervos even more than his father and as folklore recounts, was involved in a fatal altercation where he shot a member of the Cuervo family dead on the streets of Tequila back in the year 1900.

When Eladio Sauza's son, Javier, went to university in Chicago and clandestinely wed a beautiful Cuervo relative with fiery red hair, Eladio exiled his son from the family enterprise, condemning him to a life as a tour guide in Mexico City and a succession of menial jobs. It wasn't until shortly before his father's demise in 1946 that Javier was allowed to return to the family business.

It's lucky he did.

Once in charge, Javier set out to make the brand global and elevate tequila's reputation in Mexico. He was a great marketeer, recognising the value in linking tequila to Mexican culture and music. In the 1950s, he launched "Noches Tapatías", a musical variety show that featured singers from the ranchera and mariachi genres, along with no small amount of Sauza product placement. It ran for 20 years and was one of the biggest TV shows in the country along with being a game-changer for tequila in Mexico, promoting consumption as part of a popular culture that made Mexicans feel proud of the Jalisco drink. Thus, Javier became something of an ambassador for Mexican culture, travelling to Europe and Asia and extolling the culture and flavours of Mexico.

Javier also fiercely defended against copycats, especially those from Japan, which he encountered on a sales trip there. This was likely one of the contributing factors that drove him to push for the original tequila DO (Designated Origin), which was established in 1974.

Among his many achievements he launched the first *reposado* tequila (before the term was legally recognised) called Hornitos in 1950, which was also Sauza's first 100% agave bottling. On the centenary of the brand's founding, in 1973, he launched Tres Generaciones, as a tribute to his father and grandfather. Most of their product line was *mixto* however, sitting at a 70%-agave to 30%-sugar ratio at the time.

Then, in 1976, Don Javier shocked many by selling a large share of Sauza's distillery and 700 sq. km (270 sq. miles) of land to the Spanish sherry and brandy house Pedro Domecq. By 1988 Pedro Domecq had acquired all of the brand and the subsequent devaluation of the Mexican peso dealt a severe blow to the family's earnings. To add insult to injury, over time the Sauza brand slipped into foreign ownership, ultimately landing in the hands of

ABOVE Sipping tequila in the caves at Destilería La Fortaleza with Guillermo Sauza is both memorable and, depending on the amount of tequila consumed, hard to remember in its entirety.

Suntory who are, ironically, a Japanese conglomerate. Nowadays Sauza ranks around fifth or sixth in the top-selling tequila stakes and remains the second-best-known family name in tequila production.

But the story of the Sauza family does not end there.

Having navigated our way out of the small industrial town that is La Perseverencia, we head back past El Llano and onwards to the south-western edge of town, where we arrive at Destilería La Fortaleza.

We find ourselves in the kitchen of the distillery talking with its founder, Guillermo Sauza – grandson of Javier Sauza – who, with the help of the brand's long- serving ambassador, Stefano Villafranca, is trying to make us a drink while filling in the gaps in my knowledge of the Sauza family history.

"I remember coming here from when I was about six years old," says Guillermo, his gravelly voice muffled as he roots around inside a low cupboard in search of coffee. "But we had another house and I don't remember much about this factory – we were kids and we didn't have much interest in it."

When Javier sold the business in the 1970s, the family held on to some of their land and some property, totalling a modest 80 acres (32 hectares). This included an old distillery that Javier had acquired in the 1950s. At the time, he needed the additional output that the site offered but also had his eye on the hill in the middle of the land, where he could build a stately hacienda that would look out over the town of Tequila and finally cement his supremacy over the Cuervos. He named the hacienda La Fortaleza (The Fortitude) and operated the distillery as a kind of theme park celebrating the old-fashioned ways of making tequila: brick ovens, open-top wood fermenters and pot stills. The distillery closed in 1968 and all the land was turned over to dairy farming for the next 30 years.

Guillermo grew up believing he would one day become the fifth generation of the biggest tequila brand in the world, and was heartbroken when, at 20 years old, his grandfather sold it. At that time he was studying at San Diego State University, which gave him a degree and set him up for a career in consulting in the defence sector.

"I should have retired at 50," he says. Fortunately for us the pull of Mexico and tequila was too strong for him to resist. Javier Sauza died in 1990, and the distillery and hacienda became available. It took Guillermo a decade to put together a plan and to raise the necessary funds he needed to get the distillery operational again. Contrary to what you might imagine, there wasn't a huge chest of Sauza cash left lying around for him to plunder; he had only the property and his name, so the business was a startup like any other.

When he finally launched in the early 2000s, he named his brand Los Abuelos ("The Grandparents") in tribute – or perhaps protest (!) – to his grandfather. The brand quickly garnered a reputation for its quality while raising the status of the 100% agave category. The Panamanian rum brand Rob Abuelo had something to say about the name however, which is why the Destilería La Fortaleza trades under the Fortaleza brand name everywhere except Mexico, where it's still Los Abuelos.

Slowly and surely the business grew in size and reputation and, once it became profitable, Guillermo

moved to Mexico permanently and now lives in the old hacienda on the hill that his grandfather built. Fortaleza is now one of the – if not *the* – most respected tequila brands and all its production is on careful allocation to importers around the world. The distillery literally can't make enough of it.

With our coffee cups empty, we leave the office and all five of us squeeze into a golf buggy built to hold two, with Guillermo driving and an ever increasing number of dogs following behind us. As we have a designated driver, Stefano hands us a tequila each, their classic Fortaleza Blanco (40% ABV): *The aroma is brine and lime. There's also a touch of leather and a kind of smoked kippers funk. The taste is mineral and gritty; with salt and gentle nuttiness. Cleaner rather than dark. Fresh and vibrant.*

Guillermo tells me that the distillery is pretty much the way that his grandfather left it, except for the garage he added to house all the motorbikes he and Stefano like to ride. The Fortaleza buildings are a vibrant pink colour, and as well as the distillery itself they include the office, bottling line, barrel storage and space for the 140 staff who work here to eat and rest. The vast majority of the property is given over to agave however, which constitutes about 12% of Fortaleza's total requirement. There's also a miniature replica of the Golden Gate Bridge, a lake, gardens where they grow courgettes (zucchini), melons, lychees and limes and hundreds of trees that have nearly all been planted by Guillermo himself, who I soon realise is intent on adding horticulturist to a resumé that already includes biker and tequilero.

Guillermo's grand plan is to create a botanical garden of many different agave varieties and take visitors on tours around the garden in an electric bus. He stops the buggy on the southern end of the property, and the Volcán de Tequila looms large in the distance. Here we find the oldest agaves on the plantation, at around six or seven years of age. Some of them have begun their swansong, sending up enormous asparagus-like quiotes, which will soon flower if they're left unchecked. While flowering is good for the pollinators, it's bad news for tequila-makers because it steals the energy from the plant and reduces the yield.

OPPOSITE The sprouting of the quiote is the signal that the agave is fully mature and ready to be harvested soon. Normally, the flower stalk is chopped down before the plant produces flowers.

FORTALEZA

LEFT Destilería La Fortaleza is among the most respected producers of tequila in the land, and it's because it places the agave front and centre of everything it does – bottle caps and motorcycle jackets included.

"I'll see if they can cut them tomorrow," Guillermo tells us. "We will leave a few to flower here and there though."

After quiote removal, the agave continues to ripen for several months as the energy intended for flowering and seed production concentrates in the piña. Then the *pencas* (leaves) begin to turn yellow and dry, signalling optimal ripeness. The pencas can then be trimmed by the jimador and the piña transported to the distillery when needed.

Guillermo starts the buggy up and we drive back towards the distillery to see the next stages of production. The distillery building is a stark contrast to the dry, bright heat outdoors. Here, the air is humid and the light much dimmer. There's steam and noise and the smell of hot fruit and decay. All of the cooking here is done in two brick ovens. One oven has its door open and is about a quarter full of dark, roasted agave. It's currently being emptied. The bricks themselves seem to reek of cooked vegetal matter. The other oven is about halfway through its

36-hour cook time with sweet-smelling steam blasting out of the small gaps in the sides of the steel door.

The cooked agaves must be unloaded by hand and then milled to extract the remainder of their juices and separate out the fibre of the plant. Over at Arette this was done using a roller mill – basically a sequence of conveyor belts that carry the agaves into series of cylindrical cutting blades. On the first cylinder the cut is very coarse, but each subsequent cylinder, or "stage", produces a finer cut. Water is usually added through the process to help flush the sugars out of the agave fibre. These sweet juices fall through the perforated floor of the mill and are caught below and piped away for fermentation.

Arette had four stages to its mill, but some distilleries have up to seven and some have only one. In general, the more stages, the more efficiently and completely the sugar from the agave will be extracted. An extremely efficient mill might capture 99% of all the available sugars in the plant. However, efficiency can produce side effects. A very aggressive mill can also extract bitter flavours from deep within the fibre of the plant. So a compromise between taste and efficiency must be made.

At Fortaleza, the makers use a more traditional milling method, which had all but vanished from tequila 20 years ago but now is making a comeback.

A *tahona* is a traditional stone mill used in the production of tequila and mezcal. It is made of two parts: a round stone basin, which sometimes – like at Fortaleza – has guttering and pipes to collect the juice of the agaves; and a wide millstone made of *tezontle* (a type of volcanic rock) mounted on an axel connected to a turnstile in the middle of the basin. The stone is then rolled around in a circle over the cooked agaves to crush them and extract their juices. Heavy as it is, the stone at Fortaleza is powered by an engine but in other, even more traditional settings, the stone is pulled by a mule, donkey or ox.

As a technology, tahonas originated in the Middle East thousands of years ago and then made their way to Europe, probably during the Moorish conquest. There, they were used to crush olives, grapes, and sugar cane. So it follows that tahonas were introduced to Mexico after the Spanish conquest, where they were used to mill corn, cane, fruits and agaves, all of which had previously been tackled by hand – and still are in some places (as we shall see).

The tahona at Fortaleza can hold 3 tonnes of agave at a time and it's an eight-hour shift to crush it all and extract the sweet juices. They do this in three shifts, 24 hours a day. Operating a tahona is not a case of starting the engine and putting your feet up for the rest of the day. It requires constant work and supervision from a seven-man team, the workers using forks to turn over the agave fibres and flush them with water, squeezing out as much sugar as they can. "As much as they can" is just over 70% of the available sugars according to Guillermo. This means at least 25% of the sugar – and therefore 25% of the potential alcohol – is being left behind. So what's the point?

Besides the obvious artisanal nature of the process, which no doubt gets visitors excited, aficionados argue that there is a noticeable taste difference between tahona and roller mill. Some tequleros I spoke to mentioned the "minerals from the stone" imparting a "dusty" flavour into the spirit. Others suggest that the treatment of the agave fibres and the inefficiency of the extraction pays dividends in the flavour department. Additionally, using a tahona points to a commitment to quality and craft that one

would assume extends to other areas of the operation. And at Fortaleza those assumptions would be well-founded.

Fermentation here is done across eight traditional, open-top pine vats and takes around three days to complete. Then it's on to copper pot-stills, which are replicas of the original 100-year-old stills. All of the maturation for reposado and añejo expressions is on site too, totalling around 1,000 casks of maturing tequila.

"We do everything here except blow the glass," says Stefano as we emerge back into the sunny courtyard. "You want to see where we make the bottle caps?"

We head up a wrought-iron spiral staircase into a series of rooms where six workers are making Fortaleza's iconic agave piña stoppers entirely from scratch.

The shape of the piña is moulded from liquid resin and left to set for a day. Each one is hand-painted green and left to dry for another day. Then the green is sanded back to give the white "cut penca" effect, followed by a coat of varnish and another day of drying. Then the stopper is glued to the cork, which needs another day to dry. Finally someone cleans up the stopper with a knife, removing excess glue and checking overall quality. Every single stopper on every bottle of Fortaleza tequila is made this way and it takes almost a week from start to finish.

Back down the stairs we go towards our final stop: the all-important tasting room, which, at Fortaleza, is a tourist attraction in itself. Hidden in a small network of caves hewn into volcanic rock, these were once used to store barrels and farm equipment. Now they've been turned into a dimly lit bar and tasting room with a uniquely clandestine atmosphere (I'm told that the parties here are legendary).

Stefano pours us a flight of tequilas to taste starting with the Still Strength expression, which as the name suggests is undiluted with water and bottled at the strength it comes off the still. In spite of the dangerous-sounding name, this product is only 46% ABV – far lower than the average high-proof bottlings, which tend to sit in the mid-fifties. What this does mean however, is that when you buy Fortaleza Blanco the bottle has only had a small amount of water added to it to take it down to 40% ABV. *The aroma is restrained on nose with that additional alcohol tightening things up a notch. The taste is grippy at first then loosening up into lime zest, alcohol spice and soft yellow fruits. There's a hit of pineapple and a slight meatiness in the finish.*

That low still strength also means that Guillermo needs to buy more barrels for his aged expressions as, put simply,

Winter Blend, which is released in limited numbers every September and compiled of their classic Reposado blended with tequilas aged in unique cask types.

We start with the 2022 Winter Blend, aged in Oloroso and Tokaji casks (43% ABV). *Tropical and yellow fruit notes mingle with grape and honey. The agave is softened, complemented by warming yellow spices and sweet dried fruits (apricot and juicy mango) as well as soft tobacco. A delightful mustiness leads to a dry finish.*

The five of us spend at least ten minutes analysing the liquid, chatting and pulling tasting notes out of the air. Finally, we taste the 2023 Winter Blend, aged in ex-Charanda and refill Oloroso casks (43.5% ABV). *Aromas of vanilla ice cream, caramel and butterscotch greet the nose. The palate reveals more agave character, balanced sweetness, and notes of ginger and roasted fruits. It's like an elevated blanco with added robustness and length from the barrel influence.* Addie says it's like honeysuckle.

"You don't have to pick a favourite," says Stefano. "That's not the point."

With no windows in the cave and no shortage of tequila, time passes by without our knowing. When we eventually stumble outside like newborn lambs, the evening is in full swing. Before we part company Guillermo takes us out of the front door of the distillery and shows us a vacant plot of land across the road. It's part of the Sauza estate that thus far has remained untouched. This, he tells us, is where he plans to build his next distillery. He's not giving much away but confirms that it will not be another Fortaleza.

"Something different," he says, seeming to be lost in visualising whatever it is. "Something new."

there is more water in his tequila when it goes into the barrel than in a typical distillery. Cost-cutting doesn't seem to be part of the remit of this place at any stage of production, though.

Speaking of barrels, next up is Fortaleza Reposado, aged for around seven months in ex-bourbon casks. *It's nutty and figgy and has a slight tomato leaf or hot greenhouse aroma. The taste is sweet agave nectar and fresh salsa.*

Stefano heads off to Guillermo's office to retrieve more bottles and returns with two expressions of their

DON ABRAHAM

◇◇◇

La Planta

In 2006, a 90,000-acre (36,000-hectare) slab of land near the Tequila Volcano and the surrounding valley was awarded World Heritage Site status by UNESCO. This includes an expansive landscape of blue agaves, many distilleries and the towns of Tequila, El Arenal and Amatitán. Amatitán is five miles (8km) east of Tequila, and home to 16,000 people and half a dozen tequila distilleries, including the legendary Herradura brand. We have touched on three of the four "Founding Families of Tequila"so far. Herradura will introduce us to the last.

The story begins in 1870 when Félix López established the Hacienda San José del Refugio in Amatitán and began producing tequila there. In 1924, Félix López's son, Aurelio López Rosales, inherited his father's hacienda and then officially founded Tequila Herradura in 1928, allegedly after discovering an old *herradura* (horseshoe) buried in the distillery grounds, which he had mistaken for gold. The brand grew from strength to strength, becoming the first 100% agave tequila officially imported into the US, after Bing Crosby fell in love with it and promptly created an import business to ensure a supply for himself and his fellow crooners. Soon Herradura became the most respected brand in all of tequila and shorthand for quality and authenticity across America.

Gabriela de la Peña ("The Queen of Tequila") assumed control of the company in the late 1950s, and during her 40-year tenure, she oversaw significant modernisation and expansion, including a new distillery constructed alongside the original, which today is preserved as a museum. La Peña and her sons lobbied for the creation of the *reposado* classification in 1974, as well as the tequila DO. Sadly, in 2007, the brand was sold to Brown-Forman (one of the largest drinks companies in the world, in charge of Jack Daniel's among other big brands). Modern, efficiency-driven equipment was promptly installed and the quality of the tequila made at Herradura plummeted. Today, the modern Casa Herradura facility itself spans 50 acres (20 hectares) and employs over a thousand people.

While it's hard to get away from Herradura in this town (and very easy to get to it on account of the Herradura Express, which shuttles passengers from Guadalajara in an incongruously luxurious train), there are other distilleries that are harder to get to and, in my opinion, worthy of greater interest. Destilería Las Américas is one of them, and it's not the kind of place you just stumble across. Off the main road on the outskirts of town, we drive past a blue Corona-branded liquor store and up a steep cobbled street, before skidding to a halt on a hot stretch of road lined with pickup trucks and a chain-link fence. There doesn't seem to be much here at all.

Pancho marches confidently over to a big orange gate and knocks hard. A minute goes by, a few dogs amble past, and I'm starting to wonder if we have the right place. Then, suddenly, the door swings open and we are met by an old man who, judging by the stern look on his face, isn't expecting us. Pancho exchanges some polite words, the man disappears, and returns with another man who is about my age and he's smiling.

This guy is Eladio Montes Jr. and the other man was his father, also called Eladio. The Montes family have been farming agave in this region for more than a hundred years, stretching back to Abraham Montes, Eladio Jr.'s great-grandfather. Nowadays they make tequila too.

In the early years Abraham sold his agave to the Herradura in a prosperous relationship that continued for more than half a century, with each new generation taking up the mantle and learning to tend the agave fields. But things changed in the 1990s when a glut of agaves in the valley tanked the price. "We had a lot of agave for the upcoming years," says Eladio, as he walks us through the main yard of the distillery. "So in 1995 my father and uncles built a factory to make our own tequila."

The fluctuating price of agave and its ability to turn growers into tequila makers is a story that has played out countless times in these parts, and one that we will encounter again and again on our tour.

The Montes brothers were experts in agave but didn't know much about making alcohol, so they called in a favour from Guillermo Romo La Peña, son of Gabriela. He helped them set up the distillery, even going as far as sending over a stone mason to build an exact replica of the Herradura brick oven for them to cook their agave in.

It took them a few years to find their feet but by the early 2000s, they were beginning to release some great tequilas and catching the attention of some lucrative contract brands. Today they make Don Abraham and Don Montes brands for themselves and contract distil for another six to ten brands.

Eladio takes us through the yard, past a maturation warehouse, and into a large aircraft-hangar-style building where the distillery is housed. There, we see the original brick oven that was built 30 years ago, and next to it a partially built second oven. The distillery isn't producing right now while the second oven is finished, which lends a quiet eeriness to the place as we walk through.

"The guy that is making this one is the same as the guy who made the original one," say Eladio.

It turns out this man (referred to simply as "Jefe") has built in excess of 60 ovens over the past 50 years. Pancho tells us that only the other day he met a man who builds and repairs many of the roller mills in operation in the Tequila Valley. It's easy to think of tequila as simply cutting agaves down and processing them at a factory, but there are dozens of second- and third-order industries that tequila supports, from glass manufacturing, graphic design, retail, tourism, security and hospitality.

The biggest adjacent industry to tequila is the one that the Montes family has been involved with for five generations: farming. The true story of tequila begins in the fields, long before the agave reaches these walls, where the skilled hands of jimadores have been tending and harvesting agave for generations. Tequila agriculture employs something like 70,000 workers – a far larger number than the distilling side of the business. That's why the jimador is one of the more familiar faces in tequila culture. Traditionally clad in white cotton shirts with red sashes, wearing open-toed sandals, and holding a moon-shaped *coa* blade, you've seen them on tequila labels or in branding. The jimador reminds us of the powerful

connection between agave spirits and the agave itself. And through their hands-on approach to nurturing and ultimately cutting down the plant, it's true to say that more than 90% of the evolution of a typical bottle of blanco tequila occurs under their watch. All the more fitting, then, that the word *jimador* does not come from "harvester", but from the Mesoamerican word *ximador*, which means to shave, prune or sculpt.

Jimadores will typically start work at dawn and finish before the afternoon sun gets too hot. Harvesting the agaves means trimming away the fibrous *pencas* (outer leaves) and then cutting the plant off at the root, all the time being careful not to slice your foot off with the coa or acquire a long gash in your arm from the barbed

pencas. It takes about 80 swings of a coa to dismember the agave completely, and that's only if you're well trained. I have cut agaves on a few occasions, and each time, after a few minutes of hacking away, I have been gently ushered to hand back the coa out of sympathy. Just a few minutes of swinging a blade at a plant is exhausting and every wrong swing – that cuts too close or two far away – is wasted energy. Even once cut, the piñas often need chopping into smaller pieces so that they can be lifted on to a mule or carried back to a truck.

The quantity of agave a single jimador can harvest in a day varies a lot, and depends on the terrain in which the agaves are planted and the accessibility of that terrain. But in a well-organised field, it can be more than 80 plants in

a morning, which amounts to around 5 tonnes of agave. It typically takes 6–8kg (13–18lbs) of agave to make a bottle of tequila, so as a ballpark figure, a skilled jimador with a clear run of a field full of ripe agave might be harvesting 600 bottles of tequila in a single day.

Jimadores also clear weeds from around the agave to maintain the vitality of the plants and check for diseases or blight that might threaten them and other plants around it. They must *capón* (castrate) the quiote before it flowers (which causes the agave to use up valuable energy stores),

and select the agaves that are ready for harvesting. Every one of these responsibilities, if neglected, will have some negative impact on the spirit, whether it's a drop in alcoholic yield or a decrease in the flavour-producing compounds in the plant.

Though patents have been filed, currently there is no mechanised harvesting of agave in Mexico. Even the likes of Jose Cuervo, who harvests millions of plants a year, does so with an army of jimadores. One. Agave. At. A. Time.

Some of the bigger producers have incorporated machines into some of their field processes, however: Sauza uses vegetable planting machines to place juvenile agaves in the ground; some producers use machines to spread fertilisers and pesticides on their crops and to trim back leaves. These time- and labour-saving activities are easily done on flat fields, but once you get into the cactus-filled hills of the really rural areas, it's down to humans and mules to take care of things.

The rainy season is fast approaching here in Mexico and Eladio Sr. is keen to get the second oven online and working next week. Rain causes agaves to swell with water, and while this doesn't lower their sugar content it does lower the concentration of sugar in the plant. This means his workers are hauling tonnes of unnecessary water around in every plant they harvest. Swollen agave take up more space in the oven too. But for producers who buy

agave on the open market, it means they're literally getting less sugar (and more water) per peso.

The Montes family produces certified organic tequila, which remains a relatively rare thing in the tequila world. The first organic tequila, 4 Copas, was launched in 2005 and was originally made at the La Quemada distillery before production moved here to Destilería Las Américas, but it's not made here any more. Since 4 Copas, at least 30 other organic brands have launched, but owing to stringent rules implemented by the Mexican organic regulatory body Ley de Productos Orgánicos, they're produced at only a handful of distilleries. More than a dozen are made here at Las Américas.

The regulatory body states that land used for cultivation must have been free from prohibited chemical substances (typically synthetic pesticides and fertilisers) for at least three years before the first organic harvest. This means additional labour and continual attention, like setting pheromone traps to attract bugs and manually fertilising the soil with manure and other organic fertilisers.

"We have to build stone walls – like a barracks," says Eladio, "To protect the field from contamination from our neighbours." As such, it takes a workforce of up to 150 people to tend to the 1,000 hectares (2,475 acres) of agave that the three brothers collectively own. That's a lot of effort – so what's the point?

Besides the marketing side of "organic", which draws in a certain type of consumer who is willing to front the extra cash, organic farming is simply a far more sustainable approach. It promotes soil health, water conservation, biodiversity and helps reduce pollution. Recent studies have shown that organic farming produces a more flavourful end product, with increases in flavour-giving antioxidants and phytochemicals in the plant and an increased mineral uptake. Álvaro Montes (Eladio Sr.'s brother) runs the family's farming operations and is often quoted as saying, "If I grow the best agave, how could I not make the best tequila?"

The oven (soon to be ovens) at Las Américas can hold 30 tonnes of agave. This takes two days to cook, comprising 24 hours of steam and 24 hours of cooling. The agaves are processed through a roller mill and fermented in stainless steel tanks with natural yeasts. To the best of their knowledge, they are the only tequila producer that combines natural fermentation with organic agave. Eladio considers this an extension of their organic farming and part of a wider "low intervention" approach to tequila making. And while their processes are kept consistent it is ultimately the plant and the yeasts in the ferment that determine the outcome.

This brings up some interesting questions regarding contract-distilled brands and what their customers expect to receive in the bottle. In any other industry, a cavalier attitude towards consistency would be a red flag for most customers. Here at Las Américas their clients expect to find fluctuations in the end product and that is sort of the point. That said, they are not just dumping spirit into bottles at random and handing it over with a wink and a smile. After the product has been distilled twice in the huge 5,500-litre (1,450-gallon) stainless-steel stills, it is left to rest for a while before its aroma and taste are assessed. Then, it either becomes blanco tequila or, if it is a little flat or lacks vibrancy, it's sent for maturation. All the blanco tequila is rested in glass for at least three months and then any subtle differences in taste within each batch can be allocated to a customer based on their needs.

"We are selecting the tequila for each brand but not controlling its outcome," says Eladio. "If a client comes to me with a bottle of tequila and says 'I want you to make me something like this,' I tell them, 'You should go to that producer!'"

"It's an intentional selection," says Pancho, "But with the philosophy of knowing that you cannot control the whole process." There is a beauty in this, accepting that you have limited control over the natural processes of production, but that you become excellent at what you can control, namely selecting and blending the end products. And having the confidence in what you are making to be unwavering in your methods.

We walk up to the warehouse where the aged tequila is resting. Like all tequila producers, Las Américas is using oak to mature their reposado and añejo tequilas, and fortunately oak trees are naturally organic. The distillery does need to be careful about what was previously held in the oak casks, however. Most of the barrels used to make tequila are sourced from the American whiskey industry – from Wild Turkey in this case. Wild Turkey is not an organic whiskey, but because whiskey is distilled, in the eyes of Ley de Productos Orgánicos it isn't considered to harbour inorganic properties.

The same is not true of wine casks, where any traces of non-organic wine that reside in a used cask are considered contaminants to the organic process. That means the small stock of Napa Valley wine casks here at Las Américas cannot be used to produce organic certified tequila as they aren't sourced from organic wineries.

It's time to leave, and we return to the gate and begin to say our goodbyes. Then I realise in a moment of utter panic that we haven't tasted any tequila. Eladio pre-empts my request and disappears off to the office, returning with an unlabelled bottle of Don Abraham Blanco. He pours us a glass each and I sniff it. *There's a noticeable lime note on the nose, fresh and crisp, slightly peppery but soft and juicy.*

"I don't know about you," says Pancho with his nose in the glass, "But for me, this organic tequila smells like the farm – like the animals."

For me, it's fresher than that. I taste it: *Ripe yuzu, like biting fruit. There's a soft, margarita finish – an incredible clarity of flavour.*

"It's like being at an agave harvest," says Eladio.

Yes. I agree with that.

CASCAHUÍN

Algo Fermentado

With its colourful, colonial-style buildings lining narrow cobblestone streets, the town of El Arenal serves as the gateway to Tequila Valley. The central plaza comes into view, dominated by the striking parish church of Our Lady of the Rosary with its distinctive twin spires. We drive past numerous enormous murals – some of them encompassing entire street blocks – depicting every stage of tequila production with agaves being cut, cooked, crushed and, in one instance, worshipped. Many have an almost psychedelic character, their colours and shapes amplified almost beyond recognition. Local residents go about their day, and the aroma of traditional Mexican cuisine wafts from nearby restaurants and street vendors. It's a morning in Jalisco much like any other.

The Cascahuín distillery is our destination. It's located down Avenida Ferrocarril, which runs parallel to the railway line that was once used to transport barrels of tequila through town and into Guadalajara for sale. We park up and walk through the rust-coloured walls of Cascahuín. The distillery is like a castle with a central courtyard packed full of cut agave piñas that are sitting in the hot sun as the busy team loads them into the oven.

As we're sifting through and climbing over the piñas in the sunshine, Alexis appears and introduces himself. He is a younger member of the production team at Cascahuín but a formidable source of knowledge as to the goings on at this distillery.

He begins by bringing us closer to the three brick ovens (one x 12 tonnes and two x 16 tonnes), and we barely avoid a conveyor belt on wheels that the team is hastily manoeuvring into the open door of an oven like paramedics with a gurney. At this moment we can see all three stages of a brick-oven cook: loading, cooking and cooling. The cooling oven has its doors open and from it emanates the sticky-sweet aroma of stewing pineapple. Alexis offers us some slices of cooked agave and we take

a bite. They taste nothing like tequila and are more like a cross between cooked pineapple and tamarind, or molasses. They're very sweet and also very fibrous, which means that it's not practical to eat all the plant but rather chew and suck on it and then dispose of the spent fibre (spitting it on the floor seems to be totally acceptable) once you're done.

We step out of the sun and behind the ovens, into the distillery proper. It feels like climbing into an old, dark refrigerator and it's much quieter here. The place has a charming old-school vibe with its brick and masonry buildings, and each production stage tucked into its own cosy corner. Alexis tells us the distillery uses well water drawn from 200m (650ft) down for every part of production except for when they dilute their tequila to bottling strength (proofing down), which is done with demineralised water. I ask him if this is for consistency as the water is prone to change, but he tells me it's more about letting the agave character shine through.

"The family doesn't care about consistency in the taste," he says. "They know the agave changes from season to season. But they care about consistency in the process."

Cascahuín has undergone a remarkable devolutionary process over the past few decades, which has taken them out of contract brand obscurity and transformed them into one of the most respected and creatively dynamic distilleries in all of tequila.

The distillery was founded in 1953 by Salvador Rosales Briseño who had learned to make tequila at his aunt's distillery in El Arenal. The name Cascahuín means "hill of light" and is named for a hill close by. Cascahuín was fairly innocuous for its first 50 years, producing *mixto*

OPPOSITE The tahona at Cascahuín is driven by an engine – it's an incredibly labour-intensive process, requiring more than a day's worth of man hours to achieve what a roller mill can do in an hour.

tequila and contracting out to various clients including Bacardí. In 2008, that contract ended and the third generation of the family, Salvador Jr. (known as "Chava"), took a more leading role in the distillery. Chava and his father (Salvador Sr.) instigated a steady stream of upgrades (though perhaps you might call them downgrades), including steel and wooden fermenters, a *tahona* (a volcanic-stone mill), a mezcal-style pit oven, and an "ancestral" wooden still, the latter two of which are now being used to produce a type of tequila that has not been seen for a century.

"They did things the opposite way. Chava's grandfather began with concrete fermenters covered in fibreglass and roller mills," says Alexis. "Then they started adding all of the old equipment, like wood fermenters and then the tahona in 2017."

The idea of all this, Alexis tells us, is to combine traditional methods with modern knowledge. To that end Cascahuín produces two marques of spirit that begin their delineation at the milling stage, either by tahona or roller mill. They are then fermented separately and blended and distilled separately to produce their line of Blanco, Plata and Tahona tequilas.

Fermentation is perhaps the most important stage of production in the distillery. The obvious point being that there is no alcohol without fermentation, but the less obvious being that nearly all of the flavours that we find in a blanco tequila are formed during fermentation too.

Fermentation is a metabolic process in which microorganisms like yeast convert sugars into alcohol, carbon dioxide, and other byproducts, often used in the production of beverages, food and biofuels. It begins with a process called glycolysis, where yeast converts glucose (sugar) into two pyruvate molecules. Think of pyruvate as "free energy" that can be used to make other energy-providing compounds like NAD+ (nicotinamide adenine dinucleotide). In the presence of oxygen, the yeast cells use this energy to grow and multiply, producing byproducts of CO_2 and a little alcohol, plus some heat. Soon though, the available oxygen is used up, as a layer

LEFT AND ABOVE
Fermentation is where the magic of tequila production takes place and where most of the flavour in the bottle comes from.

of CO_2 sits on top of the fermentation vessel. At that point the ferment becomes anaerobic and the yeast cells can no longer convert pyruvate by the normal (aerobic) pathway. As a backup, they begin making acetaldehyde, which itself is converted into ethanol and NAD+. More CO_2 is produced, and the acetaldehyde begins to introduce flavourful properties to the ferment, as well as reacting with the alcohols that are being made to make all kinds of fruity aromas known as esters.

The variety and quantity of these flavourful compounds depends on several factors: the mineral content and pH of the agave juice, the temperature of fermentation, the type of yeast used, the Brix (sweetness) of the ferment, and time.

Brix is a unit of measurement used to indicate the sugar content in an aqueous solution. It represents the percentage of sugar by weight in a liquid, where 1 degree Brix (°Bx) equals 1 gram of sugar in 100 grams of solution. Brix is important because yeast turns sugar into alcohol and the Brix of a liquid will determine how much potential alcohol is in the juice.

If the Brix is too high (the sugar too concentrated), the yeast might be incapable of thriving in the solution – remember that syrups and jams do not ferment because their sugar levels are sufficiently high to act as a preservative. More sugar also means the yeast works more aggressively, multiplying and consuming the sugar, which generates a lot of heat that can potentially kill the yeast if it gets too hot for too long.

On the flip side, if the Brix of your agave juice is too low, the yeast is less active and the temperature of the fermentation will be cooler, possibly to the point of stalling in colder seasons. A lower Brix also means you produce a liquid with a lower concentration of alcohol, which effectively means you have more water to get rid of through distillation and that means you need bigger (or more) fermenters and stills to process it. Brix can be adjusted down by adding more water during or after milling, and adjusted up by adding the *miels dulces* ("sweet honeys") from the cooking process. Each distillery has its preferences when it comes to Brix, which can range anywhere from 6° to 18° – at Cascahuín they aim for between 9° and 15°.

So temperature is tied to Brix, but it is not only important in respect of the survival of the yeast and the completion of the ferment, but also in the flavours that are made in the fermentation tank. A longer, cooler ferment will produce a very different outcome to a shorter, warmer one; a slightly different ratio of light and heavy alcohols may be produced and very different range of flavourful compounds will undergo fabrication by these magical multicellular organisms. As a rule of thumb, cooler, longer ferments produce more flavourful outcomes.

Mineral content and pH can also play a part, with yeasts preferring a "Goldilocks" formula of mildly acidic juice and low levels of minerals and salt.

But all of the above is prone to change depending on the yeast strain that is being used. Most distilleries in tequila use a species of yeast called *Saccharomyces cerevisiae*, which is the same species – prized for its speed, efficiency and range of tolerances that is used in bread-making and brewing. Within *S. cerevisiae* there is a plethora of strains however, each with their own characteristics and application suitability. In tequila, it is common for strains with a high heat tolerance to be used, which, for example, would not be necessary or desirable for making malt whisky in Scotland. Strains are also selected for their ability to work harmoniously and sympathetically with the substrate – agave in our case. A distiller might, for example, prefer a yeast that will accentuate spice or citrus or earthy characteristics and different strains can be used to achieve this. A yeast may also be optimised for high alcohol tolerance, high Brix and rapid fermentation, which are desirable traits for the likes of Jose Cuervo and Sauza, who wish to process materials fast. Such is the effect of yeast variety on the fermentation outcome that it is quite common for distilleries to produce, maintain and fiercely protect a proprietary yeast that meets their exact efficiency and flavour-making requirements.

Alexis takes us up some steps on to a gangway that overlooks the distillery's 11 stainless-steel fermentation tanks, each with a capacity of 11,000 litres (2,900 gallons). The tanks have no top to them, so the state of the fermentation can be easily viewed from here. Some tanks are bubbling away wildly, with a gritty pale foam forming on top. Others are less active, with only a few bubbles and a darker-looking soupy liquid. Some have a sweet agave aroma, others smell more pungent or acidic. Alexis tells us that fermentation takes around four days here, and right now we are seeing its various stages from cooked agave juice right through to fermented *mosto*.

"There are our yeast creation tanks," Alexis says, pointing at some smaller steel tanks nearby. "We don't add any external yeast."

At the opposite end of the yeast property scale is natural fermentation, where the yeast culture is not controlled but instead allowed to culture by itself. In this scenario, a vast range of known and unknown yeast strains, present on the walls of the tank, in the mill, and in the air itself, descend on the liquid and orchestrate the fermentation according to their song. These yeasts may be strains of *Saccharomyces cerevisiae* or entirely different species of yeast altogether. In one study conducted in 2014 a team of scientists analysed yeast colonies from three mezcal distilleries in the state of Durango and isolated eight species of yeast and 143 strains. Of the strains, around half of them were *S. cerevisiae* and the rest *Kluyveromyces marxianus, Zygosaccharomyces bailii, Peronospora manshurica, Pichia kluyveri, Torulaspora delbrueckii, Hanseniaspora guilliermondii* and *Clavispora lusitaniae*. Interestingly, the presence of these yeasts in their respective ferments differed according to the time of the year and varied considerably between different distilleries, suggesting that distilleries that naturally ferment develop a sort of biological terroir to their product that shifts with the seasons.

At Cascahuín the process is semi-controlled: the distillery has separate tanks for breeding wild yeast cultures where agave juices are periodically added and a yeasty stew is taken out – just like a sourdough starter. Cascahuín is among a small group of tequila distilleries that use natural fermentation, and one of only a handful that make all of their products this way.

"We pitch the propagated wild yeast into the fermentation tank along with the agave juices," says Alexis. This approach allows for the further multiplication of the cells and the commencement of the proper fermentation. The alternative, which is slower but more traditional, would be to just fill the fermenter with the agave juices and allow the yeast cultures to develop in situ.

While Cascahuín is rare in their approach, there are quite a few distilleries that inoculate their ferments with a controlled strain of *S. cerevisiae*, but also use open-top fermenters and inevitably attract a broad population of yeast cultures into their ferments – albeit in lower numbers to a truly wild fermentation. And even those fermenting in closed vessels won't be able to isolate only their preferred strain of yeast. No sooner have the oven or autoclave doors opened than yeasts find their way on to the cooked agaves and begin the process of fermentation; they transport these burgeoning cultures through to the mill or *tahona* and then into the fermenters, cultivating them all the while.

Alexis walks us back down the steps and over to the oldest fermenters at the distillery, which are made of concrete. These square baths are a third of the size of the steel fermenters and have a caked mass of what looks like crusty hay sitting on top of them. They smell sour and funky, and look like they belong in a neglected corner of a dairy farm.

"What we're seeing," Alexis says, "is a mixture of juice and *bagazo* (agave fibre) from the tahona, which are fermented together – we only ferment the tahona agave in concrete."

Fibres were an inevitable part of production before the invention of roller mills and mesh filters, and would be present in both the fermentation and distillation stages of the process. But modern systems have stripped them out and helped to define the clean and fresh character of tequila that we are familiar with today. Fibres don't impart much flavour by themselves and they don't ferment easily but when they do they produce a range of alcohols, phenols, organic acids and aromatic aldehydes, that alter the character of the end product.

However, the layer of caked fibre that is floating on top of the ferment, along with the thick concrete walls of the fermenting bath, are perhaps the most important (and least obvious) factors at work here. Steel fermenters offer very little insulation, which means the fermentation is prone to behave differently with seasonal changes in temperature as well as changes that happen naturally through the fermentation process. The temperature moves up and down and so do the results. Plastic and wood are better insulators, while concrete and stone pits in the ground (we'll get there...) are very good insulators. While these materials do not impart flavour directly, each one protects and nurtures the fermentation through its insulating properties and the resulting fluctuation or stability in temperature will produce dramatically different outcomes downstream from here.

At Cascahuín, the *mosto* from the different fermentation tanks is distilled separately and then blended together or bottled for each Cascahuín expression and for their contract brands.

"You want to try it at 60%?" Alexis says, grabbing some glasses off a nearby table and collecting a sample from the stream of liquid that's gently flowing off the copper pot-still.

I smell it. *The aroma is surprisingly subdued.* Perhaps from the sensory overload of steam and funk of the distillery. *The taste is very powerful, though: hot and spicy and full of alcoholic energy.* Wow!

"Actually, I think it's more like 75%," Alexis says a little coyly.

The specific strength of the spirit changes as it comes off the still and its potency at the end will depend on when they cut the spirit and what they are making. Their Tahona expression for example (100% concrete-fermented) is distilled to an average of 48% ABV and requires only a little water adding to take it down to its bottling strength of 42% ABV. On the other hand, their Blanco is distilled up to 55% ABV and needs to be taken down to 38% ABV for the local market bottling. This, however, is a blend of 70% steel-fermented and 30% concrete-fermented.

"It's easier to understand if we taste them all," Alexis says, and he takes us outside, up an iron staircase and into Cascahuín's new tasting room. It's a minimalist space with a bar and a few tables, decorated in white marble, air-conditioned to a light chill, and altogether totally different to the warm and dank smells of fermentation and cooking in the working distillery below us.

We begin with Cascahuín Tahona Blanco (42% ABV), which as the name suggests is 100% tahona-milled and therefore 100% concrete-fermented. *It's funky and round, and boasts pronounced vegetal and savoury notes, balanced by a subtle residual sweetness. The finish is earthy.*

Then it's on to Cascahuín Blanco (40% ABV), which is 70% steel-fermented and 30% concrete-fermented. These are both distilled to an alcoholic strength of 55% ABV and then blended. *The aroma is more bright and fragrant. The agave shines through with a crisp, clean character, offering a lighter counterpoint. Floral notes dance with hints of citrus, creating a refreshing and elegant tequila.*

The Plata expression is also a mixture of steel and concrete but it is distilled to 49% ABV and bottled at 48%. When it was launched 10 years ago, it was the first modern high-proof tequila available in Mexico. *The potent alcohol on the nose gives way to a gentler, pepper-tinged palate. Salty and citric notes mingle with brine and herbal undertones, leading to a remarkably long finish.*

RIGHT When getting granular about taste and production details, it's always humbling to remind yourself that all of this begins with the agave plant.

As we move to the aged expressions, we're presented with Cascahuín Reposado (40% ABV), which is matured for six to eight months in ex-bourbon barrels. *Subtle mint and baking spices greet the nose, while soft vegetal notes linger beneath. The palate is smooth, revealing grapefruit and nutty flavours. A whisper of tobacco emerges on the finish, making this an excellent introduction to aged tequilas.*

The Cascahuín Añejo (40% ABV) follows, which has 14–16 months of maturity and retains much of the herbal, valley agave character: *Vanilla and orange aromas mingle with hints of menthol and caraway. The palate evokes memories of Murray mints, evolving into a gentle cinnamon warmth. It's a fantastic añejo that showcases the distillery's mastery of ageing.*

Finally, we reach the Cascahuín Extra Añejo (40% ABV). *This expression is a study in elegance. The dominant note of brown butter permeates both nose and palate, creating a rich, indulgent experience. Subtle oak influence adds depth without overpowering the inherent agave character.*

More tequila is offered and gratefully received, and I notice that my ability to write tasting notes soon begins to suffer. I'm certain that they must have tasted good, though, as the resulting hangover proves that I drank them in their entirety.

LOS ALTOS

The red clay soils and higher altitude of the Los Altos region seems to nurture agaves in a uniquely flavourful way. Once the domain of multigenerational families of jimadores, many of those growers have become distillers, now producing some of the biggest and best brands.

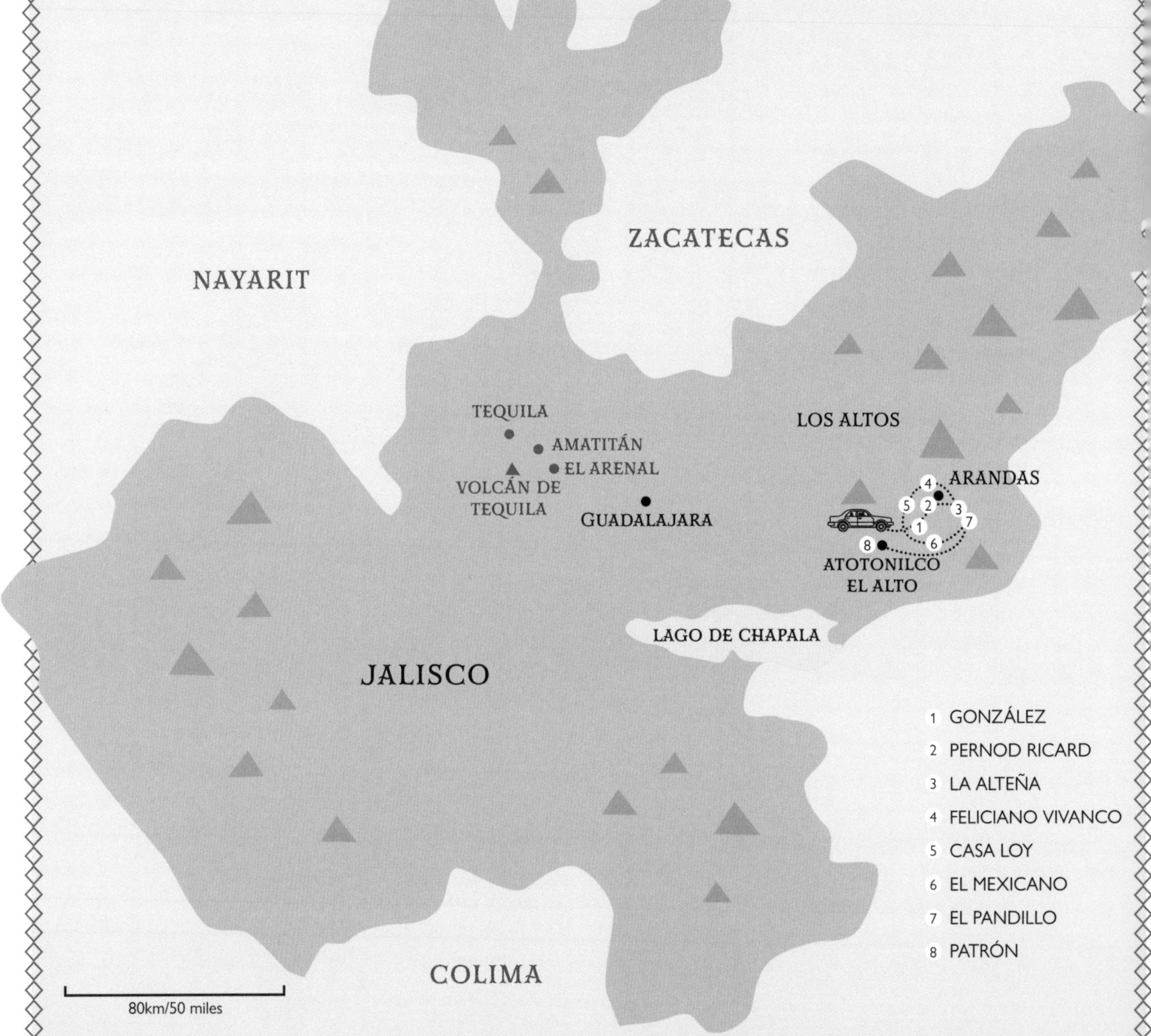

ZACATECAS

NAYARIT

TEQUILA

AMATITÁN

EL ARENAL

LOS ALTOS

VOLCÁN DE TEQUILA

GUADALAJARA

ARANDAS

4

5 2 3

1 7

6

8

ATOTONILCO EL ALTO

LAGO DE CHAPALA

JALISCO

1 GONZÁLEZ

2 PERNOD RICARD

3 LA ALTEÑA

4 FELICIANO VIVANCO

5 CASA LOY

6 EL MEXICANO

7 EL PANDILLO

8 PATRÓN

COLIMA

80km/50 miles

GONZÁLEZ

El Legado

Francisco Gonzalez Jr. is a big guy. He is sat behind a big desk in a big office built from mosaic stones and stained glass. Crystal bottles of tequila are dotted around the place and oil paintings of agave fields by the Jaliscan artist Marco Anibal hang on the walls. Behind him is a huge window that looks down on to rows of barrels filled with maturing tequila. A family photo on the shelf shows three generations of men and boys, all sat in this very office and, like a scene from Dallas, all in button-down shirts, jeans and cowboy hats.

Three leather chairs are in front of his desk and up until very recently they were empty. We are over an hour late arriving here after acquiring a puncture from an altercation with a particularly deep pot-hole during the two-hour drive from the Tequila Valley to where we are sat now, just outside the town of Atotonilco in Los Altos.

There are two distinct areas of Jalisco that dominate tequila production, the first being west of Guadalajara in the Tequila Valley, near the Tequila Volcano and around the towns of El Arenal and Amatitán and of course the town of Tequila itself. But if you head east of Guadalajara, to the eastern edge of the state, you arrive in Los Altos (The Highlands). In the past this was where agave was grown rather than distilled, but the balance of production has also been rapidly shifting further in this direction over the past few decades. This is evident in both the number of distilleries here and the average size of those distilleries. One only needs to notice (and it is hard not to) the billboard advertising and branding plastered over the frontage of bars and *licorerías* (liquor stores) to appreciate the familiar names that have grown up around here: Cazadores, Patrón, El Jimador, Espolōn – all regular entrants into the world's top 10 tequila sellers.

During our drive in we encountered the biggest billboard of them all. At a scale like something you would see on the Las Vegas strip, with flowing calligraphic script

it read "El Tierra de Don Julio". In front was the wizened old face of a Panama hat-wearing Don Julio Gonzalez, gazing out across the blue fields of Los Altos.

The man sitting in front of us now is his grandson.

"We have more than 100 years in the business," says Francisco as we take our seats. "The first tequila distillery out of Tequila Valley was established by my great-grandfather in a ranchera called El Salvador between Atotonilco and Tepatitlán. So my grandfather, Don Julio Gonzalez, was born and raised in a tequila distillery."

Julio's family were poor, as tequila wasn't very popular at the time. And living on an inaccessible hilltop meant it was hard for him to attend school, so his mother, who was a teacher, educated him at home. At 14, his father died, forcing him to start working in the distillery, which was now run by his uncle. One day, he was invited to transport tequila barrels by mule at night from the distillery to Atotonilco. From there, the barrels were taken by train to Ocotlán, an important commercial hub near Lake Chapala (Mexico's largest freshwater lake, to the southeast of Guadalajara), and then on to Mexico City. This was a tax-evasion strategy and the clandestine operation continued until he was caught one night by the police. He spent a night in jail and paid the bail with his gun. After his release, at 17, he asked a wealthy friend of his late father for a loan of 20,000 pesos to start his own business. He persisted for months until the man finally agreed. With this money, he opened his first tequila distillery. The year was 1942 and he was still just 17.

His main brand, 3 Magueyes, was launched in 1952 and enjoyed great success at the budget end of the Mexican market. Don Julio built his business, like everyone else, making *mixto* tequila, where a portion of sugar from cane was added to the agave at fermentation to bulk out the product. But in 1975 he began producing a limited quantity of 100% agave tequila strictly for consumption at family gatherings and as gifts for friends. He put it in short bottles so as not to obscure the view of guests across the dining table.

"By the 1980s he was the second or third biggest producer in the industry," says Francisco. "But in 1985 he had five strokes in a row and could no longer go on working. At age 60 he retired and my father and uncle began running the distillery."

The brothers were worried their father wouldn't be around much longer, so to celebrate his life in 1987, they launched Don Julio's 100% agave tequila recipe and named it after him. Tequila was still struggling to shake its reputation as a lower-class drink back then and wealthy folks who wouldn't admit to drinking it would often hide it under the table and prefer to be seen with whiskey, cognac or brandy. Francisco Sr. didn't want his father's name on a tequila brand that people were embarrassed to drink so he decided to create a new market and sell it as the most expensive tequila available, pricing it at double the cost of the priciest tequila at the time.

Don Julio thought he was crazy for trying to sell tequila at the price of whiskey or cognac but it worked. Don Julio became the first super-premium tequila brand in the Mexican market.

"So we didn't just change the history of the family," Francisco tells us. "It changed the history of the whole tequila industry."

In 1999 the Canadian spirits behemoth Seagram's invested an undisclosed sum in Don Julio, buying out the Gonzalez family. Seagram's were moving into the entertainment industry at the time, however, and the following year they sold all of their distilling and spirits brand assets for $8bn (£6bn) to the British spirits company Diageo and the French company Pernod Ricard. Don Julio went to Diageo and, possibly a little unsure about what to do with a tequila brand, Diageo invited Juan Beckmann from Joes Cuervo to buy into a 50% partnership with them. At that point Don Julio was selling around 300,000 cases a year. Jump forward to 2014 and sales of Don Julio had increased by a factor of three. At this point, Diageo agreed to a deal to swap their Bushmills distillery in Northern Ireland for Jose Cuervo's stake in Don Julio plus $408m (£315m). Given the million or so casks of whisky that was included in the sale, the deal was worth more than $3bn (£2.3bn) to Beckmann.

Under 100% Diageo ownership, Don Julio has continued to thrive, and in 2023 the brand sold 3.4 million cases, making it the second-biggest tequila brand in the world after Jose Cuervo.

I had the great fortune to visit Don Julio's Destilería La Primavera back in 2009. I fondly remember a very enlightening tasting with the brand's master distiller Enrique De Colsa. By that point La Primavera was already big and no doubt quite different to the place that Francisco and his brothers had kicked a football around as kids in the 1990s. Nevertheless, it maintained its brick ovens and pot stills and turned out an excellent tequila. Today, it is an absolute monster of an operation and Pancho says it's practically impossible to get tours in there. I worry that whatever they are hiding behind the walls of La Primavera today is both the secret to its massive production volume and the cause of its noticeable drop in quality over the past decade.

After the Gonzalezes sold to Seagram's they had a non-compete agreement so they sat patiently on their hands for a few years. In 2004 they got to work and began developing a new distillery on the land where their summer holiday home had once been situated. This was also around the same time that Francisco Jr. came into the business at the age of 15.

"The idea was to come back to the industry not with a distillery," says Francisco. "But with a sanctuary for the tequila in order to honour the beverage, the industry, the business that has given so much to the family, to the town, to the region."

The result is Casa de Los González, which is truly one of the most remarkable distilleries in Jalisco. In most tequila distilleries it's common to see pools of mystery liquids on cracked concrete floors, wheelbarrows of vegetal matter being pushed around, or steam blasting out of various orifices and dogs trailing around the place. But as Francisco takes us on a tour through his distillery it has more of the feel of a grand hotel lobby or museum than a place where agaves are turned into spirit.

High vaulted ceilings are supported by thick stone walls and huge stained-glass windows depict turquoise agave *pencas* and red soil, their designs painted by Francisco's mother. The floor is polished marble with a giant agave inset in a contrasting tone, almost too big to

OPPOSITE The Gonzalez family's journey has taken them from humble origins to tequila royalty. Luxurious interiors and artisanal craftsmanship now elevate the spirit once hidden under dinner tables, redefining premium tequila for a new generation of connoisseurs.

appreciate from the height of an average human's field of vision. It is a literal palace of tequila production.

This is not a distillery that is open to tours, so the architecture serves a purpose beyond aesthetics. Behind the sheen of the polished floor, the flow of production has been meticulously thought out, and engineered using Italian-manufactured equipment. The level of cleanliness is borderline obsessive, where even the brick ovens, which in any other distillery are normally caked with the residue of a thousand tonnes of baked vegetal matter, are as spotlessly clean as Francisco's office. As he puts it, "You wouldn't eat food in a dirty kitchen."

After the cooked agave is unloaded from the ovens, the entire process is handled by belts, pumps and pipes, which, wherever possible, are hidden underground. Francisco is very proud of this and points out that his mill is raised higher than most others, thus giving his staff better access to the underside for cleaning. Hidden pipes shift the agave juice to one of 13 fully insulated, 50,000-litre (13,000-gallon), closed-top steel fermenters.

"We were the first distillery to use closed-top fermenters," says Francisco. "Our entire system is designed so that nobody touches or even sees the product after milling until it is in the bottle."

The distillery uses the same proprietary yeast strain for all products and the same three (3,000-litre/800-gallon) stills with steam jackets and copper condensers. The distillate takes a narrow cut, which comes off at 53% ABV every time and the blanco is then chill-filtered to remove impurities at -7°C (19°F). No additives are used.

There is no variability in production here; everything is made the same way, and all of the brands produced here are owned or part-owned by the Gonzalez family. Besides the flagship product, Reserva de Los González, they produce a brand called Don Londrés in partnership with Post Malone's manager Dre London, and a brand called Reserva de Javier's, for an upmarket Mexican restaurant in California.

Francisco takes us through the boardroom where we see vivid portraits of Don Julio Gonzalez adorning the walls. There is a room containing old bottles of 3 Magueyes and Don Julio, along with family photos and portraits that track the Gonzalez family from small-time producers to the tequila royalty they are today.

Heading outside we walk through the gardens, where mandarin and lime trees are in fruit and sprinklers water the grass. Down some steps into what appears to be a fallout shelter, we enter a long, curved corridor, which is lined on both sides with barrels of tequila. This is the distillery's cellar, where the *añejo* products are matured. Custom built using five different layers of stone and insulating materials, this is a bunker the likes of which a doomsday prepper would be proud of and that maintains a consistent 20–21°C (68–70°F) all year round.

Out of the cellar, past a bandstand and through more manicured gardens, we come across a long row of stables. These are not intended for horses, but rather belong to members of the Gonzalez club. Francisco explains that, for $150,000 (£115,000) a year, customers can bag themselves one of only 100 spaces in one of the most exclusive tequila clubs in Mexico. This gets you your own bottle allocation (which you still have to pay for) with custom labelling, but also one of the stable spaces, which you can use as you see fit.

"It's for tequila lovers," says Francisco.

No shit.

Most of the current 33 members are big restaurant groups, leisure groups or sports societies. The stable (I realise I'm underselling it here) could therefore be used to hold private tastings or to hold private casks, or perhaps even be used as temporary accommodation (though I suspect anyone who can afford the membership might like something a bit more luxurious than a stable).

The distillery is currently turning out 220,000 cases a year but has the capacity and intention to grow to over a million cases. Interestingly, whether this is done through Reserva de Los González, or through their joint ventures, the liquid will always be the same. There is only one production stream for tequila here; it does not change according to different brands.

Back in Francisco's office he pours us a measure of Reserva de Los González Extra Añejo Cristalino (36% ABV) to try. *The aroma is a soft grapefruit candy with a touch of chamomile. The taste is very soft and mellow, with green sherbet and a touch of vanilla through the finish.*

The cristalino style is a relatively new innovation that came about in 2008 with the launch of Jose Cuervo's Maestro Dobel Cristalino and Don Julio 70. Both of these products are aged tequilas that are filtered through charcoal to remove the colour that the barrel imparts. While not an official category under the tequila NOM, with their softer flavour and sometimes lower strength, the idea was to create a "gateway tequila" that can be served on the rocks and appeal especially to women. The obvious downside of a cristalino tequila is that the maturation in cask masks much of the natural agave character, while the filtering removes yet more of it, along with some of the flavour it gains from maturation. This is why cristalinos are more akin to tequila-flavoured vodkas than blanco tequilas and their packaging tends to be styled towards vodka drinkers too. Nevertheless, the demand has proven strong and the market is now flooded with cristalino expressions. Naturally, this has triggered tequila purists, but there is even an apologetic sentiment among many cristalino-making tequila producers too, who would prefer it if people just drank their blancos.

Francisco leads us back towards our car with a brief stop by the distillery chapel, which is big enough to seat 30 distillery workers at least. Francisco crosses himself at the altar and then points out that the agave-painted tiles on the floors, walls and ceiling, if viewed from the correct angle, create an enormous crucifix effect.

Los Altos has long been a bastion of traditional Mexican Catholicism and this deeply rooted faith would prove pivotal during one of Mexico's most turbulent periods: the Cristero War of 1926–1929. As the secularising government in Mexico City sought to enforce anti-Catholic legislation, Los Altos emerged as a formidable stronghold for the resistance. The region's strategic terrain, dotted with hills and valleys, provided natural defences for the Cristero rebels, while its devout population offered unwavering support.

Local leaders like Victoriano Ramírez, known as El Catorce (The Fourteen), rallied the people of Los Altos against what they saw as unjust government intrusion. Towns such as San Julián became battlegrounds, witnessing significant Cristero victories. Even after the war's official end in 1929, pockets of resistance persisted in Los Altos well into the 1930s. This period of conflict left an indelible mark on the region, reinforcing its conservative identity and Catholic traditions.

The sense of wealth at this distillery is palpable. Even more than that, there is the feeling of something dynastic: family and power. Dallas does distilling. The Gonzalez family legacy runs deep in these parts, extending to various other distilleries and brands. Another branch of the family owns the famed Siete Leguas brand, which is made across three distilleries a couple of miles from here, in Atotonilco Los Altos.

Francisco's cousin, Eduardo "Lalo" Gonzalez, has become something of a celebrity in Texas after he launched a brand called Lalo (to honour his father rather than himself) in 2020. Lalo makes tequila at Destilería Grupo Tequilero Mexico in Arandas, and has achieved a seemingly winning combination of top-quality liquid (fermented with champagne yeast) along with minimalist, modern Mexican branding. A few years ago, Lalo sought investment to grow the brand, and can you guess who one of the investors was? That's right: Juan Beckmann from Jose Cuervo.

RIGHT Italian designer stills polished to perfection and not a single pipe or valve visible unless it needs to be. The González distillery is so clean you could eat tacos off the floor.

PERNOD RICARD

◇◇

La Industria

There's no doubt that certain families in Los Altos have profited wildly from the tequila boom. Some of the money goes back many generations when farming agave was the main industry here, but much of it has been compounded by farmers who have turned to distilling and reaped the benefits of owning their entire supply chain.

"Tequila is a workers' town," says Pancho as we blast towards Arandas at 80 miles per hour (130km/h). "Most of the owners live in Guadalajara. In Los Altos, the owners live in Los Altos."

Tequila is also naturally more touristic, with the town geared up to accept visitors and extract cash from them. With Los Altos being so spread out, there is no magnetic draw to any one particular point. Owners have stayed on their ancestral properties and built huge mansions like the ones we are driving past now.

This also means that the distilleries in Los Altos are spread miles apart from one another. Jaime Orendain mentioned this when we visited Arette (see page 12), explaining that in Tequila the distilleries congregate around areas with a good, clean water supply, which tended to mean towns and villages. In Los Altos, distilleries were built later and often among expansive stretches of established farm land, which meant seeking out a water supply within, or near to, one's own fields.

Destilería Colonial de Jalisco is something of an exception to all of this as it is one of the only distilleries to be purpose built by a multinational entity. Originally intended to produce Patrón tequila under an agreement with Seagram's (see page 74), the 140-acre (55-hectare) site was built in the late 1990s and the location on the outskirts of Arandas was chosen because it was adjacent to a 200-metre (650-ft) artesian well. The relationship with Patrón didn't work out, however, and when Seagram's sold off all of their assets in 2000, it was

Pernod Ricard that took on Destilería Colonial de Jalisco, along with two tequila brands: Olmeca and Mariachi.

Both brands had previously been made at the historic Hacienda La Martineña distillery, which is next-door to Arette, and which Seagram's bought in the 1960s. Both brands had also been neglected by Seagram's but, with their shiny new distillery in Arandas, Pernod Ricard recognised the potential of Olmeca and ploughed resources into selling and marketing it. Among other things, this meant creating the best tequila brand ambassador programme the world had seen, which drew from the bar industry's biggest names, like Dré Masso and the late Henry Besant, followed by more industry big names like Steffin Oghene and Megs Miller. With Dré and Henry came the launch of Olmeca's first 100% agave offering, Altos, along with countless bartender trips to Mexico and accompanying tales too outrageous to put in print.

Olmeca subsequently became one of the best-selling brands of the early 21st century and at one point was the best-selling tequila in Europe. Europe imports less than 10% of the annual tequila production but nevertheless has some avid enthusiasts within its ranks. Latvia, for example, is the sixth-largest importer of tequila in the world but has the second-highest per capita consumption after Mexico. Also in the top ten, but with much lower consumption rates are Panama, Singapore, Spain, Puerto Rico, Netherlands, Australia and Canada. Great Britain ranks sixteenth in the world, drinking an average of 2.4 shots of tequila a year. As for any pattern or statistical correlation between these nations, the best I could come up with is cultural diversity, tourism and good economic standing.

After passing security checks at the Pernod Ricard-owned distillery, we are met by the former master distiller, Jesús Hernández.

Jesús joined Seagram's in the 1980s and began his distilling career in California, where he made brandy and rum. When Seagram's broke ground on their new distillery in Arandas in 1995, Jesús was brought in to help design and run it, and this is where he stayed for the next 15 years until his retirement in 2013.

"I enjoy tequila so much..." he says with a shrug and a smile, "that I am still around!"

Jesús has a unique insight into the tectonic shifts of big companies within the tequila world. Having transitioned from Seagram's to Pernod Ricard, he witnessed and participated in the movement towards 100% agave, and produced a variety of brands in that time including Olmeca, Avion and Don Julio, which he liked so much he convinced the bigwigs to buy.

Outside, on an enormous patio, we inspect the huge piles of agaves that are waiting to be cooked. Here they buy *piñas* with a medium-length stub of *penca*, which Jesús says is optimal for yield and flavour complexity.

"The price of agave is low at the moment," he says. "I've seen cycles of high prices, low prices, high availability and shortages. The first one hit me just after we opened the distillery – we knew it was coming."

While the exports of tequila have been steadily increasing over the past 20 years, the price of agave and the number of agaves that are harvested is in a constant state of flux. This is the unfortunate nature of producing a spirit from a plant that takes up to eight years to mature.

As sales of tequila increase, the demand for agave increases with it and the price of agave rises. Farmers who may otherwise have been growing corn or beans recognise that it's a good time to get in on the game, so they start planting agave. Even private citizens with a small patch of land sometimes plant agave during these periods, like an investment for the future. But flash forward five or ten years and there is a glut of agave, and the prices drop as supply exceeds demand. With the price at rock bottom, nobody wants to plant agave anymore, so they shift back to growing corn and beans. A few years later there isn't enough mature agave to go around and the price goes back up again.

"You can summarise it in two words," says Jesús, "Greed and market."

This cycle has repeated itself roughly every 16 years (two agave life cycles) for the past 100 years, but the peaks and troughs are becoming more extreme. In 2003 the price of agave rose to 16 pesos (80p/$1.60) per kilogram but just five years later it had plummeted to 1 peso (5p/10 cents) per kilogram causing roughly half of all agave

farmers to go out of business. By 2019, the price shot up to an all-time high of 34 pesos (£1.30/$1.70) per kilogram and farmers were going to guard their fields at night to deter thieves. At the time of writing, the price is on a rapid downward trajectory and, in spite of the continual growth of the category, it looks set to hit close to zero pesos by 2026, where once again we can expect to see farmers going bust and agaves being used to feed livestock or simply rotting in the fields.

Besides the loss of jobs and livelihoods, this cycle has negative consequences for the environment. During boom periods some farmers take to harvesting agaves early to take advantage of the high market price, or they ramp up the use of industrial fertilisers to expedite maturation. This degrades and acidifies the soil, reducing its biodiversity and making it barren for future seasons. It can also pollute water supplies and endanger workers.

High prices negatively impact tequila quality too, as farmers looking to capitalise on the market demand harvest underripe agaves. These periods can have lasting effects on the category. One such spike in prices was responsible for the *mixto* tequila category, which was introduced in 1964 when producers lobbied to be able to use cheaper sugar sources to bolster their alcohol. And if it wasn't alternative sugars being used to extend tequila out, it was water. Sixty years ago, tequila was always bottled above 46% ABV, but the minimum strength has gradually been reduced during times of agave scarcity so that producers can dilute their products more and recoup some of the cost of their raw materials.

It may also be the low prices during 2005 to 2014 that we have to thank for the emergence of the cristalino category. Back then, distilleries were making more blanco tequila than they could sell, so they loaded the excess into barrels for maturation. Demand soon picked up for blanco tequila, but what to do about all the aged tequila sitting in cask? The innovation came in the form of cristalino, where *añejo* tequila could be recycled back into blanco by removing its colour. It's interesting to reframe the trend towards luxury cristalino tequila as purely a function of too many farmers planting agaves in 2002.

Jesús points to seven brick ovens ranging from 60 to 70 tonnes, which are used to make Altos as well as Avion (a brand that Pernod Ricard acquired a few years ago). The cook lasts a total of 38 hours with a further eight hours of resting inside the oven before the doors are opened. Meanwhile, the agaves used to make Olmeca tequila are cooked in four 30-tonne autoclaves that take 11 hours to complete a cook.

"The benefit of the autoclave is that you can really save energy," Jesús says. "But in an autoclave, 30 minutes can make all the difference between overcooked and undercooked, because it's so aggressive."

The distillery uses its own proprietary yeast that was isolated from agave many years previously and has been continually propagated ever since. Each of the three brands has eight fermenters, which are scaled according to size of the brand. This means the Avion fermenters are smaller than the Altos ones, which sit at a whopping 100,000 litres (25,000 gallons) each.

"Eight is the magic number," Jesús says. "Because of the cycle of fermentation, we are distilling between two and three fermenters each day."

There are six enormous pot stills weighing in at 10,000 litres (2,500 gallons) each. All of the distilleries we have visited thus far have used pot stills to produce tequila. A pot still is effectively a kettle that heats up the fermented *mosto,* causing the alcohol (which has a lower boiling point than water) to evaporate up to the head (top) of the still and then down into the condenser via the connecting lyne arm. In the condenser, cool water is circulated around the pipes that contain the spirit vapour and the vapour condenses back into a liquid, flows off the still and is collected. For tequila production this process is then repeated twice.

The first distillation produces a low-strength but clear liquid called *ordinario,* which typically has an alcoholic strength between 20% and 30% ABV – not strong enough to be bottled as tequila and not refined enough either. The second distillation will take the spirit up to anything from 40% to 60%, at which point it can be put in a barrel to make a *reposado* or *añejo,* have its strength adjusted to between 35% and 55% to meet Mexican bottling standards for blanco or, in some rare circumstances, be distilled again. A third distillation has the effect of further purifying the spirit: the spirit will achieve an even higher strength and its character will broadly speaking become lighter, less agave-centric, and more vodka-like.

The specific shape and materials of the still steer the character of the spirit too, and with no two distilleries having exactly the same apparatus, this is one of the variables that impacts a tequila's style. Remember that the mosto holds within it a broad range of alcohols besides ethanol as well as taste and flavour compounds with varying degrees of volatility and desirability.

Taller stills typically produce a lighter style of spirit, as it is that much harder for heavier compounds to make their way up to the head of the still. Shorter stills do the opposite and can produce denser, oilier and more heavily textured distillates. Some stills have small retorts connected to the lyne arms. These little chambers have an input pipe that comes from the head of the still and an output pipe that goes to the condenser, and sometimes a third pipe that drops back down to the base of the still. Like a safety net for heavy (and presumably undesirable) compounds, this chamber returns the compounds back to the still, while allowing lighter alcohols free passage to the condenser.

Most of the stills in tequila are made from steel, which is a durable and fairly inert material that has little effect on the taste of the spirit. But some still designs include copper components while others are made entirely from copper. Copper has a mild, purifying effect and reacts with the spirit in a way that removes sulphurous compounds from the distillate. In fact, copper stills are in a perpetual state of decay because the spirit vapour reacts with the metal which sacrifices itself to the cause of polishing the spirit character.

Distillers also have to make "cuts" to the spirit. As the spirit flows off the condenser on the second distillation, its character and composition changes over time. The distiller selects which part of the distillate they would like to keep and which they wouldn't, based on its alcoholic strength, chemical composition, aroma and taste throughout the five to nine hours it takes to distil tequila.

Generally speaking, the distiller makes three spirit cuts, which produces four distinct parts of the distillate: (1) the foreshots, which comprise the first few minutes of distillate and contain very light alcohols and other highly volatile compounds that can be toxic; (2) the *puntas* (heads), which also contain some lighter alcohols as well as very fruity and fragrant compounds; (3) the *corazón* (heart), which is the main body of the spirit and the product that can be bottled as tequila; (4) the *cola* (tails), which is the final, low-strength part of the distillation that still contains some alcohols but at a lower concentration.

"For Avion, we take a smaller heart cut," says Jesús. "And we distil it slower, less aggressively, which makes a lighter spirit too."

This is not a process of making flavour but rather selecting flavour from a palette of available options. Two different distillers can produce markedly different tequilas just by "cutting" the spirit at different times through the process. For example, Distiller #1 might make a high (early) heads cut and a high (early) tails cut. This would likely make a high-strength, perfumed, fruity and mineral-y distillate. Distiller #2 might make a low heads cut and a low tails cut, which would typically produce a lower-strength, richer, more vegetal distillate. Turning the dials and pushing the knobs on this process is where the artistry of distillation comes in to effect.

Emerging out of the distillery building, we encounter an enormous set of structures that look like they have been borrowed from an oil refinery. High steel columns rise up at least 30m (100ft), and between them a network of coloured pipes are knotted together like geometric noodles. What we're looking at is a column still, or continuous still. Jesús informs us that there are actually two of them and they are used exclusively for production of Tequila Olmeca.

The first column stills were invented in the early part of the 19th century and were originally used to make Scotch whisky. Unlike pot stills, which distil in batches, meaning they must be filled, heated, emptied and cleaned for every distillation, columns work non-stop, accepting a continuous stream of mosto and outputting a continuous stream of spirit. This reduces labour and energy costs, but also produces a higher-strength spirit at a fraction of the cost of a pot. The downside is they tend to strip out a lot of flavour in the process, which is why they are the key component in vodka production, where the removal of flavour is the ultimate goal. The high alcoholic strength also causes some producers to be indiscriminate about the agaves they use, as column stills strip out so much of the flavour of the material – good or bad. It's for this reason that columns are synonymous with mixto tequila, like Olmeca.

In tequila, columns are usually only found in big distilleries, which are making products that compete on price. In other words, it is rare to find column-distilled tequila that can compete on flavour. No wonder Jesús is quickly ushering us around the corner.

It turns out there is another reason to move on. In a separate building from the rest of the distillery, we find a smaller distillery with its own 1,000-litre (265-gallon) pots, as well as fermenters and a *tahona* (that huge

ABOVE Standing at the base of the enormous column stills at Destilería Colonial de Jalisco. These towers enable the production of tequila on a massive scale, but it comes at a cost.

volcanic stone wheel used to crush the piñas). This little setup is used to make a tequila that accounts for a small percentage of what ends up in an Olmeca Altos bottle – the exact amount being a secret that Jesús is not going to divulge.

"We blend them at just the right amount," he says with a smile. "The tahona has a slightly citrus note and a sweet taste. But when we mix it with the roller-mill tequila it adds viscosity – it's creamy. And that's what we want from this tequila."

Over in the tasting room we get to see what he means.

Altos Plata (40% ABV) *has a fresh citrus peel aroma, cool like cucumber flesh, along with fresh mint; altogether it's very green smelling. The taste has some pepperiness to it, with a molasses and cooked agave note rising up. The finish is grapefruit juice.*

Altos Reposado (40% ABV) is matured in ex-bourbon barrels for between five and seven months. *The aroma is slightly nutty, with a hint of vanilla, but repeat visits allow the agave to shine through. The taste has some baking spices to it, reminiscent of the vegetal/cinnamon sweetness of carrot cake.*

LA ALTEÑA

El Terruño

In a small *fonda* (neighbourhood spot) in Arandas, we start the day with a cinnamon-infused coffee alongside hearty huevos rancheros (crispy tortillas topped with fried eggs and spicy salsa roja). But the star of the breakfast is the birria – tender goat meat in a rich, chilli-spiced broth. Pancho teaches us how to roll tortillas into tubes and use them to scoop up the sauce. To wash it all down with, the waiter brings over bottles of homemade lime and tamarind soft drinks that they make in-house.

The town of Arandas is located in the northern part of Los Altos and has a population of 60,000. It was founded in the 18th century by the Camarena family, and that name still carries a lot of weight around here, as well as in the world of tequila. Back when the region consisted only of sparse populations of subsistent farmers and pockets of indigenous communities, the Camarenas brought the first blue agave *hijuelos* (plant shoots) to their farm, changing the economy and topography of the region forevermore. Today, Los Altos is thought to account for around 70% of the agave used in tequila production.

Pedro Camarena was born in 1861 and is another farmer and tequilero with a strong claim to being the first person to establish a distillery outside of the Tequila Valley. He and his brother actually founded two distilleries, one in Jesús María and the other in Arandas. Though neither operation survived the Mexican Revolution (1910–1920) and Cristero War (1926–1929), Pedro Camarena sired a line of renowned tequila producers who went on to open their own distilleries in the early 20th century: Pedro Camarena (Destilería El Gallito), Agustín Camarena (Destilería La Arandina) and Felipe Camarena (Destilería La Alteña).

And it's La Alteña where we are heading to now.

As we pull up into the car park, we spot a row of what look to be school busses, only they have been painted white and branded with the word Tapatio – the best-known tequila made here and one of the most loved in all of Mexico.

We're greeted by Gabby Camarena, the great-granddaughter of Felipe Camarena who founded La Alteña (which means "of the Highlands") in 1937. He launched the Tapatio brand, named after the colloquial word for a young man from Guadalajara. Felipe's son, Felipe J. Camarena Orozco, took the brand to the next level and modernised the distillery in the mid-20th century, bringing in roller mills to help it meet the demands of the market.

"By the late 1980s, my grandfather became nostalgic for the original methods his father used," says Gabby as we walk into the distillery building. "That's when he reintroduced the tahona and launched the El Tesoro de Don Felipe brand in homage to the original process."

At La Alteña they have seven brick ovens each with a 50-tonne capacity, a five-stage roller mill, and a tahona. Tapatio is made from a blend of 80% roller mill and 20% tahona, while their other brand, El Tesoro, is 100% tahona. Both brands are fermented naturally in open-top pine vats. There are 32 vats in total, each around 4,000 litres (1,000 gallons) in volume. Gabby explains that the tahona works at only around 50% efficiency of sugar extraction while the mill is 92%. But the leftover fibre from the tahona is added to the fermenters in nylon sacks, which stew in the warm *mosto* like massive teabags.

While there is scale here, the production is still very basic. There are no computers or industrial machinery, just notepads, tasting glasses and a good sense of smell.

"The distillery only got electricity in 2000," says Gabby, "and at the time that was just to power the lights."

Don Felipe passed away in 2003 and La Alteña passed into the hands of his daughters, Lilianna, Gabriella and Jennifer, and his son Carlos.

Carlos Camarena originally studied as an agronomist and took on the mantle of master distiller at La Alteña somewhat reluctantly. His passion for agaves and the land they grew on was unusual among tequileros at the time though, and knowing how to grow the best agaves put him in good stead for making the best tequila (once he learned how).

Earlier in his career, Carlos's father had developed a relationship with Robert Denton and Marilyn Smith, often hailed as the pioneering importers of tequila in the US. They initiated the introduction of the first boutique tequilas made from 100% agave – Chinaco and Caliente – and they took on El Tesoro when it was launched in 1988. Carlos collaborated closely with them, actively promoting their tequilas and working to bridge the gap between Mexico and the US through regular trips north of the border.

Besides the difference in milling between Tapatio and El Tesoro, the two products are distilled differently. La Alteña has a total of six pot stills, which vary in size. The biggest is 5,000 litres (1,300 gallons) and made from stainless steel, and the rest are made entirely from copper

ABOVE La Alteña is where terroir meets craftsmanship in Los Altos. From tahona stones to roller mills, this family-run distillery blends old-world charm with scale, and each drop of Tapatio and El Tesoro is a testament to the legacy of the Camarena family.

and range in size right down to a tiny 320-litre (85-gallon) still. Being the larger-volume product, Tapatio uses the two largest stills for its first distillation, followed by a second distillation in a 1,000-litre (265-gallon) or 600-litre (160-gallon) copper still. El Tesoro has its first distillation in those same two copper stills and then its second in two smaller copper stills.

Gabby explains that the 1,000-litre and 600-litre stills are the oldest and date back to her grandfather's time. On closer inspection, we can see where parts have been patched up, bolts have been driven through, and clamps are bracing some bits together.

Vincente Coronado is distilling today. He is a 50-year-old whip of a man with keen eyes darting between valves and flowing liquids.

"Vincente says that if this still goes," says Gabby, pointing to the old, patchwork still. "He goes."

There are in fact four Coronado brothers employed as distillers at La Alteña and they represent the third generation of Coronados to work here. Vincente's son and daughter and his niece are learning to distil here too, which makes them the fourth generation. So the Coronados are as much a part of the furniture here as the old copper stills.

The Camarenas work with other families in the fields, employing eight brothers (as *jimadores*) from the same Zuniga family.

"There are lots of families," says Gabby. "When we say we are a family business it's not only my family."

Gabby produces a horn from her pocket and uses it to scoop a sample of the blanco tequila from a vat that is collecting the distillate off the still. Vincente brings over a rolled-up banana leaf and from within it he withdraws a floating hydrometer, which can be suspended in a measuring cylinder of the spirit and used to gauge its strength.

"*Cincuenta y seis (56),*" he says.

It's one degree too strong to be called tequila, but not at all too strong for us to taste. *The aroma is sweet and pungent. It tastes sweet too, with hints of citrus rind. The finish is creamy and buttery, though.*

Gabby leads us down to the cellar, which has the feel and scale of an underground car park. It's much cooler down here but also damp, with the sound of running water echoing off the walls. The casks here are nearly all ex-bourbon, but there are some ex-Cognac barrels lurking around too (used to make El Tesoro Paradiso Extra Añejo) and even some Japanese mizunara oak barrels.

As we walk among the stacks of ageing tequila, we discover the source of the running-water sound. Across the length of an entire wall, water is emanating from cracks and flowing down into a drain. Red iron deposits are caked on to the wall and when, under instruction from Gabby, we taste the water, it is extremely metallic – like blood.

This mineral-rich spring water is used to cool the condensers in the distillery but also to dilute the agave juice for fermentation, so its character is intrinsic to the flavour profiles of Tapatio and El Tesoro. It's also used to proof down tequila for bottling.

"You wouldn't want to bottle this!" I say.

"Actually, my uncle Carlos does!" says Gabby. "At his other distillery, Los Alambiques, he takes the water for one of the workers who suffers from anaemia."

In 2007 Carlos launched a new brand of tequila called Ocho, forming a glorious partnership with one of the industry's other modern heroes: Tomas Estes. The Ocho brand was made at La Alteña for more than a decade and soon became one of the darlings of the tequila world, prized by aficionados and bartenders alike both for the men behind it and for its incredible taste credentials. The brand was purchased by Samson & Surrey in 2020, which itself was acquired by Heaven Hill (the bourbon brand) in 2022. After the acquisition a new distillery was built near Arandas called Los Alambiques, and Ocho production – along with Carlos – shifted over there. That's the short version of the story, but the story of Tomas Estes deserves a longer telling.

Tomas Estes was born in Los Angeles and worked as an English teacher for a few years. After taking a road trip through Mexico with his then wife and young son, he moved to Europe. Having grown up in LA, he was well aware of Mexican culture, but this trip inspired him to open a cantina so he sold everything he had and for $15,000, he opened Café Pacifico in Amsterdam. Europe had never seen anything like it and it became a hotspot for touring celebrities and locals alike. Further outposts soon followed: London in 1982, Paris in 1984, Cologne in 1986, Milan in 1988, the list goes on. All told, there were 18 restaurants by the late 1990s.

Tomas's passion and knowledge for agave spirits grew and he began taking frequent trips to Mexico, touring distilleries and learning all about the category. Meanwhile, he was importing pallets of tequila into Europe and introducing Europeans to a side of the category that they had never seen. Tomas began writing more about tequila and educating; in time he literally became the Ambassador for Tequila to Europe, having been granted the title by the National Chamber in Mexico. Anyone who knew Tomas knew how generous he was with his time and his tequila. He was certainly a good friend to me, and I have fond memories of trips spent with him all across Europe – he also helped me write the tequila section of my first book.

It was inevitable that Tomas would start his own tequila brand, and Carlos – with his family pedigree and technical expertise – was the perfect person with whom to celebrate agave spirits and share them with Tomas's audience. But (besides the obvious) what would be Ocho's unique selling point?

It's been a long-held belief among agave farmers and tequileros of the past that the agaves grow differently depending on the region and soil type. For example, most producers agree that Los Altos produces markedly different agaves to the Tequila Valley. The former has an elevation of 2,000m (6,500ft) and tends to be cooler. The latter has an elevation of 1,200–1,600 metres (4,000–5250 ft), is much hotter. The orientation of the land also affects the maturation time. West- and south-facing slopes receive the most intense sunlight so agaves mature a little quicker, while north-facing slopes require the longest time for agaves to mature.

"The iron in the soil in Los Altos makes the agave develop differently," says Gabby. "It's going to be more floral than the agave that grows in the Valley. Also, it can produce a juicier agave with more sugar. Agaves in the Valley tend to have more fibre, and they are more vegetal, with some green, fresh aromas and some spices."

As the industry grew in the 20th century, the big players like Cuervo, Sauza and Herradura had to begin sourcing their agaves from all over Jalisco to meet demand, and the significance of regionality was homogenised out of the product.

Carlos knew that the difference was there, though, and that it goes way beyond climate and into soil type and soil biota (the micro-organisms, animals and plant life that live in the soil). As far back as the 1990s, he used to say that he could identify every detail about the agave used for a bottle of El Tesoro by just looking at its lot number and bottling date. For their 70th anniversary, his family released a special seven-year-old tequila from their best agave field, distilled in 2000. This showed that they understood terroir long before it was a common concept in modern tequila-making. Despite this, the idea of applying terroir to distilled spirits was initially seen as crazy. "It's not wine!" people would say.

The Ocho brand used Carlos's experiences with El Tesoro and took terroir to the next level. All Ocho expressions are made from agave sourced from within the Camarena estate, which means that when we're talking about terroir here it means the specific field of agave, with each plot of land imparting its own unique terroir-driven stamp of flavour based on soil, water, sunlight and the soil biota itself. Over the years the estate has released blanco tequilas from dozens of different fields, each one showing differences in taste that have excited consumers and attracted the attention of other producers.

Carlos believes vintages are crucial for agave, noting that each field behaves differently and can only be

ABOVE Still under the stewardship of Carlos Camarena, Ocho has become one of the best-loved tequila brands and for very good reason: authenticity, transparency, and the coming together of two great tequila families.

harvested every eight to ten years. This gap allows the distillery to compare tequilas from the same field across different decades, showing how climate and soil affect the flavour. They launched their first single-field tequila in 2007 and dozens have followed since. Tomas died on 5 April 2021 and an entire industry of bartenders and tequila lovers mourned his passing.

Terroir remains a divisive topic in tequila. In 2013 a scientific paper led by Dr. Silvia G. Ceballos-Magaña at the University of Colima aimed to investigate the chemical composition of blue agave plants from five different regions in Jalisco, to assess the potential influence of terroir on tequila production. The study employed several extremely technical-sounding analytical strategies to examine the plants' chemical profiles in forensic detail.

The results revealed significant variations in composition based on the plants' geographical origin. Notably, agave plants from Los Altos demonstrated higher concentrations of sugar compared to those from the Valley. Mineral content also varied considerably between regions, with differences observed in elements such as calcium, potassium and magnesium. Additionally, the amino-acid profiles showed distinct patterns among plants from different areas.

Perhaps the most interesting and impactful of these discoveries is the variance in mineral content. This is shaped by the soil composition, which is (as you would expect) more volcanic the closer you get to a volcano. Some minerals may be absorbed by the plant but just as

a pervasive mineral note – like flint. The taste is lighter than expected, more refined and cleaner. But there is an interesting fungal, mushroom character too.

Next, Gabby pours out Tapatio Reposado (40% ABV), which is matured for approximately six months in ex-bourbon casks. *The aroma is vanilla and soft sugar, which carries on to a sweet and grippy character on the palate. Then, a welcome touch of tannin dries out the spirit a little; the linger is mossy and herbal.*

El Tesoro Reposado (40% ABV) has a little longer in cask, hitting the limit almost at 9 to 11 months. *It has a more musty note to it, like a dank warehouse smell. Bung cloth and old wood. On the taste it's more dessert-like, with fudge and a little banana. The finish is cinnamon and ginger.*

By this point we are beginning to get excited and Gabby responds exactly as she should by producing a bottle of Tapatio 110 (55% ABV) which is the distillery's high-proof offering and very similar to what we drank off the still earlier. *The aroma is wildly bright and clean, with a touch of alcohol coming through too. The taste is vegetal with sharp citrus but very agave forward. Sweetness fights spice through the long finish, which goes on for a minute.*

While we're enjoying the spirit, Gabby is rooting around the cupboards attempting to find some more experimental stuff that hasn't been released yet. She produces a bottle of El Tesoro that has been aged in Japanese mizunara wood for two months – a work in progress. *There's big cooked agave on the nose – it's pungent and mildly woody. Smoked incense and rich spice follow; it's grippy and tight, aromatic and well resolved. The long finish is sensual, heady, sweet and candied.*

importantly the soil will foster a different array of soil biota based on its mineral makeup, which will in turn produce further variances in soil composition that impact the plant.

These findings clearly demonstrate that growing agave plants in different locations influences their sweetness and botanical composition. The only question is – with all the various stages of production – how much of that carries through to the resulting tequila?

Well, there's only one way to find out, and that's by tasting lots of tequila.

The selection that Gabby lines up for us in the tasting room isn't necessarily going to inform us much about terroir, but at the very least it will broaden our appreciation of the tequila flavour in respect of production differences.

We begin by tasting Tapatio Blanco (40% ABV). *Its aroma is all fresh lime and salt with traces of cooked agave coming through. It's sweet, fragrant and delicate with some alcohol. There's also plenty of sweetness and richness, with full-flavoured and slight oily, buttery notes on the finish.*

El Tesoro Blanco (40% ABV) is a different beast. *The aroma is still fresh but with a touch more roasted agave, plus*

FELICIANO VIVANCO
Y ASOCIADOS

✦✦✦✦✦✦✦✦✦✦✦✦✦✦✦✦✦✦✦✦✦✦✦✦✦✦✦✦✦✦✦

El Sabor

Our next stop is Feliciano Vivanco y Asociados on the western edge of Arandas. This distillery is more commonly referred to as Viva Mexico, as it is the flagship brand of tequila made here but the company contract-distils many brands including Gran Dovejo, Siempre and Siembra Azul. In the circles of tequila aficionados, it is often simply referred to by its NOM, 1414, which has become shorthand for quality that belies its price point. The distillery is owned and operated by the five Vivanco brothers, who are fourth-generation agave farmers and second-generation distillers.

Entering the distillery office, Pancho introduces us to Sergio Vivanco. He is around 60 years old and as lean and long as a whip. He was once a third-division soccer player but now manages sales and marketing for the distillery, as well as hosting the odd travelling author from time to time. Sergio beckons us over to the wall of the office where various family photos are on display.

"This is my father, Feliciano," he says pointing to one of them. "Felice means 'happy' in Spanish and he was always smiling."

Like so many other Los Altos producers, Feliciano began making tequila to dodge the constant fluctuations of the agave market. It was the late 1980s and he'd earmarked a piece of land just outside of town on which to build a distillery. It had previously been used to grow beans and corn and had a small family holiday home that became the office we're standing in now. The distillery opened officially in 1994, by which time the Vivanco brothers (who had all obtained degree-level educations) were well set-up to divide up the operational pie between them. Besides Sergio, Armando does the HR and recruitment, Paulo is the architect and designer,

Feliciano Jr. handles the fields and the *jimadores* and José Manuel takes care of production. These days the family owns 17 small parcels of land that, all in all, total around 600,000 agaves.

"We are one of the small ones," says Sergio. "There are around 162 tequila producers: 14 of them are very large, 14 of them are medium, and the rest are small."

To put it in even more stark terms, the top five tequila producers account for approximately 50% of all tequila sales, and eight corporate entities own around 75% of the global market.

This disparity of scale and the resulting tension that comes from it is a defining factor in how tequila sees itself today. On the one hand, big producers have been instrumental in elevating the name of tequila and getting it on the backbar and in the speed rail of almost every cocktail bar, dive bar and hotel bar in the world. They have ploughed money into tequila tourism and helped to establish standards of production that largely serve to protect the category.

But where once the goals of big businesses were roughly aligned with that of tequila as a whole, it is beginning to feel like a rift has formed and many of the big players are taking every available opportunity to cut costs and maximise profits, usually at the cost of taste and authenticity. And as the CRT (Tequila Regulatory Council) is funded by tequila producers – on a sliding scale based on the volume of sales a producer makes – it's very easy to see how big multinationals with entire legal and lobbying departments are able to promote agendas to enact legislation that benefits their bottom lines.

This leaves the 130-or-so small producers who do not benefit from economies of scale, lack marketing money and expertise, lack the distribution networks, and ultimately cannot compete on price. They must find a niche, and fortunately for us some of them have gravitated towards quality and transparency.

"There are 22 families that make the best tequilas," says Sergio. "And all of them are small producers."

He is quick to state that these families are friends, "We get together and sip our tequilas as friends. These families feel the passion of the Mexican drink." As pretty a picture as that paints, it is hard to see in the relatively small market that sipping tequila represents (and which we are exploring extensively) how everyone can get along so warmheartedly all of the time.

Sergio walks us through the courtyard and to the back of the distillery, pointing out the stables where the family keeps 18 horses used to compete in *vaquero* (cowboy) competitions. Nearby, one of the three brick ovens is being loaded. Gesturing at the agaves, he tells us that the family takes plants from three soil types ("red, black, brown") and cuts the *pencas* to two different lengths (medium and completely shaved). This creates six variables before production has even begun.

But this is just the beginning.

They use three different cooking durations (24, 26 and 28 hours), four different levels of Brix for fermentation (8, 9, 11 and 13° Brix), five types of yeast (Champagne, wild, rum, distillers, and a proprietary

yeast), three different lengths of fermentation, and two different fermentation vessel materials (steel and wood), producing three different strengths of distillate (55, 49 and 47%). They're in the process of adding another variable to the mix too: a *tahona* is in its construction phase, seemingly only a matter of days from completion.

In one of the fermentation rooms, we encounter a wooden tub with a very long fermentation underway. On the surface is a network of beautiful patterns that have the effect of marble or some celestial formation.

"It looks like a brain," says Pancho. "It's like synapses between the neurons."

"Or like mycelium," I suggest.

This organic film is evidence of malolactic fermentation where malic acid (created during the regular fermentation) is converted into lactic acid by the beneficial bacterium *Oenococcus omni*. This can create soft and buttery flavours in the ferment that carry through to a richness and rounded mouthfeel in the finished spirit. Sometimes these bacteria (and others) are encouraged to colonise on the inside of fermentation tanks.

It's at this point that we notice music is being piped into the fermentation room. Pancho explains that the Vivancos were innovators in this department and believe that blasting classical music 24 hours a day in some way sonically activates the yeast cells, leading to a more productive ferment. Whether this is superstition or pseudoscience, or whether there really is something in it, the idea of music being a part of your drink could help people pay more attention when they drink it and that can only be a good thing.

Walking through the still house with its five copper pot-stills, Sergio emphasises that all this experimentation is not all romance and trial and error. There is real thought going into every step and they employ two graduate-level distillers from the University of Guadalajara. While flavour is paramount in everything they do, it's with a grounding in science.

Now, if all of the variables we have discussed were combined in all possible permutations, Sergio would be making at least 20,000 different blanco tequilas, which is far more than it's possible to catalogue and commercialise

LEFT The concept of "sipping tequila" was fairly outrageous 20 years ago. Now, thanks to the work of producers like the Vivancos, it's the other way around and the idea of shooting great tequila seems crazy.

in any efficient manner. But this isn't quite how it works. In most situations, production variables are proprietarily "stacked" to emphasise certain traits in the end product. Wooden fermenters, for example, are used only for very long, wild yeast ferments. The point of this is to produce broad flavour camps of tequila styles all under one roof, which can then be blended together or bottled as they are, depending on the needs of the customer.

"We are a boutique," says Sergio, "and we make the dress according to your needs."

Emerging out of the still house, Sergio sits us down on a large oak table on a sunny veranda. He's armed with a couple of bottles of tequila. He's also acquired some brandy balloons for tasting, which is not an item of glassware that I have encountered before at a distillery – even at brandy distilleries. These are generally considered a bit pompous and, ironically, quite badly suited to smelling and tasting spirits.

He pours out a measure of Viva Mexico Blanco (38% ABV) for each of us and I automatically lift the glass towards my nose to sniff it, but Sergio raises a hand to stop me.

"Has anyone ever taught you how to taste tequila?" he asks.

I hesitate for a moment, "Erm, no, actually..."

"It's important not to stress the spirit," Sergio says, turning his glass on its side and then resting it on the table, before rolling it back and forth in front of him.

ABOVE Viva Mexico, where science meets the senses. The smell of roasting agave and the sound of classical music accompany the smack of vibrant tequila on the lips.

"We must be gentle with it to open up the aroma."

After a few moments of rolling the glass back and forth, I'm beginning to wonder if he's regressed back into his pro-soccer days, but finally he slowly lifts the glass to his nose, tipping it at an angle and offering it to one nostril and then the other. This process can appear pretentious to the untrained taster, but there is a biological justification unknown even to many people who partake in it. Our autonomic nervous system spontaneously alternates the amount of airflow through our nostrils. Known as the "nasal cycle", it's thought that by slowing the airflow through one nostril, we might enhance our overall smell perception while also allowing each nostril to have a little rest.

Mimicking Sergio now, I am reminded of how pronounced the effect is. As I roll my glass back and forth, my right nostril is picking up very little at all but the left is getting an amazing cooked agave fragrance, like barbecued pineapple. Then I alternate to my right nostril again, and I'm picking up alcohol and vegetal aromas. Left nostril: green papaya, grapefruit and perhaps some chilli powder. Right nostril: nothing. And so on like this.

"You see – it's very different," he says. "It's like another glass, another product. You see?"

Finally, Sergio takes a sip, granting silent permission for the three of us to do the same. By now I'm watching Sergio like a hawk and imitating his actions so that it's Addie or Pancho who gets called out for doing something wrong and not me.

We hold the liquid in our mouths and gently move it around. Sergio pouts his lips and sucks air in, bubbling it through the tequila before swallowing. This is a technique that is used commonly in wine to help release volatile aromatic compounds, soften tannins and – much like the nasal cycle – give the outward appearance that one is assessing the wine rather than simply drinking it. I've rarely ever seen it done in spirits, though, as the bubbling action tends to kick up alcohol in your throat, which can be a bit unpleasant.

I execute a short and somewhat lacklustre bubble just to keep Sergio happy and then immediately regret it. Keeping my cool, I get back to simply moving it around gently. It's super-silky on the palate, hardly any spice, sweet and syrupy. These are the textural and taste components of the spirit: how it feels in my mouth (weight, viscosity, burn and temperature) and which taste receptors on the tongue it triggers (salt, bitter, sour, sweet, umami). These are useful sensory elements to observe but they are fairly unremarkable as long as they remain absent of the largest part of what it means to experience flavour: aroma.

With the tequila held in my mouth my epiglottis is closed. I should be extremely grateful for this as it means that when I swallow the tequila it won't enter my lungs. But a closed epiglottis also means the aroma of the tequila has no access to my nose and I can't smell it.

In other words, while it is in my mouth my brain only has access to its taste constituents. But as I swallow and then exhale deeply through my nose, the aroma of the tequila (which is coating my mouth and oesophagus) is rapidly and invisibly blasted out of my nose through a process known as "retro-nasal smell". As the aroma passes through my nasal passage, it shoots past the olfactory epithelium. This delicate tapestry of cells, located roughly between and behind your eyes and no larger than a postage stamp, is the apparatus with which everything you have ever smelled and much of what you have eaten is detected and its data passed to the brain.

We have around 400 types of olfactory receptors in the epithelium which, depending on how they're activated, can detect between potentially billions of different odours. Once transmitted to the brain and combined with data from our tongues, eyes, ears and numerous other, more subtle influences, a flavour image is created.

I find two things very interesting about this, the first being how quickly it happens – more or less instantaneously – and the second being the illusory effect that all of this complex calculation of flavour has taken place solely in the mouth.

As I exhale I detect grapefruit cordial with lime and salt. The chilli on the aroma has turned floral. Then the palate slowly dries out and a little jalapeño spice returns. As I continue to breathe through my nose, more flavours appear: a lick of roasted pineapple, soft brown sugar, then fresh citrus peel.

"This freshness is classic for Viva Mexico," says Pancho. "Now you see," says Sergio looking me dead in the eyes. "You must take your time to fully appreciate the flavours."

It does make you wonder where all of these flavours are coming from, when the base material is just a starchy, thorny plant. How can it be that through a process of cooking, fermenting and distilling that so many complex flavours that have seemingly no relation to this plant manifest themselves for our appreciation?

The first comprehensive study of tequila flavour was published in 1996 in the *Journal of Agricultural and Food Chemistry*. The authors used various strategies including sophisticated gas chromatograph-mass spectrometry (GC-MS) to isolate a total of 175 constituent aromas in tequila. Of that number only 32 were identified and five of them were considered to be key odorants. They are 3-methylbutanal (malty, nutty and chocolatey aromas), 3-methyl-1-butanol (banana, funk, pungent), beta-damascenone (fruity, floral, honey), 2-phenylethanol (rose, honey, spice), and vanillin (sweet, vanilla, creamy). However, when these compounds were combined together to "build" a tequila aroma they smelled nothing like tequila at all.

In 2005, another study explored aldehydes in tequila using high-performance liquid chromatography. They identified six aldehydes in various tequila brands, noting significant differences in levels of 2-furaldehyde (almond, bread, caramel) and 5-methylfuraldehyde (caramel,

nutty, spice) between 100% blue agave tequila and tequila *mixtos*, highlighting the impact of production strategy on these compounds on tequila's flavour profile.

Further studies in 2008, employed advanced techniques like electronic noses and headspace-SPME combined with GC-MS to analyse volatile aromas in agave-based spirits. They found many of the same results as above, but observed that minor compounds differed between the types of agave spirit, serving as authenticity markers.

These results point to a relatively clear concept of what agave spirits have in common with one another and the dominance of certain compounds in their makeup. But they also hint at something more interesting, which is the necessity of numerous lower-intensity compounds – many of which remain unidentified – that as a collective help to build the unique structure of flavour that we find in agave spirits.

Back at the table and Sergio is pouring a final tequila for us: Viva Mexico Reposado (38% ABV).

I use both nostrils to narrow down the aroma: *I'm getting nutmeg and mace, drifting into orange soda and ginger. I continue switching nostrils for some time like I'm attempting some kind of mindfulness practice. Then I take a sip – careful to pick apart the taste from the flavour, but I'm failing miserably because my mind seems to be performing billions of calculations in an instant, referencing childhood sweet shops (banana candy), my mother's baking (banana bread and pancake), botched cocktail recipes (winey with more mace) and, finally, Spanish sherry and hardware stores (carpet and rubber).*

Viva Mexico, and Viva Sabor!

We leave Viva Mexico in the mid-afternoon heat. Pancho queues up some of Pepe Jaramillo's elegant piano boleros on the car stereo and we practically float into the town of Atotonilco El Alto in search of a drink.

CASA LOY

◇◇

El Carnicero

At least five tequila distilleries produce more than 30 brands under one roof, and one of them, Destiladora del Valle de Tequila, has over 200 associated brands. More than 90% of all tequila brands are contract-distilled, and even big brands with their own distilleries buy tequila in bulk from contract distillers. Our tour is focusing more on distilleries that produce their own brands, with an emphasis on the 13 tequila distilleries that produce only one brand, like Fortaleza, Atanasio, Patrón and El Tequileño. But the true topography of tequila reveals an industry that is thick with anonymous producers, eager to attract new brands and customers, with promises of low prices and well-made liquor.

Our next stop takes us into a freshly built Death Star of tequila production, where we encounter a combination of versatility and scale like nowhere else. Tequilera Casa Loy is located on a strip of highway between the Los Altos towns of Atotonilco and Ayotlán. It was founded by Don Manuel Loy Aceves, an 88-year-old Mexican business tycoon who began his career as a butcher in nearby Ayotlán. He has since amassed a business empire encompassing pigs, poultry, limes, packaged food, agaves and, very recently, tequila. "All of the things we love in Mexico," says Pancho, as we pretend to be serious in the presence of an armed guard at the Casa Loy security gate.

Loy began planting agaves in the early 1990s and bottled and exported agave syrup for more than two decades before he made plans to build a tequila distillery. Construction on the distillery began in 2019 and the distillery opened under NOM 1633 in 2022.

The distillery produces its own brand, Casa Loy, as well as contract brands, and bulk tequila that might be picked up by one of the even bigger tequila houses and blended into their stocks.

Having parked our car and passed through another security gate, we meet Carla, our tour guide for the day.

She instructs us to don safety gear. I've visited a lot of distilleries and have found health and safety protocols to vary wildly from one to another. Safety paranoia tends to be proportionate with size – more to lose perhaps – and corporate-owned distilleries usually have strict protocols that are ostensibly designed to protect workers but also tick a number of legal boxes. Casa Loy is one of those places: high-vis jackets, hard hats and, yes, even slip-on steel-toe-capped safety boots – the irony of all this being that with enormous rubber clown shoes slipped over your normal ones, you are at a far greater risk of falling over and hurting yourself. And, of course, with all that gear on you develop a paranoia around falling objects or the potential of an exploding still, which actually makes the place feel less safe than it is.

Besides the offices and staff recuperation spaces, the entire Casa Loy operation is contained within three huge aircraft-hangar-style buildings built on a grid, with roads around and between them that add to the military-complex feel. In between buildings we are required to go through a three-stage washing process of our newly acquired shoes, as if the perfectly manicured Casa Loy campus has been dredged in some biohazardous material.

The first of these buildings houses all of the cooking equipment, or to put it more technically "hydrolisation" equipment. That's an important distinction, because there are things going on in here that cannot technically be classed as "cooking".

The first and most surprising thing we notice is a *tahona*. Stood in it are three young men who have neither hard hats nor hi-vis jackets. They are the only visible workers in the whole place, and as they turn over agave fibres and load them on to a conveyor belt that takes them up and into a big, open-top steel fermenter, they look altogether like they have been mysteriously teleported here (along with the tahona) from a mezcal distillery in Oaxaca.

Opposite the tahona are four brick ovens, each with a 60-tonne capacity, and two 40-tonne autoclaves that look like Airstream motorhomes. Carla tells us that the autoclaves can complete a cook in less than eight hours. As impressive as that is, they are not the most efficient method of converting starches into sugar at Casa Loy.

Running almost the full length of the hangar is a gigantic structure that looks like a row of steel terrace houses with interconnecting chimneys. This state-of-the-art steel slab is called a diffuser – the most controversial piece of equipment in tequila production today.

It's not easy to get to the bottom of when and where the first diffusers came to Mexico, but they were probably installed at Sauza in the late 1990s. Since then, many more have found their way into other high-volume distilleries across the Valley and Los Altos.

The idea of the diffuser was to get around the long and expensive process of heating up an oven or autoclave and paying people to load and unload it. In this way, a diffuser is somewhat analogous to a column still, in that it is a method of processing agaves that is capable of running continuously with practically no human interaction.

"I call it like a car wash for the agave," says Carla, which may be a bit misleading as this machine is doing much more than washing.

Unlike brick ovens and autoclaves, which cook the agave before it is milled, in a diffuser the agave is milled while it is raw, into a kind of raw agave slush. Carla explains that the slush (my word, not hers) passes through 12 chambers that sequentially blast high-pressure steam. This helps break down the plant fibres so that all the starch has been extracted by the time you get to the last chamber.

As the agave has not really been cooked yet, there are now a couple of options to convert the starch into sugar: the first involves boiling the raw agave liquor with enzymes; the second is a chemical process where hydrochloric acid is added to "cook" the starches. The Casa Loy processs uses the boiling method, which takes about 24 hours to complete. The obvious benefit of this process is the efficiency with which raw agave *piñas* can be turned into something fermentable.

"With the oven and autoclave, we need nine kilos (20lbs) of agave to make a litre of tequila," says Carla.

RIGHT The diffuser machine has changed the economics of tequila production, but at the cost of spirit character and authenticity.

"With the diffuser it is six or seven kilos (13–15.5lbs) and everything is automated."

The downside is that without the roasting of the agave in an oven, the end product contains little of the aromatic qualities that we associate with tequila. To that end, diffuser-originated tequilas have been proven in blind taste tests to produce an inferior-quality spirit that lacks depth and nuance. This is why most, if not all, of the tequilas on the market that are made using a diffuser machine are also packed full of additives, which attempt to give back what has been taken away. Unsurprisingly though, two wrongs do not make a right.

These production techniques are totally legal under the tequila NOM – there is no foul play at work here. But producers who use them for efficiency and financial gain risk jeopardising the name and character of tequila among consumers. It's quickly becoming a real weakness of the category, while mezcal and other agave spirits – which generally involve far fewer industrial processes – continue their march out of obscurity and into fashion.

In the past it was normal to evaluate the potential quality of a tequila by simply checking if it says 100% agave on the bottle. Now we have a situation where certain *mixto* tequilas are establishing a strong reputation for their quality, while some 100% agave tequilas are produced carelessly, with diffusers, column stills and additives.

And there's more bad news.

Brands that contract-distil and that are price conscious, which, let's face it, is everyone besides Sergio Vivanco's "22 families", are now being forced into something of a diffuser arms race, as without one they will be unable to compete on price. Besides the danger that diffusers will sully the reputation of tequila, they also demonstrate plenty of potential to financially ruin distilleries that either cannot afford them or are reluctant to use them.

As Guillermo Sauza put it to me when we met him at Fortaleza: "If you are a contract distiller using a roller mill and you're competing with a distillery with a diffuser... it doesn't look good as a long-term business strategy." He followed up by pointing at the four roller-mill distilleries currently up for sale in the Tequila Valley.

If we thought that the division in tequila between traditionally minded, quality-focused producers and scaled production in column stills and autoclaves was big, the rollout of diffusers is only going to widen that rift. The quality-focused brands will of course continue what they are doing, while also taking steps to insulate themselves

from the fallout of consumer sentiment that ultra-processed tequila will inevitably enact on the marketplace. But any producer sitting in the middle of these two camps, who uses autoclaves aggressively, who is neither authentic nor super-efficient, may be forced to pick a side or die. And that race to efficiency for the diffuser tribe will inevitably create cost-cutting measures elsewhere in production, the game being to stay within the legal confines of the NOM, while stripping back every possible cost in the process.

Right now, there are spirits being made in Jalisco from underripe agave that are processed through a diffuser, boiled up and mixed with sugar and then put through a continuous still so that any negligible semblance of agave character they might have retained has been entirely stripped. Then, this ghost of a liquor undergoes the final insult: sweeteners, colours and other enhancers are thrown into the vat – like painting a corpse – and Frankenstein's monster emerges: neither alive nor dead, but still, incredibly, by law a tequila.

Carla tells us that when you combine all of this equipment together, the distillery has the potential to produce more than 40,000 litres (10,500 gallons) of tequila a day. Multiply that by 365 and you have 14.6 million litres (3.3 million gallons) a year.

"They designed the distillery to double that though," says Carla. "There is space to install more ovens, autoclaves, diffusers, tanks and stills. And if we do mixto tequila... that is another 30% extra volume."

That would make Casa Loy capable of producing 40 million litres (10.5 million gallons) of tequila a year, which would make it one of Mexico's biggest tequila distilleries.

There are ten 65,000-litre (17,000-gallon) steel fermentation tanks here, which are inoculated with Loy's own proprietary yeast for a total fermentation time of 72 hours. Casa Loy is all about the needs of the client, though, so once you have selected your preferred cooking and milling methods, you are also welcome to bring in your own yeast and provide guidance on how you want your tequila to be distilled in Casa Loy's eight 4,000-litre (1,050-gallon) steel pot-stills.

As we move outside, we pass under the long shadow of Casa Loy's column still. Adjacent to it are three smaller columns that are used to process the waste water left over from distillation. For every litre (34oz) of tequila a distillery produces, it also makes around 10 litres (2.5 gallons) of leftover stillage or vinasses. The indiscriminate

disposal of these vinasses in soils and water bodies has received a great deal of attention of late, owing to the associated environmental impact. Casa Loy has an entire processing facility that takes the vinasse and distils it again, separating the water from the solids. The water is then recycled into the fields or further processed to be used in the distillery, and the solid matter is combined with the *bagazo* (agave fibres) and sent for composting.

Furthermore, nearly all of the power at the distillery is generated from an enormous biomass boiler that burns pine wood chips to generate steam energy. Burning wood might not seem like an environmentally sound way to produce energy, but cutting down old trees for fuel and planting new ones is a sustainable practice that produces a carbon-neutral result in the long term because the same amount of carbon dioxide that is released by the burning process is later re-absorbed by growing trees.

The upshot is that Casa Loy has an extremely low carbon footprint in proportion to its size, and is proof that not all efficiencies are bad news.

As for how these efficiencies affect the flavour of the tequila, we are about to find out. Back inside the office we take our seats in a bland meeting room and begin by tasting Casa Loy Blanco (38% ABV), the house brand, produced using roller mill, brick oven and pot stills. *The aroma has a strong fermented smell, and is grassy like silage, fermented pineapple and maybe a touch of the pungent Chinese liqueur baijou. It's dry on the palate, some gentle spice but a little flat and a short finish.*

Next is Taddel Plata (35% ABV). *It has a very light aroma, a little green with a mild, mossy pungency. Slight sharpness. Soft on the palate, little burn but a little astringency. Another short and watery finish, with the lingering taste of cooked vegetables.*

With mixed emotions of awe and disappointment, we go through the security gates and return to Atotonilco.

ABOVE Massive stills, diffusers and biomass boilers power this modern tequila giant, but the presence of a tahona and autoclaves balance industrial scale with artisanal capability.

It's dinner time so we decide to stop at Los Cuñados taqueria in the centre of town. There, we eat pork cheek tacos which, with the habanero salsa, are pretty fiery. We wash them down with a few Coronas before heading back towards the car.

On our way back, Pancho points to a run-down looking building with Lucky 8 balls painted above saloon-style doors and the words "Bar Y café" painted on the wall, "I've never been in there but it looks interesting – want to check it out?" Pancho suggests.

We walk into the place and it's dark, but not so dark that we don't notice the rails of second-hand clothing hanging on the walls along with knick-knacks and weird bits of tat – all of it for sale. The darkness does mean that we nearly step on a man lying on a mat on the floor. There is a TV on behind the bar and the floor was apparently the most comfortable viewing position.

The man leaps to attention, and soon we are drinking beers and enjoying a glass of Tapatio tequila. Then, an older woman shuffles in: she's the owner and her name is Carmen Lucia. She immediately gets busy chopping up cucumbers then squeezing lime on them and dousing them with salt and chilli powder, which we're told they had just made.

The place is a total mess: part bar, part jumble sale, part living room. But the beers are cold, the tequila of good quality, and their hospitality top notch.

We spend the next hour drinking and laughing (what we were laughing about I could not say and most of the time did not know), then finally we depart, thrilled that such a weirdly brilliant place exists at all and that we discovered it.

EL MEXICANO

◇◇

La Política

Tequila was first defined in 1949, long after Tequila town had established itself as a powerhouse of mezcal production. Written into Mexican law, tequila could be produced only in "characteristic" areas of the state of Jalisco. By 1960, the whole of the state of Jalisco was included and in 1968 neighbouring states also started to get a mention, though only in the vaguest sense.

It wasn't until 1974, however, that tequila became the first product outside of the EU to be granted Designation Origin (DO) status – a place-based protection granted to certain distinctive products from around the world. Henceforth, the Denominación de Origen Tequila (DOT) stated that any product labelled as tequila could be made only in a specific region of Mexico defined by international law. That region was the biggest DO in the world at the time, and included all of Jalisco, and parts of Michoacán, Guanajuato and Nayarit. The mezcal DO has since trumped it, though.

The DOT has expanded on various occasions and today covers all of Jalisco, seven municipalities in Guanajuato, eight in Nayarit, thirty in Michoacán, and 11 municipalities over on the Gulf of Mexico in Tamaulipas.

Mexico now has 16 products that have been granted a DO. They include vanilla from the Papantla region in Veracruz, Talavera pottery from Puebla and Tlaxcala, amber from Chiapas, mangoes from the Soconusco region of Chiapas, two types of coffee from Veracruz and Chiapas, charanda rum from Michoacán, sotol from Chihuahua and Sonora, and five agave products: one of them is a type of sisal fibre from Yucatán that is used to make ropes and rugs, the others are the four agave spirits: tequila, raicilla, mezcal and bacanora.

If you take a look at a map of Mexico (or look at page 7), you might conclude that the inclusion of Tamaulipas in the tequila DO is an interesting one, as it is about as far from Tequila as Scotland is from London. It also has no history of tequila tradition before the 20th century. The reasons the CRT (Tequila Regulatory Council) gave for including Tamaulipas have always been pretty vague, and that's because the real reason is simply a matter of politics.

In 1966, Hurricane Inés wrecked crops in Tamaulipas and the wealthy landowner Guillermo González Diaz Lombardo decided to plant blue agave, hoping to benefit from the agave industry price boom at the time. Other farmers followed suit. Around the same time, Javier Sauza (see page 17) built a new distillery in Tamaulipas to meet rising global demand for tequila, ignoring the fact that the then pre-DOT rules limited tequila production to Jalisco.

By 1972, the price of agave was falling and Sauza tried to extort González and buy the Tamaulipas agave at a rock-bottom price, but González and others held out, guided by tequila expert Guillermo Romo from Herradura. González then built his own distillery in Tamaulipas called La Gonzaleña. But in 1974, Tamaulipas was excluded from the DOT, prompting González and the farmers to sue.

González had friends in high places, and in 1976 Mexican President José López Portillo stepped in. The following year, Tamaulipas was part of the DOT. The official line of the government was that it made sense owing to cultural links, a thriving agave industry, and significant investment in the region – rather than helping out an old family friend.

The inner workings of tequila politics are never far from the minds of the people who work in the industry. Our next stop is a new distillery that is owned by a family that has seen it all, and run by a third-generation tequila maker who is not afraid to voice his opinions.

OPPOSITE Los Altos is supremely photogenic – its red, clay soil contrasting with the vivid turquoise pencas of the tequiliana agaves.

The sign reads:

RANCHO EL MEXICANO
LO MEJOR DE NUESTRA TIERRA PARA TI
DESTILADO
NOM 1588

El Mexicano is located on the highway just south of Arandas and is a beautiful site, painted the same red as Los Altos soil and built in the style of a huge colonial hacienda.

Leon's family is a joining of two successful families in the region. His mother's side came from a town in Los Altos called San José de Gracia and they were in the construction business. His father's side came from a town called Jamay on the banks of Lake Chapala, to the south, and were in the confectionery business, "So still sugar!" Leon exclaims.

His mother's side of the family owned a lot of land but not all of it was suitable for growing beans or corn, so they planted agave there.

"They used it like a savings account," he says. "You plant the agaves and eight to ten years later it's worth a lot more."

Over time, their agave stocks increased and they had contracts to sell to Sauza. But inevitably they eventually found themselves riding the waves of agave price fluctuations and, during a slump, they decided to build a distillery. Both sets of Leon's grandparents came together in partnership, plus some other investors, one of which was the local priest.

The distillery they built was called Hacienda Vieja, and this was where they launched the Cazadores brand in the late 1970s. *Cazadores* means "Hunter" and is named for the wild deer that are hunted in the area. The street where the Hacienda Vieja still stands is now named Cazadores Street on account of the early success of the brand, though its production has since moved.

At age 17, Leon's father was given the choice between candy and tequila and he made the right decision. At this time, the family was still fairly clueless where matters of tequila were concerned – a situation Leon's father took it upon himself to fix. Among his best moves was the decision to headhunt one of the Herradura master distillers, Leopoldo Solís. Solís was one of the early experts in creating tequila flavour profiles by manipulating stages of production. He became something of a mentor for Leon and between them they introduced various production elements that are considered normal today, and turned Cazadores into a highly respected brand. Their pioneering work in the 1980s and 1990s included the use of stainless-steel tanks and proprietary yeast strains for fermentation, and new oak for maturation. They also took the revolutionary decision to bottle only reposado tequila.

This was during the reposado heyday, when brands like Cazadores, Sauza and later Don Julio were bottling some of the best tequilas anyone had ever tasted.

All of these elements positioned the brand in the premium space and made it the first 100% agave tequila to top one million cases. Little wonder then that it attracted the attention of Bacardí then, which purchased the brand in 2002. After the sale, Cazadores moved production to two purpose-built distilleries connected by an underground tunnel beneath the Arandas ring-road only a mile from where we are sat.

"You can see the ugly column still from here," says Leon pointing out of the window towards Arandas. "Like Sauron's tower in Mordor."

In spite of what the Cazadores website might tell you, very little of the pre-2002 Cazadores brand remains intact. What isn't visible from Leon's office is the diffuser machine, which was installed more than a decade ago. The brand justifies the use of this by playing the sustainability card, claiming it extracts more sugar and produces less waste. In fairness, Cazadores, like Casa Loy, is one of the few tequila distilleries with a biomass boiler. Couple that with solar tubes on the roof for heating water, and you have a near carbon-neutral operation. It's just a shame the tequila doesn't taste good.

"Nothing that they say about the brand history is true," says Leon. "They are saying it is 100 years old, and was started by my grandfather José Maria, but there is nobody in my family with that name!"

When Cazadores sold, Leon's uncles kept the Hacienda Vieja distillery, which continues to produce some good tequila brands to this day: Hacienda Vieja, Mijenta and Don Felix among them. Leon's parents got the rough end of the stick, however, with a non-compete agreement that prevented them from making tequila for a few years.

"We love the tequila business," says Leon with a fierce look in his eye. "And we love to kill the monsters, so we had to enter the battle with the big guys. That's how El Mexicano started."

It's becoming clear that Cazadores was an especially appropriate name.

The distillery produced its first bottles of tequila in 2014 and its reputation for quality and consistency has attracted a range of brand contracts besides their own El Mexicano brand.

Production has options of both a brick oven and autoclaves for cooking. El Mexicano is made using an autoclave that is programmed to perform a slow, 16-hour cook with eight hours of cooling. Leon points out that the *miels dulces* (the very sweet juices that are extracted from the agave in the early part of the cook) are not separated from the autoclave like they are with a brick oven, which means the quantity of liquid in the bottom of the autoclave rises as the cook progresses. This makes for a moister cook, where the agaves at the bottom are partly boiled and the ones at the top take on more of a roast character. In spite of this, Leon says that autoclaves produce the same quality tequila as brick ovens as long as you use them properly.

"But a funny thing is that most of the clients who want a brick-oven profile want it more for marketing reasons than profile," he says.

He also thinks that tahonas are for the most part marketing devices, and that the difference in flavour between a roller mill and a tahona is actually from the fermentation of the fibres rather than the milling. "Great for tourism," he says. "But not for production."

Leon says the biggest factor determining flavour is fermentation, going so far as to suggest that diffuser tequila could be made to taste good with the right conditions and a sufficiently long fermentation (though that's unlikely to happen in a distillery that prioritises efficiency).

El Mexicano is 2,000m (6,560ft) above sea level, so there's less oxygen in the air and this affects how the microorganisms necessary for fermentation behave. Here, fermentation is carried out in open-top steel containers. They can use a range of yeast profiles but prefer a Champagne yeast for making El Mexicano.

Fermentation takes seven to eight days, which is very long for a ferment that isn't relying on wild yeasts. This amount of time pushes the ferment into malolactic territory, where softer, milky flavours are produced that carry through to the end product. "When it comes to distillation, it's just about not messing it up," says Leon. "All of the most important work has been done in the fermentation."

Distillation takes place in twenty 4,200-litre (1,100-gallon) stainless-steel pot stills here. Leon takes us through the warehouse and bottling area, grabbing some bottles to taste from an open box. The packaging of El Mexicano is quite simple, with a fairly unremarkable glass bottle, the likeness of an eagle on the label and simple, authentic typography. Even the website proudly states "We don't focus on the packaging. We focus on the agave, its process, and flavour."

Like every bottle of tequila, it also states its NOM, which in this case is 1588. There are currently around 170 registered producers of tequila in Mexico, each with their own NOM number. The NOM number tells you which producer made the bottle you are drinking, but with over 2,000 tequila brands out there you don't need to be a mathematician to work out that some distilleries are producing dozens of brands under one roof and one NOM.

BELOW Agave alchemy at 2000m (6,560ft): El Mexicano's sky-high spirits lab sees oxygen-starved yeast toil in open vats, coaxing complex flavours from thin air as steel tanks gleam under the Jalisco sun.

It's important to recognise that the NOM refers only to the producer, not the distillery. It is possible and, indeed, is the case that a producer can use the same NOM at more than one distillery and that two NOMs can be made at the same distillery.

Tequila Ocho is one example of this. It was created as a new company by Tomas Estes and Carlos Camarena, separate to La Alteña (NOM 1139), and therefore always produced under its own NOM 1474. Now that it has shifted to its own distillery, Los Alembiques, its NOM has moved too.

You would be forgiven for concluding that the NOM always corresponds to who made the tequila in the bottle. But one very important thing to note is that the NOM ignores the legal trading of tequila between registered producers. So, while a brand may fall under a specific producer's NOM, it does not necessarily mean that that producer made the product, only that they bottled it. This is a shame and a missed opportunity my opinion, as it undermines the benefits of traceability that the NOM could very easily support. How much trading of tequila goes on is anyone's guess, but certainly it is rife among the bigger producers who are understandably very cagey when it comes to talking about other people making their products. They have a lot to lose and they have the strongest lobbying power, so as with many other issues within the complex politics of tequila, things are unlikely to change any time soon.

The CRT's authority and powers stretch well beyond checking that a product comes from a specific producer, however. The CRT monitors the planting, supervision and harvesting of agaves, along with every stage of the production process, ensuring that the anticipated amount of alcohol is produced from the materials that are used. Supervision is carried out physically by a representative of the CRT as well as laboratory analysis and monitoring of certification in the national and international market. All blanco tequilas must be verified by the CRT before either can go to market, and casks of maturing tequila are sealed with a CRT label that can be removed only in the presence of a CRT representative. So, while not everyone agrees with all the rules, tequila remains one of the most strictly governed food and drink products on the planet.

We leave Arandas as the sun is setting. The windows are down and the jolly rhythms of Eliseo Robles' "Chaparra De Mi Amor" plays like a conversation between man and accordion. Pink sky smoulders above rows of blue agave in the fields we drive past and the taste of pink grapefruit lingers still in my mouth from the tequila.

Citrus is without doubt one of the more prominent flavours one can find when smelling and tasting tequila. Often it's lime, other times it's yuzu, mandarin, pomelo or grapefruit. Spirits often adopt the flavours of a culture – whether by design or not – and while it can't be claimed that citrus fruits originated in Mexico, they are certainly enjoyed here: Mexico has been the biggest producer of limes in the world for over half a century and they are the second-biggest producer of grapefruits at half a billion tonnes a year. Much of that gets exported of course, but I would wager a sizeable chunk of what is left gets mixed with tequila.

Some people mix fresh grapefruit juice (with or without soda – the Topo Chico brand, usually) and tequila; other times it's with the incredibly popular grapefruit soda called Squirt, which is almost as ubiquitous as Coca-Cola in these parts. Squirt contains only around 1% concentrated grapefruit juice (Mexican, naturally), but through the magical manipulations of the flavour industry, and no small quantity of sugar and acids, it tastes something like grapefruit and refreshes every bit as well.

In both of the above instances, the resulting drink falls under the title of Paloma – which Pancho says is the most popular tequila cocktail in the country. Gin has its tonic, whisky its ginger ale, rum its coke, and vodka its, erm… orange juice? Tequila has grapefruit.

In Mexico you can buy a Paloma practically anywhere that sells tequila, as anywhere that sells tequila will also sell Squirt, and anyone selling anything stocks ice, too. But like the other highball-style drinks I just mentioned, it's a very easy drink to put together at home, on a beach or in the back of a Jetta doing 90 miles an hour (145km/h) down a pot-holed highway.

OPPOSITE As all casks of maturing tequila are sealed with a CRT label to prevent tampering, it's a very rare occasion you can taste tequila directly from a barrel.

EL PANDILLO

El Científico Loco

At La Alteña (see page 44), we learned about the influence of the Camarena family on tequila production in Los Altos. Carlos and his sisters also have a second cousin, Mauricio Camarena, who owns and operates Destilería Tequila Supremo in Arandas where the Familia Camarena brand is made. But even closer to home, the siblings have an older brother, Felipe Camarena. With a background in civil engineering, Felipe was responsible for designing much of what we saw at La Alteña. Now he has his own distillery, El Pandillo, a place where his passion and imagination have run wild and earned him the moniker "the mad scientist of tequila".

The contents of my *tortas ahogadas* (a fried bean and stewed pork sandwich) threatens to spill on to my lap as the Jetta bumps its way down a rutted driveway, jolting and creaking to the gentle guitar strumming of Álvaro Carrillo's "Popurrí". Either side the road is framed with turquoise agaves perched on red soil which, besides a knackered pickup truck with a team of *coa*-wielding *jimadores* passing in the opposite direction, are the only signs we're headed towards a distillery.

Destilería El Pandillo was built in 2012, on an old ranch on Camarena land about a mile from La Alteña as the cuervo flies. In that short space of time, the tequilas made here (eight brands so far including Don Vincente, Volans, and its own G4 and Terralta products) have become some of the most highly regarded specimens in all of Mexico.

As the distillery comes into view, it looks like a farm. We see an ancient-looking *tahona* stone on display out the front; this, it turns out, was the original stone wheel that was used at La Alteña, which dates back to the time of Pedro Camarena and the late 19th century. All around the property there are construction materials, and mounds of dirt are lumped about the place. Pandillo has already outgrown itself.

We park in front of the distillery barn, next to what appears to be a concrete swimming pool into which water is flowing from an overhead aqueduct built on brick archways. Our guide for the day, Ali, greets us and explains that this water feature is in fact the "process water" from the distillery (the water used to cool the condensers) and it is flowing outside via gravity so that it can be cooled and then reabsorbed into the land.

This is but the first of many novel innovations that are going on at El Pandillo.

While we are standing admiring the waterfall, a huge truck pulls up loaded high with the other ingredient needed to make tequila: agave, fresh from the field. The distillery has about 90 hectares of agave-growing land but Pandillo is currently buying its agaves from other growers while their own plants mature. Ali tells us that 30° Brix is a minimum requirement of maturity for the agave they are purchasing and that translates to at least six years old.

"You see how close they have cut the agave to the heart," says Pancho, pointing to the remaining stub of the *penca* still attached to the plant. "There are three levels of cut: short, medium, long. These are medium to long cuts."

The penca of the agave contains less fermentable sugar and more waxy, fibrous substances than the juicy heart. The fibre and wax produce more methanol in the spirit, but if handled correctly during distillation can also bring some complexity. So, economically minded distillers will demand that their agaves are cut close (so that the *piñas* are almost entirely white) as the amount of sugar per kilogram is top of their priority list. Producers in the market for prioritising flavour will go for a longer cut, leaving plenty of green still on the piña. In this way, you can determine something about the mindset of the tequila distillery that you are visiting just from the length of the penca stubs left on the agave.

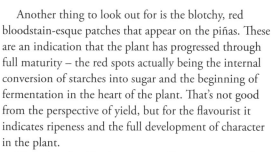

Another thing to look out for is the blotchy, red bloodstain-esque patches that appear on the piñas. These are an indication that the plant has progressed through full maturity – the red spots actually being the internal conversion of starches into sugar and the beginning of fermentation in the heart of the plant. That's not good from the perspective of yield, but for the flavourist it indicates ripeness and the full development of character in the plant.

There is a classification system of agave maturity that can be used to grade ripeness. These red-stained agaves we are seeing are known as *pinto* (stained). An agave that is fully matured but without the red spots is *maturo*. One that is nearing maturity is called *sazón* (seasoned); *entrado* means it is entering the early stages of maturity; and finally *tierno*, which means unripe.

El Pandillo produced 250,000 litres (65,000 gallons) of tequila in 2023 and is on track to double that in 2024, by increasing storage space for barrels, installing new stills, and adding additional cooking shifts. The two 50-tonne ovens work in three-day cycles to complete a cook: one day of heat, one day of resting in the oven, one day in the oven with the door open before unloading.

One of the ovens is being emptied, and as we step inside, the smell of roasted pineapple and sticky molasses is intoxicating, not only to us but also to a great number of bees that are buzzing around in the sticky-sweet gloom. Pancho says the bees are a sign of good health in the land around the distillery. Ali gives us some of the agave to taste and we notice the texture is unusually soft on account of that very long cook, "Like sweet potato," says Ali.

Next to the ovens is where the cooked agaves are milled in a machine called "Felipestein" that looks like it was taken from the set of *Mad Max*. Constructed from pieces of train suspension and the barrel of a stream roller, with steel nipples welded onto its surface, this steampunk

ABOVE Felipe Camarena's playground of peculiar pools and steampunk contraptions transforms agave into liquid gold, respecting tradition but with a liberal dose of eccentric innovation.

tahona passes back and forth over a bed of shredded agave and crushes the juices out of the fibres. Water is sprinkled over the agaves as it passes by, which takes the Brix from 30° down to 11° and means that the machine has an efficiency of 97%. It takes an hour and a half for Felipestein to process 1.5 tonnes of agave, which means an oven is emptied in less than two days.

"It's faster and more efficient than a tahona," says Ali. "But we think we get all the same benefits of flavour."

Fermentation is undertaken with a wild yeast culture that is continuously fed and drawn from special tanks. We climb up some steps and peer into the 16 stainless-steel fermentation tanks and two 18,000-litre (4,750-gallon) pine vats, in which the juices are fermented with crushed agave fibres. Once distilled, the spirit from these wooden vats makes up 6% of the liquid that goes into G4 branded bottles. Additionally, some of the steel tanks are given over to fermenting juices alongside agave fibres. In this instance they are using coarsely cut chunks of agave rather than finely shredded fibres.

Felipe Camarena's engineering background can be appreciated in the unique distillation setup too. The fermenters are raised high so that they can empty their contents by gravity. All of the stills here are made entirely from copper, consisting of a huge 6,000-litre (1,500-gallon) still (soon to be joined by another) and three 950-litre (250-gallon) stills used for producing *ordinario* (the product of the first distillation) plus three 700-litre (185-gallon) stills for the second distillation. These stills have an additional vessel about the size of a large bucket between the head of the still and the condenser, which has a pipe running from the bottom of it back down into the base of the still.

"We call it an exhaust," says Ali. "It means that the heavier alcohols and aromas drop back into the still so we produce a cleaner product."

This little modification is also the reason why at Pandillo none of the heads are removed from their product – the distillate is refined enough to stay below the regulation limits on methanol.

Ali catches some of the spirit from the stream that is flowing off the still and shares it into tasting glasses for us to try. *The aroma has an amazing orange soda note, with orange blossom and touch of vanilla cream. The taste is dry and spicy, with green apples and nice roasted agave notes. It's clean and mineral-ly through the finish.*

Ali explains that, with the exception of the slightly different fermentations for special bottles that we have seen, all of the products made here undergo the same physical processes right through to distillation.

"They are not all the same, though" he says, "And what differentiates them is the water we use."

Water plays its part in every stage of agave spirits' production, from hydrating the agave as it grows, to milling and fermentation, cooling the stills, and diluting ready for bottling. While some distilleries emphasise the quality of their water supply, its mineral content or its reliability, and others even go as far as to romanticise its source ("volcanic", "mountain spring" and so on), most are simply using whatever water is available to them and exert no active control over it other than to occasionally strip it of its minerals.

Pandillo approaches water very differently, having not one but three different types: deep well, spring, and rainwater – and a fourth if you include the municipal supply. These three water sources are very different in their mineral content and pH, with the well water being the hardest and the rainwater the softest. Recognising this and then leveraging it is the secret sauce in the tequilas made here, and it's why Felipe Camarena is famous for saying "The quality of the water is more important than the quality of the agave."

Now you might be feeling a little sceptical about how much of the flavour of a bottle of tequila can possibly come from using different types of water. So, let's do some maths. When you take a tequila off the still at 55% ABV and cut it down to 40%, almost a third of that bottle will comprise whatever water you are using to dilute the product down. Most distilleries do this with demineralised ("inert") water that is devoid of any flavour, but Pandillo uses all three of the available waters in different ratios depending on the product the distillery is making.

There's more, though. The water added after distillation is not the only water used when making tequila. There is also the water used during the milling, which accounts for a great deal of the water that ends up in the fermenter. To take the agave from 30° Brix down to 11° Brix, you have to add twice the volume of water to the amount of agave you are milling. Most of this water will be left behind in the stills, but its mineral composition and pH will affect how yeast cultures thrive or die and what flavours they produce as a by-product of their work. And that's exactly what is going on here, with each expression of tequila being produced with its own water profile.

"The deep well water is a bit more aggressive for the mouth," says Ali, "because it's more mineral rich. The rainwater is way lighter, so it's softer in the mouth and softer in the throat. The spring water is in-between, not as soft as the rainwater, not as hard as the well."

To appreciate what difference this makes to the final products, we are going to need to taste them.

Over in the tasting room we start with G4 Blanco (40% ABV), made with a blend of rainwater and spring water. It's named G4 after Felipe's sons, Alan and Luis, who are the fourth generation of Camarena distillers. *The aroma is crisp and fruity, with notes of plum and fresh green apple on the nose. The palate is balanced and clean, offering great intensity that harmonises oily texture, dry spice, and sweetness. It's a textural wonder.*

OPPOSITE The one-of-a-kind steam-roller mill at El Pandillo is like a *Mad Max* version of a tahona.

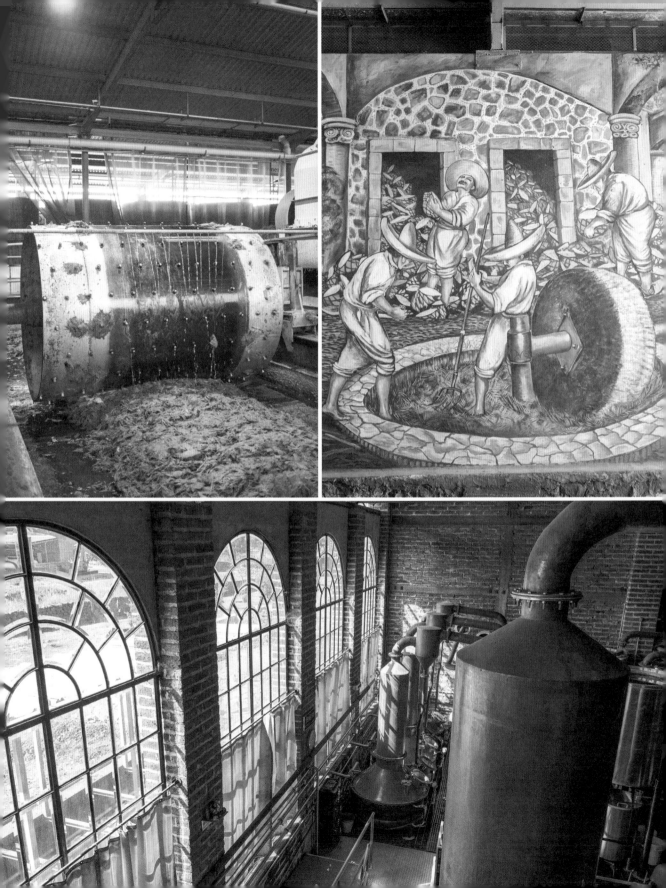

Jalisco may not sound like somewhere that gets a lot of rain, but in the rainy season of June through to September it averages around 10cm (four inches) a month. The distillery has guttering on the roof (along with solar panels that produce the distillery's electricity) and they feed into a 300,000-litre (80,000-gallon) tank for storage.

"For me," says Pancho, swirling the G4 around in his glass. "This might be the best tequila product currently being made."

Next, we sample ArteNOM Selección 1579 (40% ABV), which is an independent bottler that works with a few distilleries. ArteNOM Selección 1579 is also made with rainwater and spring water, but doesn't include any spirit made in the wooden fermenters like G4. Ali also explains that the spirit is aerated with oxygen bubbles for 20 hours prior to bottling. *The nose offers hints of soil and rain hitting dry pavement, with subtle petroleum notes and sweet nail varnish. As it opens up, the agave character shines through. The palate is dry and complex. Addie says he would wear it as a cologne.*

Moving on, we try Volans Blanco (40% ABV), which is made using all three water sources. *Aromas of butterscotch and dairy dominate, with hints of milky rhubarb custard. The palate is balanced and rich with impressive viscosity and texture and the water seems to bring about more heat in spite of the same strength. Spice notes lead to a dry, grippy and long finish. A triumph of texture and taste!*

It is astonishing to consider the differences between these tequilas where the only thing that has changed is the water source.

"Everyone said Felipe was a fool when he began playing with water," says Pancho. "They are not saying that anymore."

Next, we try G4 Blanco at 45% ABV, but this time it's made entirely from the wooden-vat fermentation with fibres, and is a blend of rainwater and spring water. *There's a slight glue-like note at first, followed by red apple, cooked piña heart, tamarind, and subtle herbal notes. The palate is full and complete, with dry grip and fullness of texture. Round agave character, hot peña, black pepper, and slight anise round out the profile.*

Ali keeps on pouring samples, as we move on to The Don Vicente (40% ABV), which uses 100% deep well water, the hardest of the three options. It also undergoes the same oxygenation process as the ArteNOM. *The aroma is perfumed and elegant on the nose, with smoking spice notes. It's feminine and sultry. The palate is floral and long, with fennel seed and aniseed, leading to a dry finish. Truly incredible.*

Finally, we taste the high-proof General (52% ABV), which is made with 100% spring water. *The higher alcohol content is evident on the nose, but the flavour is pure cooked agave – reminiscent of agave fibre in an oven. Slightly salty with sour apple notes, it offers an electric agave flavour. Outstanding.*

Minds blown and wallets emptied, we take our newly acquired stash of bottles and leave Pandillo, heading south for a couple of miles, through the town of Jesús Maria, and towards our final stop in the Los Altos region. We're on eastern edge of Jalisco here, only about 16km (10 miles) from the Guanajuato border.

Jesús Maria is a small town, filled with the usual taco stands and agricultural wholesalers (fertilisers, timber, cement), but it is also home to one big distillery that is soon to be joined by another. As we exit the town heading south we see an enormous building site, which Pancho points to and says simply, "The Rock."

It turns out that this is not a maximum-security prison, but rather the new distillery for Dwayne Johnson's tequila brand, Teremana. Launched in 2020, by my estimates this has been the fastest-growing tequila brand of the decade so far, having hit the magic one-million-cases mark in less than three years. That makes it comparable in size to established brands like Olmeca or Cazadores. It also means that Teremana has outgrown its original production site at Productos Finos de Agave. This distillery, which is run by the Lopez family, is no slouch either. They make many brands here and Johnson's team was probably drawn to it because it was the Lopezes that helped scale George Clooney's Casamigos brand from infancy up to its $1bn (£770m) valuation and subsequent sale to Diageo. If any brand can claim to have grown faster than Teremana, it would have to be Casamigos – it became a three-million-case brand in six years.

So yes, Jesús Maria is where big brands are made fast.

The new Teremana distillery is being built next-door to the Lopezes' other site and will be operated by them too. Pancho slows so we can take a look and I notice between the heavy machinery and massive red-brick walls what looks like rows of garages being built out of stone – now that's a pleasing staff perk to keep your vehicle out of the sun, but hardly essential! Then it dawns on us: they aren't garages but brick ovens. We quickly count them up... there are 32 in total.

The scale is remarkable, but so too is the commitment to authentic production techniques. It turns out that Teremana is open-top fermented and then distilled in copper pot-stills. So for anyone inclined to "smell what The Rock is cooking" you may be pleasantly surprised.

Celebrity-endorsed spirit brands are nothing new, and go back at least as far as the 1950s with Frank Sinatra and the Jack Daniel's brand. The trend really took off in the early 2000s, however, when Sean "Diddy" Combs entered a joint partnership with Cîroc Vodka, and Ryan Reynolds bought Aviation Gin. These were more than just paid advocacy deals – these celebrities actually owned a slice of the brand. In the internet age, where celebrities are never more than a tweet or Instagram post away from our eyeballs, they operate as brands unto themselves, and their aura beneficially touches any and all investments in their proximity. For the consumer this builds trust, increases visibility, offers an emotional connection, and gives a brand a point of difference, all of which make it a powerful marketing tool in the present day. Thus, joint ventures, where rock stars and actors actively invest in and co-create the brand, have become the new norm. As the rapper Jay-Z, who recently sold his stake in D'USSÉ Cognac for $750m (£575m) puts it, "I am not a businessman – I am a business, man."

ABOVE Maturation at El Pandillo take place underground, where it's quite a bit cooler. This makes for a slower ageing process that preserves more agave character.

Perhaps the earliest example of a celebrity joint venture in spirits was also a tequila brand (though not a very good one). The singer-songwriter Jimmy Buffett, known for his laid-back island lifestyle and hit song "Margaritaville", partnered with Seagram's in 2000 to launch Margaritaville Tequila. This collaboration capitalised on Buffett's tropical, carefree brand image, and his collection of over 30 Margaritaville restaurants across the US.

Other, more recent, celebrity entrants into the agave spirits' world include 818 Tequila, founded in 2020 by Kendall Jenner; Cincoro Tequila, founded in 2019 by Michael Jordan and four other NBA team owners; and Dos Hombres Mezcal, established in 2019 by actors Bryan Cranston and Aaron Paul of *Breaking Bad* fame. Fellow actor Matthew McConaughey is the latest high-profile entrant into tequila with his Pantalones brand, made at Tequilera TAP in Amatitán. But the most high-profile of all celebrity tequila brands or, indeed, of all tequila brands – period – would have to be Patrón, our next stop.

PATRÓN

◇◇

La Escala

Arriving at the Patrón distillery feels a little like a visit to Buckingham Palace in London, only there's more security and the driveway is longer. It begins with a pink terracotta archway off the highway just outside of Atotonilco El Alto. Our credentials are checked by the security guard and we are permitted entrance, into what turns out to be an even bigger driveway than we imagined – about one-kilometre long – heading south to a second security station that is itself the size of a small apartment block. More checks are made and then we are through and the Hacienda Patrón comes into full sight.

Looking like it could well be the home of Pablo Escobar, this mansion of a building is only 20 years old but modelled in the colonial style with a huge symmetrical façade and columns adorned in earthy-pink stucco and archways revealing an internal balcony across its entire breadth. The garden and courtyard in front are landscaped with palm trees, agaves and pristine lawns, along with fountains and ponds. Adjacent to the Hacienda is La Casona (The Big House), a 20-bedroom luxury hotel built for hosting VIPs and conducting private tastings.

We park the Jetta and walk through the gardens towards the hotel reception, past the life-sized bronze statues of the brand's founder, John Paul DeJoria. Opposite him is another statue of the late Francisco Alcaraz, with his trademark flop of Mancunian-esque hair and arms outspread. In one hand he is holding a stumpy bottle of Patrón tequila and in the other a small *hijuelo* (agave sapling). There's a final statue, of Ed Brown, who was Patrón's CEO for the 20 years leading up to its purchase by Bacardí in 2018. These three men, along with one other (whose statue is curiously missing) are responsible for building one of the most successful alcohol brands of the last century and selling it for a record-breaking $5.1bn (£4bn). Here's how they did it.

DeJoria was born in 1944 and brought up in Los Angeles by a single mother. The family was very poor and he had a very unremarkable start in life, embarking on a string of jobs including janitor, door-to-door encyclopedia salesman, and insurance salesman then, finally, after becoming homeless on two separate occasions, he settled down to a career in the haircare industry. By 1980 this was going well for him and he founded a company for $500 (£250) with hairdresser Paul Mitchell.

By the late 1980s, John Paul Mitchell Systems was worth millions, so when Martin Crowley, a friend who was down on his luck in the hospitality industry, returned from a trip to Jalisco with a beautiful bottle of Tequila Chinaco, DeJoria agreed to invest in a start-up tequila brand with him. Crowley and DeJoria "began speculating about which tequila the aristocrats of Mexico drank," wrote Ilana Edelstein, Crowley's longtime partner, in her book *The Patrón Way*. Then, on a visit to Jalisco, Crowley and DeJoria passed by the Siete Leguas distillery in Atotonilco El Alto and that's where everything changed.

Siete Leguas is a tequila brand named for Mexican revolutionary Pancho Villa's horse, which was said to be able to run seven leagues in a day (about 34km/21 miles – so actually nothing special, really!). The brand is owned by the González family (yes, they are related to the "Don Julio" Gonzálezes) and is celebrated for its unwavering commitment to 100% agave tequila and traditional production methods, including fermentation and distillation with agave fibres and the only *tahona* in tequila that is still pulled by a mule. Siete Leguas is also famous for not entertaining contract brands. That is, it was, until a pair of convincing Americans came along in 1989.

DeJoria and Crowley fell in love Siete Leguas' anachronistic production style and recognised its market potential in the US. While they were there, the pair met Francisco Alcaraz, a distilling consultant who was working

with the Gonzálezes at the time. Alcaraz was educated as a chemical engineer and had previously worked as a tequila inspector for ten years, visiting distilleries, checking their samples, and generally becoming a scholar of tequila production, particularly in matters where yeast and yeast nutrients were concerned.

Inspired by DeJoria's intention to make "the world's best tequila regardless of cost", Alcaraz became a linchpin in the subsequent deal that was brokered between the Americans and Siete Leguas. Lucretia González placed her trust in Alcaraz and tequila production began at Siete Leguas under his auspices.

DeJoria committed to buying 1,000 cases of Patrón with the consolation that if it all went wrong at least he'd have presents to give to friends for the next decade or so. And that looked like the way things were going to go. They launched Patrón in the US at the incomprehensibly high price of $37 (£22) a bottle, which most people thought was utterly absurd. This was at a time when

tequila was still being shot in nightclubs and thrown haphazardly into sickly sweet margaritas, and when the most expensive bottles rarely topped $15 (£9).

Crowley, who managed most of the brand's operations, convinced some high-end wine suppliers to stock it, while DeJoria worked with the Michelin-starred restaurants with whom he had good relationships. Over the years that followed, sales remained slow as the company navigated through partnerships with Jim Beam and Seagram's, facing difficulties with both owing to Patrón's small size and unique production requirements. But the brand's status was slowly growing, and in all the right circles. Celebrity endorsement helped it gain some traction when first it featured in Clint Eastwood's 1993 film *In the Line of Fire* and was then David Bowie's drink of choice in *The*

Linguini Incident. DeJoria's address book ensured that, in time, Kevin Costner, Pierce Brosnan, Sean Penn and Dennis Hopper were all seen drinking from the short bottle of tequila made by the haircare guy.

The original Patrón range included only Patrón Silver and Añejo, and the company introduced a reposado in 1992. That same year, they launched Patrón XO Cafe and Patrón Citrónge, an orange liqueur targeting margarita enthusiasts. The portfolio later grew to include Citrónge Lime and Citrónge Mango variants. As the liqueur market bloomed, Patrón introduced the Gran Patrón range partnering with the movie director Guillermo del Toro and famed crystal manufacturer Lalique. For better or worse, Patrón set the stage for luxury offerings from the likes of Clase Azul, Tequila Ley and Código, with five-digit price tags attached to them.

By the mid-1990s, production was beginning to outgrow the capabilities of Siete Leguas' tahona and mules, so plans were put into place to build a distillery on the outside of town. This would be a joint venture between Patrón and the spirits giant Seagram's, with Alcaraz on board to help with a seamless transition to the new equipment. Unfortunately, the new distillery, Destilería Colonial de Jalisco, seemed incapable of producing spirit like the stuff in Patrón bottles and, after a three-month production cycle, the tequila quality had changed beyond an acceptable margin. A legal battle ensued, which Patrón subsequently won, allowing them to build a new $5m (£3m) distillery and bring Francisco

Alcaraz on board full-time. In 2000, Ed Brown, who had previous experience with Patrón through his work at Seagram's, joined as CEO and shortly after that Martin Crowley died from a heart attack. This marked the beginning of a new era for the brand, setting the stage for unprecedented growth in the premium tequila market.

Alcaraz meticulously developed the recipe and production methods for Patrón, going back to the Siete Leguas model as a blueprint. Siete Leguas is actually a blend of spirits from two distilleries (more recently three): El Centenario distillery with its tahona and La Vencedora distillery just up the road, with its roller mills. Francisco mimicked this in the Patrón distillery, splitting production between two sides: tahona and roller mill, and then blending the results together before bottling.

This is how Tequila Patrón has been made since 2002, and we're here to take a look at how it has managed to grow from 100,000 cases to almost four million during that time.

Daphne Moreno is the Hacienda Patrón distillery ambassador and our tour guide for the day. We meet her in the foyer of La Casona and she gives us a quick look at the hotel's impressive bar, which will host some of the world's best bartenders in a few weeks in the 2024 edition of the Patrón Perfectionists cocktail competition.

Next, we head over to the Hacienda and take seats around a dining table on the balcony. We enjoy a lunch of salmon fillet with tomatoes and asparagus grown in the gardens here, followed by a mousse of Mexican coffee and

chocolate. The waiters are all impeccably dressed and the service fluid. We have to remind ourselves that this is an invitation-only table at a tequila distillery in rural Jalisco, and not a Michelin-starred restaurant in California.

As we finish our meal and embark on a tour of the production space, Daphne tells us that the distillery employs a team of 2,200 people. That's around 50% of Bacardí Global's entire production workforce, which also includes multiple Bacardí rum distilleries, Grey Goose, Bombay Sapphire, and many more. To the best of my knowledge, this makes Patrón the biggest distillery in the world based on workforce.

As a distillery gets bigger, it is normal for efficiencies to be built into the plan through economies of scale. Indeed, many large and modern distilleries employ fewer people than smaller, hands-on operations. Patrón has totally flipped this on its head and, to be honest, it is the most impressive thing about the place – as the output has got bigger, its workforce has grown linearly to accommodate it. As Daphne explains, Patrón is better thought of as a bunch of medium-sized distilleries than one big one.

Entering one of the distillery buildings really is a sight to behold. All the trappings of traditional tequila production are there, from brick ovens to tahonas, and wood fermenters... but there are just so many of them! Remarkably, the vast building we are stood in represents just one of 16 production spaces.

At the front of the building, we observe an eight-man team that is about halfway through loading up a brick oven with agaves, just as another team leapfrogs past to begin loading the next one. On the other side of those ovens, we see two huge engine-powered tahonas busy at work, and, as we walk up on to a steel gangway to get a better view of the space, we encounter a sea of fermentation vats, which, at a mere 5,000 litres (1,300 gallons) each, are all laughably small for a brand such as this. As I begin to count them up and calculate the equipment in the other spaces, the numbers are staggering.

Daphne explains that when it was first built, the tahona side of the distillery had six brick ovens, which together fed into two tahonas. The tahonas fed into 60 fermenters, which in turn supplied 11 small copper pot-stills. On the roller-mill side, there were originally three brick ovens that fed into 24 wooden fermenters and 10 stills. This model has now effectively been copied and pasted a further seven times as demand has grown, for a total of 54 brick ovens, 16 tahonas, around 160 fermenters and 80 stills on the tahona side of the distillery. The roller-mill side is scaled similarly, now with 24 brick ovens, dozens of wooden fermenters (they are bigger on the roller side) and 60 stills. So yes, with a current total of 140 stills, Patrón is the biggest distillery in the world based on that metric too.

Because of the enormous footprint that is required to house all of this equipment, it is difficult to grasp the size

BELOW You can think of Patrón as a small, traditional tequila distillery, where everything has been multiplied over and over again – including the Wellington boots.

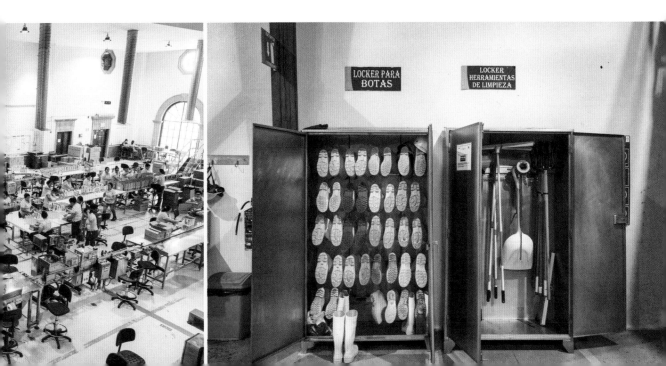

of this place. The shift changes here are illuminating. We see groups of 40 to 50 immaculately uniformed staff members moving from one place to another. Patrón has something of the feeling of a military base, where strict systems somehow orchestrate a complex range of tasks and hierarchies to interact with one another, and where everyone knows their role.

"We have entire teams dedicated to gardening, cleaning and catering," says Daphne. "Then there's water treatment, composting and security." All of that before you even get into the place that's actually making tequila.

With a workforce of this size, you need more than just a vending machine and cloakroom to satisfy their needs. And so, the distillery has vast staff canteens and rest areas for its team, as well as a medical department and physical therapy department.

As we walk along a balcony above one of the bottling halls (every bottle of Patrón is bottled here), we see around 50 ladies busy filling and hand-labelling one of the expressions. Mexican pop music is piped in to keep them entertained and we are told that every 30 minutes the production is stopped and the team partake in stretching and movement exercises designed to reduce incidents of repetitive strain and punctuate periods of boredom.

On our way through the rabbit warren of corridors, Daphne takes us into a small, private tasting room that, to our great relief, is air conditioned, and insulated from the constant noise of the distillery option.

Here we get to try blanco tequilas taken from the roller-mill and tahona sides of the distillery before they have been blended. Nosing between the two samples, it's clear that there is a big difference. *The roller mill sample is fresh and clean, with some briny note and plenty of citrus.* We get to try this at both 40% ABV and 55% ABV (still strength). *The tahona spirit is far more mineral-ly, earthy, slightly mushroomy and slightly smoky. And dare I say it, there is something of hot stone in there too.*

Before we head to the bar to drink some more tequila, Daphne takes us to the largest single part of the distillery – given over to waste management. The vast quantity of *bagazo* (agave fibre) produced by the distillery needs a home, and it obviously made more sense to process it into compost at the distillery than to be shipping it all elsewhere. So, a 12-acre (five-hectare) covered area was dedicated for composting, complete with bulldozers for turning and aeration. This large business within a business produces compost that can be used to naturally fertilise

agave fields, and Patrón produces so much of it that the distillery gives it away to farmers.

We return to La Casona and perch on stools at the enormous marble bar. We have the place to ourselves and only the blazing sunlight pouring in through the bar's high windows reminds us that this isn't a clandestine lock-in at a grand hotel.

We begin by tasting Patrón Cristalino Añejo (40% ABV). *The aroma has a kind of sparkle to it, with some delicate fragrance and minimality. There is no indication of the cask, being more herbal and minty on the taste, leading into a lime finish.*

The Cristalino is presented in a clear-glass, ribbed version of the now iconic Patrón bottle. This bottle has been a topic of some controversy in the tequila industry. The Patrón story claims that Martin Crowley discovered an old, dust-covered bottle in the Siete Leguas offices. The bottle was tall and square. Some accounts suggest it was actually a perfume bottle. The Don Julio brand thought differently and claimed that Patrón has ripped off their square bottle design. If you remember, the official Don Julio story states that Don Julio González himself instigated the shorter, stumpier bottle design so that the bottle could sit on a table and not obstruct the view of one's guests and family.

This all led to a legal dispute and a hearing at the Mexican Institute of Industry in Mexico City. The director of patents and trademarks ruled that Patrón had the right to use the bottle globally, while Don Julio could use elements of the design in Mexico.

Next, we try a cask sample of Patrón Añejo that has been matured for four years and is currently at 59.1% ABV. *The aroma is rich tobacco, leather, nutmeg and spice. On the palate there is dried fruit and soft tannins. The finish is raisins and prune, fig, hot jam, tar and slight saltiness.*

One often-overlooked element of the bottle controversy is the influence of Tonalá pottery on the Patrón and Don Julio tequila bottle design. Tonalá, a town in Jalisco known for its rich ceramic traditions dating back to pre-Hispanic times, has long been celebrated for its distinctive *bruñido* (burnished) pottery. These pieces often feature intricate designs and a unique glaze that gives them a pearlescent sheen. It's conceivable that the elegant, square shape and handcrafted feel of the Don Julio and Patrón bottle drew inspiration from this local artistic heritage.

Patrón's high-end expressions have moved much further away from the Tonalá blueprint, however. El Alto (40%

ABOVE The statue of Ed Brown at Hacienda Patrón. Brown oversaw the building of the distillery and steered the brand through a period of enormous growth in the 2000s.

ABV) is another extra-añejo expression that comes in a beautiful, long bottle, shaped and coloured like an agave *penca*. This tequila has a higher percentage of tahona spirit in it than "usual". *The aroma is agave pudding, vanilla, sponge cake and a touch of dark, musty old wood. There's also bung cloth and another shade of vanilla. The taste is nutty and caramelised, retaining some agave and melding well with old wood.*

In a similarly beautiful bottle is Patrón El Cielo (40% ABV), which is a $200 (£150) blanco tequila aimed squarely at the luxury market. It's been distilled four times. *The aroma has hints of pickle, brine and sea mist. It's not as sharp on the palate as the nose suggests. It's dry and slightly nutty. The finish is a herbal fuzz – bay leaf and oregano.*

It seems fitting to end our time in Los Altos at Patrón. This distillery is a truly remarkable marriage of traditional production and modern, industrial scale – an ostentatious theme park of tequila manufacturing.

The next part of our journey will take us first to Guadalajara and then back to Tequila Valley, to meet and explore some smaller producers and delve deeper still into the history, politics and production of this spirit.

BACK TO THE TEQUILA VALLEY

Such is the influence of the Tequila Valley that its gravitational pull requires a second visit. In the next few chapters, we will delve even deeper into the family dynasties that have shaped tequila, and meet with the new generation of young producers sculpting the future of the spirit.

ZACATECAS

NAYARIT

LOS ALTOS

TEQUILA 5

AMATITÁN

EL ARENAL

ARANDAS

VOLCÁN DE
TEQUILA

2

GUADALAJARA

ATOTONILCO
EL ALTO

LAGO DE CHAPALA

JALISCO

1 LA TEQUILEÑA

2 CALLE 23

3 ATANASIO

4 EL TEQUILEÑO

5 CABALLITO CERRERO

COLIMA

80km/50 miles

LA TEQUILEÑA

La Maduración

Sergio Mendoza is a softly spoken and charismatic man. He's a virtuoso of tequila who, along with his uncle Enrique Fonseca, is the founder of the Don Fulano brand, which launched in the year 2000 and has since become one of the most dependably brilliant expressions of tequila in Jalisco. We are meeting Sergio at the headquarters of Don Fulano in Guadalajara, because La Tequileña – the distillery where Don Fulano is made – is currently undergoing renovations.

Sergio meets us in the modern foyer of the building and walks us past the smart-looking offices and into the warehouse space out the back, where palettes of tequila are stacked on to high racks. In the corner is a small bar area that looks like it has been sliced out of a hipster coffee shop and forklifted into place. We take seats and begin a three-hour journey through time and taste.

The Fonseca family has been growing agave in Atotonilco El Alto in Los Altos since the 1880s. Over 140 years they have amassed 3,700 acres (1,500 hectares) of land and become the biggest private owners of agave in Jalisco. Sergio's uncle, Enrique Fonseca was the agricultural advisor to the CRT when the NOM was established, and one of the original advocates for tequila being made from mature agave. In 1985, he secured contracts with Sauza and Jose Cuervo to supply each with 20,000 tonnes of agave annually for the next 12 years – the biggest supply contract in tequila at that time.

Life was good, until, four and a half years later, during a price slump, both producers broke their contracts, leaving the Fonsecas with vast fields of maturing agaves and no buyers. In a desperate move, Enrique did what many other agave-growing families we have visited have done, and in 1990, he bought a distillery.

This distillery, La Tequileña, is located in Tequila town and was originally built by the Hernandez family in 1906. It was then operated by the Orendain family (of Arette

fame) before it went through a significant upgrade by Bacardí as part of their first flirtation with tequila with a brand called Xalixco (named after the old Spanish spelling of Jalisco). Things didn't work out well for Bacardí, however, and they abandoned the tequila category, returning only when they bought Cazadores in 2002.

Bacardí left the place in good shape and Enrique found himself in possession of a vast distillery housing three 40-tonne autoclaves, nine 90,000-litre (24,000-gallon) steel fermenters, five 3,500-litre (925-gallon) alembic stills and a continuous double-column still – the oldest example in a tequila distillery anywhere. It was a massive distillery by anyone's standards. Enrique had no idea how to operate any of the equipment, though, so sought advice from tequileros in Tequila Valley. Unsurprisingly, they were not forthcoming in assisting him.

"Not only because he was a foreigner from Los Altos," Sergio tells us. "But also, remember, he was the big agave farmer who didn't want to sell, and now he was looking to compete."

Undeterred, Enrique did his research. He learned that alembic stills were traditionally used for making Irish whiskey, cognac and tequila. The continuous still, invented in the 1830s and used to make whisky, allowed distillers to produce spirits with higher alcohol content and a lighter body. Scottish distillers used both stills, blending their products to create a blended whisky, which balanced richness of flavour with a lighter body. So, Enrique set off for Scotland under the guise of his honeymoon, where he visited Macallan and William Grant's Girvan distillery, and found distillers who were generous with their knowledge. Upon his return to Mexico, Enrique had a solid understanding of how to make his own tequila.

"I was very young at the time," says Sergio, "but I remember hearing what my uncle was up to with tequila.

When I was a bit older, my friends and I used to get drunk on his tequila, which my dad had cases of in the garage."

Over the 20 years that followed, Enrique brought Sergio into the business and refined his agave selection and distilling criteria to the point where, during its four or five annual production runs (the distillery is too big to be running non-stop), La Tequileña makes more than a dozen different blanco tequilas, which are blended in various ratios to make its brands: Don Fulano, Fuenteseca, Cimarron, Lapis and Cierto among them. They also still make the Xalixco brand – the same one that Bacardí abandoned along with the distillery all those years ago.

The different blanco tequilas each have their own unique style and are formulated through various combinations of fermentation with and without agave fibres, before being column-distilled through differing numbers of copper plates (producing characterful spirit from 55–65% ABV) plus combinations of copper and stainless-steel pot-stills (that is, all copper or all stainless steel; first distillation carried out in copper and the second in stainless steel, or vice versa). Don Fulano is an 80:20 blend of pot to column, whereas the Cimarron brand is more like a 60:40 balance.

And it's not only the column stills here that are being operated at odds with their intended use. The much maligned (by purists) autoclave, for example, operates at around normal atmospheric pressure at La Tequileña and the result is a cook not dissimilar to that of a brick oven, which takes a full 36 hours to complete. And why wouldn't it be? Unless we think that bricks impart a flavour into tequila, all we're really talking about here is time, temperature and pressure. Sergio considers all the steel at La Tequileña to be a feature of their tequila.

"Tequila was the first agave spirit to be cooked with steam," he says. "It is the cleanest expression of the agave, and steel allows us to achieve that objective."

If you remember, tequila producers in Mexico generally fall into two categories: small artisanal producers who create tequilas with rich, "rustic" agave flavours that are inconsistent year on year, and large-scale producers who achieve consistency but lack the essential agave character. But by blending tequila from small-batch alembic stills with that from the column still, Enrique and Sergio consistently produce tequilas rich in agave character with a delicate finish.

"The column-distilled tequilas taste tropical, like banana and papaya," says Sergio. "But our pot-distilled tequilas are rich and musty – even more so than pot-distilled tequilas from other producers."

He pours us a sample of 100% pot still and we smell it. *The aroma is spicy, like cinnamon, clove and ginger, with a rich, roasted vegetable funk.* By using the equipment to its fullest capability, Sergio and Enrique are able to create broader-spectrum liquids and mix a more diverse palette of flavours. Sergio calls this an "alphabet" of tequila styles, and at La Tequileña, they use these spirits like ingredients in a recipe to make each and every brand and expression.

In 2011, Don Fulano launched an education programme that runs three times a year in partnership with some of the other distilleries that we have visited and it is perhaps the most hands-on distillery experience that money can't buy. The programme is invitation only and mainly brings in bartenders from cocktail bars and tequila specialist venues in the US.

Only two people are hosted at a time and the schedule goes something like this: Day 1 – a full day in the agave fields working as a jimador; day 2 – a full shift on the tahona at Fortaleza; day 3 – distillation with Atanasio and then blending reposado and añejo with Don Fulano, and then over to Arette for bottling.

Don Fulano is in charge of the maturation part of this experience – and for good reason.

After the reposado boom of the 1980s, where Herradura and Cazadores impressed with gentle oak-influenced tequilas, came the rise of 100% agave tequila, which re-established blanco as the quintessential expression of agave. Following this, the idea of maturation became something of a dirty topic among aficionados who saw a barrel as a sullying of agave character. For many tequila drinkers, this sentiment remains today. Enrique was fascinated with ageing tequila from the start and believed that if one year was good, more years would be better. He was the first producer to import French wine casks, and noticed that, with the correct attention, as his tequila aged, it improved. He continued to store it in barrels for longer periods, pushing barrel ageing well beyond the normally acceptable limits of what is possible while still retaining the character of the plant.

The art of tequila maturation is a fascinating process that at its best transforms the raw, vibrant spirit into a

complex, nuanced beverage. This journey is governed by strict regulations and influenced by myriad factors, resulting in a spectrum of aged tequilas that can exhibit bolder flavours ranging from caramel and baking spice through to subtler characteristics reminiscent of tropical fruits, mushroom, tobacco, and even roasted agave. Time spent in cask can also help to soften the sharper edges of a blanco tequila, which may be desirable for particular consumers.

As a reminder, the CRT recognises three primary categories of aged tequilas: *reposado* is aged for at least two months but less than a year; *añejo* is aged for at least one year but less than three years; and *extra añejo*, is aged for a minimum of three years. Añejo tequila must be aged in oak barrels with a maximum capacity of 600 litres (150 gallons) but the most commonly used type is ex-bourbon American oak barrels, which are 200 litres (50 gallons) in capacity. Some French oak barrels are used, often sourced from wine industries, and that happens to make up most of the casks used in La Tequileña's two barrel houses. Reposado tequilas can be aged in bigger barrels, up to 25,000 litres (6,500 gallons). Known as *pipons*, these wooden (usually pine) vats are generally inactive and in the past were used to blend together batches of tequila before bottling. Smaller barrels tend to impart flavour more rapidly owing to a higher surface area-to-volume ratio.

"The origin of reposado has more to do with the transportation of tequila than the intentional ageing," says

ABOVE Don Fulano tequila challenges the dogma of column-distilled and aged tequila, proving that in the right hands no compromise on flavour is necessary.

Sergio. "Añejo is tequila playing as a brown spirit. In a way, Enrique was really the pioneer of that."

All tequila maturation must occur within the tequila DO and the age classification or numerical age statement on the bottle must reflect the youngest tequila in the blend. Every single barrel of maturing tequila has a CRT-stamped label placed over the bung of the cask. This shows how much liquid was put into the barrel, its strength, and the date the cask was filled. If the owner of the tequila wishes to bottle, blend or even taste this tequila, he or she needs to get approval from the CRT before removing the label and, once the bung goes back in, a new label is applied. This is one of the reasons why a perusal of a warehouse in Jalisco is nowhere near as much fun as it is in Scotland or the US, where cask samples are drawn and tasted freely.

The barrel influences the tequila through three primary mechanisms: the extractive effect, where the liquid absorbs compounds from the wood; the oxidative effect, where oxygen permeates the barrel, facilitating chemical reactions that soften harsh flavours and develop complexity; and the interactive effect, where compounds in the tequila react with each other and with wood extractives, creating new flavour molecules. The extractive is usually the dominant force of the three, and it's where we get compounds like vanillin, which offers sweet notes of vanilla, and guaiacol which contributes smoky, spicy characteristics. Eugenol adds clove-like, spicy nuances, furfural develops almond and caramel notes, and lactones provide coconut and woody flavours.

As is common in whisky and rum, the portion of tequila lost to evaporation during ageing is poetically referred to as the angels' share (*la parte de los ángeles* in Spanish). This natural process concentrates the remaining tequila, intensifying its flavours. The rate of evaporation is influenced by factors such as temperature, humidity and barrel size, but typically ranges from 5–15% loss per year.

Several other elements contribute to the final character of aged tequila. Previously used barrels impart different flavours compared to new oak, which means that the character of a reposado or añejo product will often be governed by the wood policy of the distillery that made it. Some distilleries rarely change their casks, which means – like a teabag that gets reused over and over – that less cask character comes across in their mature expressions. Others like the effect of a new barrel and therefore may use a cask only two or three times (or up to ten years, for example) before it's time to bring new ones in. However, most of the time a distillery will have a range of casks that produce aged tequilas that can be blended to a house style.

Then there are a multitude of other factors that play a part, like the level of heat treatment on the barrel interior, known as toasting or charring; temperature fluctuations in the warehouse, causing the wood to expand and contract, encouraging interaction between the tequila and the wood; and the specific microclimate of the ageing warehouse, which impacts evaporation rates and the development of flavour. Plus the fact that every barrel is a natural product and will, on occasion, throw up miraculous results.

To emphasise how different two product with the same label can be, Sergio pours us two reposado samples. The first is aged in a pipon vat and the second in a small French oak cask; both are made from the same blanco tequila and matured for four and a half months in total.

The pipon tequila is *full of juicy fruit on the nose, with grape, bubblegum and cherry. It maintains plenty of fruitiness in the flavour too, with seemingly very little cask character or clues that it has seen any wood at all.*

The French cask reposado is *more elegant, perfumed, refined and crisp. Addie says it has a cigar note to it. It has more barrel influence on the taste, with some gentle spice and*

patisserie character. Sergio uses a blend of these two liquids for Don Fulano Reposado.

Next, we try Don Fulano 20 (44.4% ABV), which is not a 20-year-old tequila (though Enrique has released tequilas over 20 years old under the Fuenteseca brand), but a 20th-anniversary edition aged for two years in oloroso and amontillado sherry casks. *The aroma is all apricots and plums with a touch of gooey, molasses agave. The taste is intensely sherried, with dried fruits, plum wine, baked pineapple and a hint of dried mango.*

"It's a tequila sherry bomb!" says Addie.

On a roll, we next try Don Fulano Imperial (40% ABV). Packaged in a striking blue-glass bottle, this tequila has been matured in French oak casks for 5–17 years and briefly finished in oloroso sherry butts. I'm hesitant to taste this $170 (£130) a bottle tequila, suspecting that it will be dominated by the casks and lacking in agave character. Oh my! *Roasted agave, agave honey... caramelised nuts... vegetal... how is this possible?* Then I taste it. *There's a touch of nutty sherry and dried fruits, but then there's caramelised piña, warm rubber and soft baking spices – it feels like a warm embrace.* Pancho says he can taste watermelon. *The finish is tobacco... then back again to agave. More agave follows. It's a masterpiece.*

It might be the best extra añejo I have tried. It might be the best you can try.

Aged tequilas are fantastic when sipped either neat or on ice, but they also open up the floodgates to a range of cocktail applications. Simply switch out bourbon, scotch, or aged rum for tequila and you have yourself a grown-up tequila cocktail.

An Old Fashioned (añejo tequila started over ice with a dash of bitters and a spoon of agave nectar) is a fantastic place to start, but my all-time favourite cocktail is a Manhattan and I love drinking this cocktail with tequila as the base spirit too, which is officially called a Distrito Federal – the former name of Mexico City (see page 243). You can use any good quality reposado or añejo tequila for this drink, but my preference would be to use something with a robust character as it needs to stand up well against the sweet vermouth and bitters.

Don Fulano Añejo (40% ABV) is the perfect example, aged for a minimum of 30 months in French oak casks. *The aroma is baked banana with some dried orchard fruit and baking spices. It tastes slightly coconut with some menthol character and a rich, indulgent roasted agave note. The finish is new leather and dried citrus peels.*

CALLE 23

◇◇◇

La Pionera

It's around 8pm when we arrive at Sophie Decobecq's courtly apartment in the trendy Central Zone of Guadalajara. She is the French-born maker of Calle 23 tequila and an old friend, so it doesn't feel too out of context that we are setting up a tasting on her dining table with her two young boys running around the place in their pyjamas. Her kids remind me of the childlike sense of wonder and enthusiasm that I have always admired in Sophie, and I think it is this approach, coupled with a formidable knowledge of microbiology and distillation, that has made her the world-renowned *maestras tequilera* that she is today.

Sophie learned her trade working in a research centre on yeast and lactic bacteria in Mexico in 1999, then distilled agaves in South Africa in 2000 before moving back to Mexico as a consultant in 2002, founding her Mexican company in 2003. It was while sharing a meal with friends on the Nueve Esquinas plaza in 2005, just a stone's throw from where we are sat now, that she decided to start her own tequila brand. The brand name came from an old street sign on the wall above the restaurant she was sat in: Calle 23.

Sophie doesn't own a distillery and Calle 23 is made at Destelería Hacienda Capellanía in the Los Altos region, which specialises in contract-distilled brands. Sophie's relationship is a little different to most other contract-distilled brands, however. She contracts distillery time from Capellania, meaning that twice a year she and her team move in and effectively have their own distillery for a month or so. They source their own agaves, cook, mill and ferment in their own way, and, of course, distil to their specifications before ageing in Calle 23 exclusive barrels.

"Wow!" she says pouring us a glass of tequila. "I could not believe it!" Sophie's English is fast and fluent but her French accent as strong as ever, and perfectly placed to emphasise the delight and the romance of making and blending tequila.

The thing she could not believe is not related to the thing that she is currently pouring in our glasses, and this is part of the fun of drinking with Sophie – there is a lot going on at once and it's always exciting. She has just finished telling us about a batch of tequila that has behaved in a way that she has never encountered before and she's keen for us to try it later.

But the tequila she is pouring us right now is something different: a soon-to-be released expression of Calle 23 matured in ex-Calvados barrels that is part of an exchange project with a Calvados producer in France who is currently maturing their apple spirit in ex-Calle 23 casks. Calvados-aged tequila – I ask her if this has been done before. "I don't know," she says with a shrug. "Probably not."

The aroma is crisp and bright, with green agave notes, stewed apple and some meaty, ham-like, muscularity. On the taste it's initially round and clean, but apple comes through in the finish combining with vegetal agave to make a savoury linger.

You'd be able to count on one finger the number of French women running their own tequila brands, which is not news to anyone given the obvious male dominance of field work and production roles in the industry. Women have always played a part in agave spirits' production of course, but usually in roles such as bookkeeping, preparing meals, and selling the product at market. These days there are still a great number of women employed in the tequila business, but mostly on bottling lines and in cleaning and clerical roles. Female tequileras and mezcaleras remain in short supply, but things are beginning to change and, in my experience, agave spirits' consumers seem more receptive to this change than in most other spirit categories.

On top of that, it is a well-established fact that women, on average, have a better sense of smell than men. Better noses might very well mean better tequila, which can only be better for everyone.

Carmen Villarreal, who took over the Destelerìa San Matias and the Pueblo Viejo tequila brand after her husband's untimely death in 1997, has become a pioneering female figure in the industry. As the first woman CEO of a tequila company, she transformed San Matias through her visionary leadership, appointing Rocío Rodríguez, a brilliant chemist, as maestra tequilera in 2007. Villarreal commissioned the iconic Rey Sol bottle design (shaped like a sun) and got the balance right with Pueblo Viejo's quality-to-price ratio making it a favourite among cocktail bartenders in the US. She has also been a champion of traditional production methods, installing a *tahona* and launching the Tahona brand.

Then, there is Melly Barajas, "The Queen of Tequila", who is the master distiller and founder of Vinos Y Licores Azteca. Founded in 1999, this is the only tequila distillery in Mexico that is run and operated entirely by women, from field to glass. They make the La Gritona brand and Leyenda de Mexico as well as other contract brands such as Mascota, with its bulldog-shaped bottle. Apparently, the female-only workforce wasn't intentional, it's just that only women responded to the job adverts and, as more ladies were employed, the distillery's reputation grew.

ABOVE Sophie Decobecq is one of the most recognisable voices in global tequila, challenging the male dominance of the category with delicious spirits and irrepressible energy and charm.

Perhaps you have heard of the Casa Dragones brand, which markets itself as the "#1 Sipping Tequila in the World". That brand is owned by Bertha González Nieves, who has featured in Forbes "50 Most Powerful Women in Mexico" list. I have not personally tried Casa Dragones, as it is expensive (beginning at $100/£75 a bottle), and sadly, made at a distillery that uses diffuser machines. We have of course already visited La Alteña (see page 44), where the Camarena sisters now make the Tapatio and El Tesoro brands.

Back to Calle 23, and Sophie, who is telling us that after each distillation run, she and her team of five decide which tequila will be bottled as blanco and which will undergo maturation for both reposado and añejo or used for their other limited releases.

This process involves everyone in the team sitting down and smelling and tasting the various distillates that need assessing. The tasting is always done blind, which means nobody – not even Sophie – knows which batch they are tasting, and no conferring is allowed. Tastings are conducted in the morning and the team is reminded not to eat or drink anything except water beforehand.

"I don't even brush my teeth!" says Sophie.

Just as with her tasting panels, we are tasting tequilas in the classic ISO tasting glass, which looks a lot like a miniature wine glass, narrowing near the top. The sturdy form and appropriate size of these glasses have made them the go-to for much of the spirits' industry, and as they are available more or less everywhere, they serve as a consistent tool in the spirit-taster's utility belt.

Back in 2001, the CRT commissioned the legendary Austrian glassmaker Riedel to produce tasting glasses specifically for tequila. After two tasting workshops led by Georg Riedel himself, which were attended by 30 tequila producers, officials and cognoscenti, Georg's design was designated the Official Tequila Glass by the CRT. The Riedel glass is like an elongated ISO, and actually pretty similar to a Champagne flute in its shape and size.

Honestly, though, the best glass to drink agave spirits in is the one you like. I have sampled fantastic liquids from disposable plastic cups, shot glasses (Mexico has a love affair with a particular type of ribbed shot glass that has a cross on the base), polystyrene coffee cups (with remnants of coffee still in it), half an empty Coke bottle, a horn, the shell of a cuastecomate fruit, straight from the bottle and straight from the still. All of them were an experience to be treasured. And that's all we're after at the end of the day, isn't it?

For Calle 23, the tequilas in a panel are scored out of ten based on taste and aroma and each batch is diluted with water to various strengths to see how it performs at 40%, 42%, 44% and so on. Sometimes the spirit is sweeter at lower strength and more dry and spicy at higher strength. Sometimes certain aromatic qualities will jump out more at specific strengths.

"We let the tequila pick its proof," says Sophie.

The tequila that we are drinking now, though – the one that Sophie is practically leaping around the place in excitement about – has done something very weird indeed. When Sophie's team initially ran the blind tasting, they found that their notes and scores changed dramatically between 40, 42, 46, 48 and 50% ABV.

"It was like each sample was a completely different tequila!" Sophie says.

Intrigued to see how deep the rabbit hole went, they then tasted again, diluting to all of the odd numbers between 40 and 50. More wildly different results. Sophie then homed in on the favourites and took the dilution to another degree of precision, cutting the spirit to half percentages. She continued to find differences. By the time the tastings were finished, her team were detecting noticeably different aroma and taste attributes between tequilas with only a quarter of a percentage difference in the ABV.

"It was scary, to be honest," says Sophie.

I must confess that at this point I was sceptical of what I was hearing. A difference between a few per cent is fine but 0.25%? That's the equivalent of a teaspoon of water in an entire bottle, and Sophie is saying that this was noticeable.

So we run the experiment there and then.

Like the scientist she is, Sophie produces graduated measuring cylinders. In the dim evening light of her dining room, she gets to work mixing together her favourite strengths from this same batch of tequila.

She tells us the spirit came off the still at 50.5% ABV, so using some simple maths she dilutes it with demineralised water to target specific strengths. She then starts drip feeding us samples to taste, initially giving us no information as to their strengths. As we have already tasted at least 40 tequilas already today and it's getting late, our palates are hardly the apparatus of the finely honed morning tasting that Sophie strives for, but nevertheless, we quietly sniff and sip the samples.

"The first is very elegant," says Addie. "And the fourth one has a nice peach-stone taste to it."

I smell the third one, which has a struck match, sulphur note to it, along with some pineapple and grapefruit.

Back and forth we go with more samples appearing.

"This one has a lot of agave for me," says Sophie, pointing to a glass with spirit cut to 46% ABV. I agree, it has a wildness about it too that isn't present in the other samples. As we slowly proceed through five, six, seven different iterations of strength... we come to the stark realisation that these spirits could have been made with entirely different agaves, production methods, or even at different distilleries. And yes, even the slight shift between 42.5% and 42.75% manifests some changes in the liquid.

I find this revelation to be utterly remarkable but also a little unsatisfying. In an industry that trades off methodology, where milling, fermentation and distillation offer a multitude of options that impact how a product tastes, and each brand uses its own proprietary method, the validity of all of this becomes open to criticism when one can change the character of a product by simply adding or removing a teaspoon of water. It's like saying you can undermine all of the engineering that goes into a Formula 1 car by switching out what breakfast cereal you feed the driver. It also makes you wonder if some tequilas that are not to your taste need only a little water adding or taking away to find their sweet spot.

Sophie is quick to point out that this is an outlier situation, however; she has never encountered it before and that explains why she's backflipping around the dining table in delight. This, then, opens up another thing to consider: what special sequence of events have conspired to produce a tequila with this plasticity of flavour in the presence of H_2O? The answer to that question is: we don't know. The good news for tequila geeks though is that they can ponder the hows and the whys with glass in hand, as Sophie plans on releasing this special tequila as a quintet of bottles called Los Quatros Grados ("The Four Strengths").

Such playfulness is really at the heart of what Calle 23 is doing and has always done, whether it's through the striking bottle designs that refract agave art through a reverse label on the back, or provocative taglines in the branding such as "Tequila makes me smarter" and "Agave you my heart".

To celebrate their 20th anniversary, Sophie produced 7,900 bottles of a blend of three blanco tequilas with agave sourced from Los Altos, Guanajuato and the Bajío region of Jalisco. She called it "Edicion Unica", but instead of selling it as an additional line with an inflated price, she quietly inserted all of the bottles randomly into cases of her regular blanco tequila, ensuring that those

cases would be passed on to all of her international bar and restaurant distributors. And so Sophie's secret bottles spread far and wide around the globe. This, she says, is a thank you to the bartenders who, thanks in part to Sophie's tireless energy, have been a core component of the brand's success and status.

She pours us some of the Edition Unica (40% ABV) to try: *it's heady and bright on the nose. Clean and fresh with plenty of cooked agave. The taste is long with melon and pistachio (Addie says walnut), then into bay leaf, warm and spicy. Very long finish.*

With the children sound asleep and our own minds swimming in a dream world of glass bottles, percentages and tasting notes, it's time for us to leave. Before we do, Sophie takes me into the part of her house that would normally be called the lounge or "front room" back in the UK. Hers has no sofas or television, however, and is rather more like a brand museum for Calle 23, displaying limited-edition bottles, glassware and art from the past 20 years. She hastily fills a bag with merchandise, generously palming me three tiny-handled cantarito cups that she tells me were hand-painted by a friend of hers.

We all say our goodbyes and head straight to the store on Plaza Nuevo Esquinas to procure ingredients for sangritas (see pages 230–231) so we can put the little clay cups to use – giving a polite nod to the weathered old "Calle 23" street sign that hangs above the café on the square.

BELOW If you really squint your eyes, you can just about make out the old Calle 23 street sign that inspired the name of Sophie's brand, 20 years ago.

ATANASIO

◇◇

El Profesor

René Carranza is known by many people in the Tequila Valley as "The Teacher". When he was 20 years old, he started an IT business, which brought some of the first computer equipment and IT education to the area. He sold many people their first computer and was instrumental in bringing broadband infrastructure and satellite internet connections to the communities around here. These themes of entrepreneurship, engineering, marketing and self-teaching, would play nicely into his future role as a tequilero.

One of his clients was Jose Cuervo, which offered him a taste of what the tequila industry offered as well as the spark of an idea to make his own. He visited other distilleries and was particularly inspired by Cascahuín (see pages 28–33), so invested some money and time into a small distillery in the village of San Pedro de los Landeros, a few miles east of Tequila.

Founded in 1995, this tiny operation was part of a ranch and originally created as an informal agave spirits' distillery to use up excess agaves on the Landeros family's plantations – for personal consumption and to share with friends. In 2011, the family invited René to invest in new equipment so that tequila could be made at a commercial level. René spent six years in the fields and on the stills, learning his trade step by step. Then, in 2017, he decided to make the leap to becoming a full-time tequilero. He enrolled in a distilling course and took full control of the distillery.

"The Landeros family never wanted to be involved in the tequila business," says René. "So when the prices started going up and down and contracts needed signing, they withdrew back to the fields."

The CRT officials certified Familia Landeros in 2017, named by René in honour of the family that started the place. René now produces 3,000 litres (800 gallons) of tequila in a month, which makes Familia Landeros the smallest producer we have visited and among the smallest producers of tequila in the state. To put that into perspective against the biggest producer, it is less tequila than Jose Cuervo produces in a single hour of production.

René uses a tiny three-tonne autoclave to cook his agaves, then a single-stage roller mill to cut the cooked agave before it goes into six open-top steel fermentation tanks. He uses a proprietary yeast in a fermentation that can take anywhere from five to nine days, depending on the time of the year. Distillation of the *ordinario* is done in two 2,400-litre (635-gallon) stills followed by a second distillation in a 1,200-litre (320-gallon) still.

"When orders come in for tequila, we make a production schedule," says René. "If we don't have orders, we do maintenance."

Orders are coming in, though. Atanasio is now being imported into Texas, Florida and California, and has quickly become a poorly kept secret of small-batch, quality tequila.

We sit at a table under a veranda as René grabs some bottles to taste. But something isn't right. Pancho and René are talking fast in Spanish and I can't understand what they are saying, but whatever it is Pancho is clearly a little taken aback – shocked even. They pause their conversation so that Pancho can translate, and he tells us that he and René are talking about terroir. It turns out that René is of the strong opinion that agave terroir has been overstated in tequila. He says that it is trying to force a romance into the spirit where it doesn't belong and isn't needed. "The romance is that it happened!" explains René.

OPPOSITE René Carranza's welcoming smile and generous pours of tequila belie a deep understanding in matters of agave and tequila, and his relatively recent entry on the scene means he's not afraid to ruffle feathers with his opinions.

This is tantamount to heresy, especially coming from a new entrant into the category. To take a position of terroir scepticism is to go up against the likes of Carlos Camarena and Sergio Mendoza, and challenge a sentiment that has embedded itself deeply within the hearts and minds of tequila aficionados.

What ensues is a lengthy discussion, which I will attempt to distil down for you. René's general thesis is that cooking the agave eradicates any trace of the place where the agave was grown.

"With grapes you can have an influence of the soil, because you don't have hydrolysis – they go straight into the fermenter," says René. "But with agave you have to cook it first and some agaves are sweeter, others less so, and that will degrade a large part of the characteristics of the soil and standardise the agave flavour."

Furthermore, he believes that a change in flavour could happen through subtle changes in the cooking time or temperature, wild yeast cultures getting involved, inconsistent cuts on the still and different resting periods in glass. There's also the agave itself, which might be at a slightly different level of maturity from one field to another. We know that from one vintage to another the same field tastes different, because of the changing climate and how that impacts the maturing agave. So how can we say that the soil is really the variable at work here?

Unfortunately, it is hard to prove or disprove any of this, but René thinks he has a solution. He has got his hands on a small experimental still, which he points to across the yard. It isn't much to look at, more like a haphazard stack of metal trash cans than a piece of lab-grade apparatus, but he believes it could be used to conduct trials with agaves from different fields and regions. This still is particularly suited to the task as it conducts cooking, fermentation and distillation all within the same unit. This should limit the possibility of production inconsistencies by carefully controlling temperature and time.

My opinion is that in principle the field where the agave is grown probably does make a difference, but the various steps in production quite possibly mitigate those differences. And even if they don't mitigate them, the process will not be repeatable anyway, so why distinguish the field in the first place?

But perhaps René and I are looking at this the wrong way. Is the aim to categorise tequila flavour by soil type, or is it rather just to appreciate the flavour of tequila in all its varied glory? If one parcel of land can produce an outrageously stylised expression in one year and another parcel can do that in the complete opposite direction the next year, as an appreciator of flavour that is a much better thing than both tequilas being blended together into an anonymous soup – even if that soup is tasty. Agave spirits are about the agave itself, and as blancos they are a true expression of the plant. And if truth is what we are after, any exploration into how they can change and evolve through production – from field to bottle – is worthy of investigation.

There is another terroir influence that seems to be discussed a lot amongst producers in Mexico but to my knowledge is rarely spoken about elsewhere: altitude.

"It doesn't matter where they were grown," says René. "It matters that I am distilling them at 1,300m (4,250ft)."

Many distillers mention, often as a side note, how the altitude of the distillery affects the character of the tequila they make. And with two distinct producing regions in Jalisco at different elevations, this could support an argument for terroir at the distillery level.

We know that elevation impacts production on a purely physical level. At the average elevation of 1,200m (4,000ft) that we see in the Tequila Valley, ethanol boils at 76°C (169°F); but in Mazamitla, south of Lake Chapala, where Tierra Noble Tequila is made at an altitude of 2,100m (7,000ft) above sea level – the highest for a tequila distillery – it boils at 73°C (163°F). Now that might not seem like a big difference, but a small shift upwards in cooking temperature in the still could be enough to make some taste and aroma compounds in the spirit become volatile, shifting the balance of flavour in the resulting spirit. Air pressure will also impact the pace and temperature of fermentation, as well as the microclimate of the region in respect of humidity and temperature fluctuation. And that's before we even get started on the differences in natural yeast cultures between different altitudes and of course the mineral content and hardness of the water supply.

My takeaway from this conversation is that the number of variables in tequila is huge and that the blue agave itself, at a genetic level, is the only control to the experiment. Everything else plays its part, and because of that it's hard to emphasise a single element of production – there are just so many. The best we can to is smell, sip and enjoy.

Atanasio Blanco (40% ABV) *has a bracing maritime aroma at first, with salty air and oyster, but then turns a little*

richer. On the taste, there is some alcohol, which turns into balanced black-pepper spice, mineral sting and gentle citrus zing. A clean and elegant tequila.

"When I first came to this place," says Pancho, "I could not believe that they were producing this quality of tequila in stainless steel."

Atanasio Orígenes (46% ABV) is René's high-proof expression. *It has an aroma of fresh-cut pineapple with a slight funk to it, alongside a bright, dill-pickle, vegetal pungency. Balanced and sweet on the palate, like lime pith with a long agave finish.*

More tequila is poured and I take a moment to inspect the bottles on the wall. With their simple, smart packaging they nicely reflect René's no-nonsense approach to quality. On every bottle I also notice a small circular sticker that reads "Additive Free Alliance". This label is awarded by an independent additive review body started by Grover and Scarlet Sanschagrin from the tequila comparison website Tequila Matchmaker. Beginning in 2017, the Sanschagrins were invited into distilleries to check purchase and production records and test their tequilas using laboratory equipment to check chemical composition and look for signs that additives have made their way into the bottle. The 100+ brands that have received additive-free verification from the Additive Free Alliance familiar names like Patrón, Fortaleza, Cascahuín, Don Fulano, El Tequileño and G4.

To say that the Additive Free Alliance has ruffled feathers would be a huge understatement, however, and

ABOVE Tequila Atanasio is made at the Familia Landeros distillery, which is one of the smallest distilleries in all of tequila. It's the clarity of flavour in René's products that have made them a recent hit among consumers.

to understand why that is, we need to discuss what additives are.

The tequila NOM allows up to 1% of a tequila (including 100% agave tequila) to include *abocantes* (additives) without requiring a label change. The four officially permitted additives in aged tequilas (section 4.36.1 of the NOM) are glycerin, caramel colouring, oak extract, and *jarabe* (sugar-based syrup). Officially, blanco tequilas are not permitted to have any additives, but there's a confusing loophole in the NOM that contradicts this rule. We'll get to that shortly.

In aged tequilas there may be some justification for using additives. Perhaps the barrels you are using are a little more tired one year, or the climate affected the way the oak interacted with the spirit. By allowing the addition of sugar, caramel colouring, oak extract and glycerin, brands can produce a more consistent reposado or añejo product that shows the same colour and flavour year on year.

Colour correcting is a practice used across the whisky and rum industries, and the inclusion of oak extract and sugar takes place across the cognac industry in the form or dosage. Glycerin is a semi-sweet flavour enhancer that adds texture, smoothness and mouthfeel to a spirit. It is used across the rum industry, in some types of gin and in many liqueurs. It's worth noting that glycerin is created naturally during the fermentation process of spirits so all tequilas will contain some trace of it.

The point is that the NOM is not doing anything radically different in respect of permitting additives in tequila, and there is an argument that in doing so it serves to protect the brands and the tequila category by gaining and retaining consumer trust.

However, the way the NOM has been worded has left the addition of additives open to abuse. An upper limit of 1% by weight may not sound like much, but in the world of concentrated flavourings and colourings, it is a planet-sized load of flavour and colour. A mere pin-prick of E150 (caramel colouring) can add the visual appearance of years on to a single serving of añejo tequila, while 1% of glycerin would turn your tequila into a slippery, viscous soup. Even a 1% concentration of sugar can have a remarkable effect on the taste and character of a product and some sweeteners are far more potent than sugar.

But this is just where the problems begin.

Another section (6.1.1.1) in the tequila NOM seems to contradict the earlier section that prohibits additives in blanco tequila. It states that sweeteners, colourants, aromas and/or flavourings are permitted in all types of tequila, as long as they don't exceed the 1% upper weight limit. This opens the floodgates for unscrupulous producers to add countless types of flavourings and sweeteners to their products to cover up deficiencies or rework the flavour profile of the product – even the un-aged ones.

When the NOM was established, the 1% limit might have been sufficient to keep additives in check and not muddy the natural character of the tequila beyond recognition. But modern flavourings and sweeteners produced by the likes of Bell Flavors, Multisabores and DSM–Firmenich, who service industries ranging from pet food to scented candles, can be made to extremely high concentrations, and thus the 1% limit is rendered entirely arbitrary.

Additionally, at the moment, the CRT conducts no testing for additives, with the argument being that it's hard (if not impossible) to verify whether additives, such as caramel colouring and oak extract, have been added to a product seeing as an aged, additive-free tequila will also contain colour and oak flavour derived naturally from the cask. This has inevitably led to a new breed of tequila

product; one that acquires its flavour either partially or predominantly from unnatural sources. The phenomenon is clearest to see in reposado and añejo products that seem to exhibit overt characteristics of caramel, vanilla, chocolate or baking spices.

But while flavour houses have become adept at understanding and isolating the chief components of these interactions, their deployment in aged tequilas never comes close to producing a product as naturally rounded as the real effects of maturation. The technical capability likely exists – makers could if they wanted produce flavours that are practically identical to real oak extract. But it would be expensive to do so and the competitive market for artificial flavours doesn't want it. Instead, the flavour houses blend two or three key flavour compounds, such as vanillin, oak lactone and isoamyl acetate (banana flavour) to serve as a simulacrum of maturity.

Worse still, a different range of flavours is being used widely and more secretively in blanco products to cover up deficiencies. These might include fruit aromas like grapefruit or pear, or more vegetal, cooked aromas to simulate the aroma of agave.

For some brands and their consumers, this is sufficient to give the effect of an authentic product. But it may be the case that these consumers simply don't know any better – they have never tasted an additive-free tequila and have no basis for comparison. For those of us who have, the human organoleptic machinery is our best weapon in this fight. It is every bit as proficient at identifying flavour molecules as a machine in a lab. And, where matters of authentic taste are concerned, what is missing from the product might be just as important as what is included. In the words of Sergio Mendoza from Don Fulano, the taste and aroma of tequilas that use additives take on a "hollow" effect; the flavours feel forced and lack substance, structure and complexity. By way of analogy, I might describe Van Gogh's "The Starry Night" to you as being a blue, yellow and black painting. It would give you a vague sense of the piece, but the true range of colours is far greater and my description doesn't even begin to touch on the form and detail of work. This is my feeling of flavour adulteration, where form and structure are forgotten and nuance is lost owing to a lack of myriad supporting flavours that only a natural process can currently offer.

We're now talking about mass-produced brands that are made in such a hurry and with so little care for the final outcome that they possess very little natural agave character. While the CRT does an incredible number of checks, especially for methanol, sulphur and heavy metals, according to Section 3 of the current NOM, there are no specific checks for artificial sweeteners, aromas and flavours. In this way, a lack of policing for additives has helped to perpetuate the use of diffusers, column stills and other money-saving – and flavour-negating – strategies in the production flow. You needn't worry about stripping out flavour during cooking, fermentation and distillation, when you can just add some back in afterwards.

Remember that these products can still be labelled as 100% agave because the CRT tells us that only agave sugars were used during the fermentation. But there is no getting around the fact that if they contain additives they are not made from 100% agave. Current estimates suggest that around 70% of all tequila brands contain one or more additives. At that level, a prohibition on additives is not likely to happen any time soon. The guiltiest parties are the ones with the biggest bank balances and most political clout in tequila's halls of power. In fact, an outright ban would run the risk of collapsing the industry – some of the big brands rely so heavily on additives that without them their products would become unrecognisable to consumers.

This is why the CRT was not at all happy about the arrival of the Additive Free Alliance, as it undermined its authority and challenged its values – values that are in part based on the needs and desires of their biggest funders.

First the CRT issued a statement demanding that Additive Free Alliance stickers be removed from all bottles: "We consider that any scheme offered in the market to 'certify', 'verify' or 'confirm' in any language that a certain trademark as 'ADDITIVES FREE' represents an act contrary to good customs and practices and induces error or confusion to the Tequila consumer."

Then, shortly before our arrival in Mexico, a police sting operation orchestrated by the CRT was conducted on the home and office of Scarlet and Grover in Tlaquepaque. Hundreds of bottles of tequila were seized alongside basic distillation and laboratory equipment, the accusation being that the pair was illegally producing spirits without a license. It was a stark reminder of the powers that the CRT wields and, as one high-profile tequila producer put it to me, "This was a warning shot – the police could have planted something there and made it look much, much worse."

Prior to the raid, there was another twist in the tale when, in October 2023, Patrón (the biggest additive-free

tequila brand) announced the launch of an additive-free endorsement that came directly from the CRT. Their core tequila range will now display a gold sticker stating "Additive Free, Endorsed by Consejo Regulador del Tequila." Despite this announcement, at the time of writing, the CRT has not released any official statements or detailed information regarding the programme or endorsed any other additive-free products. It is also not clear how the CRT went about testing or verifying Patrón's additive-free status.

For many of the people who are committed to seeing a greater degree of transparency, this revelation is yet more evidence of how big producers, who provide the bulk of the funding to the CRT, are granted favourable treatment by the regulator.

Just before this book went to print, the CRT threatened punitive action against a number of small tequila brands who were using the term "additive free" on their labels and in their marketing materials. The CRT warned that their product may be seized and action taken against them even if their additive-free status is mentioned on third-party websites.

The intention was obvious, and the Additive Free Alliance, not wishing to harm the small producers whose trust they had gained, effectively closed down their programme and de-listed all tequila brands from their website in October 2024.

EL TEQUILEÑO

La Mezcla

In the deepest recess of Tequila town, not far from Fortaleza and El Llano (the home of Arette), where our journey began, is the La Guarreña distillery. Owned by the Salles family, it holds a special place in the heart of Mexican tequila drinkers because it's the place that El Tequileño is made.

Throughout the 19th century, it was customary to name distilleries after their owners or location, often by appending "eña" to their name or nickname. Many examples of this are still around, from La Floreña and La Martineña to La Quintaneña and La Guarreña. Over time, the nomenclature evolved to include values or political convictions. Thus, establishments like La Perseverancia ("The Perseverance") and La Constancia ("The Constancy") emerged. Similarly, La Cofradía signifies brotherhood, La Fortaleza exudes strength, and La Quemada evokes the notion of "burned". Each name is a subtle nod to the ethos and character imbued within the spirits they produce.

It should be fairly obvious what El Tequileño means but for the avoidance of doubt, it's "someone from Tequila", and that's certainly true of the brand's founder Don Jorge Salles Cuervo. Don Jorge's father was a Texan railroad engineer but his mother was María Cuervo Salcedo, niece of one José Cuervo Labastida and daughter of Malaquías Cuervo Labastida – the gun-wielding Cuervo family "fixer", who you really did not want to mess with.

Don Jorge began operating La Guarreña in 1941 and made bulk tequila for his family's brand. By 1958, Jose Cuervo (they spell it without the accent) had expanded their operations, however, which left Don Jorge no option to bottle his own product. La Tequileña was launched on New Year's Day of 1959 and it is the only brand that La Guarreña has ever bottled. Don Jorge married Doña Minerva Camarena, forging an alliance between the two great tequila families that exploited the Cuervo knowledge of the tequila business and the Camarena expertise in the fields. This may have influenced the Salles' decision to source all of their agave from Los Altos, a commitment that remains in place even today.

Like *Game of Thrones*, alliances between the powerful families of tequila were not at all uncommon back in the day (if they weren't at war). In fact, if you go back just three or four generations, you can plot a wide family tree that draws lines between every major family in the business: Cuervo, Rosales, Salles, González, Orendain, Sauza, Camarena and Jiménez. And in many respects these historical unions have served as the foundational glue upon which the entire tequila category has been shaped and consolidated.

Don Jorge brought his son into the business in 1970 and then, after his death in 2000, his grandson Jorge Antonio "Tony" Salles – the great-great-grandnephew of José Cuervo – joined the operation in 2005. Tony has been the master distiller at La Guarreña since 2008 and he is the man shaking my hand right now in the yard at the front of the distillery.

Agaves are piled high across the patio and, as the afternoon sun beats down, a team of workers is busy chopping the larger *piñas* into smaller chunks using axes. This helps with loading them into the autoclaves and ensures that everything cooks evenly.

Tony points out that there is another task going on here too: the removal of the *cogollo* from the piña – a bitter-tasting cluster of "male" leaf fibres in the top of the plant. This is a practice we have observed at other distilleries and one that warrants further discussion. But to get to the bottom of what's going on we have to dispel a couple of myths first...

As we have already established, an agave is deemed to have reached optimal ripeness when it produces a quiote.

However, only a small percentage of the agaves used to make tequila actually produce quiotes before they are harvested. This is partly because most of the big producers are simply harvesting agaves when they are underripe – for convenience, efficiency, or to take advantage of market prices. But even some mature blue agaves, like the ones we are seeing at La Guarreña, may have failed to produce a quiote, not because they are immature but because they can't. These plants are impotent, which is a consequence of vegetative propagation in the industry, where young agaves are grown from *hijuelos* (offshoots) which are in fact genetic clones of the mother plant – a subject we will discuss in more detail shortly.

An agave is continuously generating new leaves throughout its life – as old *pencas* wither into the ground, and new, larger ones, fire upwards from the centre. The cogollo is the cone-shaped cluster of new pencas that sprouts from the top of a growing agave. Over time the leaves on the cogollo fan outward as new ones thrust upwards. The regeneration of the cogollo stops only when a quiote is formed, so for agaves without a quiote the cogollo remains intact at the time of harvest and its structure penetrates deeply into the piña.

Somewhat confusingly, piñas with a cogollo are colloquially referred to as being "male" and ones without (that is, ones that produced a quiote) as "female". Tony explains that the gendering distinguishes the "male" agaves from "female" wherein the latter have "given life" when they've produced a quiote. This is all a little misleading, however, as all agaves are monecious – meaning they have male and female sex organs. So if anyone in Mexico ever starts talking about "male" and "female" agaves to you, it's worth reminding yourself that sex has nothing to do with it and that a "male" is in fact a plant that has been cloned to the point of sterility.

Over in the fields, the cogollo is sometimes left on the piña like a unicorn's horn, as it can be used as a handle to drag the piña to a nearby truck. But once it arrives at the distillery, and if you are a tequila maker who is concerned with producing a tasty spirit, the cogollo needs removing in its entirety. This cluster of tender leaves has no starch in it but lots of fibre and wax and, if cooked, it imparts bitter flavours.

To remove it, this you need to split the agave in half and use a machete to cut out the part of the cogollo that forms on the inside the piña. Tony Salles has got into the habit of cutting the long cogollo cones and planting them in pots at the front of the distillery. "It's the most beautiful part of the agave," he says.

Tony tells us that some of the agaves we're seeing here are very old. Having been planted as three-year-old hijuelos, they have then grown for a further seven years to give a total of ten years' maturation – very old by blue agave standards. This, it is hoped, will result in some extraordinary batches of blanco tequila being produced in 2024.

"Every load we take we have a digital receipt to confirm its origin, age and sugar content," Tony says, showing me a printed copy. "This load was 807 agave, 24 tons, 25.98° Brix, planted in 2017."

The CRT will use this information, along with calculations of the sugar content after cooking and the inspection of other procedures here, to calculate how much alcohol the distillery should be making. They also combine it with earlier supplied data and satellite imaging

BELOW LEFT The process of making a tequila is a physical one where thorny agaves take on sharpened steel.

BELOW Fermentation at El Tequileño takes place in swimming-pool-sized open-top concrete tanks.

to record the location of every single plant and oversee its maturation progress. As extreme as that sounds, it is designed to eliminate fraud, where an unscrupulous grower might uproot a plant while it is still young and plant something else in its place before miraculously presenting agaves from unknown sources a few years later. To maintain this oversight, harvested agaves receive a CRT "passport" upon reaching distilleries.

The agaves used to make El Tequileño are cooked in autoclaves and these autoclaves have a fascinating story to tell. They were brought to Mexico by Tony's great-grandfather, Juan Salles, who was the lead engineer that helped build the first railroad that ran from Texas all the way to Guatemala. That's why these autoclaves are actually modified tankers from railway cars. They are much thicker-walled than a normal autoclave and only have steam injection from one end as opposed (a regular autoclave is heated all along its length). There are also no pipes coming out of the bottom for *miels dulces* (the very sweet juices extracted from the agave in the early part of the cook), so they sit in the bottom and boil the lower-down agaves. What all this means is that the cook is uneven and inefficient, but Tony considers this a feature of his tequila, not a bug.

The unique design of these autoclaves has become particularly important of late, because the brand is growing at such a rate that the distillery will soon need more ovens. That's why Tony can sometimes be seen at the scrapyard in Guadalajara, poking around the place looking for old rail cars that he can take to the distillery and convert into an autoclave.

Perhaps El Tequileño's greatest claim to fame is that it proudly produces the most loved *mixto* tequila in the industry. Mixto literally means "mixed" and is used to refer to tequilas that are made from a mixture of agave and other sugars, typically from sugar cane or corn. The term is not legally recognised and in fact actively discouraged by the CRT, as under its rules all mixtos are categorised as "tequila", while a tequila made only from agave is always labelled as "100% agave tequila".

The current rules state that "tequila" (aka mixto) must be made from a minimum of 51% agave sugars with the balance made up from any other sugar source besides other types of agave sugar (you can't sneak in other varieties of agave species into your recipe!). The most common sugar is, unsurprisingly, the cheapest, which usually means corn syrup. But in reality, you can use anything, from fruits like grapes or mangoes to the traditional *piloncillo* sugar that La Guarreña uses as part of its sugar bill. Piloncillo is a traditional, unrefined cane sugar that's a staple in Mexican cooking and baking. It's also known as *panela* and *rapadura* and is used in many Latin American and Asian dishes. The name piloncillo translates to "little pylon" or "little loaf" and refers to its conical shape. It has a flavour similar to soft brown sugar but with additional fragrant spice and molasses notes.

The Salles' choose to make their mixto tequila with a higher-than-needed 70% agave and 30% other sugars.

"For us, mixto is the one that has kept us alive," says Tony. "If you gave my grandfather the option, he would drink mixto ten times out of ten. My father, nine out of ten, mixto. Because that's the one they've been drinking all their lives."

It wasn't long ago that "100% agave" was considered a sure-fire guarantee of quality spirit, but with the arrival of diffuser machines, the aggressive use of column stills, tequila additives and the practice of harvesting immature agaves, the "100% agave" classification no longer holds as much sway – and rightly so. This has surprisingly re-opened the door for high-quality mixto tequilas that can compete on flavour and price.

And what better recognition could you ask for than being the tequila of choice in Don Javier's Batanga cocktail just around the corner at legendary tequila bar La Capilla. Tony pours us a glass of El Tequileño Blanco (40% ABV), *which has an inviting aroma of green pineapple and vegetal notes intertwined with a hint of citrus. On the palate, it is gentle and fluid, presenting a clean and crisp taste. The finish is smooth with a slight astringency but avoids any harshness.*

With the exception of the 30% added sugars, everything about the production of El Tequileño is exactly the same for mixto as it is for their range of 100% agave expressions. This means open-top ferments in concrete tanks (using a proprietary yeast extracted from mango) and double distillation in copper pot-stills.

El Tequileno Platinum (40% ABV) is the 100% agave version of the regular blanco. *Rich and bold, the nose is characterised by darker vegetal notes, which give way to a palate full of warming spice. The body is heavy, with garden herbs and the finish is long-lasting with a nice warming spice.*

Interestingly, all of the tequilas made here spend some time in cask, even the blancos. This is more of a mellowing process than a maturation one. The casks used to mellow their blancos are not very active, but time to rest after distillation does soften the sharper edges of the spirit. All of the maturation is done in Guadalajara, which means that 6,000 litres (1,600 gallons) of tequila are driven there in a tanker truck every day.

"We do a lot of reposados!" says Tony as we move into the brand-new El Tequileño tasting room across the street from the distillery. "We have five or six that we play with."

El Tequileño Reposado (38% ABV) strikes a great balance, allowing the agave to shine through prominently. *The aroma and taste reveal a fruity and nutty character, with delightful hints of mango, pineapple, hazelnut and allspice. The combination of flavours provides a rounded and satisfying experience, with a smooth and well-integrated finish.*

One expression in particular piques my interest. Reposado Rare is a tequila matured for six years in total, which might leave you wondering why it isn't bottled as an extra-añejo. The reason is that the "barrel" used to mature this tequila is about the size of a grain silo clocking in at 23,000 litres (6,000 gallons) and maximum cask size permitted for añejo is 600 litres (150 gallons). It's not uncommon for some reposados to be matured in these huge pipon vats for a couple of months to hit regulation, before receiving a liberal dose of caramel colouring prior to bottling, but six years is unheard of and that's why El Tequileño created a new category for this bottling called Reposado Rare.

They also do a Reposado Gran Reserva (40% ABV), which is a blend of reposado and añejo tequilas. *The aroma is big tomato vine, aloe vera, round and sumptuous. Flavour is like a romance between wood and agave. Nutty, crisp, vegetal and harmonised.*

The sustainability efforts at El Tequileño are impressive too. The company has its own composting facility for *bagazo* (residue after distillation) and is experimenting with producing its own natural gas to power the distillery using the leftover *vinasses* (stillage). A recent full overhaul of their packaging reduced glass usage and incorporated sustainable plant-based inks into the labels.

Throw in a 25-bedroom boutique hotel with a pool and spa next-door to the distillery, and you have a tequila distillery that really is doing it all – even a cristalino.

El Tequileño Cristalino (40% ABV) *has a subtle and inviting aroma of vanilla and cut grass. On the palate a*

ABOVE Tony Salles pours samples of still-strength El Tequileño for us with copper stills gleaming in the background.

little more agave comes through, plus black pepper and soft citrus. The finish is smooth and refined.

Finally, we taste El Tequileño Sassenach (40% ABV), a product that combines the essence of tequila with whisky-like qualities, having been initially matured for two years in American oak casks, before being finished in French oak barrels for four months. *On the palate, it reveals honeyed and jammy flavours that are quickly complemented by spiced and vegetal notes. The oak influence comes through towards the finish, providing a delightful crossover experience that is both intriguing and delicious.*

It's another hot afternoon as we head back towards Guadalajara for the evening. A non-stop diet of tequila is delicious but there's a real risk of dehydration if you don't get some alternative fluids inside you. We have

ABOVE All of the tequilas produced at El Tequileño have spent time in cask to mellow their flavour.

ABOVE El Tequileño has worked closely with Mexican street artists who have produced a dozen murals around Tequila, including the modern interpretation of the goddess Mayahuel on the left.

been seeing signs for "Cantaritos" ever since we got here, and one of these hyper-refreshing tequila and fruit-juice cocktails feels like just what we need to quench our thirst. If you're a fan of the Paloma, prepare to meet your new best friend: the Cantarito. This lively cocktail takes the classic mix of tequila, lime juice and grapefruit soda and kicks it up a notch with extra citrus juices and a pinch of salt.

The Cantarito bar we have just pulled up at is enormous. It takes us around a minute just to cross the parking lot and inside there have to be at least 400 chairs, all of them of the traditional *equipale* style, which are handmade from strips of cedar and upholstered in pig-skin leather. They originate from the town of Zacoalco de Torres, just south of Guadalajara. Right now, the seats are all empty (Pancho says it will be full in a few hours) and we choose a spot near the bar.

In a bar like this, which specialises in the drink, there are a few different variants available. We opt to share two between the three of us, going for a classic grapefruit and orange option, plus one that includes beer. The drinks cost 250 pesos (£10/$12.50) each, which is a lot for a cocktail, but they are enormous. And best of all, we get to keep the cups to take home with us.

CABALLITO CERRERO

Los Proscritos

Pancho's car is careering down a rough track, the underside scraping and the suspension slamming as we descend into the Tecuane Canyon near Amatitán. Rubén González is blasting out of the car speakers, his elegant jazz percussion ruined by the painful grinding of the Jetta. All around the valley are young blue agaves clinging to the dry hillside. And as we bounce around the place, I briefly wonder what it would be like to be flung from the open window and die via impalement on a massive blue agave penca. Our next distillery will be our last tequila (before we move on to mezcal and raicilla) so it would be fitting to perish at this point in time.

So far on our journey, we have never been far from blue agaves. They're in the fields, painted on walls, emblazoned on crockery, sculpted in stone on fountains, cast into jewellery, and have featured in quite a few of my dreams. This peculiar plant, officially dubbed *Agave tequilana* Weber was first noted by French physician Frédéric Albert Constantin Weber in 1902. Curiously, Weber's Mexican sojourn lasted a mere three years, but it was long enough to for his name to be tied to tequila for ever.

As we have learned, the ascent of tequila as a global commodity began with enterprising landowners in the Tequila Valley. The Sauzas and Cuervos recognised the potential in the local agave spirit and endeavoured to industrialise (and monopolise) its production. They formed alliances with European engineers through marriage, and by the turn of the 20th century they had brought state-of-the-art distillation technology and other efficiencies into the region. In spite of this, tequila producers faced a fundamental challenge: the slow maturation of their primary ingredient, which required up to three decades to reach harvest size. Even then, its sugar content paled in comparison to faster-growing crops like sugar cane, posing a persistent obstacle to efficient production.

Identifying an agave species that could produce maximum yields in the shortest space of the time was the key and the fructose-loaded blue agave was the solution. This plant could reach sexual maturity in as little as ten years and could reproduce by cloning itself. Furthermore, the more stressed it got and the more dehydrated it became, the more the agave thrived and the higher the concentration of sugar. Rising temperatures and selective planting in the decades that followed have accelerated the rate of maturation down to as little as five years. Weber's once anonymous plant has become the super-efficient freak of the agave world and there are now 600 million of them painting the tequila-producing regions of Mexico.

The agave itself is none the wiser. Its modus operandi remains unchanged: grow big enough to sequester the energy needed for reproduction and grow some spiky armour to protect oneself while you're at it.

Agaves have up to three modes of reproduction and most blue agaves can do all of them: seeds, which rely on pollination from insects, hummingbirds and bats; offsets, also known as pups or *hijuelos*, which are literal clones of the agave that pop up out of the ground; and bulbils, which are also clones but that grow off the *quiote* (flower stalk) and eventually fall on the ground and take root.

If nature is left to take its course, most baby agaves would naturally grow from seed. Remember that most agaves produce an impressive quiote near the end of their lives. This flower stem grows very fast, up to a few inches in a single day and reaches a height of five to ten metres (16–33ft) before producing hundreds of flower heads. After this dramatic display, pollinators such as bees and bats arrive, attracted by the nectar (note that this nectar comes from the flower head and is not the same agave nectar you buy in a store, which is made by extracting sugar from the cooked piña). As these pollinators feed, they come into contact with the flower stamens (part of

the male reproductive system), which contain pollen, and the pollen sticks to the bodies of the pollinators. When these pollinators move to another flower, some of the pollen is transferred to the stigma (part of the female reproductive system) of the new flower. Agaves are monoecious, meaning that each individual plant has both male and female reproductive organs within the same flowers, so there is a whole lot of cross-pollination going on here.

Once pollen lands on the stigma of an agave flower, it germinates and grows a pollen tube down the style to the ovary, where it delivers sperm cells to the ovules. One sperm cell fertilises an egg cell to form a zygote, which develops into a genetically unique embryo. Meanwhile, the ovule's other components form the endosperm to nourish the embryo. The fertilised ovule matures into a seed, complete with a protective seed coat, ready for dispersal. This process happens over and over again, and an average blue agave can produce in excess of 4,000 seeds if nature is left to take its course. These seeds then scatter, finding new spots to grow into the next generation of blue agave plants. The problem is that nature is never allowed to take its course.

In almost every case, the quiote is cut before the plant begins to flower (or no quiote is produced at all) lest all the sugar in the plant gets used up producing flowers and seeds. Without the flowers, there is little to no

RIGHT Agaves like it rough. This means that these plants, which are hanging on to the rocky Tecuane Canyon slopes, are likely to produce a more complex-tasting tequila.

cross-pollination and that means all of the plants are grown via vegetative propagation from hijuelos. This practice that is born out of the relentless pursuit of efficiency has been going on for more than century, and when scientists conducted studies on genetic samples from blue agave plants, they found that they contained the lowest level of genetic variation ever documented in a commercially grown crop species. To say that this is problematic would be a gross understatement.

An industry predicated on a single variety of agave consisting of identical clones is playing with fire, as this uniformity makes the entire crop vulnerable to disease. If a pathogen or insect evolves to attack one plant effectively, it can potentially devastate the entire population. The tequila industry would collapse like the vineyards in France did during the Great French Wine Blight and the potatoes in Ireland during the Irish Potato Famine.

A dry run of this already happened in 1998, when six different strains of bacteria and fungi went to work simultaneously and infected a quarter of all blue agaves, killing 200 million plants. It put dozens of farmers and tequila producers out of business and sent a warning shockwave through the industry to sort its act out.

The preventative course of action is to widen the gene pool and engender some natural defence into the agave stocks through diversity. One way of doing this is simply to let some plants flower and create diversity though cross pollination. There are two problems with this, however. The first is that the region has already lost nearly all of its natural pollinators (bats and hummingbirds), which died out or moved on decades ago when humans began chopping down quiotes before agaves had a chance to

flower. The second is that any cross pollination that could take place would largely occur between the same, genetically identical clones that make the earth on satellite imagery of Jalisco appear blue. Clones mating with clones simply makes more clones, so for this to work pollinators would need to be importing genetic information far from Los Altos and the Tequila Valley to instigate any diversity.

Another threat could arrive in the form of climate change, where a lack of genetic diversity could hamper the plants' ability to adapt to changing environmental conditions, such as shifts in climate or soil composition.

Through unsustainable and short-sighted legislation, driven by politics and capitalist warfare, the tequila industry has backed itself into a corner that it may be hard to escape from. We will explore some of the efforts being made to tackle this problem later in our journey, but one solution I will raise now is to include more species of agave in the NOM. This could alleviate the pressure on blue Weber, reinvigorate historical varieties, and ultimately mean the industry isn't putting all its piñas into one basket.

While this is very unlikely to happen, there is one renegade distillery out there that is showing us how it could work.

After a full 30 minutes of torturing Pancho's Jetta, we steer into a cluster of what appear to be abandoned farm buildings at the bottom of a gorge. Nobody is around and the sun is blazing, dust still lingering in the air from our rapid descent. Pancho directs us through a yard where we notice three metal hatches in the ground. Then, we head down a set of stone stairs, past a penned area with chickens and mules, and into a great hall of spirit production. Built by Maximiliano Jiménez in 1873, the

Santa Rita distillery has stayed in the same family, which has a distilling pedigree dating back some 400 years.

That on its own would be impressive, but add to it the fact that the distillery was built on the same site as the much older El Tecuane Taberna, which dates back to the early 1700s and is the oldest recognised *taberna* (the traditional term for a Jalisco distillery) in all of Jalisco – it's even a UNESCO heritage site.

Put it all together and it means that we have the oldest distilling dynasties in Jalisco making spirits on the oldest-known site of distillation in all of Jalisco.

El Tecuane was likely built sometime around the turn of the 18th century – long after the Spanish conquest – and the distillery has a curious mixture of Spanish and indigenous technologies. At that time, the Spanish government had placed a prohibition on spirit production in New Galicia to secure a market for their imported brandy and wines. Industrious distillers fled into remote areas of Jalisco and established illicit operations where they could make spirits for their communities. These were not typically people of Spanish descent but rather indigenous people who – if El Tecuane was anything to go by – had extensive knowledge of agave spirit production and an appetite for drinking it.

El Tecuane was built into the hillside on a series of sweeping manmade steps that harnessed gravity in the tequila-production process. On the highest step they built two huge pit ovens into which they placed a blend of agaves on red-hot stones to cook them. The cooked agaves were then crushed with a manually operated millstone of Spanish design, used for pressing olives. The sweet liquid then flowed down to a lower plateau where no less than

ABOVE The Santa Rita distillery is a working museum of tequila history, producing some of the best blue agave spirits in the land. Ironically, however, it features no mention of the word "tequila" on the products it bottles.

44 fermentation pits had been hewn from the natural volcanic rock, each capable of holding around 3,000 litres (800 gallons) of agave juice and fibre. After fermentation, the alcoholic mixture was then transported further downhill in buckets to multiple stills, which were cooled by cold water diverted from a nearby spring. There is no evidence of the stills used at El Tecuane but historians believe that they would have been of a design that pre-dates the arrival of the alembic still from Spain.

When the Santa Rita distillery was built 150 years ago (and around 150 years after the original El Tecuane Taberna), it also incorporated gravity in its design. Maximiliano Jiménez's new distillery would be both state of the art and large for its time. Those hatches in the ground that we saw in the yard were built for top-down loading into the steam ovens: arriving agave would be dropped in directly rather than carried in by hand as is the norm. Inside the distillery building, there is an old rail track with carts that was once used to move cooked agave between the mill and the fermentation vats. And through the entire length of the space runs an aqueduct, supplying the same natural spring water that El Tecuane used centuries earlier for every stage of production.

Spring water is also used in another, less obvious way. Before pumps were invented, it was necessary for someone to get into the fermentation pit or vat to stir the fibre and juice together and to assist with emptying the mixture using buckets. The work of these *batidores* (beaters) was hard and dangerous, with the risk of asphyxiation by CO_2 (or rather, lack of oxygen) a real threat. Either way, once they emerged from the pit, the beaters were often in a bit of a state, covered in sticky agave fibre and juice. The designer of Santa Rita recognised this problem and built cleaning pools adjacent to the vats that are continuously refreshed with spring water from the overhead aqueduct.

In fact, the whole place has the feeling of an enormous Roman baths with high ceilings and arches and slits cut out of the walls that offer all-day light.

As we move through the long hall and approach the far end of the distillery, we finally see life – a clutch of humans operating and observing the stills, tiny in the vast space of the place. Among them are Don Javier Jiménez and Javier Jiménez Jr., respectively the great-grandson and great-great-grandson of Maximiliano Hernandez, the distillery's founder. As it happens, we're lucky anyone is here at all seeing as the Jiménezes run a family law firm and are both full-time attorneys. The distillery and the Caballito Cerrero brand that they make here are passion projects and they produce here for only two or three months of the year. Don Javier is in his eighth decade of life but moves around the place fast, taking puffs on his morning cigar while checking spirit cuts on the stills and directing staff. He takes us into a small office space where a family tree hangs on the wall, showing 15 generations of distilling history in the region and two distilling families intertwined.

Glasses appear and spirit is poured. I'm not sure what I'm drinking at this point but it's good! *A slightly fungal mushroom note gives way to bubblegum and aloe vera – it's juicy, saline and ripe. The taste is exquisitely well formed, with papaya and blueberry giving way to sweet toffee, vanilla, cinnamon: dessert qualities.* It's an utterly phenomenal tequila, but it would soon transpire that it's not technically a tequila at all...

With the room quickly filling with cigar smoke, Don Javier explains that Maximiliano Jiménez had a daughter called Maria who married her second cousin, Alfonso, and it was their son, Alfonso Jiménez Rosales, who co-founded Herradura (Spanish for "horseshoe") in 1919, with his cousin Aurelio López Rosales. Don Alfonso Jiménez parted company from Herradura in 1950 after an unreconcilable dispute with his cousin, at which point he moved into the Santa Rita distillery and launched a new brand: Caballito Cerrero (translating as

"Wild Horse"), because, after all, a wild horse has no use for horseshoes.

After its launch in the 1950s, the Caballito Cerrero brand quickly established itself locally as a high-quality product, made from 100% agave and using traditional methods like in-ground fermentation pits and copper alembic stills. Originally marketed as a "Vino de mezcal", the label changed to include "tequila" and kept that reference despite never registering a NOM with the CRT, and despite, ironically, the Jiménezes working as legal advisors for the CRT in its early years. For this reason, Caballito Cerrero fell under the radar during the early part of the 21st century, being prized by those in the know for its outlaw status and dedication to authentic production.

That changed around six years ago.

With mounting pressure to register a NOM with the CRT, the family took the bold move to drop "tequila" from their labels and instead refer to their product as a "destilado de agave". Placing themselves outside of the CRT ecosystem could have killed the brand altogether, but Javier Jr., in particular, recognised the growing interest in mezcals and other regional agave spirits and thought the brand strong enough to flourish based on its quality and values.

"Nowadays the market is very open," says Javier. "And that's one of the reasons why we decided to stop being tequila and become an agave spirit."

Caballito Cerrero now sells for $100 (£75) a bottle in the US, placing it right at the upper end of the price bracket for a legitimate NOM tequila. It has hit legendary status among aficionados: for both its renegade ethos and its impeccable quality. This year the distillery will swing into production for just two months and make 5,000 litres (1,300 gallons) of spirit, which is nowhere near enough to meet demand. Everything made here is on allocation, with different importers and markets clambering to get their share. All of the spirit being made here today has already been sold.

And the glass in my hand confirms exactly why that is. It is their standard 46% ABV blue agave expression – a tequila in all but name – but it is one of the best blue agave spirits I have tried. And we're only getting started.

The Jiménezes also produce a tequila-style spirit made from an agave called Chato. This, they say, was once commonly used to make tequila before the DO stipulated blue agave as the only permissible base material. Some people still plant Chato now and it's likely, if not certain, that these agaves have snuck their way into tequilas we have all bought and tasted – not without historical justification but those guilty of doing so would not be concerned with that.

"We bought some land that was growing Chato," says Javier. "And decided to try it. It came out somewhere between a tequila and mezcal and now we are growing more Chato to make more."

At 46% ABV, the Chato is incredible. *A spicy aroma, with pickled jalapeño and some fermented and briny notes. The taste is softer than expected, but then a Szechuan pepper electricity holds the tongue; it's almost mineral-like, with a really bright zinginess.*

Next, we try an expression called Unicorn (because it's so rare), which is made from Chato that has been aged for 45 days and bottled at a hefty 55% ABV. *It's a magnificent liquid: sweet and honeyed, but with a pure agave pepperiness and sizzling fajita heat.*

Javier takes us down some steps to a very small cellar space nestled underneath the stills.

"This is all that I have in barrels," he says, gesturing to a small alcove stacked with a dozen or so casks. With no CRT oversight, he can happily pop the bung off a barrel and draw the 48% ABV sample.

"We have not changed the casks since the 1970s," he says. This, he agrees, will mean only the mildest interference from the barrel itself while still leveraging the benefits of oxidation in wood over a few years. *Roasted agave notes surge on the nose, then it's tropical, fragrant and intense. Damp, musty, bung cloth on the taste and a touch of cacao bitterness, but then fresh citrus and a fizzy orange hum on the finish.*

Chato Añejo by contrast has more of a roasted quality, with toasted nuts, coffee and black pepper aromas on the nose. The spice continues on the palate with ginger, nutmeg and clove, leading into a saliva-inducing, bittersweet finish.

Before leaving, Javier Sr. nimbly leads us back up the stairs and into the bottling area. Next-door there is a small room with cabinets showcasing the historical bottles of Caballito Cerrero, going right back to the 1950s. Unlike today's, these are mostly illustrated in full colour and have changed very little over the years. Only the description shifts, from vino de mezcal to tequila to destilado de agave. These shifts tell us more about the legislation of agave spirits than they do the product in the bottle. The Jimenezes have not dramatically altered the way they make spirit over the past 75 years. In the case of Caballito Cerrero, these are mere legal designations and historical

ABOVE When you technically sit outside the law, as Caballito Cerrero does, you can taste spirit straight from the barrel (as we did).

quirks. It serves as a reminder to me that labels, DOs, NOMs and classifications can be useful indicators of production or taste factors, and can help protect the quality of a certain type of product, but consumers needn't be beholden to them. It is always worth going deeper, not judging a bottle by its label, and recognising that it's people who make spirits, not lawyers. Except in the case of the Jiménezes, where it's both.

RAICILLA COUNTRY

We trace our journey through Jalisco's raicilla region, past the blue agave fields of the Tequila Valley to the pine-shaded mountain towns of Mascota and San Sebastián del Oeste and onward to the Pacific coast. The picturesque Sierra Madre and the remote *tabernas* that scatter the landscape offer glimpses into a part of Mexico's distilling history that has until recently remained hidden.

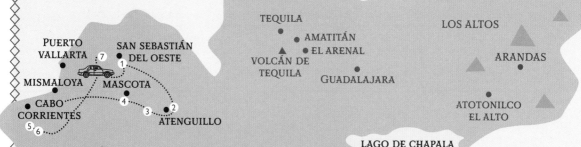

NAYARIT

ZACATECAS

TEQUILA

LOS ALTOS

AMATITÁN
EL ARENAL

VOLCÁN DE
TEQUILA

ARANDAS

GUADALAJARA

PUERTO
VALLARTA

SAN SEBASTIÁN
DEL OESTE

7

1

MISMALOYA

MASCOTA

4

CABO
CORRIENTES

3

2

ATENGUILLO

ATOTONILCO
EL ALTO

5 6

LAGO DE CHAPALA

JALISCO

1 TESORO DEL OESTE

2 LA REINA

3 LOBO DE LA SIERRA

4 MANUEL SALCEDO

5 LA GORUPA

6 LOS TRES HOMBRES

7 AYCYA

80km/50 miles

COLIMA

TESORO DEL OESTE

El Embajador

Running the gauntlet down to the Santa Rita distillery the day before had taken its toll on Pancho's long-suffering Jetta. As we headed west from Guadalajara the next morning, something didn't feel right. There was a concerning rattling noise: we had burst not one but two tyres.

They wouldn't be the last.

It was only 11am when we dropped the car into a garage and decided to get an early lunch at a small cantina. Perhaps it was just our insane schedule, but I was beginning to learn that "lunch" could take place at any time between 10am and 5pm and that breakfast and dinner are also strikingly similar to lunch, with all meals usually comprising meat, salsa and tortillas in some shape or form, and perhaps a little cheese. But who's complaining?

Back on the road, with Mexican hip-hop playing loudly over the radio, we keep heading west, out of tequila country and into the Sierra Madres mountains. The roads become narrower and twistier as we wind up into the hills, and we find the blue agaves that have been our constant companions for the past two weeks replaced by dense forests of oak, pine and fir, interspersed with stretches of scrubland. It's spring, so there are wildflowers here and there, and the occasional village with white-cement walls and red-tiled roofs. Just two hours from Guadalajara and already it feels like we're in a different country. Blue road signs marking the "Ruta de la Raicilla" display an illustration of the broad and short-leafed *Agave maximiliana*, marking this region as raicilla country.

Raicilla is the latest regional spirit of Jalisco to be officially baptised with its own legal designation of origin (DO) and, along with tequila, mezcal and bacanora, is one of only four agave spirits with protected origin status. According to the DO, raicilla can be produced within 16 municipalities on the western stretch of the state of Jalisco (Jalisco has 125 municipalities in total) and one municipality in state of Nayarit.

Within the raicilla DO, there are two regional styles: *raicilla de la costa* (coastal raicillas) and *raicilla de la sierra* (mountain raicillas). The DO does not draw a geographical line between the two regions, but the coastal raicillas tend to be near the coast and the mountain raicillas tend to be in the mountains. Each style has its preferred species of agave, and they differ in the way that they cook them too. In the mountains, the *raicilleros* (raicilla makers) use an above-ground oven that looks like huge pizza oven and is sometimes called an adobe, whereas the coastal regions tend to use pit ovens dug into the ground and of the type that have become synonymous with mezcal in Oaxaca.

Though not currently legislated, there are at least 12 species of agave used to make raicilla. The raicilla de la sierra tends to be made from the *maximiliana* and *inaequidens* agaves and raicilla de la costa tends to be made from the *rhodacantha* and *angustifolia* agaves. We will discuss the differences between these agaves (and others) later, as well as the cooking methods and how all of this impacts flavour.

Our first stop is near the picturesque town of San Sebastián del Oeste, which is a popular with American tourists who are shuttled in from cruise ships docked in nearby Puerto Vallarta. Hidden up on the hills on the western edge of town, we find the *taberna* (the traditional name given to a raicilla distillery) Tesoro del Oeste.

This is the newest distillery on our tour, having been founded in 2020. It has an Old West feel about it, being constructed from sand-coloured bricks, thick pine beams and terracotta roof tiles. All around us there is lush-green vegetation and the sounds of wildlife lurking in the hillside. Underneath the large veranda, which has maps

and framed botanical drawings of agave varieties on the wall, there is a beautiful pine bar and a huge conference table. The table is currently occupied by a dozen young men and women, who turn out to be students from the University of Guadalajara.

Outside is the white-domed adobe oven, which has a fire blazing inside it and a big pile of agaves stacked up next to it. Behind the students we can see a pair of small stainless-steel stills.

Sergio Escoto is one of the newest raicilleros in the area and he's currently standing in front of the bar talking to the students in Spanish. He's wearing a button-down shirt and *sombrero de charro* (cowboy hat), and has a handlebar moustache. All this fails to conceal the fact that he is uncharacteristically young, good-looking, and athletically built for a maker of agave spirits. And to add to his growing list of talents, it turns out he speaks fluent English, after spending some time working in bars in London during his early twenties. At that time, his family owned a small contract-distilled

tequila brand called Casco Viejo (produced at Casa Camarena) which he tried unsuccessfully to import into the UK.

Upon returning to Mexico, Sergio got into adventure sports (kiteboarding, horse riding, mountain biking) and found himself spending a lot of time in the mountains.

"We found a treasure here," he says, taking a break from his other guests. "We uncovered trails that nobody had seen for 300 years, dating back to when the Spanish were mining for minerals."

Mapping these hidden treasures (or *tesoros*) became a focal point for him, which meant clearing and transplanting thorny *maximiliana* agaves out of the way.

"You don't want to ride a bike near an agave," he says. "Those things will fucking kill you."

It was at this point that some of the locals from San Sebastián informed him that the plants he was moving – identified by locals as *lechugilla* (big lettuce) – were the maximiliana species used to distil raicilla. Knowing very little about the spirit, he delved deeper and learned that

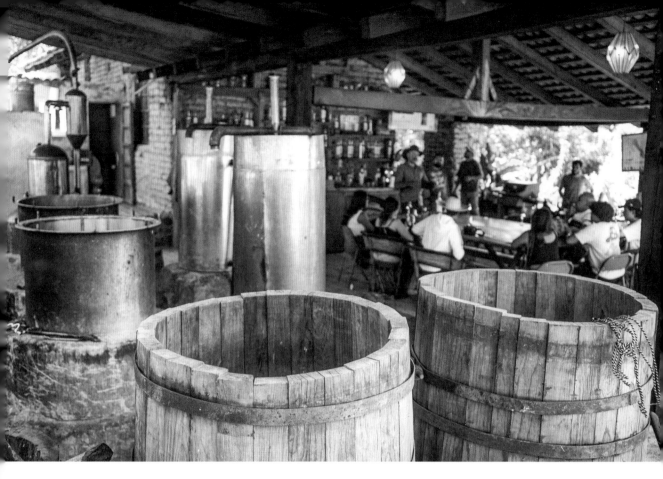

the last raicilla taberna in San Sebastián was run by a man called Juan Dueñas and it had closed down seven years previously. This information, along with his experiences in the mountains handling the plant, was stored somewhere in the back of his mind until one night, during the Covid-19 pandemic, he woke at 3am from a dream with the realisation that he needed to build a taberna.

Sergio pours us some raicilla to taste while he continues his story. The distillery currently bottles six expressions, and this one is their 100% Maximiliana (40% ABV). *The aroma is sweet and creamy, vegetal, slightly seaweed-y, with loads of fresh pineapple. The taste is delicious: candied and confected, like juicy fruits and wine gums, with a lingering vegetal agave note. It is nothing like tequila.*

Knowing practically nothing about how to make agave spirits, Sergio recruited the help of a local handyman called Chuy, who helped him build the distillery. Once the place was up and running, Sergio

noticed that Chuy seemed unusually competent at milling, fermenting and distilling the agaves, as well as harvesting them and planting them on the steep mountain slopes. It was only at this point that Chuy revealed that his surname was Dueñas and that he had grown up working at Taberna Juan Dueñas where he had been making raicilla from the age of six.

Sergio takes us over to his oven, which he tells us takes around eight hours to reach its full temperature of roughly 1,000°C (1,800°F). We timed our visit perfectly as the loading was about to begin. Along with the students, we lend a hand passing the three tonnes of agaves up to the team and they toss them in through the top door, like popping basketballs through a net. It takes only five minutes to completely fill the oven and then both the top and bottom doors are shut. Calling them "doors" suggests that they have hinges and a latch, but doors in this instance really just means "metal sheets". The top one sits over the aperture while the bottom one is propped against the hole using a wooden wedge and then wet clay is packed around the edges to seal both sheets in place. The technique here is to throw lumps of clay at the edges of each door, where it sticks and begins to bake immediately from the incredible heat that is attempting to escape. This takes around 20 minutes to complete, and even then, small wisps of smoke will emanate from tiny cracks in the baked clay.

With no oxygen getting in, the fire is snuffed out and, over the next 48 hours, the agaves will be roasted from the residual heat in the walls and floor of the oven. Once the 48 hours are up, the clay is chipped off and the hatches are opened, revealing – I would imagine – the most incredible aroma of cooked agave. Just as with tequila, the agaves need to cool for a day before they can be removed and milled ready for fermentation.

Sweaty but happy from the work of loading, Sergio grabs another bottle and pours glasses for everyone. This expression is his Platinum Assembly (46% ABV), a blend of two agave species: *maximiliana* and *inaequidens*. *The aroma smells almost dusty or earthy. The taste is supremely vegetal with a little heat, sizzling dry spice and soft fungal notes. The spirit grips the palate well with Szechuan fizz remaining for a while.*

The blends Sergio makes here are a consequence of the flow of production rather than forward planning. Right now, he is cooking *Agave angustafolia* (the same species that the preferred mezcal variety, Espadín, belongs to), which will be milled in a repurposed wood chipper, then fermented and distilled and blended with whatever the next agaves are that arrive at the taberna.

"They are all happy accidents," he says. "But this is the way it was done 300 years ago. They produced blends all the time."

No yeast is added during fermentation, it is all natural, and takes eight to ten days to complete. Sergio uses small pine and plastic fermentation vats that are basically upturned whisky barrels. There are ten of them in total, hidden away in a dark cellar space, and ranging from 200–500 litres (50–130 gallons) in capacity. The fibres are included in the fermentation and water is added periodically. Up here in the mountains, many raicillas take on a noticeably cheesy character, which is brought about by malolactic fermentation near the end

of the fermentation process, combined with a cooking method that doesn't produce so much smoke so as to mask it.

There are two 300-litre (80-gallon) steel alembic stills here. Sergio tells us that they call the first distillation *común* ("common") in raicilla circles rather than *ordinario* as with tequila. This sparks a debate between Addie and me as to whether a single distillation of agave spirits was once the norm and then at some point someone developed an improved, high-strength version. And then maybe the two versions both existed, with the double-distilled version commanding a higher price and high status, and the original, single-distilled product being lumped with the lower-ranking label of "ordinary" or "common". Pancho disagrees with this theory, asserting that ordinario likely comes from the fact that this first distillation is a common or ordinary step in the production process – a necessary intermediate stage that doesn't require the skill that the second distillation does with its cuts and gradation of strength.

All of Sergio's raicillas are rested in glass demijohns for a minimum of six months before bottling. This, as we will see, is a common practice among the best producers of raicilla and mezcal, and can result in astonishing changes in the spirit over months and years.

Before we leave, Sergio shows us a broad patio space that has coffee cherries laid out, drying in the sun. After a few days, the fruit of the cherry dries to a crispy husk, which can be removed to reveal a pair of green coffee beans inside. These are all collected and roasted and then you have yourself some coffee. Plans are afoot to make the raicilla equivalent of the hyper-successful Patron XO Cafe tequila coffee liqueur.

There's time for a quick parting glass of raicilla, but Pancho insists that this one is imbibed directly from the *penca* of a *maximiliana agave*. He carefully selects an already broken leaf from a plant that is growing near to the distillery building and then, one by one, he serves us a measure of spirit by pouring it down the concave length of the leaf and into our mouths. As fun as this is, it's not far removed from drinking diesel off the back of a scorpion, what with the agave penca being clad in thorns and the spirit being straight from the still.

We leave the taberna and head back towards the mountain town of Mascota, where Pancho has his family home and where we will be staying for the next few days. I gaze out of the passenger window and up into the hills

as we pass by them (at speed). Within the dense forests, I begin to imagine I can see old mining trails, like intricate spider webs of history, weaving their way upwards.

What I do see for sure, though, is more coffee.

It's not surprising that Sergio was processing coffee cherries back at the taberna. It is one of the chief commodities around these parts, because the combination of high altitude, sub-tropical climate and dense shade from the pines is perfect for growing it. Mexico is amongst the top ten producers of coffee in the world, though most of its output is grown further south in Oaxaca, Chiapas and Veracruz. It's also the nation we have to thank for Kahlua, which is the best-selling coffee liqueur in the world and the third-best-selling liqueur after Baileys and Malibu.

Kahlua is made from a base of Mexican sugar cane spirit, which is infused with arabica coffee, vanilla, caramel and quite a lot of sugar. In fact, in bartender circles, Kahlua was always considered to be the most

LEFT AND CENTRE Loading the adobe oven is a very hands-on process that needs to be completed quickly in order to retain the heat and avoid producing too much smoke.

sweetened liqueur on the market. It turns out it contains 400g (14oz) of sugar per litre, and as 20% of the volume is alcohol that leaves only another 40% for water and coffee solids, so it's fair to say that Kahlua is more sugar than it is anything else.

For me, though, the bigger issue than the sugar is that they didn't use agave spirit as the base. Not only that, but they haven't ever thought to release a tequila or mezcal edition. This is a missed opportunity, as agave pairs extremely well with coffee and in my book is tied with rum for being the best base spirit for an espresso martini-style drink. And to that end, I've put my money where my mouth is on page 239.

LA REINA

La Real

Beginning the day in Mascota, we eat a quick breakfast of *chilaquiles* (tortilla chips simmered in salsa, served with cheese, cream and shredded chicken) in a cantina just off the main square, and head east out of town back towards Guadalajara.

This road roughly traces the Talpa de Allende pilgrimage trail, which sees up to two million Catholics walk to Nuestra Señora del Rosario (The Statue of Our Lady of the Rosary) in Talpa every year. Many of them complete the 160-km (100-mile) journey from Guadalajara during the Holy Week in the spring, seeking blessings for health, family and personal matters. The small mountain town of Atenguillo forms part of the route, and it's here where we will meet the owner of La Reina raicilla.

Like San Sebastián del Oeste, Atenguillo draws in eco-conscious tourists and adventurers looking to explore the nearby Bosque de la Primavera. Atenguillo is a small place of only 4,000 residents, complete with colourful, picturesque streets and a sunny square.

We park and walk across the square, heading out of the light and into the warming gloom of a billiard bar. There's a bartender polishing glasses with an old rag, gnarly old boys drinking at the tables, a Mexican wrestling match being played on the TV and a row of vacant stools at the bar. It's perfect. And as it's already late morning we order beers and a raicilla. To accompany our drinks, the bartender hands us a bulls horn containing dice to play with. This game, *chuza* (also known as *cacho*) is similar to poker in that you have to score flushes, straights, full houses and so on, except the symbols of 10, jack, queen, king and ace are displayed on the faces of five dice. Looking around the place, I realise that most people in the bar are playing the same game.

Soon enough, Juan Pablo Mercado walks in to the bar and greets us. He and his partner Ana López are a young husband-and-wife duo with a forward-thinking approach to promoting raicilla. Juan grew up in Tijuana but Ana grew up right here in Atenguillo and her family are well known in the region. When she was studying at university in Guadalajara, she would bring raicilla from Atenguillo for her friends to taste. The combination of something tasty and the illicit nature of this strange mountain spirit elicited a lot of questions from her friends and inspired her to investigate more about it and drive into the mountains where it was being made. That's when she met Julio Topete Becerra and his family, and fell in love with their way of life, just as she had their raicilla.

"The family asked us to help them promote and sell their product," says Juan. "So we created a brand and managed to export 1,500 bottles to Italy."

The brand they made is called La Reina, which means "The Queen", hinting at how tequila may be the king of agave spirits in Jalisco, but raicilla is the queen.

The word raicilla probably originates from *raíces,* which means "roots". The relevance of roots, though, is open to debate. Some think it may have come about from the visual similarity of an agave piña to a root, or that it was made from agaves with visible raíces or *hijuelos* (clones) – though not all raicilla agaves produce hijuelos. Other people say that producers of old used to infuse roots into the spirit, which may sound strange but is common among manufacturers of gins and liqueurs all over the world. Some suggest it was a tactic to nominally differentiate raicilla from mezcal and evade the authorities during the Spanish Crown's prohibition, while others argue that spirits' production in this area was never forbidden. Jorge Carbajal from Hacienda Divisadero, a fifth-generation raicillero and a contributor to the DO, asserts that the name raicilla has always been in use, historically known as *vino de raicilla.*

We finish our drinks and pay our bill and head across the square to Juan's pickup truck, but not before getting a bag of the local yellow plums for the journey. The drive to the distillery is only about 16km (10 miles) but it will take an hour or more.

The plums are quickly relegated to second place, however, as, no sooner than we leave town, Juan passes around a bottle of La Reina that has been infused with cooked agave heart for us to taste. *It's the most agave thing I have ever tried, with molasses, honey and roasted qualities on the nose. The taste is cooked pineapple, charred and bittersweet but retaining structural depth from the spirit. There's a lingering taste of burnt pineapple and treacle.*

The drive is slow going but the landscape is stunning. With the dense forests now mostly below us and blue sky above, we can see many miles across the state of Jalisco. Juan has a compass map on his phone, which shows our elevation slowly climbing up as we head further into the mountains and away from civilisation.

Wondering if the flavour of agave will ever leave me, he hands over a bottle of La Reina Ancestral, one of only 190 produced and bottled at 42% ABV. *There is a strong cheese and brown butter aroma to it. The taste is beautifully refined, starting with sour cream and then turning to yoghurt, with peach and apricot. Then there's some baking spice and a green agave finish. Remarkable.*

We pass small villages and farmsteads, plus the tiny town of La Laja, but generally there is little sign of life. What I do notice are yellow signs stapled to fence posts and gates that mention "Diageo". I ask Juan what they say.

"It says 'Diageo wants your land,'" he tells me. "The big tequila companies want to grow agave here."

The soil here in the mountains has never been intensely farmed like that in the Tequila Valley and Los Altos, Juan explains; it's virgin land, so Don Julio, Cuervo and Sauza are circling around it like sharks.

"They kill everything," Juan tells us. "They put insecticides on the land, plant the agave, and leave it like that for five years without any grass growing and no fertiliser. Then they take out the agave, maybe after three or four years, and you can't do anything with the land because it is depleted."

For impoverished farm and land owners in the area, the prospect of cash up front is too tempting. The big companies pay upwards of 20,000 pesos (£800/$1,000) per hectare on a five-year term. The problem is that the land is useless when the five years are up, and the big tequila company will have already moved elsewhere. Juan tells me that the big tequila producers also sometimes use third-party contractors to take on the land, promising to grow limes or beans, and then plant agaves instead.

We finally arrive at the Rancho Nuevo, where the Topete family taberna is located. Like Tesoro del Oeste, it is a modestly sized ranch made entirely out of big chunks of timber. There is a cluster of buildings and awnings, a small bar, and a dining table big enough to seat 30 people, circled with mismatched chairs. There are quite a few people hanging around today, most of them part of the family but there are some visitors too.

Julio Topete built this taberna with his father, Maximino, in 2003. Back then, Julio was suffering from thyroiditis, which made him overly fatigued and caused him occasionally to faint. He saw numerous doctors and tried a variety of medications but none worked. Increasingly frustrated, he met a friend who owned a tequila distillery and he found that drinking the spirit made him feel better. This inspired him to start making raicilla so that he could produce a continuous supply of "medicine". This idea of raicilla as form of therapy or curative is a common theme in the mountains and for

BELOW Approaching La Reina distillery, with mountain hillsides stretching endlessly behind us, we prepare for an immersion into Atenguillo's ancient raicilla traditions.

many it is viewed more in that light than as a social drink.

"It's something people don't believe," says his wife, Silvia. "But I lived through it with him. The raicilla healed him." A few years later doctors could not find any trace of the disease that had plague Julio – he was cured.

"Drink it like medicine, not to get drunk" is what Silvia says.

In the early days they were producing only 15 bottles of raicilla a day. Now they are harvesting 12–15 acres (five or six hectares) of agaves a year and planting up to 40,000 more plants a year.

"We are putting a lot of resources into it," says Juan. "But we might not see a return for eight to eleven years."

That's the minimum length of time it takes *Agave maximiliana* to mature if it's left to its own devices. But Juan and Julio have some strategies that can speed things up, like using organic compost and cutting the weeds and grass back. This can expedite the time to maturation (when the *quiote* emerges) down to seven years. Once the quiote is cut, they leave the plants to rest for around three months before harvesting.

With its wide pencas, *maximiliana* prefers partial shade that pine trees and oaks offer and so thrives in the mountain environment. Unlike *Agave tequilana*, these agaves do not produce hijuelos so must reproduce through pollination and seed. Whether this happens naturally, via pollinators like bats and hummingbirds, or through the collection and cultivation of seeds, the result is subtle variations within the *maximiliana* species that is entirely absent from the Tequila Valley and Los Altos.

As we have already learned, all agave spirits are from the genus *Agave*, of which there are currently 299 accepted species globally. *Agave tequilana* Weber is one example of a species that is of course used to make tequila. There is also *Agave maximiliana* Baker and *Agave rhodacantha* Trel., which are both used to make raicilla, and *Agave angustifolia* Haw. which is also used in raicilla but is the predominant species grown in Oaxaca to make mezcal.

The official taxonomic classification of these plants is formed from the genus (*Agave*), the species (such as *angustifolia*) and as they are derived from Latin, the standard convention is to the put them in italics. After the genus and species comes the author citation, or the surname of the person that identified the plant (for example, Haw., which is an abbreviation of the English entomologist and botanist Adrian Hardy Haworth). For our purposes it is not necessary to include the genus and author in every single reference to a plant, so we will use only the species name (eg. *rhodacantha* and so on).

Within each species, there are often varieties, or variations. Varieties usually evolve naturally in the wild and possess specific morphological (shape and size) characteristics and/or tendencies linked to their geographical distribution. The difference between varieties is generally much smaller than it is between species, but the number of varieties is much larger. Some varieties are named after the towns that they originate from or where they are found abundantly; others are named for their visual appearance. Some take on Spanish names and others use Nahuatl or other indigenous languages.

Juan takes us up on the slopes adjacent to the distillery. The agaves here are all *maximiliana* but they are not identical to one another. Of course, some are bigger than others, but they also have slightly different physical properties and here it's these properties that are used to create varietal names: *costillona* ("ribbed"), *pico de águila* ("eagle's beak" on account of the curved thorn on the end), *punta plegada* ("folded tip" – especially concave pencas) and more than 15 others.

We elegantly stumble back down the hill and take a look at the distillery itself.

There are two adobe ovens, both of them very small and holding only 1.5 tonnes a piece. As they look so much like pizza ovens perhaps it's best to use that as a basis for comparison, in which case each oven here could hold maybe five 30-cm (12-inch) pizzas. Julio lights the oven at 7am and it's ready to cook by late afternoon. The strategy here is to rake the coals out, removing most of the fuel from the fire. The cooking therefore is almost entirely thanks to the heat stored in the walls of the oven rather than the fire itself. This is achievable in an oven of this size, where the surface-area-to-volume ratio is much smaller.

The agave piñas are tossed in like bowling balls to the back of the oven. A large slab of wood is sued as a door, which is liberally doused with water and covered in a layer of clay.

After a two-day cook, the agaves are removed. Unlike in tequila production, there is no concept of *miels amargas* or *miels dulce* (bitter and sweet juices extracted and collected during the early stages of cooking), so there's

OPPOSITE A family affair: Rancho Nuevo is a distillery but also a home where family and friends can gather and share food and drink.

no collection pipe extracting juices from the cook so that they can be discarded or retained depending on their quality. Everything is simply roasted and everything that is roasted is then sent on for milling and fermentation. From the tequilero's perspective, this means things are being retained that are undesirable, but for a raicillero, everything is an inherent part of the final product.

The cooked agave is mashed by hand in a wooden *canoas* (literally "canoes" but actually hollowed-out tree trunks). Mashing the agave is extremely hard work, where the men use a *mazo* (a long mallet) to manually crush the agave hearts, like mashing potato… 1.5 tonnes of potato. This is as traditional and primitive as milling gets, and it's as inefficient as it gets too. A great deal of the sugars held within the fibre of the agave remain in the fibre and this has consequences in the fermentation stage as different yeast cultures get to work breaking down that fibre and producing a range of flavours and alcohols.

Fermentation occurs in open, wooded containers made from pine and takes roughly eight days.

"Have a taste," Juan says. The contents of the fermentation vat looks like something you might pull out of a blocked drain. It's a fibrous mass of dried matter floating on top of a cloudy soup with the occasional bubble exploding like a zit. The flies certainly seem interested in it but, then again, they are known to gather around literal piles of shit. I hesitantly dip my finger in. The liquid is warm but not at all sticky – the sugar has

already been eaten up. Rather than give myself too much time to think about it, I pop my finger in my mouth. The taste is very sour and very far removed from the flavour of agave or raicilla. This is fascinating to me. In this purgatory between life and the afterlife, the character of the plant seems entirely lost. And yet, through the application of heat in distillation it will, like a phoenix, be born again into something beautiful that links back to its origins.

Julio's son, Oscar, takes us into the cave where the raicilla is stored in demijohns before bottling; his nine-year-old son Manuel trails behind. We begin tasting our way through various expressions that Oscar offers us freely, including a rosemary-and-fennel-seed infusion and a cannabis infusion. The stand-out is a 55%-ABV spirit that has spent three years in glass. *It has a fragrant and rich aroma, of banana candy. The taste is darker than expected, with prune and date, then green pepper and an agave nectar finish.*

Juan and Ana have been proactive in bringing bartenders and raicilla aficionados up to the ranch to work. Over a weekend of camping at the distillery, you can plant agaves, eat together, and kick back with a swim in the nearby Rio El Limón spring. However, much of what La Reina does is modern and stylish, incorporating fashion, surfing, modern Mexican music and working with top chefs in the region to create amazing food pairings. With its varying styles ranging from herbal to floral, roasted and even cheesy, food feels like a potentially great bedfellow for this spirit.

We sit around the long table with the family and help ourselves to food. There is a hot grill on which they are barbecuing tilapia. Next to it is a huge copper pan of hot oil where they are deep-frying fresh tortilla chips. Pancho is among the mothers, chopping herbs, grinding dried chillies, and passing spoons of salsa to the ladies for them try, followed by smiles and nods of approval. Addie is still walking, watching and photographing. Oscar comes over and offers me more raicilla, which I gladly accept.

The sense of community on the ranch is humbling. Back in the bar in Atenguillo, Juan had said to us when you meet the people and see what they are doing in the mountains you begin to understand why they live so far away from modern civilisation and why they do what they do. We have lost much of this in our modern world. And sitting here drinking the spirit of the land, while watching the old ladies cook and the children play, I have to hold back tears at the beautiful simplicity of it all.

LOBO DE LA SIERRA

El Viejo Lobo

On our way back towards Mascota, we pass through the tiny village of El Jacal. There's a cluster of roadside eating and drinking places here. Pancho beeps his horn and all of the ladies working there stop what they are doing and wave and cheer as we drive through. Moments later, Pancho veers off the highway to the right. My first thought is that we have blown another tyre. But we steer into a short, dusty driveway with a chain-link fence on both sides. Straight ahead there's a ramshackle looking property with exposed breeze blocks on its half-completed second floor. Next to that is an overflowing carport of sorts, out of which have emerged half a dozen wolf-like dogs.

Dogs are everywhere in Mexico and they hold a deeply rooted place in Mexican culture that goes back to ancient roles in rituals and folklore. In Aztec culture, dogs were believed to guide the souls of the dead through the underworld and they were sometimes sacrificed and buried with their owners to accompany them. The Aztec god of thunder and lightning, Xolotl, was a dog that would shape-shift into an agave plant. In Mayan culture, dogs were believed to have brought fire to mankind. The Xolo dog (Mexico's national hairless dog and one of the oldest breeds in the world) has a prominent place in the Day of the Dead celebrations. Statues and images of Xolos are often included in *ofrendas* (altars) as they are believed to guide the spirits of the dead back to the world of the living during the festival.

And then there's Cadejo, a supernatural dog that appears in Mexican folklore and can be either a protective spirit or a malevolent force, depending on its colour and the context of the encounter.

Practically every small distillery in Mexico is home to some dogs. They are used as security, to scare off wild animals and to discourage rodents and other pests. They are, of course, also great companions, and often accompany jimadores to the fields too. I came across a

book at the Don Fulano offices called *Perros y Palenques*, which is dedicated to telling the stories of dogs and their distilleries in Oaxaca. All proceeds from the book go towards raising money for the sterilisation and emergency care of local dogs.

All of that said, the wolves running towards us seem a bit overkill for what appears to be a very simple, half-built home. That is, except for the three copper alembic stills that stand in the middle of the drive with an "En Venta" (For Sale) sign stuck to them.

While the dogs circle around us sniffing, we walk up to the stills and take a closer look. They are beautifully made from hammered copper, each about the size of a washing machine. One has an inlaid plaque on the head that reads *El bien vino del cerro siempre* ("The good spirit always came from the hills"). At the bottom of the plaque, there is an agave with the word *Lechuguilla* pressed on to it. And next to that it says Gerardo Peña and *El Lobo de la Sierra* (meaning "The Mountain Wolf").

There's a shout from the house and the dogs run back up. Then Gerardo appears (now escorted by the dogs) looking altogether like someone I might choose not to make eye contact with in any normal setting: bright tartan pyjama trousers, faded sleeve top, long grey beard and long hair, Oakley sunglasses and a trucker cap.

"Allow me to introduce you to Gerardo Peña," says Pancho with what I am sure was a slight bow in Gerardo's direction. "He is one of the most respected raicilla makers in all of Jalisco."

We walk up to the house and under the veranda, and discover that this is not just a house but also a distillery. The entire living space is a long hall, with small rooms coming off the sides; at one end is a dining table, and a couple of sofas with a woman and a small child sat on them watching television. Near to where we have entered, there are two wood-fired, stone-jacketed stills, with inlaid bricks

that have been cast with "El Lobo de la Sierra" stamped into them. They are each around 200 litres (50 gallons) and made from steel, but only the heads of the stills are visible on account of the bricks. Next to them there's a thick wooden worktop made from a natural edge hardwood, with dozens of bottles sat on it in various states of consumption. Glass demijohns litter the floor.

Gerardo takes a seat next to one of the stills and speaks slowly, in English. He talks in that meandering way where you're never entirely sure if someone has finished a statement and is waiting for an answer, or if they are simply taking a moment to consider the next thing they are going to say.

It turns out Gerardo lived in the US for 25 years, then moved back to Mexico and set up a distillery in 2004. "I was distilling in the US..." he says. "I studied alcohol before and, you know, I liked it... And then I studied fermentation... and distillation."

As of summer 2023, he stopped producing raicilla, which explains why there are stills for sale on the driveway. Pancho tells us privately that Gerardo's health was suffering and that he needed to stop making spirits. While he's saying this, Gerardo lights up a Pal Mall cigarette and uncorks a nearby demijohn.

"This is the Flor de Piedra," he says, pouring the raicilla into glasses and taking a pull on his Pal Mall. "It's the type of agave... discovered by Vasquez Garcia... it's proper name is *Agave vazquezgarciae*."

It's one of six species that Gerardo used, sometimes releasing his spirits as single expressions and other times as blends of up to three. *The aroma is very herbal, with oregano, mint and smouldering spices.* "It smells like after the rain has fallen," says Pancho. *It reminds me of a forest floor, and then mandarin kicks in. The taste is spiced and sweet, with mint and black pepper.*

Pancho suggests we take a walk around the property and we move past the stills, past the sofas, past the child, and into the yard. This is a dry and sunny area with scattered tables and chairs holding plants of all types.

Some of the herbs are easy to recognise, like lavender, rosemary, oregano and coriander (cilantro). I see what looks to be a tomato plant and a couple of small lemon trees. Gerardo shows us his chilli plants: "piquín" (a citrusy, woody chilli) and "piquet de pájaro" (peppery and fragrant). There are tobacco plants and a few different types of mint.

Pancho points at a tree producing a fruit that looks a little like a dried pomegranate. "This is cuastecomate," he

says. "The hard shell of the fruit is used to make the *jícaras* bowls to drink mezcal from traditionally."

These bowls, which are very common in Oaxaca but are often used in other regional agave distilleries too, look like small coconut shells. They are usually very dark brown or black and you can carve patterns and words into them.

We try some of the fruit. It tastes a little like dark berries, reminding me of prune and raisins. Some raicilla producers make an infusion of the fruit into spirit and occasionally sweeten it into a liqueur.

Gerardo reappears with more raicilla for us to taste. This time it's a blend of three agaves, all of the *angustifolia* variety but belonging to three different sub-species: Zocal, Limeño and Cimarrón.

As Gerardo pours the raicilla, he explains that the agaves are cooked together in an adobe-style oven, above ground for around three days. He tells us that the fire is lit and left to burn until it is smokeless and the wood has turned to charcoal.

I smell the raicilla. *Initially the aroma is very gluey, like acetone. But as it sits in the glass, it turns floral, like lavender and berries. A touch of cheese too! The taste has more of that herbal character, but with a fresher, citrus note. The finish is grassy and slightly fungal.*

ABOVE Gerardo Peña, the "Mountain Wolf,' distils his raicilla in a remote workshop, surrounded by dogs and raw mountains. His now silent copper stills stand as a testament to his legacy as a true master of the craft.

"Is that the oven?" I say, pointing at the garden-shed-sized pizza oven at the end of the property.

"Yes..." Gerardo says. "Now I will turn it into a sauna."

Gerardo explains that he is going to turn it into a *temazcal*, which is a sort of Mesoamerican sauna. I am a fan of saunas and we get into a detailed discussion about how he's going to do this and he tells me of the traditional temazcal sweat lodges that evolved here independently of the Nordic sauna tradition. Temazcal comes from the Nahuatl word *temāzcalli* (house of heat), or possibly from the Aztec *teme* (to bathe) and *calli* (house). The saunas are, it turns out, built from stone in almost exactly the same way as a raicilla oven, only you don't make them quite as hot of course.

"It's not only for sweating," says Pancho. "It's also for healing and for a good connection with the earth. It's like a ritual."

Gerardo is going to strip away the concrete layer from inside his old brick oven and then fit benches and a new

door. Then he's planning on repurposing a beer keg as the fire pit in the middle. He will then pour tea on to the hot coals.

After cooking, the agaves are mechanically milled and fermented in plastic for around ten days to two weeks. Finally, they are double-distilled in the stainless-steel stills that we saw, which also contain some copper components in the condensers. The first distillation lasted seven hours and the second took ten. All of his spirits are rested for a minimum of 30 days in glass, though it's usually much longer. Interestingly, he uses gas not wood to heat his stills. Pancho thinks it's this careful and controllable management of heat that allows Gerardo to make such great spirit.

Gerardo disappears off into a back room and comes out brandishing a massive glass demijohn that has perhaps only a couple of hundred millilitres of spirit swilling around in the bottom.

"This is the *malpuntas* made out of *maximiliana*," he says. "Aged in glass for 11 years."

The *puntas* (literally "tips" or "points") are the "heads" of the spirit: the first, high-strength distillate that comes through during distillation. They are traditionally collected separately from the main body of the spirit and have become controversial from a modern production

ABOVE The *maximiliana* agave is the source of some of El Lobo's spirits, but it's the local herbs and spices that inspire its flavour.

standpoint because of the potential presence of less desirable compounds.

It's important to any reputable distiller to discard the very first drops that emanate from the still, which is oily and opaque and really quite dangerous, containing high proportions of ethyl acetate (think nail-varnish remover), acetone and acetaldehyde, all of which will give you a very bad hangover at best. The next part after that is the puntas, which has a notably different character to the spirit that comes later, being typically more floral and fruity, but often including some solvent-like aromas too, perhaps due to some residual quantities of the aforementioned less desirable compounds.

Whatever it is that gets into this part of the distillate, it has to comprise some of the most volatile components of the ferment, which evaporate more readily because they have lower boiling points. Also, because this all happens near the beginning of the distillation, less water has had a chance to carry over so the strength of the puntas is typically around the 60–65% ABV mark and sometimes even higher!

Gerardo insists that we rinse our glasses with water (we agree enthusiastically), then he pours a generous measure – hell, any measure is generous if he's not making any more. *It's sweet and floral – like lavender and moist, fungal compost. Then pine and juniper resin. I take a sip. Geranium and then pine, soft and sweet.* I add a little bit of water to it. *Agave character shines through, some citrus and a gentle floral hum of violets. This continues with a strong herbal buzz and floral notes through to the finish, which is very long. A minute or two goes by and then, mint. Wow – this is more like a gin than an agave spirit.*

As Addie and I sip the raicilla, Gerardo and Pancho continue their appraisal of the all the herbs and plants. Then suddenly it strikes me. We're tasting his garden.

All of these plants, from the chilli to the tobacco, the various types of mint and oregano – all of them are here in his raicilla. This walk around his garden is not just a perusal of a few pots of homegrown ingredients for cooking – we are smelling and tasting the palette of flavours that Gerardo imparts into his raicilla. These plants were his reference material, his muse.

"The flavour keeps changing in the glass," says Gerardo, plucking a stalk of mint from a pot. "It's always changing."

Coming from a part of the world where spirits are considered to be aged only when they are in a barrel, I feel utterly amazed at the way that this spirit has developed in mere glass. This is now an incredibly long spirit with depth and complexity.

"There's eucalyptus," says Addie.

"It's pine," says Pancho.

Whatever it is, it's green. Pancho points to the mint that Gerardo is plucking from a pot and tells us it's a special type from the area that is extremely intense, even down to the stalks. It looks like regular spearmint or water mint but the smell is very strong indeed, and immediately reminiscent of the raicilla. Pancho mentions that they have a cocktail on the menu at his bar that uses mint and we get into a discussion about mint flavour and how it is an under-recognised but ever-present aroma in many agave spirits – but not so much tequila. Gerardo gives us a handful of mint to take with us. That evening, back at Pancho's home in Mascota, we put Gerardo's mint to use.

We're going to make a version of the mint drink that Pancho serves at Farmacia Rita Perez called Yerba Buena (see page 232), which, through no coincidence whatsoever, is the name of the village adjacent to Mascota.

Some distillers differentiate only between the puntas and the main body of the spirit, but others, like Gerardo, recognise another section of distillate between them, called *malpuntas* ("bad tips"), which contain a mixture of the compounds found in the puntas as well as some of the hearts (the main part of the distillate).

The puntas can sometimes contain higher proportions of methanol too, but not usually enough to be harmful. This is partly because of the so-called "distilling backwards" phenomenon that some agave spirits claim, which means that ethanol comes through later in the distillation. We will discuss this in a later chapter.

Back to the puntas. In summary, they taste and smell quite different to the rest of the distillate. A racillero could just mix them into the main spirit and bottle it, but they are often separated out and bottled separately – in tequila it's common to re-distil them with the next batch.

"They call it the *flor* in Michoacán," says Pancho. "It is kept like the cream from the milk – a record of the fragrant, intense, expressive nature of the spirit."

Because the puntas are such a small fraction of the entire distillate, a taberna might make only one bottle of puntas for every 20 bottles of regular raicilla, and it's this rarity along with the unique flavour that makes puntas a bit of a prized delicacy among raicilleros and aficionados.

MANUEL SALCEDO

El Creador

Founded in 1525 by the Spanish conquistador Francisco Cortés de San Buenaventura, the mountain town of Mascota, besides being where Pancho's family comes from, has a rich colonial history. The name "Mascota" is believed to derive from the Teco Indian word "Amaxacotlán", meaning "place of deer and snakes". The town played a significant role in the region's gold and silver mining industry during the colonial era, but nowadays most of its economy comes from agriculture (beans, chillies, tomatoes, avocados, blackberries, strawberries and corn) and increasingly from tourism, because for those looking to have an authentic, rural Jalisco experience, you can't ask for much more.

Hidden down one of the back streets, just a minute's walk from the plaza and in the morning shade of the church tower, is a small raicilla taberna belonging to Manuel Salcedo. Manuel has been making raicilla for 30 years, beginning in the 1990s when the word raicilla was scarcely uttered outside of these parts. In that time, Manuel has become a legend of raicilla production, he has twice served as the president of the CMPR (Mexican Raicilla Promotion Council – see page 144) and has operated and built numerous tabernas. The first one was in El Carrizo, just north of the town of Mascota, then he built one at his sister's house in Rincón de Mirandillas, to the south of Mascota, then one in Cimarrón Chico to the east.

In 2004, he modified a distillery with his friend Rubén Peña Fuentes, before moving into his current location in 2018. As well as building his own tabernas, he has commissioned a dozen more adobe ovens for other distillers in the sierra and built stills for them (including Sergio's oven and stills at Tesoro del Oeste).

If you drew a Venn diagram of racilla production in the mountains, you will see Manuel Salcedo's name right in the middle of it.

Taberna Salcedo is not the prettiest of operations. There is a big oven that looks like a termite nest and sheets of steel and lengths of timber stacked along a wonky brick wall. As we arrive, we see a team of three workers unloading cooked agave from the oven and putting it through the mill. It's early in the day but judging by the big piles of milled agave being loaded onto wheelbarrows, it looks as though this has been going on here for hours. The electric-powered mill is a very small device with just one set of blades that produces a coarse cut. Manuel is operating the mill, and using an old Coke bottle to pour water into the teeth of the device as the agaves are loaded. Manuel's son is hacking the cooked agaves into smaller chunks with a machete and passing them to his father. The third man is in the oven itself, tossing the gooey agave hearts onto the patio next to the mill.

Spotting us lurking in the wings, Manuel hands over his milling duties and walks towards us. In spite of the messy work, his gingham shirt is spotlessly clean and his pencil moustache has not a hair out of place. After exchanging greetings with us, he begins telling us about his oven: it's a new model that he has recently built that holds seven tonnes of agave. The design is unusual because the oven is perfectly round and built from a combination of stone and steel mesh, with concrete plastered on the inside and outside for additional insulation.

Manuel says most ovens in the past were square or oval because it was easier to shape the materials that way, but he says the perfectly round design causes less burn on the agaves. He thinks that this has something to do with depriving the oven of airflow through more consistent loading. I recall Gerardo "Los Lobos" Peña explaining to me that you can get a relatively smoke-free flavour from the adobe oven because the design quickly deprives the fire of oxygen. The technique is to load the oven fast, and that way the fire is smothered by the agaves and has no oxygen

to burn. If you load slowly or create pockets of air in the corners, the hot coals will use the oxygen and burn the agaves. So everything has to be engineered and actioned to load fast and load completely if you want to avoid a smoky effect, as most raicilla producers in the mountains do.

Manuel has his own fields and has been planting and growing *maximiliana* agaves for more than 30 years. It can take 10–20 years for these plants to hit maturity, but he has been around long enough to have seen the seeds he has planted turn into mature plants that have produced more seeds and more mature plants.

Water is an issue here, Manuel explains to us, because, like much of Mexico, the municipal supply is either contaminated or contains high amounts of chemicals to combat the contaminants. It's for the latter reason that Manuel has to bring in spring water from the nearby town of El Agostadero.

"You can't work with it," he says, speaking of the chlorinated local supply.

ABOVE A ramshackle yard where the termites have taken over? No. This is the taberna of Manuel Salcedo, a legend in raicilla production and the go-to guy for building distilleries in the mountains.

Water is added only at two stages of raicilla production: when milling the agave and for adjusting the spirit to bottling strength. He tells us that the cooked agave is at around 35–40° Brix. With the addition of the water during milling, it roughly halves to around 14–18° Brix.

Manuel ferments the agave naturally, which typically takes 10–14 days. He prefers to use stainless-steel vessels for fermentation, which he says is more efficient, but he has experimented with wood, concrete and plastic vessels in the past.

"They do taste different," he says, confirming what we have learned in tequila. "It's not the taste of the material – it's the reaction of the yeast with the material." He then goes on to describe how the heat generated in the steel fermenter causes the yeast to stick to the sides and produces a different array of flavours.

We walk inside the distillery building. To the side is a small bottling room and a little bar; there are the remnants of breakfast on a plastic dining table and evidence of a recent birthday party for Manuel's two-year-old granddaughter. On a small table is a microwave, a drill, children's toys and demijohns of raicilla. The distillery itself proves to be an impressively clean setup, made almost entirely from stainless steel. All of the fermentation and distillation equipment has been fabricated by Manuel personally. Even the wheelbarrow used for transporting the milled agave is welded steel because "the agaves destroy the enamel on regular wheelbarrows".

During fermentation, that unusually sweet agave juice ramps right up to around 12% ABV. This is high, but it is necessary for Manuel's unique production process. Distillation is carried out in four 500-litre (130-gallon) stainless-steel stills from his own design. They are built in the style of Jamaican rum stills (although Manuel doesn't seem to be aware of this when I point it out) and might be the only ones of their type being used to make raicilla and perhaps any agave spirits.

The design uses the usual pot for boiling the *mosto*, connected by a lyne arm to the condenser, which turns the spirit vapour back into liquid. However, built into the lyne arm is a sealed 5-litre (1.5-gallon) steel vessel called a retort. It actually looks a bit like the vessel we saw on the stills at El Pandillo (see pages 66–71), which allowed heavier alcohols to fall down a pipe and back into the base of the still. This device has no pipe leading back to the still, though, and is instead partially filled with finished raicilla at the start of each distillation run. As the alcohol from the still begins to evaporate, it enters the retort and the vapour partially condenses, with only the higher alcohols boiling off and moving into the condenser.

In this way it acts almost like a second distillation, increasing the strength of the spirit and, in Manuel's words, "removes some of the heavy metals". What this all means is that Manuel can turn a 12% mosto into a 55%-ABV spirit from a single distillation run.

"With a single distillation, you have more aromas and flavours," he says. "In the second distillation, you lose a lot of that, and it takes on a different flavour."

This approach is partly what gives Jamaican rum its unique, heavy style, so it's exciting to see it being used

to make agave spirits. Manuel tells me he does do double distillations from time to time, which come off at 70% ABV, and he occasionally uses this high-strength spirit to adjust the bottling strength of his raicilla.

"How many stills have you built in total?" I ask him.

"I've made them for almost everyone in the area," he replies. "First, I made four for Giralindo, then I made four for Chiquito, then I made four for Lalo, three for another man, two for a shaman, then another three… another two…" he begins to trail off and then finishes. "I've made about 30 stills."

With Pancho doing his best to interpret, our conversation delves into finer details of his distillation process – understanding how and when he decides to cut his spirits, dilution and spirit character, and what effect the copper coils in his condensers have. Manuel possesses a formidable combination of being both extremely well versed in the agricultural side of his business and also a talented engineer and chemist. Eventually words prove insufficient and he disappears off to get a bottle.

The first raicilla we are trying is simply called Sierra Mascota; it's 41% ABV. *It smells like forest fruit at first, blackcurrant leaf and blackberry (another example of local flavours finding their way into spirit aromas). It's also green and herbal. The taste is juicy and yet drying, with berry tannins. Green (lime) sherbet and soft vegetal notes follow.*

Manuel produces a bunch of different brands for different local markets and they all share the same agave, same cook, and same fermentation. The differentiation is found in the distillation, in when he cuts the spirit off the still and how much he dilutes it afterwards. He takes a lid off a tank and uses a *carrizo* (a bamboo-like reed) to draw liquid out by putting his finger over the end. Then, with the horn of a ram in the other hand he lets the stream of liquid flow out of the bamboo and into the horn. As it hits, it forms bubbles on the surface. At first, I assume that this is all just for show, but when Pancho shuffles in for a closer look and he and Manuel begin taking sharp inhalations of breath, it's clear there's more going on here.

The bubbles tell the raicillero something about both the strength and the quality of the spirit. Large bubbles that

OPPOSITE Humility and ability: Manuel's stills are designed to extract the essence of the *maximiliana* agave, representing a perfect union of engineering and tradition.

129
MANUEL SALCEDO

burst quickly mean that the spirit is low in strength and therefore poor quality. Finer bubbles suggest a higher alcoholic strength as the surface tension shifts based on the water/alcohol mix. Long before hydrometers were available in rural Mexico, this was how makers of spirits checked their distillate. And some distillers, like Manuel, can estimate the strength of a spirit off the still within one or two degrees of error.

Additionally, the longer the bubbles hold the more viscous or oily the raicilla is assumed to be. This is probably the result of dissolved fatty acids in the liquid helping to form stable bubbles in the spirit. Oiliness is generally considered a favourable trait for those seeking flavour and length of finish, so small bubbles that hold for a long time is what you're after. You can conduct this test yourself using a regular straw and dropping a stream of liquid into a glass.

Next, we try and bottle called La Sulla, which is 44% ABV. *It's much lighter on the nose, with soft agave notes, fresh*

ABOVE Hand crafted – practically every component of Manuel's taberna has been designed, cut, hammered, welded and stuck together using his own hands. The result is a spirit that's as robust as the hands that made it.

and well defined. The taste is grippy and dry, spiced like hot agave fresh from the oven, with a hint of forest fruits and some lactic funk. It has a long and very dry finish. In fact, both the raicillas share a dryness in the finish, like a wine tannin, that really makes you want to take another sip!

Manuel also produces a range of liqueurs, which see local fruits being infused into raicilla with the addition of sugar. One of them is *guayabita* (little guava), which has distinctive red-grape character to it. Then there's *zarzamora* (the Spanish word for blackberry). The fact that he seems to have chosen fruits that already seem present in the flavour profile of his raicillas is not lost on me.

Manuel's raicilla has made it out of Mexico. It can be found as 100% maximiliana in the LA-based brand

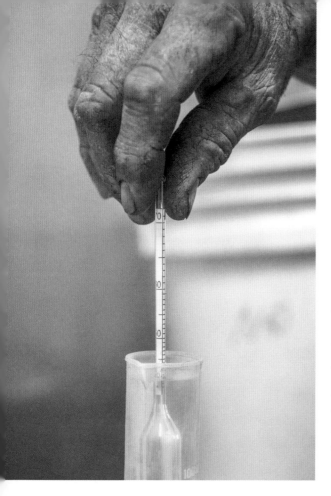

a raicilla specialist bar owned by a friend of Pancho's. There, we are plied with various raicillas both from the mountains and the coast, and just like the vast landscape of the raicilla region, the flavours of the category open up in front of us: toasted spice, dried oregano, feta cheese, dusty slate, pine needle, strawberry and rose.

We stumble out of the place and into Mascota's town plaza, which has come alive with activity. As the sun sets, the bandstand is adorned with twinkling lights and hosts a rancho band in their finest charro outfits, silver embroidery glinting in the evening glow. The lead singer's rich voice blends with the strumming guitars, vibrant trumpets and violins, filling the warm air with an intoxicating sound.

It's late in the evening but families gather, children are playing, and elderly couples walk laps of the plaza. Vendors offer cups of frothy *horchata* and steaming *elotes* (grilled corn). Young couples dance in front of the bandstand. The music, sometimes soulful and sometimes spirited, seems to bind the community together.

We wolf down some street tacos and head into one of the bars on the square, which has a balcony with views of the plaza. In need of a longer, more refreshing drink, I revert to a classic that any bar with an agave spirit can make: tequila & tonic (see page 235).

Raicilla De Una. It's also been bottled by Esteban Morales' brand La Venenosa (see page 159), but only as a very special one-off product called Los Gigantes.

The story behind this bottle is one of friendship, patience and one very big agave plant. Twenty years ago, Manuel and his friend Ruben Peña Fuentes started a joint farming project with two adjacent farms on the same field. They were both growing *maximiliana* agaves and needed a way to define the boundary between each other's plants. Instead of building a fence or a wall, they planted four *americana* agaves (sometimes referred to as the "century plant") in a line. This is a large architectural species of agave and these particular plants became freakishly big over the 15 years that followed. A few years ago, they were harvested and turned into raicilla. With the piña of one plant reaching 880kg (1 tonne), the spirit was rightfully bottled under the name "Los Gigantes".

We return home and get cleaned up, then head out for an evening in Mascota. Our first port of call is Los Agaves,

LA GORUPA

La Costa

Following our last evening in Mascota, Pancho decided that we – and more importantly, the Jetta – needed a day off, so we pootle slowly to the coast of Jalisco well aware that the car was slowly dying. In the middle of the afternoon, we arrived at Bucerías, which is a coastal suburb of the thriving touristic purgatory that is Puerto Vallarta. There, we met Pancho's friend, Luis, who is a sculptor that lives an idyllic life with his partner just across the border into Nayarit. We swam in the ocean, ate delicious seafood and then drank and danced until the sun began to rise.

In the morning, Luis deemed neither Pancho nor his Jetta capable of driving the challenging coastal roads that the day would present us with, so we fall into his Mitsubishi 4x4, which makes up in terrain handling what it lacks in air conditioning and comfort.

It's now mid-morning, and as the crescendo of our hangovers climax and conversation dwindles, we wind our way south and the coastal road unfolds like a snake. To our right, the Pacific stretches endlessly, while the Sierra Madre mountains rise up to our left, coated in lush-green vegetation. We pass through charming fishing villages like Boca de Tomatlán, where colourful boats bob in turquoise waters and stop briefly for a much-needed beer and some birria. All the while, the jungle presses close, a vibrant tapestry of greens punctuated with the vivid hues of bougainvillea and orchids.

Farther along, we catch sight of Mismaloya, home to the famous La Joalla de Mismaloya hotel, where John Huston's 1964 *The Night of the Iguana* was filmed. Huston and the movie's star Richard Burton were said to have drunk copious quantities of raicilla during the shoot. Richard Burton once described to a reporter, "If you drink [raicilla] straight down you can feel it going into each individual intestine." Huston believed this effect was owing to the fact the taberna "left the needles in".

Our next stop is near the village of Llano Grande in the coastal region Cabo Corrientes, not far from El Tuito. This is a quiet and peaceful part of the state, popular with US travellers who come for yoga or to take *ayahuasca* (the plant-based psychoactive drink). It's also popular with the cartels, which are especially active around these parts. I can tell you that there's nothing like a couple of cartel trucks sandwiching you from in front and behind on the highway to shock you out of a hangover's melancholy. On this occasion they gave us no trouble, though.

After more than two hours of driving, Luis finally pulls into a ramshackle yard and comes to a stop – I've already resigned myself to the likelihood that whatever we're going to see here cannot possibly balance the suffering we experienced on the journey to get here.

We can see three men sitting like statues under a small veranda. The oldest looks to be about 70 and the youngest is a teenager. The third man is somewhere between them in age. They are three generations of the Hernández family: Alberto, Sergio and Christian.

While Pancho gently negotiates an interview with the men, I take in the surroundings.

And what I see is nothing like I have ever seen before in a distillery.

All of the stills we have seen up until now have been made from copper or steel, in the classic alembic fashion. These types of still were brought here by Europeans in the 17th century, but their design goes back more than a thousand years, to the Middle East. Alembic stills form the basic design of distillation equipment used across rum, whisky and gin production to this day.

But the two stills here are of an entirely different shape – so as to be almost unrecognisable as stills – and made from a different material: wood.

The base of the still, where the fermented agave goes, is a large copper cauldron, which is basically invisible to us as it is set into a stone structure. Underneath the copper cauldron there is a stove built into the stonework where a fire is lit and this heats the copper and its contents – nothing too unusual so far.

But on top of the copper cauldron – and forming the main body of the still – there is a hollowed-out tree trunk. On top of that sits another copper bowl with water in it. As the mosto is heated, the alcohol vapours rise up through the hollow trunk until they hit the bowl at the top. The bowl has cool water in it, which is being constantly replenished using a basic plumbing system feeding more cool water from a nearby spring. So it is that the alcohol vapours condense onto the underside of this bowl and drip down. Here's the clever part, though: suspended in the middle of the tree trunk is a wooden paddle called a *cuchara* (spoon). The cuchara rests at an angle, slotting into a hole in the trunk, which in turn connects to a reed on the outside, serving as a pipe. Thus, as the condensing liquid drips off the underside of the copper bowl it doesn't fall back to the bottom of the still but rather onto the cuchara and out through the pipe. A jerry can is positioned to catch the alcohol.

Around the edges of the equipment, where copper meets wood or wood meets stone, a crusty resin has been stuck on to seal any gaps. It turns out this is made from a paste of agave hearts mixed with denim fibre, and we watch Sergio karate-chop the fibres into the corners of the still as it is running to seal in any cracks where spirit vapour is escaping.

The whole thing is about as primitive a distillation setup as I can conceive of.

We have been here less than a minute and Pancho has clearly worked some magic with Alberto, as he has relaxed and is now pouring raicilla into *jícaras* (see page 123) and passing them around. *It smells sweet and lightly smoked.* It's straight from the still and warm from the distillation. *There are tropical notes here: papaya and guava. The taste is sticky, with a slight tobacco note on the finish.*

Coastal raicillas are said to be a little more fruity, citric and saline than their mountain counterparts. This may be because of differences in cooking or the species of agave employed, but it could also be the growing conditions, where some of that sea air lends a salty seasoning to the soil that translates through to the plant's biology.

As we have discussed already, the type of oven also matters. However, La Gorupa is using an oven more typical of that used in the mountains, being made of stone

ABOVE La Gorupa is coastal raicilla at its finest. The Hernández family's primitive yet effective distillation methods yield spirits that capture the essence of Jalisco's seaside terroir, one bathtub-sized fermentation at a time.

and above ground. The differentiation of oven type was historically a matter of materials and their availability. The stone and clay required to make a brick oven simply wasn't available on the coast, so raicilleros made pit ovens, which are less efficient and require more time to heat, fill and empty. The adobe oven here has a capacity of three tonnes and the cook takes a total of four days with the added twist of 60 litres (16 gallons) of water being thrown into

the oven after the first two hours. Pancho seems to think that this is a very unusual strategy.

Don Alberto's taberna was built only in 2009, which may explain the atypical oven. Before 2000 he was a corn and bean farmer but around the turn of the century, he decided to get into agaves and began planting them in the area we are in now. He had a wait on his hands of course, as it takes up to ten years for the angustifolia agaves he mostly uses to mature. When they did finally mature, he didn't have his own taberna to distil in, so he rented space at a taberna in nearby Mascotita.

"I took everything from here, the agaves, the firewood, everything," says Alberto. "But for every four gallons I made, the owner of the taberna took four gallons in payment – so I decided to fight, to make my own."

As we sip the raicilla, everyone's eyes turn back to the stills with their steam and smoke and incredible mixture of construction materials.

The stills we're seeing here are of a design that has remained unchanged in Mexico for 400 years but has a history that goes back further than that. Commonly called a Filipino still or Ancestral still, this basic design was introduced to Mexico by Asian immigrants during the late-16th century and therefore pre-dates the arrival of alembics. These types of still continue to be used today in the Philippines to make a coconut palm distillate called *lambanóg*. The discussion of how Asian stills got here and how they integrated into the indigenous culture of Mexico is a fascinating one and we shall return to it later in our journey.

Fermentation is done with all of the agave fibre in plastic barrels, but we are unable to see these as they are behind a closed and locked door. This fairly dry mixture is left to sit and begin to ferment for three days. Then the tanks are topped up with water, which flows down the hill by gravity from a series of connected pipes. Then the door is shut and locked for two weeks. In this part of Jalisco, there is a great deal of superstition and respect granted to the fermentation process. Nobody is allowed in there and, crucially, women are not allowed to even visit the taberna.

"It is very delicate," explains Alberto. "If women come they 'mix it' and it stops." I press Alberto more on this topic – what is the effect of a woman on fermentation? Pancho uses the analogy of when the grandmothers make

atole (the sweet and spiced cornmeal drink that is traditionally fermented) and insist that nobody enters the kitchen as it will halt the process.

Alberto agrees with this, stating that by simply entering the fermentation room, a person can impact the behaviour of the natural airborne yeasts that are responsible for the fermentation process. As far as women go, he says, this effect is amplified by their menstrual cycles. Outside of the time of fermentation, it is fine for women to be there.

I cast my mind back to our visit to Tesoro del Oeste, when Pancho told me we could not see the fermentation. At the time I had thought the room was perhaps in a state of disarray or not very photogenic. But now it was clear to me that the room was in fact sealed shut and that nobody was permitted to go in there. After a few raicillas, Sergio did eventually invite us in, but only under the instruction that we "please be quiet", which I had considered to be something of a joke at the time. Once in there, it became clear he was serious. Few words were spoken. He showed us inside one of the barrels which was full of fibrous agave matter, bubbling away like a witch's brew in the dark. Carefully, he massaged the mixture with his hands, causing it to fizz even more as the strong aromas of vinegar and old fruit, and the sting of CO_2 filled the air. It was like watching a priest partake in some holy anointment or religious ceremony.

The reverence afforded to fermentation is not entirely without some scientific backing. People and animals carry with them their own unique yeast and bacteria flora that can invade a fermentation tank. Whether a menstruating woman has the power to abruptly halt a fermentation shifts into the realm of folklore and superstition for me. When it comes to noise though, we have seen tequila distilleries piping classical music into their fermenters, so if we are to believe that music can change the course of a ferment, why not shouting as well?

Beyond the simple production of spirits, there is a rich cultural tapestry to agave spirits comprising a blend of indigenous beliefs, Catholic influences and practical observations, reflecting the complex history of the region. Many of these observances are subtle, but when you visit a lot of traditional tabernas, the patterns of behaviour begin to show themselves.

Some mezcal producers, like Xiaman, in Oaxaca only harvest agave during the full moon. They believe this practice results in higher sugar content and better flavour. This superstition may have roots in ancient Aztec and

OPPOSITE From barn to bottle: The rustic charm of this taberna is captured perfectly in the spirit it makes.

LEFT "Excuse me sir, I'm English and I am lost – can you tell me the way to Taberna Gorupa?"

Zapotec lunar calendars and their influence on agriculture. However, it probably fits nicely into the roughly four-week cycle that it takes to make a mezcal from scratch. Of course, it may also share its origins with "moonshining" – that being the illicit production of spirits by moonlight.

In the Yucatán, some mezcal producers believe in the presence of *aluxes* (mythical, Mayan sprite-like creatures) who guard their agave fields. The producers leave small offerings to keep the spirits happy and ensure a good harvest. This belief is deeply rooted in Mayan folklore.

In parts of Guerrero, it's considered a good omen if a bat flies over the agave field at dusk. Bats are seen as protectors of the agave, possibly because of their role in pollinating certain agave species.

Some mezcaleros in Durango believe that distilling during a thunderstorm will result in a bitter, unpalatable mezcal. They may in fact pause production if they hear thunder. This superstition could be linked to practical concerns about temperature and humidity changes affecting fermentation or, indeed, a distillery getting struck by lightning and burning to the ground!

Catholic adherence is present in many distilleries across the country, ranging from the small church we saw at Reserva de los González, through to likenesses of the Virgin Mary near their stills, believing her presence blesses the spirit and protects against evil influences. Catholic adherence is so ubiquitous in these parts that it is unusual not to see some reference to it in a distillery. It's interesting to see how this is intertwined with older belief systems, like here at La Gorupa, where animal horns fixed to the walls above the locked door of the fermentation room serve as a warning to predators both natural (jaguars and pumas) and supernatural (who knows...).

"What type of agave are we drinking?" I ask. Alberto explains that when they first started planting, they were ignorant to the differences between plants and that he believed he could sell the agaves to tequila producers. It was a few years later that he found out he wasn't growing *Agave tequilana* and he'd need to find another use for his crop.

"We never knew, hey, I'm planting this variety or that variety," he says. "Chino Guero, Alto, Prieto, Pencudo." These were all new names that he learned when the University of Chapingo helped him identify his plants. It turned out that the Hernandezes were using 16 varieties of *angustifolia* and *rhodacantha*. Now they replant from *hijuelo* across 5 acres (2 hectares) of land and select a range of varieties that are blended together to make raicilla.

Alberto produces only in the dry season, which means he can complete five cooking cycles, totalling just 750 litres (200 gallons) of racilla across an entire year. I'm shocked when I realise that we have drunk almost a litre of his raicilla between us since we got here – as a percentage of annual production it's the equivalent of visiting Jose Cuervo and drinking 250,000 bottles of tequila.

It's remarkable to think that this humble operation is producing a spirit that is now enjoyed across all of Jalisco and, in fact, all of Mexico. On some rare occasions it has been exhibited at international bar shows, enjoyed at consumer events, and poured and mixed in some of the best cocktail bars in the world. And here we are right now, seeing it being made by three generations of men, in a dilapidated yard, in the middle of nowhere.

There's no way these products would have found their way out of Jalisco, let alone into the high echelons of the bar world, were it not for independent bottlers of agave spirits. We will explore the world of independent bottlers later in our journey – its champions and its darker, exploitative side.

Before we leave, though, we have to do some of our own independent bottling. Empty Coke and Topo Chico bottles are filled with raicilla and we pay Alberto for his spirit, and his time.

LA GORUPA

LOS TRES HOMBRES

‹‹‹

La Intoxicación

If we thought La Gorupa was hard to get to, tracking down the next taberna felt like we were conquistadors on a days' long expedition for gold in the hills.

As we bump down a rough track that appears to lead nowhere, there are fallen trees both sides and freshly cut stumps from those that blocked the path not long ago. Luis tells us about a recent storm that hit the coast and caused all manner of damage to plants and property, including the agaves. This road is impassable in the rainy season he tells us, just as we hit a ford in the base of the valley.

An entire family on a quad bike bounce past us after half an hour or so – proof that there is something at the end of this track. From there it's only leather-skinned riders on horseback who stare down at us with grim curiosity.

The road is truly dreadful. The Jetta would never have made it. Pancho is not his normal cheerful self and I begin to wonder if it's because he missed the opportunity to have killed the car once and for all.

Finally, we pass through the village of El Agodón. There are a few buildings clustered together and around 20 people of all ages eating lunch on a veranda. We keep our distance and park up. Pancho hops out and walks over to ask for directions. Arms fly up and point to the north road. Then, there's the sound of friendly voices, followed by laughter. A minute later Pancho trots back over grinning. He has cups filled with raicilla and a bowl of fresh ceviche and toastada.

Then we were all grinning.

It was only another 15 minutes driving before we finally hit the town of Chacala. Perhaps it took longer, but it's amazing how the generosity of food and the green, tropical taste of raicilla makes everything and everyone feel that much better.

Chacala came upon us as an absurdly metropolitan place compared with the places we had seen over the past few hours. There is a town square, a garage, shops. We stop to ask a uniformed school boy for directions. He points to the northeast and tells us "Avenue Mexico".

Five more minutes and we are here.

Two flimsy, wire-mesh gates block the entrance and a simple wooden sign reads Los Tres Hombres. Hills rise up all around us, peppered with agaves and cacti of all types. Pancho opens the gate and Luis drives us through, the wheels kicking up the soft, sandy soil of the driveway. Luis parks the car and we get out, our view monetarily blocked by the settling dust cloud we just created. Music is blaring from a speaker somewhere on a hill ahead. It's a classic ranchera song, "Las Mañanitas" by Vincente Fernández, which tells the story of a man who wakes up at dawn to greet his lover with flowers.

We walk towards the music while the dust cloud settles and an incredible sight materialises in front of us.

There's a large veranda supported by gnarly Montezuma cypress branches. Two wooden stills the size of dustbins are working hard, smoke billowing from their ovens below, and steam escaping from the copper dish condensers on top. Behind them are plastic fermentation vessels and jerry cans, along with a massive log that has been hollowed out like a canoe. Hammocks are strung up here and there and plastic bottles are dotted around on surfaces. To the right, outside of the protection of the veranda, is an enormous pit in the ground. It's empty but has a great pile of black rocks and dry logs stacked up around its perimeter.

Also under the veranda are three men.

The first of them is Adrián Rodriguez. He's 80 years old but has the weathered look of a man who could throttle a jaguar to death if he needed to. In spite of that, he has friendly eyes and a bushy white moustache that conceals a grin. Then, there's his son, Pablo Rodrigo Rodriguez. He seems to be doing most of the work around the place: pasting agave fibre into cracks around the head

of the still, loading the fire, then washing his hands in a warm copper dish condenser. Another man is sitting on a chair, sipping from what appears to be a half empty plastic water bottle (it later turns out it isn't water). I don't catch his name but he seems happy, if a little distracted.

But wait. There's a fourth man, who looks like he could be in his late 70s. It's hard to tell, because he is lying on the hot dirt floor. And he appears dead.

The man's name is Margarito, and we're told he got up early that morning just like the lover in "Las Mañanitas". But instead of going out to buy flowers for his lover, he drank five large glasses of *puntas* in quick succession. He passed out, and we are assured that he is in fact alive and that this is not at all unusual for Margarito.

Adrián is the owner of the taberna but he allows friends to come and make raicilla here when they have

ABOVE Los Tres Hombres, where agaves grow wild, the still's always smoking and the raicilla tastes like spiced rocket fuel. Warning: may cause spontaneous siesta syndrome.

completed the harvest of their plants. The man with the half-empty plastic bottle is one such friend. He is distilling a variety of agave called Amarillo Pura which, as the name suggests (*amarillo* meaning "yellow" in Spanish), is yellow. Pablo marches over with a jerry can half filled with the puntas from the current distillation. He grabs a dirty coffee cup, briefly cleans it with raicilla, then pours a large cup, which I distribute into smaller cups for everyone. The first thing I notice is that it has some colour to it, which I don't think has come from leftover coffee grounds in the cup. Pablo explains that the carrizo pipe on the still that directs the flow of liquid out and into the collection vessel is imparting a soft, green hue to the spirit.

I put my nose deep in the coffee cup. *The aroma is very perfumed: lots of floral and acetone notes but also hot, smoked pineapple.*

"Oh, this one is very sweet," says Pancho. "You can feel it's strong – intense. It has a lot of spirit. Mmm."

It's very hot on the palate, and actually still warm from the still. There's paraffin, beeswax polish and then, eventually there's some cooked agave.

Reaching into my bag for a swig of water to wash it down, I am immediately reminded of the quote from Graham Greene's 1940 novel *The Power and the Glory*. "The plainclothes priest took a healthy slug of raicilla causing his throat to spontaneously combust. Then, his eyes watering with religious fervor, he reached down, grabbed my Pepsi and poured its entire contents down his scorched gullet. Then he emitted an enormous burp and said, 'This is very good!'"

"It's 65%" says Pablo, pouring the spirit between two plastic cups like a theatrical bartender and assessing the bubbles. We're all surprised at that, then he explains that during the first few minutes when the spirit comes off the still it can be up to 80 or even 90%, but then it drops off quickly.

Much like I will if I keep drinking it. Much like Margarito did.

Adrián tells us that he learned to make raicilla at the age of 14 from his adopted uncle. I ask him how things have changed over the years and how he remembers production from back then. He points first to changes in fermentation. Sixty years ago, they used to ferment the *mezcales* (he refers to the agaves as mezcales) in the same wooden *parota* canoes that were used for *majar* (crushing) the cooked agave by hand.

"That is *parota*," he says, pointing to a broad and bushy tree with leaves like ferns. He then points at two other trees, "*ceiba* and *narrayanes*," which he tells us were also used for making canoes. They would seal them with a resin called *brea* and this was the established tradition for a long time. Prior to that, Adrián recalls how his grandfather produced raicilla by fermenting the cooked agave in leather sacks.

Now Adrián ferments in plastic, which, despite being less authentic, he prefers on account of its durability and consistency.

"Raicilla used to be contraband," he says. "But it was the lifestyle of the people here and the source of much of the work."

The main industries in this region were raicilla, coconuts and *chicle* (a natural gum that is collected from various species of native trees), but all of them have suffered greatly over the past few decades. The federal government provided funds to support them but corrupt politicians in the area took back-handers from big companies in Puerto Vallarta, crushing smaller businesses and the communities who relied on the jobs to support themselves. Tourism is now beginning to take over and many of the traditional industries that made the area so desirable are ironically dying out.

"We are united though," says Adrián. "They got the Denomination of Origin together and we are in companionship." He explains that consumers now know the geography of raicilla: the coastal region and the mountain region. And they can make informed decisions about what they like and why they like it. "In your way you will choose your taste. The two regions are different, but both are very good. Very tasty."

Leaving Pablo in charge of the distillation (and Margarito), Adrián takes us on a short walk up into the

hills where his agaves are growing. Gringos as we are, the heat makes walking uncomfortable but the 80-year-old raicillero strides ahead of us in blue jeans.

"I have 36 varieties of agave in total," he says, with not a hint of arrogance. "We can see six of them right here. This is Serrano, that one Serrano Percudo, Douro, Amarillo, Cerello, Cerello Margot..." He continues on, pointing at plants that look very similar to one another besides their varying ages.

Pancho is absolutely enthralled. With each different variety we stop and observe the subtle changes in the plant. And, of course, Addie takes pictures of every one of them. Some have wider leaves, some leaves are longer. On some plants the leaves are like troughs; on some they're flat. The barbs along the leaves vary in how hooked they are, how long, how sharp, as well as how many. The thorns on the end range from a little prickly to like a fucking needle. Colours vary from mustard yellow through to olive, cactus green, dusty blue and everything in-between.

"They are the same family but the quality is different." Adrián replies, running his hand along the razor-sharp penca of a nearby agave.

What Adrián is actually showing us is a whole load of varieties of one agave species: *rhodacantha*. Mezcaleros and raicilleros have a tradition of assigning varietal names to individual plants based on physical characteristics and the location where they are growing. An agave growing on a south-facing slope may be assigned a different name to one in a shaded spot on top of the hill. Or an agave with slight yellow markings on its pencas may be given a different name to one without. Mix up just those two variables and you have yet more names.

This can get very confusing, as varietal names can transcend species. Amarillo is one such example, which

is commonly used to signify any agave that is yellow in colour. Lechuguilla ("big lettuce") can be misleading too, as it can be applied to certain agave species that have a lettuce-like shape, but *Agave lechuguilla* is also a species in its own right. Add to that the fact that spirits made in the state of Chihuahua are often called Lechuguilla, and you sometimes have a lot of unpicking to do to get to the bottom of what people are actually talking about.

Cimarrón might be the most confusing of all. It means "wild" but can colloquially refer to: the agave species *salmiana*; to any species of agave growing in the wild; or even to a mezcal that simply tastes wild!

It's worth noting that Adrián's idea of what constitutes a variety may differ to the ideas of a taxonomist, who may wish to see proof of heritability (that its morphological characteristics can be genetically passed on) to grant a plant varietal status. But for a raicillero, a plant might need only to manifest certain growth and taste characteristics to be worthy of distinction.

It's easy to be dismissive of this pseudo-taxonomy as random mutation between individual plants, but to Adrián and many other raicilleros, these plants are like children (though some of them are the age of teenagers), each with its own unique needs, and each subtly different from the rest. Adrián is involved in an intimate dance with nature that has played out in these lands for thousands of years. The commercialisation of agave spirits has done an effective job of making us forget that growing and harvesting these plants for food, drink and fibre was once a symbiotic process, not only between man and agave, but with the land, with other flora and fauna, and even with the microbes in the soil. And perhaps this connection is beyond the scope of what science can currently teach us.

Some of Adrián's "children" are not looking so healthy, though. Their pencas are dried up and eaten out from the

OPPOSITE AND LEFT
Adrián and Pablo are the masters of raicilla at this taberna, but that doesn't mean that I can't pretend to be king of the agaves.

base up, with only the inner leaves still reaching up for dear life.

They are diseased.

There are various pests and diseases that can afflict agave plants. Adrián seems none the wiser as to what is happening to his plants but he estimates that he is losing around 5% of all plants to what he calls "*la plaga*".

"The worst affected is the Amarillo," he says. "I think it is because it is the most similar to the blue Weber agave."

Pancho thinks that the problem here has been caused by a species of weevil (*Scyphophorus acupunctatus*), which are small black bugs with a long aardvark-like snout. They bore into the plant causing significant damage and ultimately death. Also on the most-wanted list are nematodes, which are microscopic worms that attack the roots of the agave, leading to root rot and overall poor plant health. Agave mites (*Oligonychus pratensis*) are tiny pests that feed on the sap of the agave leaves, causing yellowing, browning and reduced growth. Scale insects attach themselves to the agave leaves and stems.

I am no expert, but I can see no sign of bugs or insects here and I suspect the issue might be invisible to the naked eye – a fungal or bacterial infection in the plant. Agaves are susceptible to soil-borne fungi such. *Fusarium oxysporum*, for example, causes Fusarium wilt, which causes the water-carrying vessels of the plant to become blocked so that the plant's core rots and eventually dies.

There are other fungal diseases that can cause issues with the development of the plant but won't necessarily be fatal. Leaf spot, caused by *Phyllosticta*, results in dark spots on the leaves, reducing the plant's ability to photosynthesise and weakening it over time. Root rot, often caused by *Phytophthora*, affects the roots of the agave, leading to poor nutrient uptake and plant decline. Anthracnose, a fungal infection caused by *Colletotrichum*, leads to dark lesions on the leaves, causing extensive leaf damage and reduced plant vigour. Additionally, *Botrytis cinerea*, known as grey mould, can infect agave plants, particularly in humid conditions, leading to leaf and flower rot.

Effective management of these pests and diseases involves regular monitoring of good practices, such as proper spacing and watering – all of which Adrián is doing. What he is not doing is smothering the ground and plants in pesticides or other biological control treatments.

The University of Guadalajara has been over to take samples of his plants to identify what the problem might be. From their findings they have instructed Adrián on how to make composts and build furrows into the land that might serve to protect the plants. What they're describing sounds something like a firewall for plants.

The state of Jalisco uses more herbicides and pesticides than any other in Mexico, and the big agrochemical companies like Monsanto and Dow have enjoyed an increasing presence in the countryside here over the past half-century. Every small village and town around the state has at least one of the following: taco stand, auto repair, a convenience store selling Coke and beer, a hardware store, and some place with a big sign painted on the wall advertising the sale of fertilisers and pesticides.

The hills where Adrián's agaves grow are left to their own devices, with trees, weeds, cacti and shrubs filling up the spaces between. Would he like to rid himself of whatever disease is afflicting his plants? Yes. Would he do it to the detriment of the land for years to come? No.

As we descend back towards the taberna, we can see Pablo still working: testing the spirit as it flows off the still, stoking the fire, which is still crackling away, and pressing fibres into gaps in the still head. Margarito is in the same position on the ground, but is now moving his arms around in front of his face as if he has discovered hands for the first time, and he is happily talking to them.

Margarito becomes the butt of all the jokes from here on in, and I find myself laughing at jibes spoken in Spanish that I somehow still understand. There is a healthy brotherhood among these men, and this taberna serves as not only a place to make agave spirits, but also a place to warm human spirits; to listen to music, drink, laugh and connect with nature and one another. Ultimately, though, it is about respect – for the land, for the plants and the livelihood they bring to those who dedicate themselves to them, as has been the way for centuries.

AYCYA

El Futuro

"These are the seeds of the *maximiliana*," says Jorge Luis, as he digs his hands into a bathtub-sized trough scooping out handfuls of the black and white kernels. "The black ones that have been pollinated and are viable and the white ones are virgins – they are no use."

"How many plants did these seeds come from?" I ask.

"Two."

"How many seeds are there?"

He considers for a moment and then, with a shrug, replies, "About 30,000."

We are visiting our final raicilla taberna and, in contrast to the other places we have been, it is an impressively modern example of what the category currently has to offer. With its Japanese-style shoji glass windows and concrete design, Taberna Aycya looks more like a Nordic spa or hipster publishing house than a place where wild agaves are turned into liquor. That said, its location is the same centuries-old terrain as its forebears: hidden away in the mountains at the end of another long, rough track. The co-owner of this place, Jorge Luis Aguirre, is more of that time too. Looking like he has stepped off the set of a 1960s' Mexican Western movie, he is the perfect anachronism to all the glass and steel.

This is where the Aycya brand is made, established in 2018 by raicillero Jorge Luis in partnership with brothers Pedro and Diego Fernandez del Valle, who both have backgrounds in the hospitality industry in Puerto Vallarta. With not even 60 years of age between them, they have built a beautiful and versatile distillery that, when coupled with Jorge Luis's knowledge of agaves, is an exciting taste of where the future of raicilla might be headed.

Watching Jorge Luis scoop up great handfuls of seeds, it's crazy to consider that two plants could sire potentially three orders of magnitude more offspring than a typical blue agave does from hijuelos, just from being left to flower for a few weeks.

Across the yard is the only other building within miles: Jorge Luis's home where he lives with his dogs. In front of that there are dozens of raised beds with nascent agaves growing in pots. We walk along the rows of young plants and note even at this young age the differences in their shapes and colours. There are 20,000 juvenile agaves here and another 60,000 growing in the surrounding hills. These include the species *maximiliana*, *angustifolia*, *inaequidens* and *valenciana*.

The baby agaves undergo a full year of growth in pots before they're planted in the mountains. Then, depending on the individual plant, it's a 7–15 year wait for them to reach maturity. Right now, however, Jorge Luis has only mature *maximiliana* agaves, and the two expressions of Aycya that he is currently bottling are both made from this plant.

Maximiliana is about the only thing that the two products have in common, as this distillery is really two completely different distilleries operating under one roof.

Production of their ancestral product (which is bottled as Aycya Madurada) is similar to what we have seen at the previous two tabernas: an above-ground three-tonne adobe oven, small plastic fermentation barrels and distillation in Filipino-style parota wood stills that look totally out of place in such a modern setting.

For the artisanal raicilla (bottled as Aycya Joven) they use a completely different set of equipment including a seven-tonne pressurised steel oven (an autoclave, basically), a steel mill to separate the juices from fibre, closed steel tanks, which are where the juices are naturally fermented, and 600-litre (160-gallon) stainless-steel alembic pots, which are where double distillation takes place.

Aycya Joven is still a small-scale production in comparison to all but the smallest tequila distilleries, but for a raicilla taberna located an hour down a bumpy track, it's both big and state of the art. Aycya is therefore something of a proving ground to see whether authentic raicilla can be made in a modern fashion and at scale. The beauty being there is a small-scale, traditional production flow operating at its side for comparison.

"I began in the taberna at age seven," says Jorge Luis, as we take seat inside the distillery and prepare to taste some raicilla. "I used to love eating the *mezcal dulce* (cooked agave) and would go after school to help my great-grandfather unload the oven."

Jorge Luis took to working weekends and holidays at the taberna under the tutelage of his grandfather, Don Margarito Aguerre Gomez. By the time he was 14, Jorge Luis was being given to the opportunity to find and harvest his own agaves and use the taberna to cook, ferment and distil them. His first batch came out perfectly, and the whole family knew they it had a new maestro in the house.

"In those days they didn't call it raicilla, it was *vino del cerro* or *vino de lechuguilla*, because there were no permits and that's also why they made it hidden, down by the stream."

Jorge Luis worked with his grandfather until he was 18 and then joined Jesús "Lalo" Sánchez at the Hacienda Don Lalín taberna in San Sebastián. There, he got to learn from one of the best in the business, and also had the chance to travel to Michoacán, Oaxaca and Guerrero to take courses and better understand how different regions produced their mezcals. This was quite an eye-opening experience, as he had been brought up making raicilla from a single ordinario distillation, which he insists can produce a delicious-tasting raicilla if the agaves are good and the distiller is competent.

Single distillation raicillas have a bad reputation and most of the time it's warranted. They are commonly made by adding a liberal dose of *piloncillo* (cane sugar) to the fermentation to bolster the alcohol content and increase the strength of the resulting distillate or by simply adding cheap alcohol to the still before distillation. These products are then sold for 100 pesos (£4/$5) a bottle and have the quality to match the price tag.

"As soon as you smell it, you can tell it's had other things added," says Jorge Luis.

Jorge Luis accepts that double distillation makes a more polished, refined product, but he is not ruling out the possibility of releasing a single-distilled product in the future that would, of course, be made from 100% agave.

Right now, though, he pours us a sample of Aycya Ancestral (48% ABV). *The aroma has a good hit of baked fruit, with green cucumber and pineapple, plus some floral notes. Taste brings about far more heads, plus a light amount of smoke. The finish has a little glue and a hum of cheesy funk. It's wild and slightly trippy.*

Artisanal and ancestral are recent terms used to describe production methods in agave spirits and differentiate more traditionally produced products from those that use modern equipment. As it stands, they have no legal grounding in raicilla, but that will likely change in the near future. When it does, it will be a contentious subject. It's worth reviewing some history to understand why.

Up until the turn of the century, production of raicilla was very small indeed, typically using only wild agaves, and destined mainly for family and local consumption. Then, in 2000, the El Consejo Mexicano Promotor de la Raicilla (CMPR) was established with the vision to bring together producers and work to generate better conditions and knowledge for the production and marketing of the drink and, more recently, to ensure adherence to the DO. The original president of the CMPR was Jorge Dueñas, whose surname you might remember from our visit to Tesoro del Oeste (see page 111). They now have an office in Mascota along with the tasting room called La Taberna.

The CMPR has no legal jurisdiction over how raicilla is made. Neither does the raicilla DO, which can make only recommendations on how raicilla should be labelled and mandate where it is made. Currently there is no regulatory council – no CRT equivalent – for raicilla. That looks set to change, however. A draft NOM has been written and it's only a matter of time until it is approved by the Mexican government and at that point a "CRR" will likely be formed to oversee production practices, monitor agriculture, conduct lab tests and legally enforce compliance with the NOM.

The draft NOM proposes three classifications of raicilla that have effectively been copied and pasted from the mezcal NOM. The first two of these are:

Artisanal Raicilla: Agave must be cooked in a pit oven or above-ground oven with firewood or gas. Mechanical shredders are allowed. Pot distillation in stills no larger than 500 litres (130 gallons) is mandated. Stills can be

OPPOSITE Jorge Luis – the future of raicilla? At Aycya, he blends tradition with modernity, crafting spirits in both rustic barrels and sleek stills, and bottling a classic product in modern packaging.

stainless steel. We have seen examples of this at Tesoro del Oeste and the taberna of Manuel Salcedo.

Ancestral Tradition Raicilla: Requires cooking in a pit oven or in an above-ground oven, milling with mallets or a stone wheel, and distillation in wood-fired clay-and-wood pot stills. Agave fibre must be included in both fermentation and (first) distillation. We have seen examples of this at Los Tres Hombres and La Gorupa.

The draft NOM is not without its critics, who have seen the loopholes and misclassifications of tequila and mezcal and how they can be exploited. There are, for example, a lot of grey areas in the current document, such as limits on the species of agave that can be used. Five are currently listed (*maximiliana*, *rhodacantha*, *angustifolia*, *inaequidens* and *valenciana*), but the language in the document also states "among others". This may serve to protect a handful of producers who have been harvesting alternative species for years, and whose unique biology provides special characteristics to the final product, but it also leaves the door open to species not native to the region to be thrown in the oven (that is, whichever agave happens to be cheapest at the time).

Further breathing space for unprincipled behaviour is permitted in the third proposed category of raicilla. Ironically titled "Classic Raicilla" (ironic because there is very little "classic" about it) this allows for cooking the agave in autoclaves, extraction with roller mills, fermentation in stainless steel, and distilling in a stainless-steel pots or even columns. Interestingly, this is where Jorge Luis's flagship product would probably sit if the classifications were to be ratified. And that product just so happens to be what is in my tasting glass right now.

Aycya Joven (42% ABV) *has the aroma of fresh pink grapefruit, salted fruit and lime. This continues on the palate with sweetness of grapefruit and then a richer, oily quality. Turpentine and some habanero spice follow and there's more of that oily, juniper-y, resiny character on the finish.*

Overall, it feels like a product that sits somewhere between tequila and raicilla. It does show that it's possible to make a delicious spirit from *maximiliana* agaves using steel and steam, and products like this could serve as a gateway to raicilla appreciation without going straight in to the high-strength puntas. But does raicilla really need semi-committal gateway products to lure consumers in, or should it trade on its own inherent good taste?

I'm not overly concerned about Jorge Luis's Joven product. He is a skilled and sympathetic producer of spirits and, regardless of the equipment he's using, his craft is one of an artisan. But the draft "Classic Raicilla" categorisation leaves ample room for abuse from less principled parties. Permitting the use of column stills, for example, offers no benefits to this category other than lowering production costs and granting a competitive advantage to bland-tasting raicilla. We know that this is how the scenario will play out as we have already seen it in the tequila and mezcal categories, which have been systemically denatured and denigrated through legally permissible strategies to cut costs and dispose of flavour and authenticity.

By granting raicilla column stills and autoclaves, we would be sowing the seeds of the category's destruction before its development has even got started. Why give producers the opportunity to shirk tradition in place of profits?

Speaking of tequila, one example of a "Classic Raicilla" that is already being imported into the US is the La Cristana brand. This product certainly looks the part. The bottle is wrapped in paper and has a handcrafted appeal to it. But, there is no mention of a specific taberna, the method of distillation, or the type of agave used to make it. Just a cryptic reference to Doña Crista of Rincón de Mirandilla, which is a village in the mountains. Dig a little deeper into what's going on here and you discover that La Cristana is owned by Agavera Camichines, which is a shell corporation of Jose Cuervo.

The sharks are circling it seems, and I wouldn't be surprised to see the other big spirit companies investing in or starting up raicilla brands in the coming years – if they haven't already.

In danger of falling deeper into a death spiral of politics and bad ideas, Jorge Luis awakens me, by pouring a measure of a yet-to-be released reposado, which has been aged for six months in ex-brandy casks. This is based on the artisanal Aycya formula spirit. *The aroma is gentle vanilla, then tomato leaf, and dry barrow notes. Very high fidelity. Precision. Long fruity salsa, toasted nuts, soft aromatic spice and sweet candied fruit.*

As more spirits are offered (Jorge Luis is making a fantastic cane-juice-based rum as well), my uneasiness fades away slowly. With craftspeople like Jorge Luis at the forefront of racilla's future, we are in safe hands. And this brand and distillery take on a new meaning to me as the perfect representation of the present and future of the raicilla category.

There's the contemporary architecture and brand, primed for Instagram snapshots and back-bar placement and plans are afoot to install a visitors' centre, tasting room, restaurant and possibly even a hotel. This represents raicilla's potential future, its opportunity to bring in tourists, its ability to attract money and to scale, and how it may build desirability to international consumers. You could market a successful brand using these principles (the vodka category does it all the time), but without the passion, skill and patience that Jorge Luis brings to the table you would be left with a brand lacking in authenticity. He holds the key to the past, to the tradition of raicilla and therefore the authenticity of the brand that should carry it through to great success in the future. Not to mention the ability to make tasty liquids, which ought to remain near the top of any brand's priorities.

It is encouraging to see this blend of old and new at work, and it's exciting to imagine how it will continue to play out as the brand develops. Raicilla needs investment in facilitates, marketing, branding and PR if it is to be recognised on an international stage. If we wish to share and enjoy the spirits made by the likes of Adrián at Los Tres Hombres and Manuel Salcedo in Mascota there is a requirement for importers and agencies to invest their time and money into elevating these products out of obscurity. But these efforts must be applied mindfully so as not to blemish the name of raicilla and negate its significance to the communities of western Jalisco. It must pay these people a fair price, treat them with dignity, and support expensive and time-consuming endeavours to grow and harvest responsibly, so that they, above all else, ensure the cultural legacy for the next generation.

We finish with a final sample of 100% Chico Aguillar raicilla, which is among the first non-*maximiliana* agave distillates to be made at the distillery. *The aroma has a sour funk; dry and dusty. Incredibly oily on the palate, full and bright. But so much glue and high alcohol too!* It's a challenging drink – not a commercial bestseller – and for that I am strangely thankful.

The car radio fails to get a signal until we re-join the highway and head into Puerto Vallarta. For the next stage of our trip, we will be travelling south along the Pacific coastline, leaving the state of Jalisco for the first time, though only briefly. Not far down the road from Puerto Vallarta, with the dramatic guitar battle of *Malagueña Salerosa* filling our ears, Pancho suddenly swerves off the road and nearly crashes into the front of a street vendor selling coconut water. "I love this stuff!" he exclaims, and he's out of the car before we've stopped moving.

Piles of coconuts are stacked under a shabby awning, and a stout woman wearing an apron is hacking them open with a machete. Despite their modern-day prevalence, coconuts are not indigenous to Mexico. They were brought here on galleon ships from the Philippines, arriving at the ports of Acapulco and Colima, which is about 100km (60 miles) south of where we are standing. From there, they multiplied until coconut palms populated the entire west coast.

The stout woman's strategy seems to be to extract the water and bottle it, then chill on it on ice in a cooler until it's sold. She opens the cooler to reveal plastic bottles with their translucent contents covered in condensation. On a hot day like this, it looks to be just about the most refreshing thing imaginable.

Just about…

Pancho and I exchange a knowing look and I jump back in the car to retrieve a bottle of raicilla and a couple of the limes that have been rolling around in the boot for the past day. I pour a slug of raicilla into three empty plastic cups while Pancho borrows the machete off the lady to cut limes and squeeze their juices into the cups. He dumps the spent lime shells in there too and then the lady tops up with chilled coconut water. The three of us slurp happily on the drinks for a minute, looking at each other with silent appreciation. The coconut lady remains as stoic as ever.

The next part of our journey will take us through Colima, and into the birthplace of agave spirits in Mexico. There, we will discover that ideas, just like coconuts, have an incredible capacity for multiplying and moving long distances. Especially when those ideas (like coconuts) are delicious.

SOUTHERN JALISCO

The south of Jalisco conceals a certain magic in the spirits that are made here,
perhaps because it maintains the oldest agave spirits-producing tradition. All of this
in spite of having no legally classifiable raicilla, mezcal or tequila distilleries.
Intrigued? You should be.

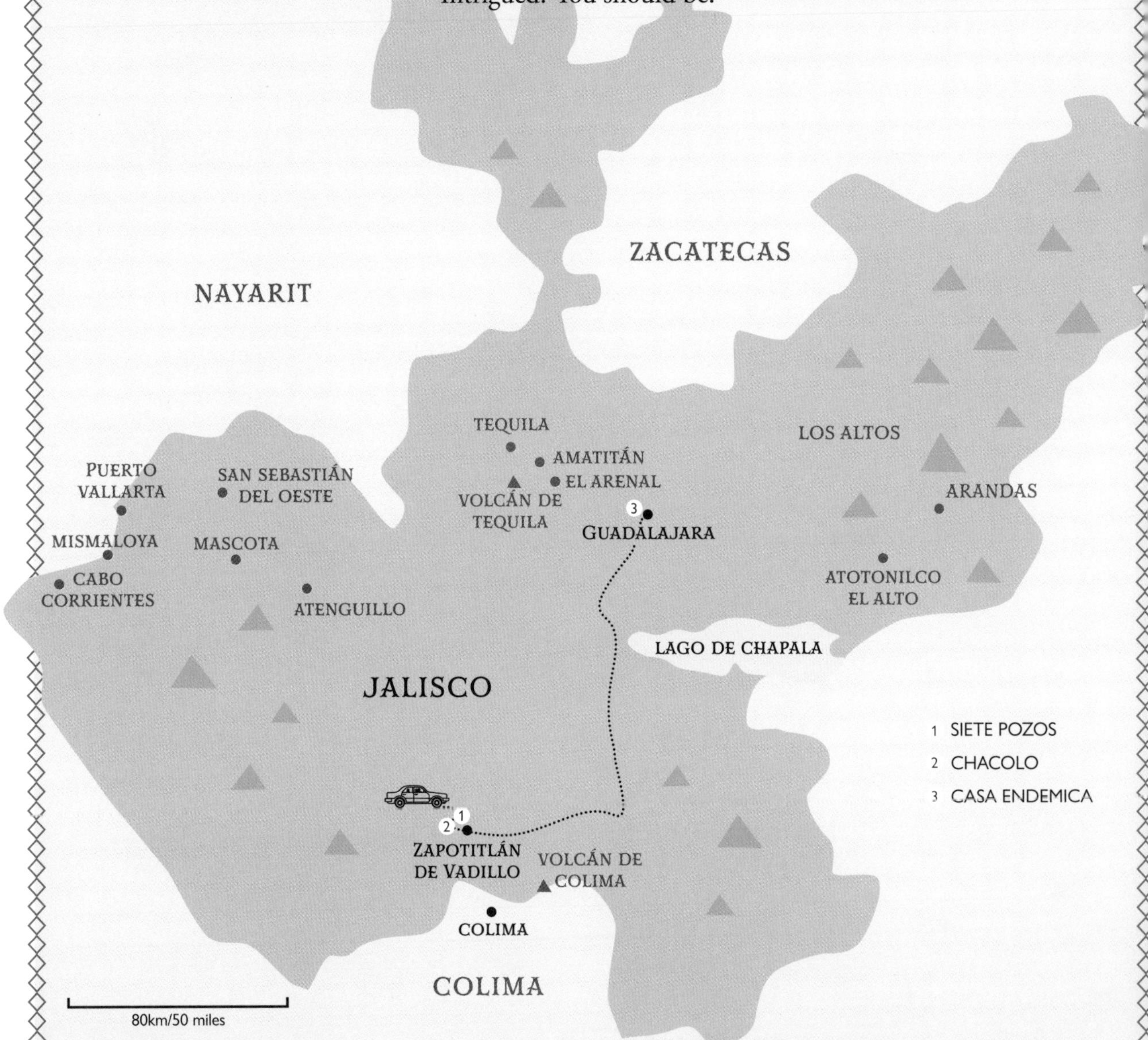

ZACATECAS

NAYARIT

TEQUILA

AMATITÁN
EL ARENAL

LOS ALTOS

PUERTO
VALLARTA

SAN SEBASTIÁN
DEL OESTE

VOLCÁN DE
TEQUILA

ARANDAS

MISMALOYA

MASCOTA

GUADALAJARA

3

CABO
CORRIENTES

ATENGUILLO

ATOTONILCO
EL ALTO

LAGO DE CHAPALA

JALISCO

1 SIETE POZOS

2 CHACOLO

3 CASA ENDEMICA

2 1

ZAPOTITLÁN
DE VADILLO

VOLCÁN DE
COLIMA

COLIMA

COLIMA

80km/50 miles

SIETE POZOS

<svg>~~~~~~</svg>

La Historia

As we cross the Colima-Jalisco border the next morning, the majestic Sierra de Manantlán looms before us, its green slopes shrouded in a thin veil of mist. To our right, the imposing silhouette of the most active volcano in Mexico – Volcán de Colima – pierces the sky, its snow-capped peak catching the first golden rays of the rising sun. This area is home to indigenous Nahua and Otomí communities, as well as some of the oldest varieties of corn and cultivated beans in the world. Down in the valley is the municipality of Tuxcacueso (or Tuxca), which is generally agreed to be the birthplace of agave spirits.

Agaves have furnished the geography of this area for millennia, and the rich and fertile volcanic soil of the Tuxca region claims at least seven indigenous species. They are in both the physical and written geography of the area. A few years ago, researchers from the University of Colima conducted a survey of the region and recorded every town or village in the foothills around the volcano that had some relation to the agave, including mentions of *ixtle* (the fibre from the agave). The list was long and included familiar sounding names like La Mezcala, La Mezcalera, La Mezcales, Mezcalitos, Los Mezcales, Las Tabernas, La Taberna and Tabernillas, along with Ixtlahuacán and Ixtlan.

This connection to the plant is also reflected in the archaeology of the region. Agave-themed pottery designs span at least 1,500 years of history, from the Ortiz phase around 400BCE to the Chanal phase in 1100CE, reflecting the plant's enduring importance to ancestral peoples.

Agaves were used as nutrition in the form of agave nectar (from the flower), tea (from the roots), sweets, vinegar and alcoholic beverages, like the fermented agave beer *pulque*, and as construction materials for habitations, fences to secure plots of land, and both the needle and the thread for clothing. It has been turned into balms and

ointments for the skin, combs for hair, and putty and glue. Suffice it to say there's practically no area of ancestral life in Mesoamerica that agave didn't play a part in.

Recent excavations at an archaeological site in Colima uncovered fascinating ceramic pieces adorned with intricate drawings of various agave species, curiously placed only on the base of the vessels. These vessels are thought to have been served to elderly men and women, symbolising the transcendent role of the plants in the afterlife. Biologists have meticulously identified the agave species depicted on these artefacts and two species stand out: *maximiliana* and *angustifolia*. Further evidence of the use of agaves in these ancient cultures has been found in figurines that portray the work of harvesting and carrying agave *piñas*, as well as ritualised drinking and ceremonial activities.

So it's little wonder that when the technology to distil spirits arrived here attention turned to making the first *vino de mezcals*. The question is, though, where did this technology come from?

The obvious assumption would be that the Spanish introduced it. After all, the knowledge to distil was present in Europe as far back as the 12th century and production of the first brandies and whiskies was already well underway by the time Columbus landed on Hispaniola in 1492. The 16th century brought distillation with alembic stills to South America via the Portuguese. But the Spanish saw no need to introduce the technology to the Americas. They viewed the indigenous people as heathens and banned ritual consumption of pulque to avoid competition with their own imported wines, which also served as a means of religious assimilation to the Catholic faith.

So the best explanation is that pot stills came not from the East and across the Atlantic Ocean, but from the West and the Pacific.

The Philippines was a Spanish colony from 1565 to 1898, which led to the establishment of the Manila Galleon Trade where sailors, soldiers and labourers took the three-and-a-half-month voyage to New Spain (renamed as Mexico in 1821). Some were attracted by economic opportunity; others had very little choice in the matter. Once they landed, the travellers worked in various sectors such as shipbuilding, agriculture and mining. Many Filipinos intermarried with locals, contributing to the rich cultural mosaic we see in Mexico today.

Their migration also facilitated significant cultural exchange, including culinary practices and artisanal skills that remain in place. Among the other things that they brought were coconut palms, which were agriculturally suited to the Central American coast and a promising source of nutrition, as well as a means of promoting cultural integration. Crucially though, the Filipinos also brought distillation equipment with them, which may have initially been intended for distilling fresh water from seawater but inevitably ended up being used to make spirits. It's no secret that sailors like a drink, and it probably didn't take them long to begin distilling their own Filipino *lambanóg* (coconut palm liquor) in their new home in New Spain.

Lambanóg is a traditional Filipino spirit that dates back at least 700 years. To make it, you collect fresh sap from the flower buds of coconut trees. A tapper climbs the tree, makes cuts on the flower buds, and the sap flows into containers. This sap is then poured into big vessels where it ferments naturally at which point it is known by the Filipino name for coconut wine, *tuba*. The fermentation takes a few days and then it's sent for distillation.

The wooden ancestral stills we have seen in western Jalisco, which are used to make raicilla, are based on the same design originating in the Philippines in the 15th century. These stills are small and cylindrical and have a bowl for condensation on top and a spoon or paddle that is used to catch the falling spirit and direct it out of the body of the still. Sometimes they are made from hollowed tree trunks, sometimes from staves of a wood braced together like a barrel. There are further regional iterations on this design that we will explore in more depth later.

By the year 1600, coconut wine distillation was already well established in Colima. One document from around that time states the following: "In this valley of Caxitlán the Chinese Indians make *vino de cocos*. They use it to inebriate the *indios naturales* ('natural Indians') in nearby towns and *naboríos indios* ('free Indians')." Further clarification was given on the term *vino*, stating that it was a misrepresentation of the product, as these were indeed distilled liquors.

By 1612 the number of legal vino de cocos haciendas in Colima exceeded 60, with much of the product being sent to mining towns whose workforces had apparently developed a substantial dependency on the spirit. Alcohol consumption took on a prominent role as it often does when people migrate and cultures mix, as imported wines and brandies were either unavailable or too expensive, miners opted for the fermented agave sap pulque or for vino de cocos.

Never one to turn down an economic opportunity, the Real Audiencia (the instrument of Spanish royal power) in Guadalajara promptly banned the production of vinos de cocos to help promote consumption of imported Spanish wines and brandies.

This single act may have been the catalyst for the development of the first agave spirits. With distillation in coastal towns now being policed by the Spanish government, distillers moved their equipment into the hills and valleys of more rural areas. The Filipino stills were perfectly suited to this, as they themselves were developed from portable stills that may have originally been used by nomadic Mongols in yurts. Thus, they were small and could be easily dismantled and transported by mules to wherever there was a nearby water source and coverage to avert prying eyes. The only problem was that coconut palms won't grow away from the coast. But agaves do.

As indigenous and immigrant cultures mixed, new ideas fermented and new ingredients were tested and tasted. The abundance of agave and its cultural significance made it the perfect candidate for distillation. And within a single generation, production and trade of these early mezcal liquors moved north through historic cultural trading routes. These tended to track river systems that had been used to transport salt, chocolate, cotton, pottery, seashells, snails and jewellery since pre-Columbian times. For early mezcaleros, they offered not only a means of transport but also a steady supply of water. And it was through this trade network that distillation eventually found its way north, into the Tequila Valley.

En route, the indigenous populations adopted various techniques through observation, and modified them with their own unique skills and available materials. The use of tree trunks, agave leaves and inflorescences, wooden spoons, earthenware pottery, agave threads and agave gums mixed with clays tells the story of how Asian-style distillation methods blended with Mesoamerican culture to produce the most diverse methods of distillation in the world.

And this is where it began.

Driving down the mountain pass, we are following a similar route to that of industrious distillers of the 17th century. Perhaps they were Filipino immigrants, who felt compelled to continue their distilling tradition. Or they may have been native Mesoamericans armed with new insights about how to capture the essence of their maguey. Or maybe it was both – as cultures intertwined and new generations were born, Fillipino and Mexican technology and tradition came together at last.

We are heading into the town of Zapotitlán de Vadillo, in the heart of Tuxcacueso just a few miles north of the Colima border. The population of Zapotitlán is 7,000 and many if not most of its inhabitants are involved in the cultivation of agaves and production of agave products. Despite being a southern Jalisco municipality, the spirits made in Tuxcacueso do not fall under the raicilla DO and cannot be called tequila either because – with one or two exceptions – they do not use blue *tequiliana* agaves. Neither can they be called mezcals, as the mezcal DO – despite being the largest Designation of Origin in the world – does not include the state of Jalisco within its boundaries.

This relegates them to the classification of "Destilado de Agave", which is a legitimate category of spirit under the NOM that can be produced from any type of agave, anywhere in Mexico as long as it is made from a minimum of 51% agave sugars and bottled above an ABV of 35%.

There is of course an enormous irony in all of this, seeing as the DO neglects to include the area that likely birthed mezcal. And in a legal respect, it is the birthplace of spirits in Mexico. When the Prussian explorer and naturalist Alexander von Humboldt published a "Political Essay on the Kingdom of New Spain" in 1811, he identified this region as among the first to effectively levy a tax on agave spirits' production in Mexico, and many of the families that would go on to establish distilleries further north, in Tequila, can trace their roots back to this district in southern Jalisco, nestled between the coastal area known for vino de cocos and the modern centres of tequila production. Thus, the recognition of the historical significance of the Tuxca region and the potential for a tuxca DO has become one of the recent hot topics for the agave spirits' industry.

We discover the entrance to the Taberna Siete Pozos is via a small gate on the side of a residential street, perched on a steep embankment in Zapotitlán de Vadillo. No sooner have we parked up than we are greeted by the smiling faces of the owners of the taberna, the Vilasco sisters, Lucretia and Alejandra. They take us down a sloped path, through the garden of the property, which is known to them as La Huertita. The property once belonged to their grandmother, Sara, and has been used as a place to gather to commemorate births, marriages and deaths in the family for generations.

The sisters are the sixth-generation family members of a 100-year-old luxury leather business, specialising in bags and boots made from crocodile and alligator hides. A great deal of their business is done in the US and on cruise ships, so when the Covid-19 pandemic hit in early 2020, their company all but ceased trading overnight. Taking advice (and money) from their father, who is a long-time collector of agave spirits from the region, they saw the rising tide of mezcal and raicilla and decided to build a taberna on their grandmother's plot of land.

Under the tiled-roof veranda of the distillery, we are introduced to José Partida, who was brought into the project to build and operate the new taberna – a challenge that he was born to do.

"I come from a family of distillers," he says modestly. "Me and my brothers."

That's an understatement.

The Partida family are very well known around here, being fifth-generation agave stewards and producers of some of the best agave spirits in the world. José is one of nine Partida brothers and his father is Don Macario Partida, who produces the Chacolo brand that we will see on our next stop.

José built the taberna with pine fermentation vessels and wood-fired alembic stills, which right now are partially dismantled with their condensation coils exposed. All around are plastic jerry cans filled with liquids, and just outside is a pit oven. We take a seat at a wooden table and Pancho gets to work dousing fresh

RIGHT Wooden Filipino stills and ancient pits whisper secrets of bygone distillers, while the Vilasco sisters are breathing new life into a forgotten style, challenging the industry with feminine finesse.

cucumber slices and mango that the sisters have prepared for us with ground chilli, salt and lime, and we munch happily on them as Alejandra hands out cold beers and pours us samples of their spirit.

The aroma is slightly smoky and musty, like new carpet. There's a touch of red wine, then some light tropical notes. Blue cheese also starts to come through after a while. Barbecued cucumber, asparagus and some hot glue follow. What we are tasting is Indio Alonso Tuxca Artesenal (45% ABV), which is made from the Cimarrón (*Agave angustifolia*), Cuaquizoca and Salmiana (*Agave inaequidens*) varieties of agave.

"Salmiana is a touch of joy for me," says Pancho. "Every time I drink it, it makes me very happy!"

But this is just one of two products that the Vilasco sisters currently bottle. The story of the other one is where things begin to get interesting.

The first distillations of Indio Alonso took place in 2021. Soon after the spirit had been bottled, the Vilasco sisters' uncle – who was apparently unaware of what had been going on – announced that he had an old plot of land on the other side of town that they should see.

"He said, 'I think this land is for you,'" says Lucretia. "It turned out that our great-grandfather, Salvador Vilasco, had once owned a distillery there. When we learned this, everything... vibrated!"

The old taberna known simply as Los Pozos (The Pits) was like a 19th-century WeWork for mezcaleros. Local distillers would bring their agaves to be roasted and distilled there and they could pay for the service with a portion of the spirit they made. Lucretia thinks that it may have served as a kind of agave spirits' academy too, where information was shared and skills improved.

"Can we see it?" I ask.

"Of course!" the sisters say in unison.

We head back towards the cars and up through the garden. Lucretia draws our attention to the trees in the garden: mango, plum, avocado, guava and mesquite. The plums here are apparently some of the best in Mexico, and Lucretia tells us there is even a local cocktail that combines them with agave spirit called Faustina (see page 246 for my twist on this).

We all hop into a pickup truck, the sisters in the front cabin and José, Pancho, Addie and me in the back. We drive out of the hills and down into one of the tributaries of the Armería River gorge. The afternoon sun is blazing but the wind chill of the moving car feels delightful. We park by another gate and follow a set of old stone steps cut into the hillside, leading down past Lineño agaves lining the pathway. At the bottom we see wooden Filipino stills and *canoas* (hollowed-out tree trunks) for mashing agaves.

The area opens out into a terrace built from cobbles of river stone, all of it set into the hillside and under a canopy of trees. Built into the ground are a bunch of what appear to be wells, with round wooden covers placed over the top. These are the *siete pozos* (seven pits) from which the brand takes its name. Similar to the

fermentation pits we encountered at the El Tecuane, the UNESCO World Heritage site adjacent to Destilería Santa Rita, where Caballito Cerrero (see page 101) is produced, they were built perhaps 250 years ago for the sole purpose of turning cooked agaves into alcohol on an industrial scale. Given the engineering effort it must have taken to have carved and lined these pits, they indicate a significant commitment to the production of spirits by whomever built the place.

A similar degree of love and dedication was required from the sisters to restore the old taberna, which had remained unused and unloved for decades. With the help of another local mezcalero, Refugio Pineda, they painstakingly made the pits watertight, built new parota wood stills, and committed to producing tuxca spirit here in the ancestral way, with no electricity – only buckets and elbow grease.

José tells me that the pozos create a faster fermentation environment as the insulation is consistent and there is minimal contact with air once the wooden lid is dragged over the top. Here, they still use the Filipino word *tuba* to describe the fermentation.

Gazing down towards the dry river bed, it's depressing to think that this taberna would have once been directly adjacent to the river. In recent years it has all but dried up as aggressive farming in the region has sucked the water away to irrigate crops. Today, the taberna's supply comes from plastic tubes, like a life-support system for a terminal illness.

The Siete Pozos brand is made from Ixterro Amarillo (*Agave rhodacantha*) and Lineño (*Agave angustifolia*) and production is extremely small, totalling less than 1,000 litres (265 gallons) in a year. Lucretia pours samples for us to try. *The aroma is gluey at first, then gives a slight sweet wine note. The taste is spicy with hot red pepper, then a cheesy note comes through – a slight tang of malolactic fermentation. Chilli spice finish.*

As we head back up the ancient stone steps, I reflect on the challenges that the sisters face: establishing two new spirits brands in a competitive market that doesn't recognise their product as mezcal, pushing for recognition of tuxca in the form of a DO, and all the while overcoming the stigma of being female in an industry where clients request to see the maestro of the taberna, falsely assuming Lucretia and Alejandra are employed in sales or PR.

But from this timeless base, in what is possibly the birthplace of agave spirits, they are slowly overcoming adversity, challenging norms, celebrating ancestral production, and doing it all with smiles on their faces.

CHACOLO

◇◇

El Magico

The next day we find ourselves winding our way down a rough track, past huge candelabra cacti that we learn are *Pachycereus weberi*, named after Frédéric Albert Constantin Weber of blue agave fame.

The taberna we are here to see reveals itself as a simple operation with a covered parking area, a small bar with a plastic dining table out front, and a little outdoor kitchen where two older ladies are kneading tortilla dough. Behind them is a modest-sized pit oven and then the distillery proper, where we can see smoke emanating from underneath a couple of wooden Filipino stills.

We are greeted by Miguel Angel Partida and then his father, Don Macario. They take us for a walk through the fields near the taberna. As I'm a gringo and have arrived unprepared, Don Macario loans me his hat. It's only then that I notice he is missing an eye. I would later find out from Pancho that he lost it in a fight many years ago, and that the other guy... well, he lost more than just an eye.

A private audience with Don Macario as he talks us through his plants is a true honour. This man might be the most remarkable producer of agave spirits in all of Mexico. He is a living testament to the producers of the past and the spirit of ancestral Mexican agriculture and mezcal production. Despite being in his late 80s, he frequently embarks on hikes around the Cerro Grande in the Sierra de Manantlán to seek out wild agave populations, carefully selecting shoots to propagate back at the farm. Through careful breeding to produce seeds and propagation of *hijeulos* today, he cultivates 24 different of *angustifolia* and *rhodacantha* varieties and is effectively maintaining a living gene bank of local plant diversity. We have seen variety numbers like these mentioned when we were at some raicilla tabernas, but they were often used casually to describe the same agave growing on different parts of the farm. Here at Chacolo it's the real deal.

The care Don Macario puts into his agave cultivation is matched only by his expertise as a distiller of mezcal. He has a keen eye for identifying the agave plants that will produce the most flavourful mezcals and through a process of careful selection, reproduction and approval, he continually refines his stock, choosing only the best individual plants to carry forward his legacy of quality.

"A lot of the *mezcales* have disappeared," he says as we walk among the plants near the distillery. "For example, Ixtero Verde. People stopped using it for its old purpose, to make fibres, and they let it end. Fortunately, a researcher who came to Mexico brought me two plants from San Cristobal. Now we have a lot of those plants again."

Outside of tequila production, it not uncommon to hear producers of agave spirits (including raicilla and mezcal) refer to the agaves themselves as *mezcales*. This makes sense, because the word mezcal comes from the two Nahuatl words *metl* and *ixcalli*, meaning "cooked agave." Once this mezcal was fermented and distilled it became *vino de mezcal* ("wine of the cooked agave") and then it was only a matter of time before the *vino* part was dropped for ease of use.

The indigenous peoples of Mexico had lots of different names for the agave. In the Otomi language it is *uadá*, in Zapotec it's *doba*, and it was called *akamba* in Purépecha. Incidentally, it was the Swedish naturalist Carl Linnaeus who, in 1753, coined the word agave, taken the Greek word *agavos*, which means "illustrious or admirable".

Another frequently used word for agave is *maguey*, which was taken by the Spanish from the Taíno people, indigenous to various Caribbean islands. There they used it to describe aloe vera; the Spanish, upon seeing agaves in Mexico mistook them for the same plant and imposed the word on the indigenous people. Maguey is still used by many producers of agave spirits today as well as agave-

spirits advocates who are probably unaware of its roots as a colonialist imposition and like it for its indigenous sounding phonemes. The word maguey sometimes features on bottles where it is commonly used to indicate the local name of the variety (or varieties) of agave used to make the product. For example, Chacolo Chancuellar, which distinguishes itself with a turquoise label, is made from *Agave angustifolia* and the "maguey" Chancuellar, a variety of the *angustifolia* species.

We walk past another huge agave, which Don Macario identifies as Ixtero Maria. He estimates that the piña on the plant might weigh 250kg (550 lbs), but laments that it will probably offer relatively low amounts of fermentable sugar and that it's fibrous and hard to work with. At 16 years old, he thinks it has another four or five years to go before it produces a quiote. Even at over 20 years of age, the Partidas are in no rush to cut them down. They wait a minimum of three years after the quiote is *capón* ("castrated") before they harvest the plant fully. This, they believe, gives their heirloom varieties a long period of development in the field that translates through to their product.

We take a seat under a straw canopy to eat some lunch of stewed pork with beans and blue corn tortilla cooked on a skillet on an open fire. Macario's wife has expertly cracked an egg onto some of the tortillas and places another over the top before cooking the "sandwiches" on a hot stone griddle, creating a kind of tortilla-egg toastie. Not even Pancho has seen this done before.

"There were a lot of tabernas hidden in the canyons around here," says Don Macario pouring us a glass of Chacolo Lineno, "because they tried to hide as much as possible to make some money, but also to have some alcohol for the hard times and for births, weddings and deaths. So when the people all around knew that the government would come, they took as much as possible, hid it and destroyed everything they couldn't take."

The aroma of the spirit is slightly sherried with nuts and dried fruit. There is a floridity to it as well. On the palate it's warm and toasted with a smack of green, chlorophyll dryness.

Chacolo is the colloquial name for a person who comes from the city of Zapotitlán, but it wasn't the original name of the brand. Miguel explains that he began taking the Partida mezcal to fairs in Guadalajara and Mexico City in 2008, packaged in soda bottles for people to try. The response was overwhelmingly positive.

"They said, 'You should bottle it,'" says Miguel, "'and if it's mezcal, you should put a label on it that says it's mezcal to make it sell better.'"

Miguel returned the following year with bottles of "Don Macario Mezcal from Zapotitlán" but when people realised he was from southern Jalisco they told him he couldn't bottle mezcal in Jalisco, and that in Jalisco people make tequila. He insisted his product wasn't tequila, and then did his research and discovered to his surprise that he could not make mezcal – the drink of his ancestors – in his ancestral home in Jalisco. Nevertheless, he continued to do so until he got a letter from the government telling him to stop and threatening court action if he didn't. The Partidas pulled the product and began working on new labelling, but during the interim someone registered a trademark for the "Don Macario" brand name (along with 40 other trademarks) and tried to sell it back to the Partidas for a high price.

"So we thought of another name, another bottle," says Miguel. "In short, a renewed way of going on the market."

The "Chacolo" brand was registered in 2013 and in the ten years since has become just about the most respected three-syllable word in all of agave spirits. Given what they have been through with the mezcal DO, I wonder how the

Partidas feel about the proposal for a Denomination of Origin (DO) for tuxca. On the face of it, a DO seems to present an opportunity to recognise and protect a unique regional tradition. As we have learned, both the type of agaves and the soil and microclimate they are grown in, as well as the yeasts that inhabit the area collude to produce unique outcomes in the end spirit. Just as relevant here, however, is the historical significance of tuxca as the birthplace of agave spirits. A DO might serve to protect this, by providing legal safeguards for local producers and ensuring that only spirits made within the designated area could bear the tuxca name.

Furthermore, a DO could significantly boost tourism in southern Jalisco. As we have seen with other Mexican agave spirits, official recognition often leads to increased interest from spirits' enthusiasts, bartenders and tourists. This influx could provide economic benefits to local communities and help sustain traditional production methods.

Finally, a DO could also elevate the status of tuxca on the global stage, celebrating its unique identity and potentially affording any brand displaying the tuxca name increased value and marketability. It could help to educate consumers on agave spirits in general, and assist in making a timeline of development. Jesús Israel Nava Solano, head of tourism for Zapotitlán, has already begun discussions with the CRT about getting this off the ground, and there are multiple proposals on what a tuxca DO could look like.

But there's much more to this than it first seems.

Miguel points out that the term *tuxca* originates from the city of Colima, which is a two-hour drive south and in a different state. Tuxca was originally used as shorthand in Colima to signify mezcal arriving in clay jugs from Zapotitlán de Vadillo and Tuxcacuesco – similar to the way that tequila became synonymous with mezcal from Tequila. However, the folks of Zapotitlán and Tuxcacuesco have never called their spirit tuxca; they've always referred to it as vino mezcal. So, essentially, tuxca is a name tied to the destination, Colima, rather than the origin.

"Certain people want to take advantage of everything," says Miguel. "Most of the people pushing for it are not even producers, they are just looking to commercialise the opportunity."

The concern that a DO could be exploited by opportunists seeking to capitalise on the region's hard-earned reputation is understandable given what has happened to tequila and what is currently happening to mezcal in Oaxaca. Evidence seems to suggest that once a DO is granted, it leads to increased production, which causes the deforestation of wild agave, disruption of ecosystems, decreased biodiversity and increasingly slippery production standards. One proposed DO seeks to include parts of Colima in the definition, in spite of there being scant evidence of any tradition of agave spirits' production there.

"Both the big tequileros and the mezcaleros don't like distilleries where there is no denomination," says Miguel. "It's plain to see that the tequileros want to deforest and destroy the agaves we work with. They only want their *tequiliana*. They want to finish us."

The animosity here is understandable. The Partida family and others are stewards of this land and have spent decades building prestige through quality of production, environmental sustainability and educational initiatives, such as the annual festival they hold that features prominent speakers from the world of agriculture and mezcal. They worry that a DO could allow outsiders – and possibly those funded by or owned by the big tequila and mezcal brands – to either appropriate this prestige without adhering to traditional methods, or simply to turn over the fertile volcanic soil the region has to growing *Agave tequiliana* just like they are attempting to do in the western part of the state.

So determined are the Partidas to refute a tuxca DO that they have collected over a thousand signatures protesting it. "The best way to destroy a traditional mezcal is to create a Denomination of Origin," says Don Macario. "Now the fight is not only against the government. Sometimes it's against the other producers around here because they have a very cheap product and they use sugar cane in their distillations."

He believes that the Mexican government, while publicly supporting DOs, has allowed powerful industry leaders to manipulate these initiatives repeatedly. This mismanagement began with early changes to quality regulations in the tequila industry (allowing the use of alternative sugars and changes to bottling strength) and continues now with the broader distilled-agave market.

A particularly egregious example occurred in late 2011. With support from the big players in tequila and mezcal, the Mexican Institute of Industrial Property (IMPI) proposed legislation to trademark the term "agave" and

OPPOSITE Miguel Angel has taken his family's brand from rural Jalisco and into the hands of spirits aficionados across the world.

LEFT Three generations of Partidas represent a tradition of spirits' production that has been passed down for hundreds of years.

shortly afterwards, the Ministry of Economy suggested regulating agave spirits outside of DO regulations through a measure called NOM 186. This would have forced mezcal producers outside DO areas to use "Agavacea" instead of agave on labels and in advertising. Additionally, it sought to limit agave harvesting zones and restricted the production to just six agave species, despite dozens being traditionally used.

These proposals faced significant backlash. Petitions circulated both in Mexico and internationally to stop the legislation. In an unexpected turn of events, government officials suspended the proposals in early 2012 and this transnational effort successfully countered the industrial elites' attempts to control the market.

For powerful companies committed to turning profits for their shareholders and growing their market share, these political moves may feel justified once you characterise those who will be negatively impacted as poorly educated souls scratching out a meagre existence producing dangerous moonshine. But in understanding the truth behind what the Partidas and others are attempting to preserve, the behaviour of Big Tequila should more accurately be classed as cultural genocide.

The conversation moves on and we find ourselves gathered around the wooden distillation pots. Miguel's brother silently stokes the fire and then sits down to rest. A thin ribbon of spirit continues to flow from the *carrizo* pipe and into a small plastic receptacle. While we have seen primitive distillation setups already on our tour, there is something about this place that is special. It is eerily quiet here, with only the sounds of the crackling fire and the bubbling liquor. There is no wind, no sign of wildlife, no roads, no other visible habitation in any direction. The trees and cacti are massive; the land feels old, and the people are patient and methodical.

Miguel is sat in front of me, pouring his spirit between two *cuernito* cups made from the horns of a ram. He looks me in the eye while he does it. Then he looks at the spirit, observes its *perlas* (the pearl-like bubbles) for a moment, nods approvingly, and passes one of the horns to me. "Each distillate of the agave is treated differently," he says. "And the strength decides itself when the perlas close – we have learned this from our grandfathers." I hold the horn like a sacred idol, careful to ensure that Miguel sees me give it the respect it deserves. *The aroma is winey and fresh, with a sense of vitality. Curry leaf and pomegranate seed. The taste is resin-like and tropical, with a touch of mango and pineapple. Then agave starts to come through as the spirit goes down my throat, leaving a medicinal note of sasparilla. Unbelievable!*

"I don't know what it is," says Pancho, turning to us with wild eyes as he weaves the Jetta along the track and out of the taberna. "But the agave spirit from this part of Jalisco – it gives me a high!"

I hadn't noticed until now, but he is right, and Addie agrees too. What we are feeling is not the usual effects of alcohol consumption, but rather something warmer and slightly psychedelic. I must stress that I'm not suggesting that drugs are infused into these products or that they are in anyway harmful beyond that of any other alcoholic beverage. But something felt different – and it felt good!

With Manu Chao blasting out of the stereo and all the windows down, we fly down the highway and back north, towards Guadalajara. The evening sun is setting in as we break into a fresh bottle of Chacolo Cimarron.

The aroma is musky, with that joss-stick headiness of a hippy shop. Oily and bright on the palate, there's more toasted spice, incense, and some meatiness and muscularity. And yet it's still fresh. Utterly incredible.

Perhaps Pancho would have noticed the enormous pot hole and swerved to avoid it had we not been enjoying ourselves so much, but he didn't, and the car crashed into it, instantly blowing the front left tyre. We skidded to a halt on the edge of the highway, but not even a roadside tyre change on a dark highway could break our spirits. Maybe that had something to do with the bottle of Chacolo, which granted a level of cool and calm unknown to science. All the while, the music continued to play, the passing headlights conjuring up a dance floor on the tarmac.

CASA ENDEMICA

El Cartógrafo

We have been discussing the good, the bad and the ugly of Designated Origins (DOs) a lot over the past few chapters and comparing their cultural and historical relevance to their modern legal application. Before we embark on the next stage of our journey, where we will explore the mezcal tabernas and palenques of Michoacán and Oaxaca, Pancho suggests that we visit his friend Esteban Morales in Guadalajara to talk about this more.

Esteban began his career as a chef, but in 2010 turned his attention to agave spirits with a special focus on raicilla. He founded a company called La Venenosa with a mission to uncover and champion raicilla producers and bring their products out of rural villages and towns into the hands of tequila and mezcal aficionados. In fact, we have La Venenosa to thank for introducing the world to the spirits of Gerardo "Los Lobos" Peña and Alberto Hernandez from La Gorupa, as well as other respected raicilleros like Arturo Campos and Ruben Peña Fuentes.

La Venenosa now sits within a broader portfolio of spirits brands called Casa Endemica, which includes Derrumbes mezcals and La Higuera *sotol* (a spirit produced from the *Dasylirion* plant and chiefly made in Chihuahua, Durango and Coahuila), as well as other products that don't neatly slot into a particular category of DO.

As we arrive at Casa Endemica's Guadalajara office near the end of the day, most of the staff are on their way home. Esteban greets us on the pavement and walks us inside, closing up the shutters, locking the doors, and leading us past pallets stacked high with cases of raicilla and mezcal of many types. The office has an incredible bar area with a formidable collection of agave spirits that Esteban describes as "tools" to help him and his team plot a map of flavour and time and to understand why and how each region developed different spirits. The differences can then be compared to the DOs for each category, and some insight can be found concerning

where certain producing regions have slipped through the cracks. Then the question becomes "Why?" and the answer to that usually involves some form of economic or political influence.

We take seats at the bar and Esteban pours a series of raicillas and mezcals for us to taste. A six-metre-high (20-ft) stack of barrels is organised next to the bar, with the end caps on each one marked "Nodo". Esteban tells us that Nodo is a new brand that he has launched in partnership with the Bañuelos family who are based in the village of Huitzila, just five miles (8km) north of the Jalisco border, in the state of Zacatecas. "I love maps," he says, sliding our glasses across the bar and laying out a map of Jalisco.

When viewed from above, Jalisco is a sprawling blob of a state but it's shaped something like a distorted horseshoe, with a thick base and arms that reach north on both sides. Esteban points to Guadalajara, which is near the top of the base, in-between the two arms. He points to Tequila, around 50km (30 miles) west of Guadalajara, and then to the northern border with Zacatecas, which, if you travel east, drops down and forms the other side of the Jalisco horseshoe.

"The production of Nodo happens here," he says, pointing at the southernmost tip of Zacatecas. "The distillery is surrounded by Jalisco and only five minutes from the border – but you cannot make tequila here."

The border is defined, in part, by the mountains, rivers and canyons of the Sierra Occidental, but in practice, he says, the people who live in the southern part of Zacatecas are culturally identical to those who live a few miles over the border in Jalisco. In fact, there are families that own farmland both sides of the border and communities that function between the two states. They have been growing blue agaves in southern Zacatecas for decades, before the tequila DO or the CRT came into existence. When the tequila DO was established in the 1970s, the decision to not include any municipalities in Zacatecas probably benefited the main tequila producers, who may have seen Zacatecas as a threat, or saw the blue agave grown there as a commodity they wanted to keep for their own products.

"Zacatecas is very long," says Esteban. "So the north of the state is a completely different culture to the south. The Bañuelos family uses a mixture of underground ovens, autoclave and a *tahona*, along with alembic pots and blue agave grown only 50km (30 miles) from Tequila."

This means the family is able to make products that are indistinguishable from other modern tequilas, as well as products that are highly representative of historical tequila. More so, in fact, than any tequila producer is currently making (with the possible exception of Cascahuín – see page 28).

Zacatecas opted to join the mezcal DO when it was being established in the 1990s, but this plunged the Bañuelos family into an identity crisis, whereby they are making a product labelled as mezcal that tastes like tequila. Hence the name Nodo – "no DO".

"Then there is the blue agave itself," says Esteban, frowning. "Why?"

We can see from fieldwork conducted in the late 19th and early 20th centuries that many agave varieties were once used to make tequila. An 1887 study produced by Lazaro Perez referenced nine varieties including Chino, Azul (Blue), Vernejo, Siguin, Moraneño, Chato, Mano Largas, Opilote and Piedemula. Farming accounts well into the early 20th century document seven or eight varieties. Then, from 1949, only one. The Second World War brought about a change in philosophy, directed towards consistency, mass production, and standardised quality for the masses. Put simply, the blue agave produced the most amount of yield in the shortest space of time.

"The logic was correct," says Esteban. "But when applied to our industry you end up with... monoculture."

Esteban's maps lead us into a deeper conversation around the tequila DO, and its credibility as a protected area of production. As we have already established, the DO includes Jalisco and certain municipalities in Nayarit, Michoacán and Guanajuato. It is sometimes referred to as "Jalisco-plus", and in colonial times once constituted a large part of the region called Nueva Galicia, which also included Zacatecas. Some say this makes it a culturally unified area in spite of modern state borders. However,

cultures can and do cross borders, but the traditions and practices of different regions of the same state can vary just as wildly as the geography, and probably partly because of the geography.

"Jalisco is the best example of the Mexican identity," says Pancho. "It is a fusion of many indigenous cultures and the European. It's in the music, the food, the *charrería* (horsemanship) and it's in the agave spirits."

"I have a map for that too!" says Esteban.

This map is much smaller and more basic. It is a perfect circle, 500km (300 miles) across, with Guadalajara in the centre. The map was created by John Pint, who is a cave explorer based in Jalisco. Having spent a few decades travelling around the region, Pint began to question how there could be so much geological and botanical diversity so close to his home. After researching, he discovered that Mexico has five distinct ecosystems: arid scrublands, tropical evergreen forests, tropical deciduous forests, grasslands and temperate forests. These regions include the cactus-rich Sonoran desert, the rainforests of Quintana Roo, the thorn forests of Sinaloa, grasslands from Ciudad Juárez to Aguascalientes and the oaks and pines of the mountains.

Amazingly, all five of these distinct regions converge within a 250-km (150-mile) radius of Guadalajara, making it one of the most geographically diverse spots of land on the planet. Pint's map is now known as the "Magic Circle", and through coincidence alone, the same circle more or less covers the various states and municipalities in which tequila can be made (and yes, it does include the southern part of Zacatecas).

"When you have all this biological richness, the humans adapt differently," says Esteban. "This is where all the richness of cultures in the area comes from but also the endless number of agaves that have adapted to their environment too."

Esteban is obsessed with these maps, and how the geography and politics have resolved themselves into state lines and DOs that, to a varying extent, reflect the unique cultural diversity and traditions of the people who live here. It's this fascination that led him to partner with Sergio Mendoza from Don Fulano to make a mezcal brand called Derrumbes, which celebrates the cultural

OPPOSITE A rare photo of Addie Chinn and me, accompanied as usual by bottles of tequila, guns and animal heads.

and geographical diversity of Mexico by featuring mezcals from Oaxaca, San Luis Potosí, Durango, Tamaulipas, Zacatecas and Michoacán. The word "derrumbes" ("landslide") seems perfectly apt inspiration for the brand and its philosophy.

Inevitably our conversation moves towards the Filipino stills we have seen being used to make raicilla and other regional spirits in Jalisco. We talk about the transition from vinos de cocos to vinos de mezcals and how still designs took on regional variations as they spread into different states and through different communities.

Just as I am beginning to feel like I finally have a grasp on the evolutionary story of distillation in Mexico, Esteban drops a bombshell.

From behind the bar, he produces what appear to be two vases made from red terracotta clay. These, he explains, are replicas of pottery jars that were found in Colima burial sites in the 1930s. The person who was buried there was thought to be a high-ranking member of the ancient Capacha people who lived in the region between 3,000 and 4,000 years ago.

Both jars consist of a connected bulbous upper and lower section, with a spout section on top. One is the shape of a gourd and the other has three stirrups and looks like a clay model of a triffid.

In any other context it would be hard to imagine what these jars might have been used for outside of their obvious ornamental value – but they attracted the attention of the British biochemist Joseph Needham, who proposed in 1980 that Native Americans in the west-central highlands of Mexico might have been micro-distilling spirits as early as 1,500BCE. Needham suggested that these jars bore a striking resemblance to old stills found in Mongolia and asserted that "...if [these jars were] surmounted by a cooling bowl and provided with a little catch-cup inside, alcohol could certainly have been distilled in them."

To prove his hypothesis, Needham travelled around Mexico visiting indigenous communities and carefully illustrating their stills to see if he could draw a link between them and the ancient Capacha vessels. His illustrations of stills from San Luis Potosí and the Huichol people who live just north of Jalisco helped to establish the connection between imported Filipino stills and the equipment used in rural communities today. His illustrations also bore striking similarities to the Capacha gourd-shaped jars.

If Needham's hypothesis was correct, these jars would be the distillation equivalent of finding the Holy Grail and so completely rewrite our understanding of the state of technology in the ancient period of Mesoamerica. Indeed, they would serve as the earliest-known distillation technology on Earth, predating similar practices in China and the Middle East by more than 2,000 years, and the arrival of European and Middle Eastern stills in Mexico by 3,000 years.

"It's not proven," says Esteban with a smile. "But it's part of the discussion. Obviously, there are people who don't believe this is possible – they don't believe in the intelligence of indigenous people."

To test whether the jars could indeed be used to make spirits, a few years ago a crack team of artisans in Southern Jalisco conducted experiments using replicas of two Capacha vessels: a gourd type and a stirrup (or triffid) type. Both were crafted from Colima clay by expert potter Guillermo Rios, using traditional pre-Hispanic techniques.

Using a traditional outdoor kitchen and materials and utensils available only in ancient times, a micro-distillery was set up. A stone hearth fuelled by firewood provided heat, with local cook Margarita Rivera Nava maintaining temperatures of 165–175°F (74–79°C). Who else but Don Macario Partida from Chacolo supplied the agave ferment that was poured into the vessels.

For the stirrup-type vessel, a small receptacle was placed inside to collect distillate drops. In the gourd-type piece, another receptacle was suspended from fibre cords pressed into the upper hollow. Once water-filled bowls were installed, the entire system was sealed with corn dough to prevent steam from escaping. The distilling process continued for about two hours and was repeated five times.

The stirrup-type vessel yielded an average of 47ml of distillate at a strength of 32% ABV. The gourd-type vessel collected 72ml of distillate with 20% ABV. It was a paltry quantity of liquor but the question of whether the Capacha vessels could have been used as proto-stills had been answered.

A couple of problems remained, though.

Following the experiment, the jars were sent to a lab to test for chemical biomarkers from the agave distillation that could be compared to samples taken from the ancient jars. If a match was found it could support the theory that the excavated jars were used to boil agaves. The results came back inconclusive, showing none of the

expected markers and no evidence to suggest that other native natural products of the region (e.g., maize, hog plum, prickly pear, and so on) had been cooked in the ancient jars either.

More importantly, perhaps, was that the internal collection cup that is required to collect the distillate is a hypothesised item. In spite of further burial sites being excavated and more jars unearthed, archaeologists are yet to find a Capacha jar accompanied by a collection cup, and only one example of a potential condensing bowl has been discovered near a jar in a burial site. Without all three of the necessary Capacha-still components together (jar, bowl, cup), it might be a stretch to assume the jars were made for distillation.

Some archaeologists also reference the elaborate and decorative design of the jars and that they only pop up in burial sites of high-ranking individuals. These clues may suggest a more ceremonial or sacred purpose than the production of spirits.

"Shall we finish the conversation with a drink?" says Esteban. "I have a small bottle of lambanóg made from coconut tuba in clay pots in the south of Jalisco."

This spirit was produced by Arturo Campos and designed to imitate the style of late-16th century traditional liquor made in the Philippines by distilling coconut sap, or *tuba* as closely as possible. Thus it

provides a taste of perhaps the first spirits to be made on Mexican soil. Arturo was chosen both because of his ancestral equipment and because, in Pancho's words, "He definitely has some Filipino DNA!"

"We found a guy who extracts the coconut sap and sells tuba," says Esteban. "So we organised a full three days of extracting and then stored it and sent it to Arturo as fast as possible because it was very much alive and constantly changing."

The aroma is much flatter than with agave spirits, but still pungent, nutty and slightly citrus. The taste is far more one-dimensional, with some sweetness and a gentle acidity to the finish, but missing spice and texture.

"Now you understand why mezcal took over from lambanóg," says Esteban with a smile.

MICHOACÁN

Leaving Jalisco on the next stage of our journey, we cross into Michoacán and begin our tour of mezcal distilleries. This state neighbours Jalisco to the south and serves as a stepping stone towards the mezcal powerhouse that is Oaxaca – our final destination. Michoacán's mezcal tradition is not as well known as that of Oaxaca, but it is old, and here we will find producers making incredible spirits and who are fiercely intent on keeping it that way.

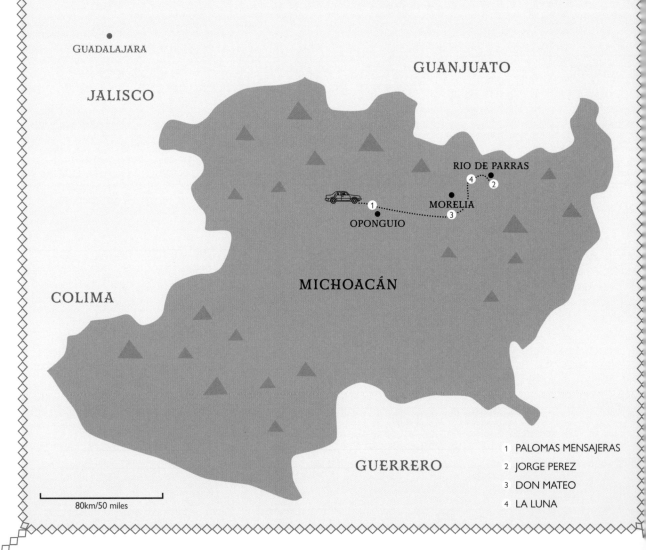

GUADALAJARA

GUANJUATO

JALISCO

RIO DE PARRAS

MORELIA

OPONGUIO

MICHOACÁN

COLIMA

GUERRERO

80km/50 miles

1 PALOMAS MENSAJERAS
2 JORGE PEREZ
3 DON MATEO
4 LA LUNA

PALOMAS MENSAJERAS

Los Hermanos

We spend most of the day driving. The towns blur past in a kaleidoscope of dust and noise, each one weirder than the last. Some of them have a peculiar eeriness about them, like the town of Santiago Azajo, where nobody is on the street, no music plays and doors are kept shut. Pancho tells us that it's home to almost entirely indigenous people, who are distrustful and superstitious of out-of-towners.

As the blue agaves once again dwindle in number, in the distance we see a trio of huge tornado-like dust devils tracking our vector. The metaphor isn't lost on us.

South of here is Tierra Caliente, a region of hot, arid land where Michoacán *charanda* rum is produced. Made from cane juice in the *agricole* fashion, its tradition goes back far enough to have earned it DO status in 2013. Spanish-speaking nations have a tendency towards producing lighter rums in the now well-established Cuban style, but charanda is a welcome exception. There were hundreds of charanda distilleries, but our love affair with avocados has wiped out most of the sugar-cane-growing land in favour of "green gold" orchards. Michoacán now produces almost half of the global supply of avocados.

Of the handful of charanda producers left, Charanda Uruapan stands out as the most renowned, holding the unique distinction of being the sole brand to breach US markets. It's imported by Texas-based Heavy Métl Imports, which have a small but perfectly formed roster of brands including Caballito Cerrero and Chacolo, plus our next stop on the banks of Lake Pátzcuaro, Palomas Mensajeras.

Palomas Mensajeras ("Messenger Pigeons") was founded by Don Miguel Perez Resendiz in 2007, its name taken from a line from "Que Lindo Es Michoacán", one of his favourite folk songs. The line itself translates as: "Messenger Doves, stop your flight if you're heading to paradise… you're already above it. Oh Michoacán!"

Don Miguel is a fourth-generation mezcalero, who moved to Oponguio on Lake Pátzcuaro in the 1990s. He worked at another *viñata* (the name given to mezcal distilleries in Michoacán) for ten years and I heard he was briefly jailed for producing without a permit before that. Don Miguel founded the Palomas Mensajeras brand in 2007. Most of the day-to-day running of the viñata is done by Miguel's sons, Miguel Jr. and Melltón. Melltón is the more jovial of the pair, cracking jokes and slapping backs; Miguel is a little more serious. They are both big guys and probably quite handy in a fight. The family live at the viñata, which appears to be an old garage or gas station, evident not only from a broad forecourt and large shutter doors but also from the dozen or so vehicles that, even now, are parked in every available space. If ever Palomas needed to find space to expand its operation from the current 3,500 litres (925 gallons) of mezcal it produces a year, all it would have to do is reverse a few vehicles out of the way.

This love affair with vehicles and combustion extends into the production of their spirits and even into the oily texture of the mezcal itself. A massively over-specified mill, built from a machine intended to turn corn into animal feed, is used to coarsely chop the cooked agaves. This noisy contraption is jerry-rigged to a diesel engine. The transmission and gear stick are taken from a 1978 Datsun and the mill speed is controlled by switching gears.

Adjacent to the mill, next to a pickup truck and a battered old VW, are two deep pit ovens, more cylindrical than the shallow pits that are common in Oaxaca. These were designed to combat the soft clay soil on the banks of the lake, but had the unintended effect of retaining heat better and requiring less fuel to operate. One of these pits has a capacity of five tonnes and the other is ten tonnes. White oak is used to fuel the fire, then rocks are thrown on top, next the agaves, then a layer of tule palm fibre, followed by a layer of sand. A cook takes three days.

In Michoacán, the preferred agave for producing mezcal is *Agave cupreata* Trel. Known locally as maguey chino (curly hair), *cupreata* takes around 15 years to mature and produces no *hijuelos*. This means that the plants must be grown from seed, which is more time consuming and costly. *Cupreata* is native to the states of Michoacán and Guerrero and was first identified by US botanist William Trelease, who differentiated around 20% of all known agave species, including *rhodacantha,* which the Palomas also use in some recipes.

Don Miguel brought back *rhodacantha* (maguey Mexicano) seeds from a trip to Oaxaca a few decades ago and then harvested additional seeds from those plants once they reached maturity. They now have a sustainable supply of *rhodacantha* growing on their land in spite of its non-native status in Michoacán. Another species they use is the slow-growing *inaequidens,* which we have seen at Los Tres Hombres. The local variety name for this agave is Alto and there's a love/hate relationship with it because it takes at least 15 years to reach maturity, at which point the *piña* may weigh 500kg (1,100lbs) but produces only a mere 6–8 litres (1.5–2 gallons) of mezcal – that's about 10% the yield of a blue agave. In fact, it is one of the worst-performing agaves commonly used to make mezcal – but it tastes great! The Perezes are also experimenting with *tequilana* agaves (though this part of Michoacán is not in the tequila DO) as well as *salmiana*.

Miguel pours glasses of Palomas' Ensemble, a blend of their three main varieties: Chino, Alto and Mexicana at 47% ABV. This is a "hot blend" he tells us, meaning that the three varieties were cooked, fermented and distilled together, rather than in a "cold blend" where each variety is produced separately and blended together afterwards. This sample was produced in 2011 and has had more than a decade in glass demijohn to mature.

"It's velvety," says Pancho with a grin. *The aroma has a very light smokiness, but otherwise it feels green like (bell) pepper and plump. There's prune and date on the palate, sumac, tamarind and dried tomato. It's sticky yet dry – like velvet! And it has a very North African style to it. The finish is raisins with a lick of honey.*

After milling, the juice and fibre is transferred to stainless-steel fermenters. We peer inside these vats, with their mass of fibrous chunks like bits of hairy animal hide. There is a low-level fizzing noise emanating from the vats, though the sound may just be coming the great number of flies. The agave is dry and crusty-looking and smells like decaying vegetal matter. "These have had three days," says Miguel. "They are becoming thirsty for water."

After the initial fermentation has started naturally the fibres expand as the volume of CO_2 increases. Like an increasingly self-aware vat of sludge, this mass of material threatens to overflow the tank and walk out of the door if Miguel doesn't intercept. He tops the tanks up with water, which flushes out the sugars, releases the gas and pushes the fermentation into its later stages.

He decides that these tanks need water right this moment and disappears. The next thing we know he's opened up the huge roller shutter and is reversing a water truck into the building. He then unravels a long hose and we spend the next 30 minutes pumping gallons of water into the tanks, in a process that produces plenty of froth as Miguel stirs the liquor, like a gondolier with a paddle.

We get into a pattern of me topping up the water and Miguel doing the stirring. Pancho passes around glasses of 100% chino (*Agave cupreata*) for us to taste as it corresponds with the agaves that are fermenting. *The aroma is herbal and green, with roasted courgette, mint and jalapeño. The taste has notes of green olive oil, bright and slippery. It lingers around for a while – delicious!*

There are three stills here, each of them 200 litres (50 gallons) in capacity and based on the Filipino blueprint. This means they are made from wood with a metal cooling dish on top, but unlike the hollow trunk designs, we have seen before, they are constructed in a conical barrel shape, using staves and steel bands. Known as Tarascan stills, they take their name from the Tarascan Empire, which thrived in the Lake Pátzcuaro basin before Spanish colonisation in the 1500s. We'll revisit this still design in more detail later.

Down some steps behind the stills, Miguel shows us the wood-fired ovens that heat the stills, and adjacent to this is a cellar stacked with glass demijohns of maturing mezcal. It's a cramped space with only the dimmest of light but we spend time here tasting five or six different mezcals, including some 100% blue agave. One of them, distilled in 2015, *has an aroma of light smoke and gentle maritime notes. The taste is sweet and heady, with a slight anise flavour – dry and resonant. It's nutty and slightly vegetal.*

Miguel pops the lid off a plastic barrel about the size of a whisky cask and invites us to stick our noses in and smell. I didn't need to get close to know that the barrel contained cannabis and – judging by the potency of the smell – probably more cannabis that I have ever seen in my life. "Four kilograms," says Miguel, "into 80 litres of mezcal."

Dark red in colour, it reeks of marijuana. Pancho pours some large measures and we begin sipping. *It's all weed to begin with, followed by rosemary and sage, but with that intoxicating funk. The finish brings in more vegetal agave notes and a little sweetness.*

Cannabis was legalised for cultivation and recreational use in Mexico in 2023, so there's nothing illegal going on here. Even prior to legalisation, Michoacán was one of the biggest growing states. Now that the practice of growing is legal, an entire kilogram costs just 500 pesos (£20/$25).

Some time passes, and more mezcal is consumed. Miguel is still doing various tasks: checking water, moving collection vessels, organising wood. The sun begins to set and the lake is holding a haze in the air that matches the one inside my head. The plastic chair I'm sat on is backed up against the wheel of a utility vehicle and there are open bottles of mezcal littering the table in front of us.

Miguel's wife appears at the perfect moment with an evening snack of fried wheat tortillas coated in sugar with sugar-cane syrup splurged over the top. They are like giant Crunchy Nut corn flakes, thick and hot, and about as dense a form of calories that mankind could conceive. They take the edge off the booze and cannabis but only enough to throw myself into Pancho's car and head to wherever it is we're sleeping tonight.

I wake up, my head pounding, mouth dry as sandpaper. The room has a balcony and I stumble over to it like a newborn lamb, squinting against the harsh morning light. The world slowly comes into focus with an uninterrupted view of Lake Pátzcuaro, its waters a rich, muddy brown – like old sepia photographs of Mexico come to life. The murky expanse shimmers under the rising sun, its surface broken only by gentle ripples.

In the distance are dark silhouettes of men standing on small boats – the butterfly fishermen of Lake Pátzcuaro. Their movements are slow, deliberate, almost hypnotic as they raise their enormous nets high before swooping them down into the brown waters. The scene is dreamlike, caught between the haze of my hangover and the surreal beauty of this ancient practice. I blink, wondering if I'm still asleep. I am trudely brought back to reality when I realise that wherever it is I've slept last night has no running water or electricity.

Miguel arrives and offers to take us for breakfast and then on to the fields to see some agave being harvested. Pancho seems to think that the fields are sort of en route to our next stop, Morelia – the state capital – so the plan is for us to follow Miguel in Pancho's Jetta, see the fields with him then leave him to head home as we go on.

ABOVE If I had to summarise Palomas Mensajeras in one statement, it would be: family, trucks and utterly delicious agave spirits.

That was the plan, but the reality – and from the perspective of anyone in the area – it was like a high-speed car chase.

For reasons that remain unknown to me, Miguel drove like a maniac that morning. As we hit speeds of up to 100mph (160km/h), his overtaking etiquette ramps up from aggressively dangerous to plain suicidal. Pancho, with no other choice but to follow suit, also becomes a racing-car driver. The music is muted, all conversation stops, save from the occasional, "Fucking hell, Miguel." From Pancho.

After 20 minutes of this I decide to temper my nerves and hangover with a healthy slug of mezcal. If I'm going down this morning, it might as well be with something tasty on my lips. Addie passes me a bottle of Palomas' 100% Mexicano (*rhodacantha*) at 48% ABV. *It smells of pine resin,*

LEFT Cooked agave piñas on a table on the distillery forecourt give passers by the chance to try before they buy.

pine needles and forest floors. There's a touch of dank compost and a little smoke. It smells like fear! The taste is oily with a hint of citrus, juniper and geranium. The finish smacks with spice and a gentle, vegetal hum.

Finally, with the euphoric afterglow of a rollercoaster ride ended, we park up in the town of Villa Madero. Here, we get a quick breakfast of *aporreadillo*, a classic Michoacán breakfast of ground pork cooked in a mole sauce with scrambled eggs, hot sauce and tortillas. After the near-death experience of the morning's drive, it is the most delicious thing I have ever tasted.

We load into Miguel's vehicle for the final stretch of the journey: a bizarrely slow drive into Etúcuaro, the mezcal capital of Michoacán. This modestly sized town has at least 60 viñatas of various sizes operating within its orbit. In fact, the vast majority of Michoacán's 160,000 litres (40,000 gallons) of annual mezcal production comes from this place. The quality of mezcal produced here sadly reflects this. Pancho and Miguel warn us that much is made in a commercially driven fashion with little regard for taste.

The town is plastered with advertisements and signage for numerous viñatas and the streets are dotted with hardware stores selling agricultural hardware, machetes and

trinchera (the local name for a *coa*-style blade) and various other tools to dismember and transport agaves. Miguel stops briefly so that we can grab some cold beers along with purple potato and pumpkin-flavoured ice creams from his cousin's shop, and then we head over to the fields.

We descend into a long valley and park up where we are greeted by the smiling face of his brother, Meli, waiting by a pickup truck half-filled with *piñas*. It's only 11am and he has had a busy morning. We all crack open a beer and take a walk on to the hot and dusty slopes. A couple of minutes later we stop near a large chino agave, where Meli downs the rest of his beer and begins to murderously sharpen his trinchera with a stone. Then, he attacks the plant.

After all these weeks of appreciating the flavours of the agave, observing them at every stage of maturity and watching them create life with their flowers – of identifying their many varieties, their texture and colour, the elegance of their leaves, their serrated edges and thorny end – and seeing them growing by the sides of the road, walking among them in the in hills, and dreaming of agaves most nights, I find myself here, on this rocky slope, watching a man hack *pencas* off this old plant. It feels like witnessing the slaughter of a defenceless old woman.

I've heard that in some parts of Jalisco, *jimadores* whisper blessings to the agave before harvesting. They believe this practice ensures a smooth fermentation process and a superior final product. This likely originated from indigenous beliefs about the sacred nature of agave and the importance of respecting plant spirits. I whisper my own blessing to the plant that Meli is chopping away at, even as it is disembodied and stripped of its dignity. It's brutal. For a brief moment, I consider abstaining from consuming agave products but then remind myself that tequila and mezcal fall under that category and that's crazy talk. Perhaps it is the magic of the flavours that this plant is capable of producing, though I have never viewed grapes and wine in the same way. Whatever it is, I'm slipping into a state of spiritual bond with these plants. Each one has its own physical quirks and its own unique history. Ultimately, I am left with a feeling of respect and gratitude, that the life of this plant has ended but that its essence will be preserved for us to enjoy, and that the work of the mezcalero should always be undertaken with care and consideration.

PALOMAS MENSAJERAS

JORGE PEREZ

El Rey

I'm not the first person to be intoxicated by the spiritual pull of the agave. For the Aztecs, agaves were powerfully tied to their religion. Like the River Nile to the ancient Egyptians, bison to the Native Americans, and the Sun to the Incas, agaves claimed special status in a religious context. The sharp tips of pencas were used for bloodletting rituals, where Aztecs would pierce their skin as an offering to the gods; agave fibres were used to make brushes for ritual purification and clothing for religious ceremony, and the sap was used for religious healing. Most significantly, the agave was itself deified in the form of the goddess Mayahuel.

In Aztec tradition, Mayahuel was known for her fertility and as the ruler of the agave. She was a benign goddess, who brought love to mankind and lifted spirits with her presence, embodying the products derived from maguey, such as mezcal (cooked agave in this context) and pulque.

The story goes that Mayahuel lived in the sky, hidden by her wicked grandmother Tzitzímitl, a monstrous star demon. One day, the honourable Quetzalcoatl, a green-feathered serpent, encountered Mayahuel and instantly fell in love. They fled together to Mesoamerica, but when Tzitzímitl discovered her granddaughter's absence, she unleashed her wrath. To hide, Quetzalcoatl and Mayahuel transformed into a tree, but Tzitzímitl recognised them, split the tree, and tore Mayahuel apart. Quetzalcoatl, grieving deeply, buried her remains, from which the first agave plant grew. This plant, believed to contain Mayahuel's blood, introduced pulque and mezcal, bringing prosperity to the land.

In another version, Mayahuel, trapped by her grandmother, sang sad but seductive songs. Her voice attracted Ehecatl, the wind god, who whisked her away in a passionate whirlwind. They transformed into an agave plant to hide from Tzitzímitl, who eventually found and split the plant. Ehecatl managed to save a small spire,

planting it near a volcano. His tears, blessed by the rain god Tlaloc, nurtured the spire, leading to Mayahuel's rebirth as the maguey plant. When lightning split the plant, it released mezcal to bring joy to the Aztec people.

Mayahuel was also said to be married to Patecatl, the "lord of the root of pulque" and god of healing. Together, they had 400 *coñejo* (rabbit) children, the Centzon Totochtin, or "gods of drunkenness". Each rabbit god represented the many personalities people could exhibit when intoxicated. Mayahuel, known as "the woman of the 400 breasts", fed her children pulque, which made her a symbol of abundance too.

The 400 Coñejos mezcal brand is named after this ancient mythology, and thanks to the marketing clout of its owner, Jose Cuervo, it saw more growth than any other mezcal brand between 2022 and 2023 and is now the best-selling mezcal in Mexico and fourth across the world. Jose Cuervo also owns another mezcal brand, called Creyente, but sadly (and predictably), both products are one-dimensional, and therefore best avoided.

But the same cannot be said for the products made at the next distillery we visit.

Viñata Salto Bonito is run by Jorge Perez and his family. It has become a beacon of ancestral mezcal production in Michoacán and has established a strong international reputation, for which it is bottled under Mezonte and Siembra brands.

The only problem is how you find the place.

We have been driving back and forth through the small town of Rio de Parras for some time, searching for any sign of the distillery. Google Maps has sent us off in the wrong direction, and every person we stop and ask tells us "It's just down the road there – you can't miss it."

Finally, Pancho pulls up outside a small bungalow with a large gate next to it. He gets out and knocks on the front door and we wait for a minute. Nothing happens. Then a curtain on the window twitches and the face of a lady in her late 60s appears. It's clearly the wrong place.

Pancho says hello and they have a conversation in Spanish. The head disappears from the window and Pancho gets in the car. Then, the gate opens and we drive through, into a yard, around the corner, and under a washing line. The space opens out to reveal a full working distillery.

The lady, who is wearing a vibrant pink dress, introduces herself as Josephine Perez. She is Jorge's wife and mother to Miguel Perez, who takes care of the brand's marketing. Neither Jorge nor Miguel are around at the moment, so Josephine leads us into the distillery, where she beings showing us the fermentation pits and the Filipino stills. She takes us down some steps and loads logs on the fire under the stills as if she were vacuuming the living room.

There are two boys working here: Miguel, her 14-year-old grandson, and his friend Sergio. They are working at the distillery during the school holidays.

"We are not here for the money," says Miguel. "We are here to learn." Miguel will one day be the sixth-generation mezcalero of the Perez family. "They go to school also," says Josephine. "But it's important they don't neglect the tradition of making mezcal."

The boys show us the ten-tonne pit oven where the agaves are cooked. These days the use of plastic sheets to cover the cooking agave hearts is disappointingly ubiquitous but it is a practical means of protecting the agaves. Here, though, the Perezes go down the traditional route of loading branches of pine trees over the top and then smothering them in dirt. The last cook was more than a week ago so the agaves are all fermenting or distilling now. Prior to that they were mashed by hand with a *mazo* (wooden hammer) in a *hielgo* (the term used for a canoe here). Fermentation takes around 12 days and is done in a combination of concrete pits and steel; distillation is in Tarascan pot stills. Many components of the distillery have been ingeniously thought out. Cables, weights and levers abound, each with its own purpose to balance some load or to lock something in position. Every piece of wood, rope and rock has a function no matter how primitive it appears.

The boys have been working since 4am, loading the fermented agave into the stills using buckets, tending to the wood fire under the stills, and then sealing the stills shut for distillation. Miguel complains that the agave they are distilling (a wild variety) has low strength because of its low sugar content. He tastes the *ordinario* as it runs off the

ABOVE The small town of Rio de Parras conceals a rich culture of mezcal production in Michoacán.

still and spits it on the ground, then returns to playing dominoes with his friend.

In the past, it wasn't uncommon for mezcaleros to work for three straight days to process their fermented agave into spirit. It was part of the tradition and considered "bad" for the mezcal if they stopped.

While we were talking to the boys, Josephine had disappeared but is now back and armed with a tray loaded with mezcal for us to drink.

We begin with an ensemble of Chino, Alto and Pulquero, the latter an agave from Oaxaca that was previously classified by the CRM (the mezcal regulatory authority) as *Agave salmiana* but is now believed to be a variety of *Agave atrovirens*. *The aroma has very fresh blue agave notes, with some citrus and salt alongside greener characteristics. It's incredibly fresh and fragrant. The finish becomes more perfumed with orris root, violet and rose.*

"The Pulquero doesn't have much sugar," says Josephine, "but it produces a lot of flavour."

The next one is an Organic expression made from 100% Alto agave that rested in the field for four years after the *quiote* was *capón* (castrated).

"Mmm..." says Pancho. "Wow! It's like strawberries, raspberries and plums."

The aroma is very fruity indeed, cherry and forest fruits. There's blackcurrant too. Then, on the taste, cherry stones, big and round, some oiliness, more fruit, roasted courgette (zucchini), and a very long finish. Outstanding!

At that moment, Jorge Perez walks in. Like his wife, he is dressed immaculately, with polished shoes, a button-down shirt and a broad sombrero. He's a tall, mild-mannered man with keen eyes. We introduce ourselves and compliment him on his mezcal, assuming that because of his smart attire, this is his day off. To our surprise, he gets straight to work tasting spirits, manoeuvring equipment and carrying around buckets.

Josephine disappears to get more mezcal and the boys stoke the fire and relax into a game of dominoes.

"She has a cave somewhere," I say.

"Yes, with a candle," says Pancho.

"Here she comes," says Addie as the old lady totters towards us with another tray full of drinks.

"Snake, coyote and rabbit," she announces proudly.

Don Jorge's mezcals are incredible, but the Perez family have become particularly well known for their *pechuga* mezcals. The word *pechuga* translates to "poultry breast" (as in a fillet of chicken) and it comes from the practice of placing or suspending animal meat in the still, which is then either cooked by the rising vapour or boiled in the base; it lends an unctuous texture and a very mildly meaty flavour to the mezcal. Chicken and turkey breasts are the most common, but pechuga mezcals are now being produced with practically any meat or botanical ingredient

you can imagine, from local berries and herbs to slabs of goat and snakes. You can think of it as a bit like the flavouring of gin, where the spirit is redistilled with flavourful ingredients. The difference is that with pechuga there are basically no rules and anything goes.

The coyote pechuga that Jorge makes is distilled with the gutted carcass of a coyote.

"We remove the hair and wash the meat," says Jorge. "Then everything goes in there: the liver, the heart, the head, the eyes."

I am not squeamish when it comes to these things, but the prospect of drinking a dog-infused mezcal gin doesn't exactly get my mouth salivating. Addie, as a vegetarian, steadfastly refuses his glass. *There is a distinct animal fat note to the aroma with sage and subtle citrus. More floral aromas continue. The taste is big and bold: it's nutty, with walnut, hazelnut, then a dank forest-floor spice. The finish is peanut shell and cherry. It's very tasty!*

The origins of pechuga are steeped in intrigue and misinformation. At first glance you might think of pechuga-making as an archaic practice, perhaps as a means to infuse some medicinal or spiritual properties into the mezcal or for killing two birds (if you'll excuse the pun) at a time and cooking one's dinner while working the still. Or simply, because it tasted good. But there has never been much evidence to support any of these theories, which has led some cynics (and one brand ambassador I met during our trip) to conclude that the practice of pechuga-ing a mezcal is at best a recent marketing innovation brought about by the Del Maguey brand, which began importing pechuga mezcals into the US back in 2000, and at worst a rewriting of Mexican history that has no grounding in fact.

Well it's time to debunk that.

After some extensive research, the earliest written reference to pechuga I can find dates back 150 years to 1863, in D. Manuel Payno's article titled "Memoir on the Mexican Maguey and Its Various Products" published in *Boletín de la Sociedad Mexicana de Geografía y Estadística*.

The text references a spirit known as *vino de pechuga*, a predecessor to what we now recognise as pechuga mezcal made by incorporating chicken and various undisclosed ingredients into the distillation process. Interestingly, the passage highlights that this early version of pechuga was not for everyday consumption but primarily as a gift or for celebratory events. This suggests that even in its early days, pechuga was viewed as a premium or ceremonial spirit, set apart from more common varieties of mezcal.

Another early reference from 1872 in *Gacete Médica de Mexico* provides some further insight into how and where pechuga was made: "The mezcal from the States of San Luis and Zacatecas, even the one called pechuga, is less rich in alcohol, but richer in aromatic principles of the maguey, and abounds in the imperfect distillation which occurs in the deformed stills used in these localities."

Later advertisements from the 1870s give the first indication that pechuga was commercially available, particularly in the Tequila region but also in other Mexican states, including Zacatecas, San Luis Potosí, Guanajuato, and Querétaro. Judging by the adverts, pechuga was generally twice as expensive as regular mezcal, possibly because of its perceived higher quality or rarity.

The production methods varied, with some sources suggesting that pechuga was made by distilling mezcal with chicken or veal legs. Additionally, fruit peels were sometimes added to enhance the aroma. One reference calls for the use of a "fat hen" to supply the necessary breast, and that it should be macerated in the mezcal for 15–20 days before the product is distilled. Variations

included "Pechuga Almendrado" (with almonds) and "Pechuga Naranjado" (orange-flavoured). Interestingly, Pechuga Almendrado was often marketed as being especially suitable for women because of its smoothness.

Pechuga was sometimes marketed as "legitimate", suggesting the presence of imitations and a counterfeit industry. In some circles, it was referred to as "*mezcal de sustancia*" (mezcal of substance), highlighting its perceived superiority. Pechuga was attributed various medicinal properties, being recommended for ailments ranging from chronic diarrhoea to women's health issues. These perceived health benefits likely contributed to its popularity and premium pricing. By 1881, it was being exported to the US, marking its entry into the international market. It gained recognition in international competitions, including an award at the 1878 Paris Universal Exposition.

The popularity of pechuga, particularly Pechuga Almendrado, continued well into the 20th century. By the 1930s, it was being advertised regularly in Mexican publications, suggesting its enduring appeal to consumers. This rich history demonstrates pechuga's status as a premium mezcal variant, with its production methods, varieties, and cultural significance evolving over time, incorporating an astounding array of ingredients and cementing mezcal as the most diverse category of spirit the world over. A survey of the pechuga mezcals on the market today throws up dozens of animal products, from goat organs to rattlesnake tails, each conveying unique characteristics to the product.

Next Josephine pours us a pechuga made with *tlacuache*, a type of possum that is native to Mexico. In Mexican folklore it is believed that the tlacuache has the ability to clean the blood. It derives its name from the Nahuatl language, meaning "the little one that eats fire". The story goes that the tlacuache risked certain death by retrieving fire from the underworld for the benefit of humankind. The brave fellow that was used to flavour this mezcal certainly took one for the team.

The aroma is very smoky, with barbecue flavours and a big, wild character. It smells rough, like animal pelt and leather. The taste is also smoky, with notes of bacon and hot leather, leading into a waxy finish with moss and flint.

There are vegetarian pechugas too (much to Addie's relief), which incorporate a broad spectrum of wild fruits, roots, barks, herbs, grains and flowers. Many of these can be found only in Mexico – capulín cherries, uvalama berries, cactus fruit and Mexican tarragon among them. Common spices and grains also play a role – more than 30 non-agave plant species present such as the Lima pechuga that Josephine is pouring us now. *The aroma is permanent marker, oily and resolute. The taste is very intense. It's oily and bitter with some green fruit and lime rind. Hot and spicy.*

Next is an orange pechuga, which Pancho says Jorge Perez is very famous for. *It smells of burnt orange peel and the citric buzz of a cosmopolitan cocktail. It's slightly soapy on the palate with a weird perfumed note – orange blossom, perhaps. The taste has a fuzzy orange-peel character, then a long, margarita and triple-sec finish.*

Many of these ingredients have roots in ancient Mesoamerican cuisine, with some used to flavour *pulque*, an agave-based fermented beverage, for thousands of years. Some have a tradition in alternative medicine, though these days the medicinal virtues of pechuga are not commonly touted.

Next, we try a mezcal that has been distilled with chocolate – literally bars of chocolate. *The aroma takes on a dark, coffee roast character, but it's also green and smoked. The taste is like pain au chocolate and the finish drifts into cigarette and roasted nuts.*

Some producers have even gone down the route of distilling agave hearts as a botanical. Over at Chacolo they periodically release a "Triple Destilado" product that is distilled a third time before being rested in glass for four years. The tale goes that during one production run, some cooked agave inadvertently fell into a batch of double-distilled mezcal, altering its colour. Rather than discard the batch, the Partidas decided to redistil it in an attempt to clarify the liquid. To their surprise and delight, they found the resulting triple-distilled spirit to be exceptional, leading to the birth of this unique mezcal style.

Another part of the agave that is occasionally distilled is the roasted quiote, which contains quite a lot of sugar. In agave-growing regions it is often sold on the street as it can be used to make cakes and desserts, or sliced up and eaten like candy. The distillation of this part of the plant is uncommon, though, except in Michoacán.

Jorge tells us that the quiotes are cooked alongside the agave piña, but after the cook they are picked out and mashed up separately. This is because the fermentation is notably colder than regular agave fermentation with seemingly different yeast cultures going to work. The two ferments are then mixed together and distilled to make quiote mezcal.

ABOVE Jorge Perez has cleverly designed his taberna to be time-saving while adhering to tradition.

Careful to clarify that we are now drinking quiote mezcal and not coyote mezcal, Addie and I take in the aroma of the spirit... *It's super buttery, with freshly baked croissant or buttered brioche. The taste is much greener and more vegetal, moving into a mineral character as it develops. The finish is steely and tight.*

As the afternoon progresses, the work at the distillery continues around us. Don Jorge complains that the *hielgo* (milling canoe) is taking its toll and likely to be switched for a mechanical mill in the near future. Pancho tells him about a taberna he visited where the mezcalero had attached a bicycle to a machine that pummelled agaves like pistons in an engine. Jorge laughs at this.

Soon Jorge is up out of his chair and helping his grandson Miguel, winching up the trunk of the Tarascan still to reveal the hot metal pot below. Miguel hands him buckets of fermented *mosto* and he loads them into the still. Here, family is everything.

DON MATEO

El Conservacionista

Armed police are a regular feature in Michoacán. Many of them are federal officers, sent to supplement or oversee local law enforcement, especially in areas where local police are considered compromised – which is to say, everywhere. Cartel activity is rife in these parts, and there have been numerous instances of local and state police in Michoacán being infiltrated by or collaborating with drug cartels. "*Plata o promo*" (silver or lead) goes the saying, offering either bribes or death. Earlier today we were behind a souped-up cartel truck with a skull painted on the back and two dangerous-looking guys stood high up top, presumably with automatic weapons just out of sight. Tourists don't get troubled too much by the cartels, but Pancho has already expressed how fortunate we have been up until this point to have avoided a stop-and-search by the police, which can go on for hours if you don't pay your way.

So it feels like we're tempting fate when we slow down to ask moody-looking officers for directions to Viñata Don Mateo. On this occasion the police are neither helpful nor a hinderance, but shortly thereafter we find the road that takes us into the forested hills and en route to what is arguably Michoacán's most famous distillery.

As for exactly where we are, I can only say that it's about 45 minutes south of Morelia, the state capital, and the place where we stayed last night. The mountains rise with lush pine forests lending an almost alpine feel to the landscape.

When the mezcal DO was established in 1994, only the states of Oaxaca, Guerrero, Durango, San Luis Potosí and Zacatecas were permitted to bottle mezcal. Michoacán was incorporated in 2012 and Don Mateo de la Sierra became the first brand in the state to be officially recognised and the first to be exported to the US. Guanajuato was the next state to join the DO in 2015, Tamaulipas and Puebla followed in 2018 and most recently the tiny states of Aguascalientes, Estado de Mexico (Mexico City) and Morelos were brought in. That makes 12 states at the time

of writing, though more will undoubtedly join in the future, further increasing the size of what is already by far the biggest DO of any kind in the world.

There is of course some justification for adding new states. Mezcal production had no state borders in the past and occurred all over Mexico. But as long as Jalisco is excluded from the DO, the legitimacy of the designation will always remain in question, and ongoing changes to the current DO only serve to highlight its absence. The politicking in tequila's halls of power is unlikely to let Jalisco join any time soon.

There are now thousands of registered mezcal producers in Mexico and probably tens of thousands of unregistered producers are hiding in the hills, operating out of garages, or bottling their mezcal under another name. Indeed, if we were to give equal footing to the viñatas of Michoacán and palenques of Oaxaca as we have to the tequila distilleries of Jalisco purely on a percentage basis, you would be holding a cube-shaped book in your hands right now!

Michoacán is the third-biggest mezcal producer after Oaxaca and Puebla, but accounts for just 1.5% of the total. This share has been growing, though, and as the category is expanding at something like 15% a year (save for a blip in 2022–2023), Michoacán is riding a wave of opportunity and doing it in style. There are now around 700 viñatas across the state, so you'd be forgiven for assuming it's easy to track down one of its most famous names.

Finally, we see a signpost to Viñata Don Mateo, which takes us off the mountain road and on to a gravel track, descending the hillside with some sketchy turns that send the suspension of the Jetta crashing against chassis. Just as it feels like there's nowhere left for the track to go, we arrive.

We park outside the main gate next to a sad-looking old dog on a chain. What with the gate, green forest, growling animal and huge mound of dirt with smoke emanating from it, I'm getting a *Jurassic Park* feeling.

This viñata is not old but the Vieyra family who own it have been producing mezcal in various locations since the mid-19th century. It's now run by sixth-generation Vierya, Emilio, with the help of his mother Doña Delia and his 23-year-old son, José Manuel. Emilio is away, so José Manuel is looking after us today. He's wearing a t-shirt depicting the moustachioed face of Don Mateo Vieyra and I briefly wonder how many people walk around with a picture of their great-great-great-grandfather on their chest.

It's now lunchtime and José Manuel tells us that he and his grandmother have been awake all night getting the fire ready and loading the ten tonnes of agaves, then covering it with *petate* (woven palm fibres) before topping it with plastic, dirt, and some heavy bits of timber to press it down.

As we circle around the great mound of smoky dirt, he tells us some of his recent family history including the passing of his grandfather, Emilio Sr., in 2018, who is still very much here in spirit if not in body. Born in Michoacán, Emilio Sr. worked in California and Texas for a decade in agriculture and wine production. He came back home to marry Doña Delia, but they soon moved back to Texas. Emilio Jr. was born in Houston and lived there for two years before his family permanently returned to Michoacán. This means that Emilio Jr. holds both US and Mexican citizenship, a fact that sometimes leads the workers at the viñata to jokingly call him "gringo".

Doña Delia has taken on the role of matriarch of the operation and is something of a mezcal celebrity, as a *cocinera tradicional* (traditional chef) and in her role in preparing the pechuga mezcal recipes at the viñata. Here the pechuga is made from Cenizo or Cupreata agaves and includes ingredients like iguana, deer or turkey, and a secret

blend of herbs and spices, including lemongrass, mint and cinnamon, grown in a small garden adjacent to the kitchen. This pechuga mezcal is reportedly the top-selling product for the family in the US market, showcasing the combined skills of Emilio and his mother in creating high-quality, traditional mezcal. José Manuel pours us some to try, bottled at 45% ABV. *The aroma is very fruity and slightly smoked, with green agave notes and some baking spice probably from the cinnamon. The taste has a balanced sweetness – dry and herbal, then leaving a savoury oiliness through the finish.*

Doña Delia invites us over to see the kitchen and garden, where she points to various herbs, fruits and flowers, explaining their symbiosis with one another and how they detract pests and encourage growth. She explains that there are no less than five different organisations in Michoacán aimed at promoting the role of women in mezcal production. Some of them support the wives, mothers and daughters of mezcal maestros, while others promote the women who actively work in production.

"I am the president of one of them – Mujeres Mezcaleras y Magalleras de Michoacán," she says.

This organisation comprises 25 women, four of whom are *maestras de mezcal*. Many of them have studied marketing, distilling or sales and work as ambassadors and administrators. Indeed, some own their own viñatas.

Over at the kitchen, Delia pours us a sample of their Manso Sahuayo (48% ABV) expression made from a currently unclassified agave species that is indigenous to the

Sahuayo region of Michoacán, not far from the Jalisco border. *The aroma begins quite flat and soft, but soon opens up to be fungal – like good compost. There's a touch of leather too. It's incredibly dry on the palate, like electricity with no hint of sweetness. This shifts to sizzling spice and a long, very dry finish.*

While Doña Delia prepares some *corundas* (triangular tamales) with *salsa de jocoque* (a mint and yoghurt dip) and *gorditas* (stuffed corn cakes), José Manuel takes us through the rest of the distillery step by step. The cooking process continues for 6–7 days, with the mound slowly reducing in size as the agaves soften and are crushed under their own weight. After cooking, the agave is milled by machine and then fermentation takes place in four large 3,000-litre (800-gallon) square wooden fermenters, lasting for 6–8 days. Such is the influence of *charanda* rum in Michoacán, the viñata is also producing rum, using local sugar cane in a separate 1,000-litre (265-gallon) wooden fermenter.

As with the last viñata we visted, the stills here are a Tarascan design – a truncated cone shape with steel bands holding the staves together. Like Filipino stills, a pan sits on top of the still containing cool water for condensation and a paddle directs the flow of distillate off the side of the still.

The Tarascans were one of the few Mesoamerican civilisations that successfully resisted Aztec domination. Their civilisation was renowned for its sophistication in architecture, craftsmanship and metallurgy, and its isolation in the elevated volcanic landscapes of western Mexico allowed it to develop unique characteristics that set it apart from other Mesoamerican societies. This seems to have extended into the unique stave-built stills that have survived in Michoacán.

José Manuel leads us to a brick staircase that descends down to a *cava* (cellar). He produces a set of keys to unlock a sturdy wooden door, above which there is a hammered copper plaque showing a likeness of his late grandfather, Don Emilio, and the inscription "Cava En Su Honor". We enter the small bunker that is fitted with wooden racks and stacked high with glass demijohns of crystal-clear mezcal totalling 100 or more. Each flagon has a laminated tag around its neck, which details the type of agave, where it was grown, when it was harvested, when it was distilled, and its strength. As we browse the collection, we see that some of the spirits go back 20 years or more. José Manuel pours out a nearly empty demijohn of Cupreata silvestre mezcal. It was filled back in 2010 and is 53% ABV. *The aroma has a gentle hum of spice with very little smoke and a slight mineral note, then it's green and herbal, like pine*

needles. There are some apple bubblegum and tropical aromas too. The taste is almost effervescent, with green papaya, pickled green (bell) pepper and plenty of zingy spice.

In Michoacán, *silvestre* means "wild agave", distinguishing it from cultivated varieties. Mezcal made from silvestres typically has a markedly different taste compared to its cultivated counterparts, because of genetic diversity and unique environmental conditions.

"The silvestre pulls in the flavours from the plants around it," says José Manuel. "You can taste the forest."

The Vieryas grow about 80% of the agaves they need on an old ranch called El Limón located around 1.5 hours south of here. "Ranch" is perhaps underselling it, though, as El Limón is basically a 400-acre (160-hectare) nature reserve. Its high-altitude environment features sandy soil and moderate rainfall and the agaves grow among grazing livestock with pine needles, moss, and red sandy clay carpeting the forest floor. The woodlands are full of wild plants that are close relatives or ancestors of many crops that have sustained Mexican families for nearly 10,000 years, some of which can be found only here.

Many of the agaves grown at El Limón are wild while others are agriculturally grown agaves bred from wild stocks, with their subtle colour and shape variances speaking of their diversity. Due to the remote location, harvesting and transporting the agaves to the distillery can be challenging, often requiring traditional methods like packing agaves onto mules or donkeys and slowly walking to a waiting truck.

Recent years have seen the concept of truly wild agave questioned, as farmers gravitate towards cultivating agaves that were once wild but are now farmed. On the one hand, this trend has helped to preserve and diversify threatened wild varieties by breeding them "in captivity", and helped to prevent the over-harvesting of wild agaves like Tobala in Oaxaca's central valley. But it's also created marketing challenges in verifying whether agaves used in mezcal production are genuinely wild. For most consumers, the agave variety listed on the label provides sufficient information about the bottle's contents. However, for high-end purchases, authenticating the wild status of the agave has become increasingly important.

Preserving these wild varieties through breeding and sustainable harvesting, as well as other ancestral plants in El Limón, has become part of the mission statement and a major focal point for Emilio as it was for his late father. It is so often the case that where multigenerational, family-owned businesses are concerned, sustainability and conservation become intrinsic to the operation. As with Doña Delia's careful management of her kitchen garden, this extends beyond simply harvesting the right plants at the right time, and into a holistic approach to conservation and a responsible use of ingredients and the ecosystems they support. Over at El Limón this includes at least 85 species of birds and three types of bat, one of which is on the endangered species' list.

Long before anyone thought to make mezcal, *magueyero* bats (aka Mexican long-nosed bats) had a symbiotic partnership with agaves. These little pollinators flitted from flower to flower on mature plants, inserting their long, nimble tongues to take the nectar, inadvertently carrying the pollen away on their furry bodies. This interaction kept the bats fed but it also facilitated the creation of seeds with unique DNA within the pollinated plants, which meant genetically diverse agave populations.

You will recall that over in Tequila there has been more than 100 years of intense farming that has seen producers planting blue agave and cutting the quiotes before they have a chance to flower. This, of course, means no food for bats, which becomes a major problem for bat populations that rely on agave flower nectar to survive. This problem extends beyond tequila and into mezcal, particularly with the ubiquitous Espadín variety, which is now too becoming a monoculture crop that is cloned and farmed just like the blue Weber. Responsible farming practices are the key to protecting agaves and ensuring a prosperous and delicious future for all of us. Enter the Bat Friendly project. This initiative promotes agave management practices that support our bat friends. By allowing 5% of the agave population to flower, these bats get their nectar fix, and in return, they pollinate the plants, which in turn produce genetically unique offspring. It's a win-win: bats get food, agaves get pollinated, and we get healthier, more resilient crops for our agave spirits.

Don Mateo de la Sierra was one of the founding members of this initiative when it launched in 2016 and Emilio Vierya is on the board of directors. Another founding member, and someone who has a close relationship with the Vieryas, is David Suro Piñera, the owner of Tequilas restaurant in Philadelphia, US, and the founder of the Tequila Exchange Project, which connects bartenders to the tequila industry through an immersion into Jalisco's distilleries, fields, libraries and regulatory offices. He is also the co-author of *Agave Spirits: The Past, Present, and Future of Mezcals,* which devotes much space

to highlight the need for responsible farming practices in tequila production to protect pollinators and agaves alike. Finally, he is the owner of Siembra spirits, an independent bottler of agave spirits imported into the US, which includes some of the distilleries we have visited in its portfolio.

Siembra Azul was their first product, launched in 2005 as a contract-distilled tequila made by the Vivanco family at Viva Mexico and was designed to highlight – in the words of their own mission statement – transparency, traceability and terroir. Since then, Siembra added Siembra Valles to the roster, another tequila produced at Cascahuín's Arenal distillery in the Tequila Valley. Unlike Siembra Azul, Valles is made using dedicated cooking and distilling equipment based on ancestral pit ovens and wooden stills more commonly seen in raicilla and mezcal production. We actually walked past this distillery, which was partly designed by Jorge Perez, when we visited Cascahuín, but as Siembra Valles is made only a couple of times a year, it was almost inevitable that it would be silent on our visit (and it was).

Siembra also produces a roster of mezcals under the Siembra Metl brand. These are definitely worth checking out as they feature spirits produced here, at Viñata Don Mateo, and spirits made by the Famila Perez at Viñata Salto Bonito.

There's just enough time to taste one more mezcal before we need to leave. In spite of their all-nighter, Doña Delia and José Manuel need to get back to Morelia to open up their bottle shop. José Manuel pours us another silvestre, this one at 50% ABV and produced in 2015. *The aroma practically jumps out of the glass: vibrant and grassy. The taste is deeply complex, with wet stone minerality, a notable forest-floor note, anise and just a little smoke.*

The two of them jump into Delia's bright orange VW campervan, which does a remarkably good job of traversing the steep mountain track as we follow behind in the Jetta. Soon we converge on the bustling centre of Morelia, where we park up and pop our heads into their store to buy some bottles. Saying our goodbyes to Delia and José Manuel, we cross the street and fall into a small cantina where we order *sopa tarasca*, which is a tomato soup with a mildly spicy kick, with tortilla strips and beans adding texture. The *charales* arrives next – a plate of tiny fried fish, which we snack on alongside glasses of mezcal and the strained vocals of the Michoacán band La Nobleza De Aguililla piped through tinny speakers.

LA LUNA

El Emprendedor

Our final destination in Michoacán takes us north again, close to Rio de Parras where we visited the Perez family at Salto Bonito. Here, we find Lake Cuitzeo, the second biggest lake in Mexico, which marks the boundary between the states of Michoacán and Guanajuato.

Just south of the Cuitzeo is La Luna, Michoacán's biggest mezcal producer. As we draw near to the town of Indaparapeo the distillery comes into sight, its scale apparent from the bountiful fields of agaves flourishing on the rolling hills around it, its high walls, security guard and the six-metre-high (20-ft) gate. For a moment it feels like we are back in Los Altos and tequila country.

La Luna will turn out an impressive 20,000 litres (5,250 gallons) of mezcal in 2024, accounting for around 15% of the state's total. Remarkably, this distillery was built in only 2020 and the La Luna brand is not even ten years old.

It was founded by a father-and-son duo, both called Salvador Chavez, whose ancestral home is 160km (100 miles) west of here in Cotija, on the border into southern Jalisco. Looking for a better life, Salvador Sr. emigrated to the US in 1984 with his wife and young daughter, doing so illegally and dangerously via coyote trucks in the dead of night. They eventually gained citizenship and Salvador Jr. was born a US citizen and grew up in Sonoma in California. In 2008, the family opened a popular restaurant in Sonoma County called Café Picazo, and Salvador Jr. began to take a keen interest in spirits from his ancestral home.

Frequent trips to Michoacán found him a mezcalero he liked and he began bottling and importing *cupreata* mezcal sourced from a single distillery in Michoacán, under the La Luna brand. By 2017, he was bringing tequila and rum over to the US too, and La Luna was beginning to take off. Quality and a consistent supply became an issue, however, so Salvador made plans to build his own viñata on the site of his father's childhood home in Cotija. One

viñata then became two when Salvador Jr. began producing at Destiladora Las Azucenas in the mezcal capital of Etúcuaro too. A third production location was added where we are now, in Indaparapeo, which began as a tenancy agreement in 2019 but now is owned outright and very much expanded in its size. For a time La Luna was being produced at these three locations, but now that the new distillery in Indaparapeo is fully operational, all La Luna products are being made here – and there are a lot of them!

After parking up and passing security, we walk through the electric gate and into a broad courtyard containing office buildings, a bottling hall and stables that are home to half a dozen horses. The distillery's operations manager Adrián Gallegos, greets us. His story is as interesting as Salvador's, as the pair first met in 2016 when, like Pancho, Adrián was a taxi driver who happened to work a lot with the agave spirits industry. Seeing the potential in Adrián, Salvador brought him on board. Adrián now lives on site and runs production for the Mexican side of the business.

We hop into his pickup truck and drive back out of the gate and up the track to the huge, covered production space. Out the front is a small garden of agaves of various varieties, plus a deep pool where the water from the condensers is channelled. It has an actual living crocodile in it. I've seen turtles in condensers before in Haiti, but I have to admit this is the first time I've seen a crocodile in a distillery.

There are eight pit ovens at this distillery varying in size but with a total capacity of 100 tonnes. Adrián explains that, if you are going to build a big distillery, you need lots of small ovens rather than one big one. The bigger the oven, the less even the cook. Agaves on the outside of a big oven are just physically much further from the heat source and likely end up with only a mild blanching, while the innermost agaves would experience

incredible temperatures from what would surely be a very large fire.

The number of agaves piled on top would create another problem in the form of excess pressure. As they cook and lose their structural integrity, the agaves on top will squeeze thos beneath very hard, probably resulting in a very dry husk that would produce off-notes in its flavour and lose much of its sugar content in the process.

Finally, small ovens work better from a production-flow point of view. Each oven might fill four fermenters, which in turn feed eight stills and ultimately produce a set amount of mezcal that can be sent for bottling. Having a range of sizes also means smaller batches of individual agave varieties can be cooked. In this way you are able to manage the workflow to ensure your equipment is being maximised but not overloaded and that cooked agaves or fermentation tanks are not sat around for days on end because you have created a bottleneck in the system.

ABOVE Maguey Bruto growing outside the taberna. Just out of shot is the crocodile who Adrián describes as "an angry bastard".

Adrián tells us that, such is the size of La Luna, other mezcaleros nearby were concerned that they were going to use all of the local supply of wood in their pits and to power their stills. It led to petty complaints about the brand's many expressions, which some producers labelled as ridiculous and vanity projects.

"This is why we had to get out of Etúcuaro," says Adrián. "The people there are resistant to change and to producing different styles of mezcal."

La Luna are planning to grow to 30,000 litres (8,000 gallons) a month in 2025, by which point they will employ a team of 160 people. To keep the business sustainable, they are working with only certified wood suppliers and will soon be replanting everything they cut down. Additionally, all of their *vinasses* and *bagazo* are sent away for processing into compost or they are turned into fuel.

After a five-day cook, a repurposed wood chipper is used for milling the cooked agaves. They also use another very unusual device for extracting the agave juice, which Pancho calls a *trapiche*, though that is also the Spanish word for "mill" so doesn't describe it fully. It is basically a giant hammock into which the cooked agaves are placed. The cords of the trapiche are then twisted using an engine. Like wringing out a cloth, the twisting tightens the mesh of the hammock and crushes the contents, extracting the juices and leaving behind the larger chunks of fibre. This trapiche might be the only example of such a device in the state. Pancho says they originate from San Luis Potosí but that "almost nobody has them anymore".

The trapiche is used only for La Luna's flagship product, Black Label, which undergoes a faster production flow than other products and therefore benefits from the higher Brix (sugar concentration) that the trapiche can provide. Fermentation of Black Label takes place in plastic for the same reason, while everything else is fermented in wood. Around 70% of all production is La Luna Black Label.

There are 24 copper alembic stills here, which are used to produce Black Label, but the viñata also features some Tarascan wooden stills as well as a clay pot still. This is the first clay still we have encountered so far, as they are uncommon in Jalisco and Michoacán and more typical of Oaxaca. This one is tiny, at around 50 litres (13 gallons), and used only for very small batches of one-off products. We'll discuss clay stills in more detail soon.

The distillery is currently pausing its operations as the patio where agave piñas are normally unloaded is instead littered with piles of young agave hijuelos. A team of women are taking the baby plants and trimming them of their root hairs and any withered leaves before they are taken back to the fields and planted in rows.

"The trimming stresses the plant," says Adrián. "It becomes dehydrated so that when you replant it, it thrives quickly and grows new pencas."

Adrián tells us that these plants are all of the Manso Sahuayo variety, which, alongside blue (*tequilana*) and Chino (*cupreata*) make up the recipe that goes into a bottle of La Luna Black Label.

Manso Sahuayo and blue agaves both produce hijuelos that can be harvested from the mother plant and cultivated in the way we are observing now. Black Label was once a 100% Chino expression, however, which required a little more work because those plants don't produce offshoots.

We have encountered *cupreata* at all of the Michoacán viñatas we have visited and you can think of it a bit like the *tequilana* of this state. But the fact that it can be grown only from seed makes it far more labour-intensive to cultivate. Each individual plant requires planting and nurturing from seed, or you have to track down and monitor the plants that have grown naturally in the wild.

The *cupreata* looks totally different to most other mezcal-producing agaves. It has broad, lemon-sole-shaped pencas compared with the diabolical spears of an *angustifolia* or rhodacantha. They are arranged in the same Fibonacci sequence as every other agave but the curve of these spiny paddles lends a softer, more organic profile than the vivid fractals of *tequilana*.

The experimental approach here means that La Luna have worked with *cupreata* (both cultivated and in its wild form, silvestre), *salmiana* (the Verde variety), *tequilana* (blue), *inaequidens* (the Bruto variety), *angustifolia* (Espadín and Espadíncillo) and the Manso Sahuayo variety.

The basic product range at La Luna includes half a dozen different agave varieties and ensembles (blends), but extends to dozens of interestingly flavoured mezcals that have been distilled in the pechuga style. Many of these products have been made in partnership with high-profile restaurants and agave spirits' bars in the US and elsewhere, which have worked with the team here to produce their own unique expression, using La Luna's full range of equipment and imagination.

This quick-fire, experimental strategy has garnered La Luna no shortage of attention – good and bad. Advocates of La Luna love that the brand is pushing the boundaries of mezcal in its use of agaves that are non-native to Michoacán, and in its imaginative pechugas with approachable flavours that may bring new consumers into the mezcal category. But La Luna critics think the brand has misplaced traditional production values and quality consistency in favour of marketing trickery and vanity projects.

Adrián walks us along the patio, past the piles of hijuelos, and over to a small, covered structure that conceals a ladder leading underground. He gestures for us to clamber down. At the bottom we find ourselves in a hidden tasting area equipped with a bar and at least 500 bottles of mezcal. This mezcal bunker holds practically every bottle La Luna have ever produced, in multiple quantities – 96 expressions in total.

"What do you want to try?" says Adrián.

"All of them" seems a bit ambitious but, hey – you have to start somewhere. We begin with a sample of their 100% Chino Silvestre (wild) (48.5% ABV) *The aroma has a fresh, toothpaste and green sherbet appeal; fresh lime peel. There is a slight apple-candy note on the taste, with beautifully integrated spice, being both creamy and sweet.*

Next, we try a watermelon and chilli pechuga made with blue agave and Bruto, which is a variety of *inaequidens* that grows at high altitude near Cotija and around Patzcuaro in central Michoacán. Like its sibling, Alto, which we have previously encountered, it is a massive agave that produces a very low yield.

The aroma is not especially watermelon-y but it is certainly fresh and speaks of red things: (bell) pepper, tomato, raspberry. The taste is sweet and has a certain hum of tropical alongside strawberry and cranberry flavours.

While Pancho and Adrián discuss the possibility of doing a crocodile meat pechuga for his bar in Guadalajara, Addie and I taste La Luna Espadíncillo (48.5% ABV). *It has an initial medicinal note of cough syrup with some menthol brightness. The taste has spice, more iodine and medicinal flavours. It's very short-lived but with an intense sweetness, then a dry aniseed note kicks in just when you think it's over.*

Next is Café de Olla pechuga, produced in the clay pot still with cinnamon, orange peel, piloncillo sugar, chilli and coffee as botanicals. *The aroma is unabashedly that of cinnamon, supported by ground ginger and green cardamom. The taste is drier than the aroma suggests: there's*

ABOVE LEFT The remarkable trapiche "hammock" squeezer.

ABOVE Just a small selection of the enormous range of mezcals that La Luna have produced, but I have no memory of this place (got to get a Gandalf quote in one of these books).

definitely cinnamon, then coffee, along with a touch of green eucalyptus.

More spirits are poured and my tasting notes become incoherent and eventually non-existent as the joy of simply drinking and laughing takes over. The realisation that we need to climb back out of this bunker dawns on us, and as we emerge back into the cruel light of day and say our goodbyes it's with a pang of regret that I realise we tasted only 10% of La Luna's massive range. An excuse for a return visit.

The evening is beginning to close in as the Jetta's wheels skid down the track, sending a plume of dust and smoke into the air. Pancho drives hard for an hour and the sound of Willie Colón's "Pedro Navaja" blasts from the speaker, its frantic jazz tempo furthering the sense that we are embroiled in a high-speed car chase.

Soon we near Mexico City and skirt around the northern edge of its sprawling expanse. We pass by the Pyramid of the Sun (the third biggest pyramid in the world) in Teotihuacán. This ancient city dates back 2,000 years and was one of the largest pre-Columbian cities in the Americas. The Teotichuacán people are something of an enigma, however – nobody knows if they had a written language or why the city was abandoned by 750CE.

What we do know is that they liked a drink.

Scientists conducted an analysis of pottery fragments found in Teotihuacán to investigate the diet and culture of its inhabitants. Employing a technique called "absorbed organic residue analysis", they examined over 300 pottery shards dating from between 200 to 550CE, taken from both within and near the ancient city. The fragments were first cleaned and then ground down into powder, which was then analysed for substances that might have been absorbed by the unglazed ceramic.

The focus was on detecting residues of *Zymomonas mobilis*, a bacterium involved in alcohol production that gives pulque its alcoholic content. The study yielded significant results as the researchers discovered 14 pottery fragments that contained the earliest direct chemical evidence of *pulque* production in Central America. Their findings suggest that this fermented beverage made from agave sap was stored in specialised vase-like containers sealed with pine resin.

Further archaeological evidence hints at an even earlier history with the Otomí people, whom you may remember being mentioned during our time near the Volcán de Colima. Ancient Mayan glyphs going back as far as 2000BCE from the region show what appears to be a fermented agave beverage that was consumed orally but was also used for enemas. The name *pulque* is thought to come from the Nahuatl word *poliuhqui* meaning "decomposed".

The Aztec Empire, which thrived in the late 15th and early 16th century, provides us with the most detailed historical records of pulque production and consumption. The Aztecs revered the agave plant and considered pulque sacred owing to its mind-altering properties. Strict rules governed its consumption, because excessive intake was seen as dangerous divine possession. Pulque was also believed to have medicinal properties, used to treat various ailments including digestive issues and malnutrition. In Aztec times, the elderly were encouraged to drink pulque to balance their bodily "heat", reflecting Mesoamerican beliefs similar to Old World "humour" theories about maintaining harmony through balanced influences.

The Florentine Codex, a 2,500-page, 16th-century ethnographic work by Friar Bernardino de Sahagún, included over 2,000 illustrations by native artists, and depicts the era's culture including detailed pulque production methods.

Our evening journey to Puebla should have taken five or six hours. Pancho did it in four, complaining only once that he needed "a red wine".

Once settled into our lodging, we head out for drinks and stop by a pulque bar called El Nahual, named for the shapeshifting spirit-animal from Mesoamerican folk religion. This place has an extensive menu of pulques most of them being flavoured with fruits, herbs and spices. Pancho opts for the classic unflavoured, Addie takes a lemon-flavoured one, and I go for papaya.

Like with mezcal, pulque can be made from a range of agave species but the most common is *Agave americana* – probably on account of its size. Once the plant is mature and the quiote cut, the harvester cuts away some of the pencas to expose the centre of the plant. A cavity is then carved into the piña, and, over a period of several days the *tlachiquero* (pulque harvester) siphons off the juices from the plant using a narrow tool called an *acocote*.

Once the juice is collected, it is transferred to fermentation vessels, traditionally made of animal skins or large wooden barrels. Natural fermentation occurs because of the presence of wild yeasts and bacteria in the environment, transforming the sweet sap into pulque. This fermentation process can take anywhere from a few days to a week, resulting in a slightly viscous, milky-white beverage with a distinctive tangy flavour and an alcohol content of about 4–6%. Pulque is often enjoyed fresh, as its flavour and quality can degrade rapidly over time. This is also why it is not generally exported or even drunk far from its place of production – transportation and storage of it would require pasteurisation.

Our drinks arrive in handled jars, broad and opaque. I take a sip through the wide straw. It's thick and creamy, with plenty of fruit flavour and quite a lot of added sweetness. It's like a big glass of mildly boozy, fruit yoghurt. Pancho's unflavoured version is milky white and more viscous. I taste it and the flavour is yeasty and less sweet, sitting somewhere between sourdough starter and beer.

The Mexican historian Fernando de Alva Ixtlilxochitl documented a pre-Columbian legend about pulque's origins in the 17th century. According to the tale, the Toltec man Papantzin discovered pulque-making from agave in 843CE. His daughter, Xochitl, presented pulque to King Tecpancaltzin, who was so impressed that he took her as his queen. Their son, Meconetzin, eventually became the Toltec king, all thanks to his grandfather discovering pulque.

OAXACA

Oaxaca is the beating heart of mezcal in Mexico, with a rich history rooted in indigenous traditions. On this part of our journey, we will explore some of Oaxaca's most remote *palenques* (the name given to mezcal distilleries here) and witness some of the rarest and longest-living agaves being transformed into memorable spirits.

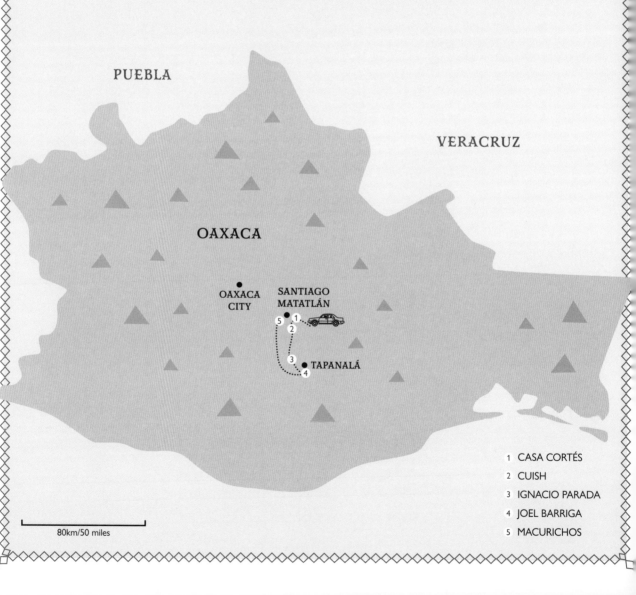

PUEBLA

VERACRUZ

OAXACA

OAXACA CITY

SANTIAGO MATATLÁN

5   1
    2

3   TAPANALÁ
    4

80km/50 miles

1 CASA CORTÉS

2 CUISH

3 IGNACIO PARADA

4 JOEL BARRIGA

5 MACURICHOS

CASA CORTÉS

◇◇◇

La Inspiración

We awake early the next morning and make our escape from Puebla, heading south for the Oaxaca border. The cheerful trumpets and accordions of the band Los Xochimilcas accompany much of our journey. "Pulque Para Dos" sees the accordion take centre-stage, weaving a playful tune that's impossible not to tap your foot to and you can almost detect the sound of glasses of pulque being clinked together.

The landscape soon becomes mountainous again, with organ-pipe cactuses standing like sentinels on every available patch of the endless, arid mountains. In fact, there's little sign of life besides the cacti, which conceal a hidden treasure of at least 20 indigenous agave species – more than any other place in the world.

The mezcal NOM states that mezcal must be made from 100% agave (there is no *mixto* category here) and that it can be made from any plant from the agave genus, which according to the Royal Botanical Gardens, Kew (UK) currently includes 299 confirmed species. Of that number, about 40 are known to have been used to make mezcal constituting at least 70 magueys or varietal names. We have encountered some of these species already: *Agave cupreata*, *Agave salmiana*, *Agave rhodacantha* and *Agave inaequidens*. But these plants make up no more than a couple of per cent of the total production volume of mezcal. In Oaxaca, we will encounter the balance, in the varieties Tobalá (*Agave potatorum*), Cuishe and Madrecuishe (*Agave karwinskii*) and the agave that really pays the bills down south: Espadín.

The widespread adoption of Espadín began in the 1960s when mezcal production in the central Oaxaca valleys slowly shifted from local consumption to broader export and commercialisation. This transition led to a favouring of the faster-growing, more predictable and higher-yielding Espadín over wild and semi-cultivated varieties. As demand for mezcal has surged globally, especially since the early 2000s, the pressure to produce at scale has further entrenched Espadín's position as the dominant agave in mezcal bottles.

Espadín is a variety of *Agave angustifolia* and it gets its name from a fancy Spanish dress sword, which itself takes its name from a small fish on account of its sword-shaped *pencas*. In 2023, COMERCAM (the mezcal regulatory council) reported that 86% of all mezcal was being made from Espadín agaves.

If this is beginning to sound a lot like the situation that has played out in Jalisco with tequila over the past 100 years, rest assured that the parallels do not end there. Espadín looks a lot like a blue agave in both its shape and size, except that its pencas are an olive green as opposed to the dusty blue of *tequilana*. It matures at a similar rate as the blue too, produces *hijuelos* like blue, yields a similar amount of spirit to blue, and is now farmed aggressively and unsustainably like blue too.

Pancho hints that Espadín and blue Weber may be genetically closer than we think, and that some experts believe the blue Weber is in fact another variant of *angustifolia* and not a species in its own right. If this were true, blue Weber would still be classed as its own distinct variety, but its sanctification as *angustifolia* by botanists would effectively nullify the *tequilana* species and bring about some serious soul searching in Jalisco.

Grab a bottle of Espadín mezcal and taste it next to a tequila and you won't find much in common. But production techniques have a huge part to play in this. The tequila industry is built on steam power, which produces the heady jalapeño and grapefruit notes that we know and love. Espadín is generally used in mezcal production on a much smaller scale with more artisanal methods that bring about earthy and pungent notes in the spirit. However, when you taste mezcals made from blue Weber agaves using artisanal mezcal techniques you begin to entertain the idea that blue Weber is maybe not so unique after all.

One thing we do know is that Espadín is close enough to blue Weber in style to be a tequila stand-in when needed. During periods of high prices, tequila producers have knowingly – and illegitimately – sourced cheaper Espadín agaves from Oaxaca and shipped them north to make their tequila. The last time this happened in a significant way was in the 1990s, and it spurred many farmers in Oaxaca to plant Espadín to meet the new demand. Then a few years passed, the economy changed in the north, and the next thing anyone knew, tequila didn't need Espadín any more and the value of agave in Oaxaca bottomed out. Just as this cycle of supply and demand has built some of the best-known producers of tequila in the 1990s it contributed to the regrowth of the mezcal industry Oaxaca too.

These days, the CRT seems to be policing the use of illegal agaves in tequila more closely, monitoring fields with satellites and in theory at least producing a fully traceable flow of production. But during times of high prices and scarcity, there are still accounts of authorities intercepting tarpaulin-covered trucks heading north to Jalisco, stacked high with Espadín agaves. One has to assume that many more trucks complete the journey without detection.

Pancho's VW Jetta is one vehicle that is currently very easy to detect. It has been losing power up the hills for some time now, with occasional blasts of smoke emanating from the exhaust and streams of cars overtaking us with horns blaring. Pancho suspects the fuel pump is blocked, and he blames the last fuel station we stopped at for selling adulterated gasoline. He turns up the music (a frantic jazz piano and brass number) to drown out the spluttering emanating from the engine. The possibility of breaking down on a remote piece of mountain highway when it's 36°C (97°F) outside is becoming ever more real.

After an hour or so of stalling and restarting, we finally see a service station. Pulling up outside, Pancho removes the fuel cap to put some injector cleaning fluid in. An immediate and forceful explosion of fuel sprays out, splashing us and two sinister-looking armed police. With the problem seemingly – if somewhat dramatically – fixed we grab some pork scratchings, which Pancho douses in lime juice and hot sauces, and load back into the car for the final straight into Oaxaca – stinking of gasoline and crispy pork.

You can think of the state of Oaxaca like a doughnut, ringed almost entirely with mountains but with a flat central core. Oaxaca City is in the most northerly part of the middle bit known as the Valles Centrales. This region includes some of the biggest mezcal-producing towns and regions in Mexico, including Santiago Matatlán, Tlacolula, Ocotlán, Ejutla and Zimatlán. Each has its own subtle variations of mezcal style brought about by unique climate, topography, tradition and agaves.

Oaxaca City itself is not a big production hub but it certainly knows how to sell the spirit. The city centre is a UNESCO World Heritage site thanks to its immaculately presented Spanish colonial architecture. Colourful buildings line cobblestone streets, housing art galleries, museums and bustling markets. Oaxaca's culinary scene is legendary, offering some of the best food in Mexico and regional specialties such as *mole* (a rich, fruity, cocoa-imbued savoury sauce), *tlayudas* (big, thin, toasted tortillas with toppings) and *chapulines* (toasted grasshoppers). The city is a mezcal-drinker's paradise, with numerous mezcalerías, cantinas and brand tasting rooms, and offices promoting and exporting the stuff.

For now we are passing straight through the city and on to our first palenque, which is located 20 minutes southeast of the city, in the town of Santiago Matatlán.

Viewed from above, Matatlán would appear to be a fairly unassuming place with a wide highway running through its centre and a network of narrow perpendicular streets. Viewed from within, however, it is like a Las Vegas strip of mezcal palenques. This small town with a population of 2,500 residents is home to some of the biggest mezcal brands: Ilegal, Montelobos, Casamigos and Sombra, and 400 Conejos. Respectively owned (or part owned) by Bacardí, Campari, Diageo and Jose Cuervo, all of these brands were either started by or have been purchased by massive spirits conglomerates. They account for more than a quarter of the entire mezcal market, and the biggest slice owned by a single brand belongs to Del Maguey, founded in 1994 by artist Ron Cooper. This was the brand that introduced the concept of single palenque mezcals to the world and, with its striking label design and liquid, providence made it the darling of agave spirits for more than two decades. Hence it became a prime target for a buyout, and in 2017 the French spirits giant Pernod Ricard did just that – lock, stock and smoky barrel.

The trade magazine *Drinks International (DI)* conducts an annual brand report that surveys 100 world-class bars around the globe on brands they stock, which are the best-selling, and which brands the bars see as exciting or trending right now. Of the 100 bars surveyed in 2024, 96 of them stocked at least one mezcal and 80 of them stocked at least three.

DI found that in 2019, two-thirds of bars that stocked mezcal carried Del Maguey. This figure dropped to 44% in 2020 and 38% in 2021, and in 2024 (at the time of writing) sits at around 19%. Del Maguey still holds around 12% of the total mezcal market and, while its grip has loosened, that market has got bigger.

In 2023 Mexico produced 12.2 million litres (3.2 million gallons) of mezcal compared to just 2.5 million litres (660,000 gallons) in 2013. This constitutes an average annual growth of 13.6% year on year, which, while still making it a relatively small category, makes mezcal one of the fastest-growing spirits in the world today.

The welcome sign for Santiago Matatlán above the highway reads "Bienvenidos a Santiago Matatlán 'Capital Mundial del Mezcal'" with what looks to be a genuinely workable copper alembic still perched on top. Current estimates suggest that there are 250 palenques in and around Santiago Matatalán, which makes it not only the mezcal capital of the world, but the distilling capital of the world too.

The town's distilling history goes back centuries but the past 60 years have been a rollercoaster ride and, by all accounts, the town has been utterly transformed since the turn of the century. Where once stood only family-run operations, now hundreds of brands vie for supremacy, their logos and billboards plastered across any available surface. The narrow streets can be clogged with lorries transporting agave *piñas* and finished products and many of the old adobe houses have been replaced or expanded to accommodate larger production facilities, their walls adorned with murals depicting agave plants and mezcal bottles – a nod to tradition amid the march of progress.

We are meeting the team from Casa Cortés, a brand that works with 19 different families across the various producing regions of Oaxaca to bottle and sell their mezcal. The Cortés family are from Matatalán, however, and have six generations of mezcal production behind them. The family operate a couple of small palenques in town: De Cortés and El As.

We have just pulled up at De Cortés and we are met by the brand's founder, Rolando Cortés, and his colleague Matt Morrison.

The palenque is very small, with a pair of copper alembic stills, wooden fermenters, and a mule-drawn *tahona*. De Cortés has been in the family for generations and was previously run by Rolando's grandfather. El As, their other Matatlán palenque, is much newer having been built in 2011, but on a patch of land adjacent to Rolando's father's old palenque. Both are fully operational, with El As now being run by one of Rolando's brothers, Francisco, and De Cortés under the care of mezcalero Gregorio Martínez. Being the oldest of the two, De Cortés is also used as a HQ to showcase the three brands that sit within the Casa Cortés stable: Agave de Cortés, El Jolgorio and Nuestra Soledad.

"In the 1990s, we used to see the palenques full of dust and everything without movement," says Rolando. "There weren't as many buildings as there are now. Sometimes you would pass between the river and the terraces, and you would see the palenques all abandoned."

Go back 100 years and Oaxaca represented only around 4% of the total market share of mezcal production. Distilling was endemic, of course, but all of the palenques were very small and not all of them registered. Now it is by far the biggest, producing more than 90% of everything bottled as mezcal. This dramatic change in the economy of the state has wrought huge social and cultural change. Mezcal has seen its status shift from an agricultural observance passed between generations, to a dangerous intoxicant produced by indigenous peoples deserving of persecution, to a premium spirit of unmatched provenance and flavour prized by drinks' geeks across the planet, and now as the commoditised property of multinational companies.

The 1970s was a particularly rough time for mezcaleros in Oaxaca's central valleys. In a shameful targeting of indigenous communities – very likely egged on by the tequila mafia in Jalisco – the Mexican government conducted raids on small-scale producers, dumping mezcal down the drain and destroying the distillation equipment of those unable to pay taxes or obtain permits. Rolando recalls how his father, Don José, would return home some evenings beside himself with grief after seeing the knives of government officials stabbed into his stills. These crackdowns had the desired effect, Matatlán went from having 460 tiny palenques in the 1960s to just 12 by the end of the century.

The collapse of the local economy and the shame that came with it, caused a significant migration of people to the US, with many producers, including Rolando's brothers, leaving their homes permanently. Rolando, being the youngest, remained in Matatlán. Witnessing all this inspired him to take on the mantle of mezcalero himself, to reinstate some pride into the community and help to support the families economically. This ethos remains the driving force behind Casa Cortés to this day.

"At that time my father would not let me come to the palenque because it was seen as low-status work," he says. "And we were banned from speaking Zapotec too, because it was a symbol of not advancing – you had to speak Spanish to progress in life."

Of course, Rolando did what any son would do and rebelled against his father.

"The thing that is most prohibited is what you look for," he says. "My grandfather used to make mezcal where we are standing right now and this is where I began – he taught me Zapotec and was my mezcal teacher."

Making mezcal at the family palenque in Matatlán, Rolando found a connection with the land, the seasons, and the agaves. In time, he became familiar with every stage of production and launched his first brand, Agave de Cortés, in 2006.

Agave de Cortés has three core expressions: Joven, Reposado and Añejo. Joven (unaged) mezcals make up 97% of the mezcal market but the NOM recognises reposado and añejo classifications, which follow the same guidance as tequila. These products are unusual, however, and rejected by many enthusiasts for being inauthentic and bland-tasting, but Rolando bottles both types under the Agave de Cortés brand. He points to raids in the 1980s when mezcal was commonly hidden in barrels as historical justification for a style that some local people still have a taste for.

A few years after launching his brand, Rolando met with Edgar Guzman Corrales in Oaxaca. Edgar invited him to join the beginning of a group called the Sistema Producto Maguey Mezcal, an organisation to support mezcal-producing communities. There he met Jaime Muñoz, a restaurateur and the owner of the longstanding mezcal brand Danzantes, as well as Graciela Angeles from the brand Real Minero. With a shared passion for elevating the name and reputation of mezcal, the trio lobbied for the planned Tequila Museum in Mexico City to include "Mezcal" in its title. And it's thanks to their efforts that anyone visiting Plaza Garabaldi today will see the enormous container ship of a building proudly signed Museo del Tequila y el Mezcal.

It was while celebrating their success at the Los Danzantes restaurant in the Coyoacán district in Mexico City that Rolando had his eyes truly opened to the world of mezcal. "I came from Matatlán and was the fifth-generation mezcalero so I thought I knew everything," says Rolando, "but the server at the restaurant gave me all these new magueys to try – Cuish, Arroqueño, Largo – and I felt like a neophyte!"

The Agave de Cortés brand was then and remains today focused entirely on Matatlán and Espadín. However, tasting these new magueys, Rolando was beginning to appreciate there was more to mezcal. It's hard to imagine now that someone who grew up in Oaxaca their entire life could have been shielded from the huge variety of agaves traditionally used to make the spirit, and it paints a depressing picture of how much the industry had declined at the turn of the century.

Rolando immediately went to his father to learn more, at which point José Cortés showed him his scarred hands and regaled Rolando with tales of agaves shaped like exploding stars, with pencas like broad paddles, and spines that can slice through leather. This spurred Rolando into action and he began travelling the state, seeking out new mezcaleros with stories to tell. Ultimately, this all led to the creating of a new brand in 2010: El Jolgorio. The brand's name means "revelry", and reflects the celebratory nature of mezcal in Oaxacan culture and the part it plays in funerals, births, weddings and so on. The range has featured more than a dozen different producing families across ten locations around the state, and numerous agave varieties.

It was under the El Jolgorio brand that Rolando released his first pechuga expression, although his father José took some convincing.

"When I went to ask him if I could sell a pechuga, my father said 'no,'" he says. "'That is our mezcal,' he said, not for other people."

Eventually José relented, but only under the proviso that every bottle of pechuga he sold was commemorated to the family's saint. El Jolgorio Pechuga (47% ABV) is made from Espadín agaves with pineapple, orange and plantain, plus turkey breast. Rolando pours some to try: *The aroma is meaty, brown agave, then some tropical fruit notes and dark berries. The taste is sweet and creamy, with a*

OPPOSITE Espadín agaves dominate the Central Valleys of Oaxaca today, but what's less common to see is a collection of Espadín inflorescences.

touch of ash and some mineral notes too. It finishes with a nutty note of caraway seed.

Nuestra Soledad, another brand under Casa Cortés that was launched in 2010, focuses on regional expressions of Espadín. By featuring only one type of agave, the brand aims to showcase the influence of different terroirs on the flavour and experience of mezcal, while also addressing concerns about the exploitation of wild agaves by using cultivated Espadín only.

"Ultimately our goal is to conserve the traditional process," says Rolando. "To care for the culture, to take care of the *maestro mescaleros* – for us the most important thing is to protect the culture."

In recent years, Casa Cortés has made efforts to highlight women's contributions to mezcal production. Rolando's niece, Monica, now serves as the face of the company, and in 2021, *maestra mezcalera* Justina Ruiz Perez joined as their first female mezcal producer.

We finish with a special glass of Tepeztate mezcal that was produced in 2013 and has spent 11 years in glass. The

ABOVE A standard afternoon tasting session for three dedicated agave spirits' road trippers.

agave itself would have been something like 17 years old when harvested, which makes for a clear-coloured spirit that was 28 years in the making.

"I'm an eternal fan of Tepeztate," says Matt as we put our noses into the glass.

"*Qué chingón!*" (awesome) says Pancho. *The aroma is intensely floral, to the point of being honeyed and sweet-smelling. The taste initially continues this theme with rose and orange blossom. Then barbecued vegetables arise, aubergine (eggplant) and smoky beans. The finish is waxy and generously long.*

CUISH

El Artista

On our second day in Oaxaca, we return to Matatlán, to visit one of the newest palenques on the block. It's owned by Felix Hernandez Monterossa, the co-founder of Mezcal Cuish, which began life as a mezcalería in Oaxaca City in 2009. Remarkably, this was the first modern tasting room of its kind to promote and educate consumers on traditional mezcal production in the city.

Cuish started bottling mezcal from five small producers across Oaxaca. Over time, clients grew in number to 17. And then, in 2018, Felix became one, refurbishing an old family property in Matatlán and turning it into a palenque known as Familia Monterossa. It's our next stop, but rather cryptically Felix has requested we meet him in Matatlán's central plaza to show us something special.

He's waiting for us in a battered old VW Beetle – just about the most fashionable vehicle you can own in Mexico. As if the car wasn't cool enough, he steps out looking like a Mexican Indiana Jones, in a button-down shirt, weathered trousers, a small sombrero and leather sandals. We introduce ourselves and he walks us over to the town hall, stepping into the cool shade of the foyer. As our eyes adjust, the wall reveals an enormous, painted mural that is at least six metres wide and three high (20 x 10ft).

The piece is like a "Where's Wally" of mezcal. There are more than 100 painted figures partaking in agriculture, crafts, religious ceremony, celebration, mourning and, most notably, the production of mezcal. It depicts jimadores cutting down at least five different types of agave, more agaves with full quiotes in flower and bats and hummingbirds among them; a roasting pit, wood fermenters, clay stills and demijohns of mezcal. Felix points out the shape-changing Tlahuelpuchi (of Mexican folklore) dark silhouettes of displaced indigenous people walking in the distance, and a pair of huge sandal-wearing feet trampling the width of the scene which, to my eyes, represents the recent march of commercialisation of Oaxacan culture.

Equal parts love letter and lament, even among the rich and diverse range of Mexican street art we've seen, this is a magnificent piece of work – both in its storytelling and its scale. Felix is a man of few words, but when he reveals to us that he is the artist who painted it, it's obvious that he has a lot to say about his home.

Feeling somewhat in awe of the man, we return to the car and head five minutes down the road to the Cuish palenque. Serving as both a bottling space for their sourced mezcals and a production space for their own, this is a small operation with a lot going on.

The agaves are cooked in an underground pit oven, milled by horse-drawn tahona, fermented with open air yeasts in cypress and pine vats, and double-distilled in copper pot-stills. We take a seat near the tahona with tasting glasses and a few bottles.

RIGHT Felix's enormous mural in Matatlán is a visual spectacle dedicated to the tradition of mezcal production in Oaxaca.

Felix tells us that his parents ran a mezcal *expendio* (small shop) from 1988–1994 in the location where the palenque now stands. It was during the hard times, when many palenques closed, that Felix's uncle, Cornelio Monterrosa, was inspired to establish the Union de Palenqueros (which later became the Asociación de Productores del Mezcal Tradicional Oaxaqueño A.C.) – a group dedicated to protecting traditional Oaxacan mezcal. One of the ways they did this was to promote and preserve non-Espadín agaves, whether cultivated or wild. This later became the inspiration for Felix's mezcaleria and the Cuish brand which champions lesser-known agave varieties such as Tepeztate, Pichmetl (*Agave marmorata*), Jabali, Belato (a wild agave with orange or red pencas) and of course their namesake (with the additional "e"), Cuishe.

Cuishe is a wild agave belonging to the *Agave karwinskii* species and is thus close relative of Madrecuishe, Barril (barrel) and Largo (long) magueys/varieties. Unlike the image of an agave that most of us store in our heads, with its broad, ground-hugging leaves, *karwinskii* grows in a distinctive cylindrical, stalk-shaped form. Its leaves spread from the top, making it look more like a palm tree than an agave.

The piñas of these plants run the full length of the trunk, which means they are shaped like cucumbers. This cucumber, though, is typically longer than the person who harvested it. This also makes it a uniquely photogenic agave piña, so jimadores pose with them like proud fishermen with a tuna.

Of course, the unique shape also influences how the plant grows and matures, and the flavour profile of the mezcal it produces. Cuishe tends to be slightly smaller than its close relative, Madrecuishe, but its compact size hides an intensity of flavour that is hard to beat. Felix pours a sample of Cuishe mezcal for us. Bottled at 48% ABV, it's produced by Francisco Garcia León in San Guillermo, Miahuatlán. *The aroma is slightly fizzy, with aromatic orange and some lime. It tastes floral and slightly soapy – there's lavender, geranium, and it feels very bright, oily and clean. Fantastic precision of flavour.*

"When we first opened 15 years ago, the Cuishe was a very undervalued agave variety," says Felix. "They used to dry it out and use it as fire wood."

In the past, the large haciendas in Oaxaca and Jalisco promoted the use of cultivated varieties, particularly blue Webrt and Espadín. This preference wasn't just about agriculture though – it carried undertones of classism and racial prejudice too: wild agaves for the indigenous communities; cultivated for those with Spanish ancestry.

"The tequila hacienda was seen as the successful model," says Felix, "and if you weren't working in that model you were primitive and backwards. But my grandfather would produce mezcal using wild agaves. They were all just referred to as *cimarrón* (wild) to producers in the towns and cities. It was a derogatory term."

Felix recalls how his grandmother used to say that real mezcal was different because it was made from the *loma* (hill). And the one they cultivated in the valley, was "another flavour".

Our sudden obsession with single-variety mezcals is an excusable one. By controlling variety, we can experience the joy of internally categorising the many and varied flavours of mezcal, and form opinions about what we like and predictions about how things might taste. Challenging those predictions is, then, the really fun part, as new and surprising flavours are discovered within the framework of variety and species.

This is not how mezcals were made in the past, though.

"My grandmother told me that all of my grandfather's mezcals were ensembles," says Felix. "They would use whatever was ripe and mature – everything was an ensemble and everything was wild."

To a mezcalero in the 1950s, the idea of traipsing around tracking down one species of agave and carrying the plants back to the palenque to make a single-variety expression would seem ludicrous. What all this means, of course, is that the authentic approach to operating a modern-traditional palenque – the most honest expression of mezcal, if you like – would use a random mixture of wild agaves.

This approach wouldn't have the same marketing ring to it, of course, no matter how hard you beat the drum of authenticity. Regardless of their historical credentials, ensembles have the feeling of something homogenised and mass-produced about them – or that something inferior is being masked by something else. As corporate-owned brands with big budgets vie for supremacy, Oaxaca's most authentic palenques have a big enough challenge on their hands promoting their traditional approach without forfeiting one of their greatest tools: distinctive flavour.

Felix brandishes another bottle, "This is very unique," he says, pointing at the label that indicates it is a Madrecuishe mezcal and then below it the statement "Técnica: Tumbado". *The aroma is slightly cheesy, with a*

tonne of red fruits and pungent, decaying, tropical notes. On the taste it's almost effervescent, oily and rich – a true rollercoaster of texture and flavour. It finishes with spice and soft, smoky notes.

Felix explains that a man named Jarquin Aquino owns a palenque in the town of La Chaga, in the south. There, he practices an unusual harvesting method that does crazy things to the flavour of the mezcal. The Madrecuishe agave is *capón* (castrated) once it reaches maturity, which takes around eight years. The plant is then left for a year or two to mature and concentrate its sugars. Then, in the late autumn (the time of year is important here), they chop the base of the plant and let the agave lie in the fields for three to four months with its pencas intact (a practice called *tumbado*). It's during this maturation on the ground that the agave attracts moulds and fungi, which catalyse radical new flavours in the mezcal it produces.

Felix thinks it was a technique going back to the 19th century, which died out because of the theft risk of leaving prime agaves in the fields for months. Madrecuishe is special because it is happy with this treatment of being felled and left to rot, unlike almost any other plant.

More recently, Felix launched another brand called Agua Del Sol, bottled outside of the mezcal NOM as a Distillado de Agave. For this brand, he sources spirits from across Oaxaca – the brand was born out of the Covid-19 pandemic when it was necessary to produce something more affordable for his customers. One way of cutting costs was to not pay the fees associated with certifying a mezcal. Soon after launching Agua del Sol, Felix recognised an opportunity to begin bottling spirits that couldn't be certified as mezcals because they exceed the legal limit of methanol.

Methanol gets a bad rap in spirits. Horror stories abound of poisonings through dodgy bottles of liquid spiked with methanol, which makes many of us conclude that methanol is uniquely dangerous and should be limited where possible. The truth, however, is it's not possible to create dangerous quantities of methanol in the production of most commercial spirits – mezcal and tequila included. And, in fact, small amounts of methanol are pretty much harmless when they're in the presence of their sibling, ethanol. This is why patients suffering from methanol poisoning are administered vodka (ethanol) to help slow methanol metabolism down and so reduce toxic build-up.

In Mexico, methanol is limited to a maximum of 300mg per 100ml for tequila and mezcal. The US on the other hand permits up to twice the amount of methanol in its products and, in Europe, some fruit brandies are permitted four times the Mexican limit. So as with many aspects of the regulation/legislation of alcohol in Mexico, the relatively low Mexican limit is baffling, particularly as tequila and mezcal contain naturally more methanol than most other distilled spirits.

When fermenting with substantial organic matter, such as agave fibres, more methanol is produced than with cereals or grapes. This is because a compound (lignin) in the fibrous structure of the plant is broken down by enzymes and releases methanol as a by-product. Lignin occurs in higher concentrations in trees and very fibrous plants, which is why it was once used to make industrial methanol and why methanol is also known as "wood alcohol". All agave spirits are susceptible to this, but traditionally made products that are fermented with the fibre will see the highest levels.

The overregulation of methanol has had some negative downstream effects on how the industry operates, pushing some producers to take steps to limit methanol production and selection in their processes. This means there has been a shift towards using more modern, flavour-reducing practices, like diffusers and column stills, or simply adding additional water to their tequila before bottling to dilute the methanol out. On the other side of the industry, like the small palenques of rural Oaxaca, it has vilified producers who practice spirits' production in a traditional manner and in some cases it has prevented them from bottling and marketing their products.

This Mexican methanol problem is further compounded by a strange chemical phenomenon of so-called "reverse distillation" where the alcohols in the *mosto* apparently boil in reverse order. To understand what's going on here, a little science is needed. Methanol has a boiling point of 64.7°C (148.5°F), which is lower than that of pure ethanol (78.4°C/173.1°F) so it should be among the first compounds to vaporise and pass through the still. For most spirits, this process is straightforward and a large chunk of methanol is captured in the early stage of distillation and discarded or re-distilled. However, it's not quite as simple as that in Mexico. Here's why. Certain compounds have an affinity for others. At certain concentrations, ethanol is very fond of water making it nearly impossible to separate them completely. Even if a distiller could isolate pure ethanol, it would quickly absorb moisture from the air until the mixture contained about

4% water by volume. This is called an azeotrope: a mixture of two compounds at a specific ratio that have a very strong attraction and behave as if they are one. This alters the boiling point of the two chemicals, and depending on the chemicals, an azeotrope's boiling point can be higher or lower than either component's normal boiling point.

Water and ethanol form a "minimum" boiling azeotrope, named that way because it boils at 78.2°C (172.8°F), which is far lower than that of pure water and 0.2°C lower than the boiling point of pure ethanol. Methanol and ethanol also form an azeotrope which occurs at a concentration of 92% ethanol and 8% methanol with a boiling point of 78.2°C, which is significantly higher than that of methanol on its own and again, slightly lower than ethanol. What all this means is that a great deal of methanol produced during the fermentation of agave fibres forms an azeotrope with ethanol in the still and is carried through inseparably from it. The only practical way to limit this would be to produce less methanol during fermentation, but that would mean cleaning out as much fibre from the juices as possible and thus dramatically altering the character of the resulting product.

On a positive note, the fact that so much of the ethanol in agave spirits comes off the still later in the distillation is one of the reasons why the *puntas* (heads) don't contain dangerously high levels of methanol in mezcal and raicilla.

The Mexican regulatory authority's ignorance to the basic chemistry involved in agave distillation, and general vilification of methanol, is yet another example of special treatment being awarded to large-scale producers with no

ABOVE Celebrating the diversity of wild agaves and exploring the outer realms of agave spirit character, Cuish is one of the most exciting mezcal brands out there right now.

interest in preserving the historical characteristics of the national spirit. As we have so often seen on our journey, the regulations seem almost purposely designed to demonise, discount or destroy the artisans of the industry who carry the torch of traditional production and upon whose backs the industry has been built.

"There has always been the issue of methanol in mezcal," says Felix, "and sometimes there are incredible batches that are too high in methanol and we cannot bottle them as mezcal without blending or diluting them. Agua del Sol is the workaround."

As we say our goodbyes holding half a dozen bottles of Cuish, I reflect on the small revolution that Felix is waging. His commitment to interesting agaves, his beautifully unconventional bottles, his game-changing mezcalerías. But in a way, Agua del Sol is the truest representation of what he's trying to achieve. This brand removes the baggage and preconception that comes with being a "mezcal" in the growing marketplace of big brands. It places itself at an accessible price point so that it can be enjoyed by anyone, and, above all, it emphasises great distillers, agaves and the lowest interventions possible with the finished liquid.

The only shame in all of this is that it cannot be called by its true name: mezcal.

IGNACIO PARADA

◇◇

El Maestro Escondido

The history of the Zapotec and Mixtec people in Oaxaca goes back 3,500 years, which makes their respective languages among the longest continuously spoken dialects in the world. Both groups built impressive cities in the south of Mexico, like Monte Albán and Mitla (the former also being the name of the first brand of mezcal to be exported from Mexico in 1975), which flanked what is now Oaxaca City to the east and west.

Oaxaca City, which was originally named Antequera by the Spanish, was founded by Juan Peláez de Berrio and Hernando de Soto, under the authority of the Spanish Crown, with the site chosen for its location in a fertile valley and its proximity to existing indigenous settlements.

The city grew rapidly during the 20th century thanks to an increased focus on cultural preservation and the tourism that followed. There are no high-rises in Oaxaca City on account of occasional seismic activity, so instead the city sprawls into the surrounding hills in glorious technicolour, like a patchwork quilt of culture laid over a lumpy mattress. Through the middle runs the Atoyac River, which, along with its tributaries, has supported farming in the region for centuries.

The subject of water in Oaxaca has become a serious topic for public health, agriculture and lately politics too. The elections are on their way across all of Mexico and billboards and posters promoting politicians are an ever-present feature of the geography in this state and the rest. These posters promise all the usual things that politicians promise and fail to deliver, but in Oaxaca a great deal of the messaging is centred around water and its quality. The city of Oaxaca has experienced record-breaking temperatures in recent years, resulting in empty wells and forest fires. Agricultural areas surrounding Oaxaca have reported up to 100% crop loss owing to drought. Public water delivery has become unreliable, with some areas receiving water less than every 40 days. The situation has

sparked protests and a surge in private water-truck usage, some of which are illegally sourcing water from contaminated rivers and reservoirs. The crime of "water theft" has reared up in response to *huachicoleros* who siphon off the water from wells, reservoirs and tanks that are meant to supply the public water services.

The crisis extends beyond the city, affecting rural communities and traditional farming practices. The shift towards monoculture agave farming for industrial-scale mezcal production has contributed to deforestation, further exacerbating water runoff issues and greenhouse-gas emissions. Industrial practices in mezcal production have also raised concerns about water pollution, as runoff from fertilisers and disposal of *vinasses* (leftover from the stills) can pollute water systems if not handled correctly.

One billboard with the smiling face of a female politician reads: *Volviendo a abrir las válvulas en los campos* ("Turning the valves on in the fields"). Estimates for the total amount of water needed to grow an agave to full maturity vary, but research and agricultural reports suggest it could take anywhere from 500–1,000 litres (130–265 gallons) of water per plant over its entire life cycle.

The good news is that agaves are well adapted to arid climates and store water efficiently, so their water needs are much lower than other crops like maize or wheat. Agaves open special stomata pores to take in CO_2 at night and close up in the day to retain moisture. In addition, their pencas are coated in a waxy layer that reflects heat but allows for photosynthesis – a protein called mayahuelin protects them from extreme heat by causing the pores on the leaf to close almost entirely like nature's version of a thermoplastic. Then consider that each penca is basically a paddle or a piece of elegant guttering, designed to catch rainwater and direct its flow in, towards the centre of the plant where its roots are located. Succulents are aptly named: the plant physiologist Park Nobel estimated they are eight times as efficient at using rainwater than most annual crops like grains or tomatoes. Young plants still need regular watering, though, with each seedling requiring approximately one litre of water per week for its first year.

Over in the palenque, a mezcalero needs about a litre of water (34oz) to ferment a kilogram (2¼lbs) of agave and more to cool condensers and for cleaning. Crunch the numbers and it takes approximately 10 litres (2.5 gallons) of water to produce 1 litre of mezcal. Most palenques have their own well to pull from, but the well water has to come from somewhere and there are concerns that the water table is dropping to an unsustainable level. In Matatlán there are two community wells that service domestic and commercial properties, and palenques are charged a higher price for their water supply. In Don Chucho's palenque in Zoquitlán the community relies on mountain spring water, but in recent times the authorities have needed to put pipes in the river to supply the town.

Some mezcal producers are taking a proactive approach to these issues. Brands like Salvadores and Los Ocotales are implementing reforestation projects and rainwater-capture systems. Los Ocotales is building a new palenque that will operate solely on rainwater, and Rolando Cortes is exploring rainwater capture at his De Cortes palenque too. Community-based solutions are also emerging. In 2022 Pensador Mezcals funded a new well in San Isidro Guishe, while the Neta brand, which works with about 20 palenques in the south, near Miahuatlán, is collaborating with Isla Urbana to build water cisterns in Logoche.

The water crisis in Oaxaca adds to the growing list of challenges faced by the mezcal industry today. Already grappling with the threat of commodification and cultural appropriation, mezcaleros are confronting environmental threats including agave diseases, soil degradation and species extinction because of over-harvesting. These problems are further compounded by persistent poverty among local producers. Oaxaca is the third poorest state in Mexico, with other mezcal-producing states of Guerrero, Puebla and Michoacán also in the bottom five.

Established at the same time as the mezcal DO, in 1994, the mezcal NOM lays out the rules that mezcaleros must abide by to have their product certified. As is consistent with every other legal document to do with agave spirits, the NOM is quite contentious, both in its content and in the way it is policed. However, it was rewritten – and most agree, improved – in 2017 with the main change being the introduction of three distinct categories of mezcal.

Mezcal: The broadest category, allowing industrial production methods. Controversially, it permits non-traditional techniques like using continuous stills and diffusers. This approach mirrors issues faced in the tequila industry, potentially diluting the traditional essence of mezcal. The category currently represents about 5% of mezcal producers.

Mezcal Artesanal: Agaves must be roasted in a pit or above-ground stone oven, fermentation must take place with fibres included in stone, earth, wood, clay or leather vessels (steel is not permitted), and distillation can occur in a copper alembic, wooden, or clay pot still. Mechanical shredders are allowed. This category encompasses about 95% of all registered mezcal producers.

Mezcal Ancestral: Similar to Artesanal except the agaves must be roasted in a pit oven, milled by hand or tahona, and specifically distilled in clay pot stills. While this is the most authentic method of production for Oaxaca, it controversially precludes producers using Filipino-still derivatives in other states. Ancestral mezcal represent just 0.35% of all registered producers in 2023, but this might tell us more about who is registering rather than providing an accurate portrayal of production methods across the entire spectrum of agave spirits' distilleries.

As with tequila, certified bottles of mezcal include a NOM number on them, which indicates the distillery or corporate entity that is bottling the product.

Originally all commercially produced mezcal was regulated by non-profit agency COMERCAM, which, about ten years ago, rebranded themselves as the CRM to mirror tequila's CRT certifying body but have recently reverted to COMERCAM. COMERCAM/CRM have never had the sole rights to certify mezcal, but they were the first organisation to be certified a certifier, so to speak, and thus are largest and most influential certifying body in the land. But in 2018 a regulatory spanner was thrown in the works when the Mexican government began approving several other organisations to certify mezcal. This naturally challenged COMERCAM's certification monopoly, but according to them they still stamp around 96% of all certified mezcal brands.

With a situation as confusing as this, and a framework of production that doesn't do much to support smaller producers, it's no wonder that some palenques are choosing to jump ship, forgo their certification fees, and remove "Mezcal" from their bottles.

The most high-profile example of this is Real Minero, owned by the Angeles family which has a long history of mezcal production in Santa Catarina Minas, 20km (12 miles) south of Oaxaca City. Real Minero produces some of the most highly regarded spirits in the state using authentic production methods including clay pot-stills. In 2020, the brand began a transition away from using the term "mezcal" on their labels. They replaced the "ancestral" designation with "traditional" and eventually departed from the official certification process. Consequently, their products are now labelled as "Destilado de Agave".

As more and more high-profile, quality-driven brands jump ship, we may find ourselves on the verge of an agave spirits' revolution and mass decertification from the category. This would be quite an ironic turn of events, as so many of the palenques that have lately been cherished by aficionados sought certification only so that they could be bottled as mezcal and engage with the export market.

The next palenque we're visiting is one such example.

We are sticking with the Cortés family for now, taking the four-hour journey into the southern mountains of Oaxaca and the town of Santa María Zoquitlán. Matt Morrison (whom we met at Casa Cortés) tells us that a new road that goes all the way to the ocean has just opened and it will cut what was a five or six-hour drive in half. There's a sense of mixed feelings about this road, however, as it will inevitably create a flow of tourists (like us!) into towns and villages that have enjoyed seclusion and privacy for centuries. Zoquitlán is one such place, and as we approach the town, it appears like a jewel in the palm of a hand, where the surrounding peaks are tree-covered fingers pointing at the sky. The town is flanked by two converging river valleys and its steep hillsides are visibly studded with rare agaves, such as Jabalí and Tepeztate.

Rolando Cortés tells me he first came to Zoquitlán in 2007 off the back of his mezcal epiphany at Danzantes restaurant. It wasn't a sourcing trip or part of a plan to expand his brand, but a pilgrimage to seek out and learn from one of the state's legendary producers. The town had a reputation for being dangerous, though, and Rolando's father cautioned him not to go. "It was considered a town that takes its own justice," says Rolando. "And I always heard that if you come here you won't get out alive."

The man he was looking for was called Ignacio Parada, said to be the operator of the last remaining (unregistered) palenque in town. The quality of his mezcal was well known in the area, as well as his cultivation and sourcing of many varieties of agave including Espadín, Tepeztate, Jabalí, Tobalá and Madrecuishe.

Rolando rolled into Zoquitlán with his friend Daniel who, regrettably, "had the look of a judge or politician about him". They came across an old woman who was immediately suspicious of what they were up to, assuming that the pair of men from the valleys were federal police looking to shut things down or hustle for a bribe. After some negotiation and placation, she directed them to the river and told them to follow it to the palenque. Upon finding the palenque, the man attending it said he had never heard of Ignacio Parada and that his name was Chucho. Things turned nasty for a moment, negotiations were made, and eventually Chucho served Rolando a Cuishe mezcal. "It took me back to my childhood," says Rolando. "It smelled like wet dirt – it was incredible."

Over a series of meetings spanning years, Chucho shared stories with Rolando about his family, about his daughter who was studying in high school, about his son, who had emigrated to the US, and about his desire to see them reunited and living and working together. Many mezcals were shared and, one day, Rolando posed the question to him: "Why don't you want to be recognised so that people know you are making incredible mezcal?"

Don Chucho agreed to supply Rolando with mezcal and this was the seed of the beginning of the El Jolgorio brand. It was only when Don Chucho came to sign the papers to register his palenque that Rolando saw his real name: Ignacio Parada – the legendary mezcalero he had been searching for all along.

Ignacio's was the first palenque to join the Casa Cortés family back in 2012. Since then, Chucho has produced a range of expressions across a variety of agave types. The palenque is still owned and operated by Ignacio with the help of his son, Jose, who has returned home. Besides bottling some spirit for the town, they produce it only for Rolando. "In the end, he was the first one who is not from the bloodline," says Rolando. We're standing in Ignacio's palenque and Ignacio himself is next to Rolando, armed with a big plastic jug half filled with mezcal. "But he is more than that," says Rolando looking fondly at the man.

OPPOSITE The man, the legend, Ignacio "Don Chucho" Parada has spent a lifetime making mezcal and has become extremely adept at it. His spirits speak of the wild and dangerous nature of the mountains.

"He is a part of everything we do – he is a part of the family." Ignacio pours us samples of one of his recently distilled spirits – Espadín puntas made two days ago and sitting at a weighty 65% ABV. *The aroma is bright and fresh and not as aggressive as you might expect at this strength. Alcohol is certainly there on the palate, but more in its taste than in raw heat. There's a lick of smoke and roasted green veg. The peppery finish lasts a while.*

Thanks in part to Ignacio's skill and Rolando's publicity of him and of Zoquitlán, the revival of mezcal in the town is well underway. There are now ten palenques, and a new generation of energised, ambitious mezcaleros to go with them. Matt tells us that many of the next generation have learned much of their trade on the internet, and are innovating a diverse range of styles as they find their feet.

Ignacio tells us that he has a family-distilling history in this region that goes back at least to the 1700s. Now in his 50s, he learned to distil with his brothers at ten and worked and owned previous palenques before he built Zoqui in 2015. He picked the location to be nearer to his agaves, personally constructing a wooden mould for his tahona into which he poured a mixture of gravel and concrete. Nearby is an eight-tonne pit oven in which he roasts the agaves.

After milling in the tahona, the agaves are transferred to wooden fermenters. These are a mixture of pine and Mexican cypress (known locally as Sabino) with one of the latter being more than 100 years old. The crushed agaves undergo an initial aerobic fermentation without water, which allows the natural yeasts to multiply among the fibres. Once the colony is established, water is poured over the fermenting fibres, which circulates some of the sugars and the yeasts and is accompanied by a satisfying frothing and bubbling from the fermenting tank.

Ignacio tells us that he usually harvests agaves before they sprout a quiote because he thinks they actually have more fermentable sugar than after the quiote is cut. He also says that wild agaves from the hills ferment much faster than cultivated ones, which he puts down to the lower concentration of sugar in the wild ones. "The ones that come from the hills take only three days," he says with a shrug. "The Espadín can take eight days depending on the season and the amount of water added."

Among the other tricks up his sleeves, Ignacio is making a mango spirit distilled entirely from fermented mangos. Motivated into action by our interest in it, Ignacio disappears and returns with a massive plastic jug and pours out samples for us to try. *The aroma is undeniably mango,* but more of a dried and slightly fermented/rotten version of the fruit rather than crisp and tropical. The taste is nice, with plenty of heat and some nice curried notes.

We pile back into the minibus and take a 30-minute drive further into the mountains, to see where some of the agaves that Ignacio is using are grown. The vehicle comes to a halt high on a mountain ridge. Compared to the air-conditioned sanctuary of the bus, the hill feels almost electric in the heat of the mid-afternoon sun. Twiggy trees and organ-pipe cacti bake, while lizards scuttle out of sight and a pair of hummingbirds zooms between the foliage.

We take a short walk along a narrow trail and find ourselves on the edge of a small outcrop with incredible views in all directions on to the surrounding valley. The river that runs through it is all but dried up, and land and even the air has taken on a sepia hue. Rolando says there has been no rain here for two years – a reminder of how climate change is impacting the water crisis in Oaxaca – but that when it does the vegetation turns a lush green. Here, between patches of scrub and cacti, we can see hundreds of agaves dotted around the landscape.

There are a handful up here on the ridge too.

"This is a Jabalí," says Matt, pointing at a nearby agave with many, relatively short, spear-like pencas – like the leaves of a pineapple. Jabalí belongs to the *Agave convallis* species and has a reputation for being hard to deal with as it contains proteins that cause it to expand during fermentation and distillation, and has even led to some stills being damaged as Jabalí mosto expands like a bomb. This aggressive nature is reflected in the spirit it makes, which Pancho describes as "wild and chaotic".

"That big fucker is a Tepeztate," says Matt, pointing at a huge agave, with its pencas like pointy elephant ears draped over rocks in undignified folds. We spy another Tepeztate, which has the stub of a quiote showing, indicating that it will be harvested soon.

"Those ones that look like starbursts," says Matt, pointing at an agave that looks like a palm, "those are Madrecuishe – hey Chucho, do you have any?" Ignacio walks towards us with a serious look on his face. He stops in front of us, and pulls out a plastic water bottle filled with clear liquid. "Of course," he says with a grin, and fills our glasses with a generous pour. *The aroma is earthy, like hot sand and dust, then cooked grapefruit comes through followed by freshly milled sawdust. The taste is wild and medicinal: eucalyptus and menthol with burnt courgette (zucchini). The finish is very savoury.*

UNNAMED PALENQUE

Most of the mezcal distilleries we have visited belong to the 400 or so mezcal brands that have found their way across the border into the US as a fully exported brand. However, this means there are more than 2,000 distilleries that are producing mezcal only for local consumption and thus remain basically unknown to the outside world. This constitutes the majority of the people working in agave spirits: tens of thousands of people, and communities, working daily in the production of a spirit that you and I have never heard of and, for most of them, are never likely to either.

I wanted to meet some of these people and see them at work, so this morning we got up early and headed to the fields near Ejutla to see some agaves being harvested and to visit a nearby palenque.

Not far from the highway to the north of town, we park up near a pair of pickup trucks, both of them stacked high with agave hearts already. The men are a few hundred metres further into the fields, moving slowly and deliberately among the cacti and agaves, which, in the morning light appear to be the luminescent green-like flora of an alien planet. Two men are harvesting agaves while another is watering some of the smaller plants that were put in the field only recently. There are no pipes or irrigation system, instead he fills buckets from a tank in the pickup truck and walks through the field to the waiting plants. These plants are the Tobalá variety (*Agave potatorum*) and have even shorter and wider leaves than *maximiliana*, making them look altogether like very large cabbages.

These are hard men, with skin weathered by dozens of hot summers, hands callused by a million cuts, clothes sun-bleached and with holes or patches from days spent lifting and carrying the piñas from one place to the next.

The role of the jimador is not well-paid. While the tequila industry occasionally reports that some of its workers can earn up to $100 (£75) a day, these people are unusual, and a typical labourer will pocket more like $20–$30 (£15–23) a day and sometimes even less.

For an industry that celebrates the craft of the jimador and readily uses his likeness on bottles and in marketing, it is a shamefully meagre compensation for their work.

In the book *Agave Spirits*, David Suro Piñera makes a depressing observation that one tonne of agave might produce somewhere in the region of 2,600 tequila or mezcal cocktails in a typical US bar, each of which could be sold for $15 (£12). Thus, the total revenue produced by the tonne of agave at the end of the supply chain is $40,000 (£30,000). I mentioned back when we visited Don Abraham that a skilled jimador might cut 80 agave plants or up to six tonnes in a day and at a daily rate of $25 (£20), he is earning around $4 (£3) per tonne. Therefore, the labourer is earning 0.01% of the retail value of the product.

Ah, yes, but think of all the production stages, the bottling, marketing, import, transport, taxes, staff costs and so on! This is how supply chain works after all, with each link in the chain adding in their own margin to cover labour, overheads and profits. The percentage margin at the beginning shrinks down to very small numbers.

While this is true, consider the bartenders' tip, which is added on at the very end of the supply chain, almost as an afterthought. If you crunch the maths, the tip constitutes 162,500% more than what the jimador earns per kilo of agave. To put it another way, if just 10% of the bartenders in the US donated just 10% of their tips derived only from agave spirit drinks, they could increase the salary of every jimador in Mexico by a factor of five.

One thing I have learned while being around mezcaleros is the importance of recognising that mezcal is not made in the palenque but in the fields. These are people of the fields, guardians of agave and custodians of an ancient tradition. The field is where they belong, while the palenque serves as a ceremonial temple – where human and plant come together at last.

The final agave of the morning is a *salmiana* that is proving a challenge. The pencas have been trimmed but the root is still in the ground. One of the jimadores, a man named Abel, has jammed his coa blade into the base of the plant at ground level and is now whacking it like a chisel with a sledgehammer. Meanwhile, his co-worker, Alfonso, attempts push the plant out of the ground by pressing his weight against it. Finally, with a crack like the felling of a tree, the plant relents and topples over. It must be at least 100kg (220lbs) so now they must split it into pieces so that it can be carried back to the truck.

An hour later we have arrived at their palenque, which is a small place set into a courtyard with a single alembic still, half a dozen wooden fermenters, and a pit oven. This morning's harvest makes up the final few plants that will be roasted in this oven today.

Being that we are nearing the end of our journey, it is surprising that this will be the first time that we have seen a pit oven being prepared and loaded. But when you consider the steps of production in most of these places, plus the seasonal flow of making spirits, this two-hour process might only occur once a month. After all, the pit can take days to empty if the agave is milled by hand or tahona. And even then, the fermenters will be filled and might take a week or two before they can be emptied. But even then, the fermenters can be emptied only as quickly as the stills can be run. This whole "batch" process is basically a series of bottlenecks that need to be accounted for along the way. And all of it means, unless you have a lot of equipment, you can't just keep cooking agave all the time.

So here we are.

The pit is around five metres (16ft) wide and less than two metres (6.5ft) deep. In the bottom there's a large stack of black volcanic rocks giving off an enormous amount of heat. Underneath them we can see the red glow of a smouldering fire that was lit at 4am – about 8 hours ago.

The specific type of wood used for these fires tends to vary according to availability, but each imparts its own flavour. Some prefer mesquite, others oak, guamúchil or sabino. As a BBQ pit master will tell you, different woods impact both heat and smoke quality. And on that note, let's not forget that it's the Mesoamerican culinary tradition of grilling and smoking food, known as *barbacoa*, that we have to thank for the word "barbecue".

In some respects, wood is as important to the mezcalero as the agave – without it there's no fire to roast the agaves or heat the stills. Along with fresh water, this trinity of materials has defined the historic locations of tabernas and palenques just as it has the villages for the people who make them.

Around the edge of the pit, the agaves are stacked more than a metre high, leaving enough of a gap between them and the edge of the pit so you can walk around it and another gap in the wall so you can get in there. With its concentric circles of wood, fire and rock, the whole thing is set up like some sort of religious sacrifice.

The three guys who have been preparing the oven while we were in the fields are laying about in the shade, but now they suddenly kick into action. Trousers are dusted off, Coca Cola and Squirt bottles drained of their contents, and very few words are exchanged. You can feel the tension building as the rocks near the correct temperature and smoke from the fire has all but gone. Some of these agaves have been in the ground for more than ten years, then carefully harvested and brought here for this exact moment.

The agaves are mixed varieties and will produce an ensemble expression. While single-variety mezcals are the trend today, the methods at work here – where mature agaves are harvested regardless of their species – is far truer to the ancestral methods of producing mezcal.

Alfonso produces a wheelbarrow loaded with moist agave fibres – the *bagazo* (residue from the previous distillation). He rolls it into the inner perimeter of the oven and starts throwing it on the rocks with a pitchfork. Not all over, just in the parts where the glow of the embers can be seen clearly. The fibres smoke and sizzle as they land. I'm trying to figure out the pattern of where and why he is disturbing the fibres and begin to see that he is identifying parts of the fire that allow oxygen to penetrate on to the coals. The idea here is to snuff out the flames as quickly as possible by removing oxygen, otherwise the fire will burn the agaves and cause flames to rear up.

Next, it's time to start loading on the piñas. Addie is photographing furiously and I am taking notes; wary of not getting too close to the pit while the men do their work. That's when Abel beckons me over.

"Put one on," he says, in clear English. "Just one."

I had been keenly observing the process thus far, and it was already impressed with the artistry of it all. It is not just a case of throwing agaves into a pit. You have to build solid walls around the edge and fill in the centre gradually. This ensures that no air can get through to the fire but also that you are cooking the maximum quantity of agaves in the given space. It also prevents the whole thing collapsing under its own weight and semi-cooked agave spilling out all over the dusty yard.

So I grab a medium-sized piña – maybe 20kg (45lbs) – and load it in like a brick in the circular wall we're building. I give Abel a smile and he smiles back. I grab another one and load it on. Then another. At this point it felt rude to stop, so I continued. After a while Abel instructs me – in action more than language – to stack the piñas with the root-end facing towards the centre of the fire, as it is denser and requires more heat. We're working as a team now, each building our own section of the wall with our own stack of agaves. Pancho is working too and Addie has put his cameras down and is getting involved as well.

For me, the labour of lifting and stacking the agaves is not so bad. They are a manageable shape and size and the stubs of pencas give you something to grip on to. But the heat of the rocks is really something. After around 20 minutes, we have covered the rocks with agave and the heat is more tolerable but that is when the smoke really starts. In that instant, I realise why some mezcal tastes smoky. Huge plumes of it drift this way and that, stinging

ABOVE Loading an Oaxacan pit oven makes it very clear exactly from where the smoky quality found in mezcal originates.

my eyes and blinding my vision. I don't want to complain, though – gringo as I am – so continue with my work. Abel and Alfonso exchange words across the pit and look at me, laughing. "You want a job?!" says Alfonso.

Shortly after that the work pauses – the critical first stage complete. The owner of the palenque, Javier, has been carrying his young daughter since we started. Now he's carrying a bottle of mezcal and some *copitas* too. He pours out a large measure for all of us and we waste no time getting acquainted with it. *It's warm and sticky in the palate, blending with the acrid smoke from the air and the salty sweat on my lips.* It's not the most refreshing drink I can think of at this moment, but I am grateful of the pause in the work and the reminder of why we are doing it.

I accept a second one just to be sure.

Abel and Alfonso are chatting to each other and it's only at this point that I realise they are not speaking Spanish.

"Zapotec?" I say. "Yes, I do not speak Spanish," comes the response from Abel. "But my English is okay."

I clink my copita onto his and ask how to say "cheers" in Zapotec. "*Dixeebe*," he says (pronounced "dishbey").

All told it took around 45 minutes to load five tonnes of agave into the pit and, by the time we finished, it was piled nearly three metres (ten feet) high. My work is done, but for the team there is still a lot left to do.

They drag in plastic sheets and layer them over the top of the agave pile. The final step of building the oven is perhaps the most labour intensive of them all. With the plastic sheets in place the team begins carting barrows of dirt over to the mound and shovelling it on top. This creates a layer of insulation as well as some pressure to keep the sheets in place. Of course, the dirt wants to slide off the top, so a significant amount is needed in order to cover the whole mound. Wood is then piled on top of the dirt to create a downward pressure and hold the dirt and sheets in place.

In some mezcal palenques, it's common practice to place a wooden cross on top of the oven. This practice seems to be a curious mashup of Christian symbolism and older spiritual practices. The cross is said to demonstrate respect for the earth and the maguey itself, and serves as a symbolic request to grant a successful cook.

As the men pile the dirt on top, my forearms start tingling. I head to the bathroom to clean up.

"Be careful!" says Alfonso. "Don't rub them!"

The sap of many agaves is a powerful irritant on the skin and the loading work has created tiny scratches and scuffs where the sap has begun to trigger a reaction. Some agaves are more irritating than others and its said by some that the degree to which it aggravates the skin can be an indicator of how much sugar is in the plant – the stronger the irritant, the lower the sugar. Alfonso warns me that rubbing the skin with soap and water would make it worse, but with my arms caked in dirt and sticky sap it seems like the right thing to do. The dermatitis that I developed from that 30 minutes of loading stayed on my skin for over a month.

Not far south of Ejutla is Miahuatlán, another big mezcal town. It's sheltered by the southern mountains, which results in a warmer, drier climate that of course affects the agaves grown there and has led to distinctive mezcal-production methods. Both Miahuatlán and Ejutla have become synonymous with a type of still called a *refrescador*. This looks like a classic alembic still, with a steel or copper head connected to a separate coiled condenser by a pipe, but it also has a condensing jacket surrounding the head of the still that is filled with cool water, that causes reflux, as the alcohol vapours rise up the head of the still and fall back down again. If the still is made from copper this can encourage prolonged contact between the spirit vapour and copper, which can help to remove off notes. But what it also does is increase the alcohol concentration in the spirit vapour, as the heavier compounds (like water) fall back down to the base of the still. In effect, it produces a continuous chain of micro-distillations, allowing only the lightest alcohols to pass through to the condensation coil. The upshot of all this is that you can take a fermented mosto of, let's say, 7% ABV and distil it up to and above 40% ABV in a single distillation run. "To me, it's less polished," says Pancho. "And it's not as oily either."

The story of how these stills got here is not entirely clear, but the best explanation I hear is that in the 1930s there was an inventor who built the first refrescadors and went around Mexico trying to sell them. Only one mezcalero in Ejutla bought one because they were very expensive, but he soon began turning out some of the best mezcal anyone had tasted. Then everyone wanted one and the mezcalero became the local sales guy for refrescador stills. He managed to sell a bunch of them in Ejutla and Miahuatlán but never gained much traction in the rest of the state, and that's why only those two areas have them today.

It's still morning when we leave the palenque and walk past a small market stand with local vendors offering homemade *tamales* (filled cornmeal dough) wrapped in banana leaves, still steaming from their cooking baskets. The sharp tang of pickled vegetables cuts through the air from the jars of *escabeche* lined up neatly on rough wooden tables. In the shade of a gnarled mesquite tree, a group of workers shares a jug of *agua fresca*, the chunks of watermelon and mint leaves floating temptingly in the rosy liquid.

Pancho grabs a bundle of freshly cooked tamales and we load into the car, stuffing them into our mouths as it bumps down the road. The bumping continues even as we merge back on to the highway, and it's at this point we notice the bonnet of the Jetta is bouncing up and down in an unnatural fashion. Worried that it might fly off, we pull to a stop at the side of the road and discover that we have burst another tyre. Not only that, but whatever pothole caused the puncture has also destroyed the suspension, causing the entire strut to detach from its housing and hammer the bonnet like a pneumatic drill. We change the tyre and slowly limp back to Oaxaca City where Pancho drops the Jetta off at a garage for repair (again).

JOEL BARRIGA

◇◇

La Comunidad

On our penultimate morning in Oaxaca, Pancho receives a phone call from the garage where the Jetta is being repaired. It's not good news. The long-suffering vehicle needs a new suspension strut and the damage done to the subframe has made it unroadworthy in any case. Pancho doesn't seem at all phased by the news – further evidence in my eyes that he wanted to kill the car all along – so we hop in a taxi and head into the centre of town to the offices of the mezcal brand Vago.

Vago was founded in 2013 by Judah Kuper, a Colorado native who had spent most of his younger life surfing and snowboarding around the world. In 2010 he got injured surfing off the Oaxaca coast and landed himself in hospital where he met his future wife, Valentina, who was working as a nurse there. The pair fell in love. Judah went to the mountain village of Candelaria Yegolé to visit Valentina's father, Aquilino Garcia, to ask for her hand in marriage. It turns out that Aquilino was a third-generation mezcal producer so naturally he served Judah a mezcal that became Judah's first ever sip of *puntas*. Judah fell in love all over again and became fascinated with the ancestral production methods of his product.

Judah and Valentina opened a small cantina where they began serving Aquilino's spirit, and the response was overwhelmingly positive. Judah's best friend, Dylan Sloan, convinced him to bottle the mezcal and invested $7,000 (£5,500) into the business. Judah took only nine months to get the business off the ground and exported his first bottles to Texas in 2013.

Initially, Mezcal Vago focused on distributing Aquilino's mezcals but over time they expanded to work with a further three mezcal producers from different parts of the southern Oaxacan mountains. These four mezcaleros extol different regional styles of production and a range of agave varieties but also represent a sustainable approach to sourcing agaves and supporting the families that make the spirits – because some of them are literally family.

With Aquilino's passing in 2019, Temo and Mateo García have taken over from their father at Candelaria Yegolé near Zoquitlán. Their most popular product is called Elote and it is basically a corn pechuga made using heirloom corn kernels that are toasted on a *comal* and placed in the still with Espadín *ordinario* for the second distillation. Meanwhile, Tío Rey, based in Sola de Vega, produces mezcal in traditional clay pot-stills making him one of the very few producers of Ancestral mezcal. Don Emigdio in Miahuatlán employs refrescador stills, which can produce a finished spirit in a single distillation. Finally, Joel Barriga's palenque, Hacienda Tapanala, nestled high in the mountains, is our destination for the day.

"We call them communities," he says. "But they are really just extended families living in the same village. Most of them have been there longer than records exist."

It's roughly a four-hour drive from Oaxaca City to Hacienda Tapanala through some tough mountain terrain. Fortunately, we have Andres Cruz, the national ambassador for Vago as both our host and driver for the day.

Much like Casa Cortés, Vago is a mezcal brand that is committed to traditional production methods and working directly with mezcal producers so as to contribute to the economic development of the communities where their mezcal is produced. Andres explains that the brand has stuck with the same four families for ten years now and has no plans to work with any others.

After loading into his Vago-branded Hilux, we leave the city and make a quick stop for some late breakfast at a roadside cantina. Andres orders *tlayudas*, which are something like Mexican pizzas, being comprised of a wide, thin, toasted tortilla with toppings including fried beans, meat, cheese and whatever else is at hand.

This sets up nicely for a spectacular journey through the mountains, taking in breathtaking views along a track that seems to be on a never-ending ascent into the sky. The Jetta could never have managed it, but Pancho would have tried – if only to kill it. Every new turn offers a treat for the eyes and Addie's camera shutter fires relentlessly. After around an hour of this, we summit the range and find ourselves driving among the clouds on a winding track that weaves between great mounds of rock, which appear wrinkled like rhino hide as the morning light catches their profile. If feels as though we have driven to another planet. How anyone can live in such a remote location is beyond me, let alone run a business producing a spirit that is now being exported around the world.

The village of Tapanala is built upon the ruins of a former hacienda and these days is essentially populated entirely by the Barriga family, with Don Joel as the head along with his six sons and their families. Here, they are almost entirely self-sufficient for their food, growing everything from limes and sugar cane through to rearing a range of livestock for milk and meat. There are around 20 children in the village, all of them siblings or cousins. There is an elementary school to support their early learning, but older children tend to move to Zoquitlán to attend high school, or they begin working in the village.

"Joel is the oldest of our mezcaleros and he really seems to have things figured out," says Andres as we step out of the car and approach the house. "He's just enjoying his grandchildren, going out and put fences on his land, growing his cows, growing his agave, making mezcal."

Joel, his wife, one of his sons and three grandchildren of varying ages greet us. Their modest home is clearly a happy place, and despite their remote location, we get a very warm welcome.

We start the tour by taking a hike up into the hills adjacent to the village. The water supply for the houses and palenque is a spring that emerges half a kilometre (1500ft) up the slope. It's a dusty, technically challenging hike up the hill, past many cacti and agaves. We walk alongside an old brick aqueduct that once serviced the hacienda but has since collapsed. Arriving at the spring, we see that water is now transported down the hill through plastic pipes.

On the walk back down, Andres and Joel point out some of the Tepeztate agaves that are growing wild on the hills amid the trees and shrubby undergrowth.

Tepeztate has broad, pale green pencas with a particularly rugged and tough texture, like elephant skin.

They gracelessly twist and collapse under their own weight, which is why the Tepeztate love hills and rocks – they serve as resting places to drape their leaves over and anchors for the roots to adhere to. The hills also allow rainwater to run off, which prevents the agave from swelling up and keeps the sugar concentrated.

Full maturation for these agaves can take an incredible 25 years. If they were cultivated and weeded around and maybe fertilised from time to time, they might mature in half that time, but Joel is quick to point out that they would have only half of the complexity of a plant that has undergone a lifetime of struggle on the slopes.

"When we harvest the wild agaves, you can tell they will make good mezcal," says Joel. "The smell as you cut them is intoxicating – sweet and complex."

The long maturation of Tepeztate is one of the reasons why Joel is harvesting only very small amounts (around ten plants a year) because he is mindful of maintaining a community of these plants for reproduction. There's a fine balance at play here, where over-harvesting in a single year could mean it's unsustainable to harvest again for an entire generation.

"You see those blue flags over there?" Andres points up, high on the hill. "Those are to mark the agaves that should not be cut." It takes me a moment but then I notice strips of blue plastic dotted around in the tree canopy that could easily be mistaken for random bits of litter. In fact, they are placed very near old tepeztate agaves that are nearing full maturity. Tepeztates do not produce *hijuelos* (clones) from their roots so need to pollinate and seed if they are to reproduce. These flags indicate the Tepeztate agaves that should not be harvested but instead left to produce a flower and hopefully seed the next generation of plants naturally. By the time those plants are mature, Joel will likely be gone and his grandchildren will be making mezcal.

We have already discussed the threat that some agave species face as a result of over-harvesting and poor sustainability practices. The industry is in a quandary, though. Demand for non-Espadín varieties is high and the prices consumers are willing to pay reflect this. Who then are we to tell a mezcalero to act responsibly when he is simply responding to market demand and looking to feed his children?

COMERCAM recently reported that 18 of the known 58 varieties of agave used to make mezcal are threatened to the point of extinction, including the species *potatorum*, *karwinskii* and *cupreata*.

Recent studies suggest that endangered species would need up to a third of their plants to reach full sexual reproductive maturity (produce a flower stalk) for the plants to stand a chance of surviving in the wild. Demand for single-variety expressions is placing further pressure on these plants.

With 90% of mezcal being made from Espadín already, we are well along the way to seeing this single variety become the de facto agave in the same way *tequilana* has. Only this time it's through the unintentional extinction of wild species rather than political pressure from industrial producers.

Here at Tapanala, Joel is growing cultivated Mexicano (*rhodacantha*), Espadín (*angustifolia*) and buying in Jabalí (*corvallis*) from nearby Miahuatlán.

We return to the family home where Joel finds some mezcal for us to try. Joyfully we realise it is a 100% Tepeztate expression, made from wild agaves just like the ones we have seen on the hills. *The aroma is raw and very green, leading into an intensely floral character with a touch a violet and geranium. The green note continues in the taste, with eucalyptus, lime and apple.*

Joel's wife serves us a lunch of freshly made tortillas, beef steak, radishes, *asadero* (a hard, salty, mozzarella-style cheese) and frijoles made from black delgado beans and toasted avocado leaves, all, of course, grown on the farm.

Our conversation for the next half an hour is focused only on the food. Sitting there drinking mezcal and sharing food while laughing with one another in spite of the language barrier, I wonder if there is a better life than this? It is a simple life, for sure. The Barriga home is little more than a courtyard with small adjoining rooms, one of them serving as a chapel for prayer. Corrugated iron forms part of the kitchen roof and other sections of the property are in a semi-completed or partially demolished state.

It's not an easy life, but consider the rewards. Providing for family and community. Working with animals. Finding a connection with the land and making something spectacular from it.

Awoken from my reverie in the best possible way, Andres produces a bottle of 100% Cuishe mezcal produced by Don Joel. *The aroma is medicinal and herbal, with liquorice (licorice) root sweetness and caraway, cinnamon spice and star anise. Very more-ish.*

RIGHT The Barrigas are a self-sufficient family community, but when you visit, you become part of the family too.

After lunch we take a short truck ride over to see the palenque. It is a familiar setup, with a mule-pulled tahona, wooden fermenters and alembic stills. The tahona is loaded with crushed agaves but its mule is taking a short break from work.

"His name is Macho," says Joel as I stroke his face. "Como esta, Macho?" I say, with no response.

"No es bueno!" says Joel on his behalf with a laugh.

Joel tells me Macho works for around 14 days straight after a cook is completed, which is the time it takes to crush all of their agaves. After that he gets two weeks of rest in the field and then the next round begins.

Besides Macho, there is no real difference between the tahona here and those we saw in Jalisco at Cascahuín, Fortaleza, Patrón and more. There is a difference in the way they are used, however. In traditional mezcal production, no water is added to the tahona while it is milling the agave – you might think of it as a "dry"

ABOVE Macho the donkey giving us some side-eye while he takes a well-earned pause from pulling the tahona. Meanwhile, the agave fibres are turned to ensure maximum extraction.

milling. Yes, there is some juice in the agave itself, but in general it looks more like crushing herbs in a pestle and mortar than it does juicing oranges.

We have talked about tahonas quite a lot through our journey, both as a traditional method of crushing agaves and as a symbol of authenticity. Some of the tequileros and mezcaleros we have met have espoused the benefits in flavour that a tahona offers, noting that it brings about a pronounced stone or mineral flavour in the spirit. I am naturally cautious about accepting these claims as fact because, after all, we're just cutting up agaves here, right?

Keen to understand more, I explored some scientific papers to see if I could get a better understanding of what difference the tahona makes versus the mill.

It turns out that the tahona does indeed yield higher concentrations of complex compounds like terpenes and furans, and produces more "minor compounds", such as limonene and pentyl butanoate. This results in richer, more complex flavours and aromas. In contrast, mechanical milling produces higher concentrations of major compounds like methanol and acetaldehyde. Basically, a tahona appears to amplify subtle flavours by extracting less of the dominant plant flavours. This creates complexity, similar to how a sauce with many ingredients often tastes richer than one with only a few dominant flavours.

Don Joel employs one of two copper pot-stills, each with a capacity of 300 litres (80 gallons), which are heated by a natural wood fire. The first distillation process spans approximately five hours, with the *ordinario* (first distillate) beginning to flow from the still after around 30 minutes, yielding 55 litres (15 gallons). As distillation progresses over the next hour, an additional 10 to 15 litres (2.5–4 gallons) are produced, though these are reserved and redistilled with the next batch of *tepache* (ferment) because they are weaker in flavour. This is not a common practice in the production of agave spirits but it is similar to the re-distillation of feints that is standard practice in single malt whisky in Scotland and elsewhere. After the entire batch of tepache completes its initial distillation, it is returned to the still for the second distillation, known here as *resacado*.

Joel lets me draw samples of mezcal from a jug, using a *carrizo* straw and we observe the *perlas* (bubbles) form and fall away. It's a mezcal made from Tobola (*Agave potatorum*), which is minuscule in size compared to its compatriots but famously produces a very intense liquor. *The aroma has a slight banana character to it, along with overripe fruit-bowl smells. Chilli spice comes through on the taste, and a slight touch of nail varnish remover. The finish is clean, dry and mineral.*

The wooden fermenters are fizzing away, and the fire under the copper alembic stills is burning bright. Meanwhile, a worker gently taps Macho on his hind quarters to keep the tahona stone moving. Pancho asks Joel if he has ever considered adding a scoop behind the tahona that could help turn the fibre and speed up the process. The answer that comes back is simple but it speaks volumes – "No."

Maintaining tradition is not always about social responsibility or preservation of culture, or even about flavour, efficiency or consistency. Sometimes it's just the

ABOVE Practising my carrizo-straw technique, then assessing the perlas of the mezcal in a cuastecomate cup.

way, and if the way works, it will continue to be the way. That's just the way it is. In many ways, this is what makes Hacienda Tapanala unique – the rest of the world has changed, but this place hasn't.

MACURICHOS

◇◇◇

La Comunion

A few miles north of Matatlán is the Guilá Naquitz Cave. This archaeological site has yielded some of the earliest evidence of plant domestication by humans, dating back around 9,000 years. It's a cornerstone in our understanding of early human–plant interactions in Mesoamerica.

When the cave was excavated in the late 1960s and revealed a treasure trove of well-preserved organic materials, as well as a small roasting pit. Among the most significant were charred agave fibres and *quids* – chewed plant material that had been spat out. These remains, dated to around 8,000–7,000BCE, provide irrefutable evidence of agave utilisation by early Mesoamerican hunter-gatherer societies, highlighting a relationship between humans and agaves that may have been ongoing for tens of thousands of years. Sites in Chihuahua and Coahuila dating back more than 4,000 years have uncovered large quantities of agaves suggesting it was a staple food in the diet of whoever lived there. Over the years that have followed, indigenous people have developed ways to eat and drink practically every part of the agave with little left to waste.

Besides the roasted heart, pencas, roots and flower stalks, the sweet and tender blossoms, which go by names such as *bayuazas, cayaquias, huertos, gulumbos, hualumbos, machetes* or *jiviveres*, would also become cherished ingredients in traditional cuisine and beverages. Soon the seeds were cooked and eaten whole or ground down into a type of flour. More recently, even the thin, translucent skin of the agave penca, known as *mixiote*, has been used to wrap meat or other ingredients into a dumpling-like parcel. And then, if all else fails, why not eat one of the many and varied types of bug that can call an agave home, including *chinicuiles* (red maguey worm), *meocuiles* (white maguey worm), *escamoles* (ant larvae) and *cuchama* (agave weevil). These insects were a vital source of protein in a region where livestock was not widely raised before the arrival of the Europeans.

Our final stop is in the centre of Matatlán on the main highway. It's a palenque called El Sabino, better known by the brands it makes, which are fierce defendants of ancestral production: Libertador, Tempestad and Macurichos.

"The first time I visited Oaxaca, I went to maybe 20 palenques," says Pancho as we approach the palenque gate, his eyes suddenly wide and shining. "I arrived here and had a personal epiphany. We sat here and we drank... maybe 15 different mezcals. We got drunk together and he opened this place to me. I was totally hooked by the energy of the place – I spent an extraordinary amount of money – and that was the day I realised I had to open a mezcal bar."

We enter the gates and are greeted by the distillery peacock and the sounds of running water burbling and children playing. With its pale stone walls, terracotta roof tiles and timber bar, it's like we've time-travelled back to a grand house in the city of Monte Albán. Gonzalo Martinez, the owner of the palenque, greets us and shakes our hands. He is a fifth-generation mezcalero, though his family has no record or knowledge of anyone doing anything other than farming agaves and making mezcal. Ever.

As we take a seat at the palenque bar, Gonzalo pours a glass of Macurichos Tobalá (*Agave potatorum*) mezcal bottled at 48% ABV. *It's fragrant and sweet, with raisin box and smoked almond, burnt brandy and Xmas pudding. There's a slight funky, almost rancid note to the taste (in a good way), then smoked red (bell) pepper. The finish is robust and powerful.*

As we sip on the liquid, he wastes no time in sharing his feelings on the crisis that Oaxacan mezcal is facing. Agaves are being swept up by big distilleries he says and leaving smaller ones without the raw materials to produce. Mezcal has become a commodity to be bought and marketed, its traditions respected only in so far as to benefit its sale. As it becomes the property of big corporate entities, attention turns to profitability at the detriment of quality and

authenticity, not to mention the livelihoods of the people who make it. Many new brands are either vanity projects for rich businessmen or celebrities looking to make a quick buck off the back of mezcal's popularity. "I saw it coming," he says with a sadness in his voice. "The plant talks to you – they warn you – they understand that things are not the same as in the past. As I walked among them in the morning dew, they told me a crisis was coming. That was a year ago. I see with my people today living and suffering. A lot of people don't have a job right now. They are pioneers in mezcal. And owners. Owners of the tradition."

He pours us a glass of Macurichos pechuga mezcal, this one made using coyote and bottled at 58% ABV. *The aroma is of incense and perfume, then a strange latex scent comes wafting in. A return visit gives agave, sweet and sticky. The taste has notable brawn and animal notes to it, with heat and more of that plastic. It's like a werewolf wearing a condom.*

The threat that mezcal faces is not only from within. Gonzalez tells us that the other day he met a pair of Americans visiting Oaxaca with the sole purpose of collecting seeds from wild agaves and taking them to California. They made no secret of the fact that they were planning on growing the agaves there to make an agave spirit. Agave spirits are now being bottled in India, Australia and the US and while these new products may recognise Mexico as the originator of the tradition, and they cannot use the word mezcal thanks to the DO, from Gonzalo's perspective they have taken a part of his culture – his family. "They think that the drink is alcohol," he says. "But it is not. This is something deeper."

Gonzalo believes that mezcal is in a war right now, fought across battle lines of economics, authenticity and identity. To that end he has written a book – the first to be

ABOVE Macurichos, where ancient agave lore meets holy spirit. In this peaceful palenque, Gonzalo Martinez distills liquid verses, each bottle a poem to the agave that made it.

penned by a mezcalero – called *Largo Trecho* (Long Walk) and describes the journey that his people and agaves have taken and the production of spirits in Oaxaca.

While Pancho and Gonzalo talk some more, Addie and I take a look around the palenque, armed with full glasses of Macurichos' blend of Tepeztate and Tobasiche (*Agave karwinskii*) magueys. *The aroma is like melon rinds, with light smoke, a touch of grapefruit, pineapple and salt. Slightly salty, spicy and dry. Parma ham and melon salad. It's perfumed, like olive oil and sea salt. Manzanilla sherry finish.*

Above the seven-tonne earthen pit-oven is a huge mural of the god Mayahuel. An ornate window sends a shaft of light down onto the stack of wood and rocks, as if the heavens are blessing the production of mezcal at El Sabino.

The agaves are of course milled in a tahona, then fermented in wooden vats, each of which has its name painted on its side in Zapotec. There are four copper alembic stills, but the stars of the show here are the clay pot-stills, each of them tiny and arranged like spiritual offerings with the rhythmic drip of mezcal from the carrizo tubes flowing like sacred water, a slow and steady baptism of the soul. There is something very special about this place and it reflects Gonzalo's spiritual nature.

While these clay pot-stills may look like something you would encounter in a Japanese Zen garden, they are as Mexican as they come. My mind is drawn back to the clay Capacha jars that Esteban introduced us to at Casa Endemica, and then to the illustrations I have seen taken from the Florentine Codex showing foaming clay jars of pulque. The only difference here is that this one is being heated and distilled.

Distillation is at the heart of all spirits' production and nowhere comes close to the diversity of stills we have seen in Mexico. Constructed from hollowed-out tree trunks, barrel staves, clay pots, and hammered metal, just as these still designs shape the unique character of the spirits they make, they also offer a fascinating exploration of technology and anthropology in the Americas.

Despite the vast range of distillation equipment we have seen, there are other still types that we have not encountered: Duranganese stills (made from wood, but instead of using an internal paddle are connected through a carrizo tube to a condenser coil, like an alembic still), Potosí stills (modelled after the Capacha pots with an internal collection vessel) and Huichol stills, which are like Potosí stills only they are buried underground.

The Huichol people are an indigenous group native to the Sierra Madre Occidental, inhabiting a small area on the borders between the states of Jalisco, Nayarit, Zacatecas and Durango. They are probably best known for their spiritual practices centred around the *peyote* cactus – the source of the psychoactive drug mescaline.

Norwegian explorer Carl Lumholtz first documented the Huichol still during his late 19th-century expeditions in Mexico. He noted its unique design, suggesting that their appearance was "so rustic that it implied pre-Columbian knowledge of distillation". This sparked scholarly debate about its origins and whether the Huichol people possessed a more ancient knowledge of distillation.

Then in 1937, two researchers exploring the technical evolution of distillation in Mongolia described Mongolian stills with internal receivers, which closely resembled the Huichol still. This came about at roughly the same time that the Capacha pots were discovered in Colima and prompted a re-evaluation of the Huichol still's origins, suggesting a possible transcontinental distillation tradition linking Asia to the Americas that predated Columbus.

To operate a Huichol still, you dig a small hole in the ground and light a fire. Then you lower in the base of the still, which is shaped like a lightbulb and would typically be made from a single piece of hand-moulded clay. Next you load the fermented agave in there and then build the head of the still on top. The head is made from thin, flexible materials like *zacate* (wild grass), pine-leaf cords, branches and trunks, all insulated with wet clay. Your collection vessel is then suspended in the head using agave-fibre cords.

On top of that goes the condenser, and the whole thing has mud and stones packed around it leaving only the condenser visible. With no oxygen, the fire goes out. But this doesn't matter as the heat is absorbed by the base of the still as it has nowhere else to go. Thus, the Huichol is a very efficient method of distillation. As everything is closed, no spirit cuts are made and the process is just left to run its course. Eventually everything cools down and when you lift the condensation dish off the top you should be presented with a collection vessel filled with alcohol.

One thing that all of these ancestral stills have in common is their size – they are small. These small designs are consistent with that of stills made and used in China during the Mongol period of the 13th and 14th centuries. Stills were designed to be small because they needed to be portable. Mongols moved around a lot and had a keen interest in portable still technology, because *kumiss* (fermented horse milk), their preferred drink, wouldn't last long, but distillation inside a yurt or tent allowed it to be enjoyed year-round. When these portable-still designs arrived in Mexico, they offered the perfect solution for thirsty colonial-era distillers who wanted to evade the Spanish authorities and pack up quickly and move elsewhere if the need arose. This may also have been why pits were so often preferred for cooking, fermenting and distilling, as they could easily be concealed and returned to at a later date, if necessary.

But how did these stills come to be in Mexico? One theory is that they were simply a regional interpretation of the Filipino still. But if this is true, the end result is strikingly similar to the stills being used by Mongols 700 years ago. The alternative seems too fantastical to even put into writing. As one anthropological study on proto-distillation in Mesoamerica put it, "The alcohol bridge that exists between Asia and America supports a hypothesis in a history that is yet to be written."

We return to the bar to find Pancho and Gonzalo still deep in conversation. Taking our glasses, Gonzalo leads us into the cellar where his mezcals are matured in glass, though "cellar" is a gross misclassification of this space. It is like a chapel, with an "altar" at the end and a congregation of hundreds of glass demijohns of mezcal. It is as holy a place as I have ever been, as the lingering scent of earth and agave hangs in the room like incense. There is a timelessness here, a sense that what happens in this room is more than just a process – it is a ritual, an act of devotion that connects past, present and future.

In the dim light, Gonzalo pours us a glass from one of the demijohns, a rare blend of Tepeztato and *Agave sanpedroensis* matured for a total of 13 years. I treat the liquid with all the respect of a holy communion. *The aroma is like light coconut water and aloe. The taste is soft and oily and the rising spice and heat. Then it becomes viscous, juicy and saline. More coconut through the finish, along with banana skin, black pepper and green papaya.*

Gonzalo picks up his book from the "altar" and, like a priest reading his sermon, offers to read us a passage. As he begins, his voice carries a new kind of weight, one that is even more sorrowful. And as Pancho translates, he matches the emotion of Gonzalo, who does not stop or slow down, as doing so he would in some way betray the sanctity of the words he is saying:

Mezcal is my refuge. It's my shelter.

I remember a few years ago, I was at a family reunion for a wedding. There's a tradition where all the relatives contribute something for the future. That day, some of us were given the task of gathering and grinding ingredients for the mole. We walked together to the grinding place, grinding cacao for the chocolate and for the mole.

On the way, our conversations were varied, but in Matatlán, you always end up talking about mezcal. The oldest among us asked a guy from another community who was engaged to a girl in town, "Your grandfather-in-law is building a palenque, right? Who's going to be in charge of it?" Without hesitation, the young man replied, "Me, I'll do it. Making mezcal is easy. I've seen it. You just throw the agaves in the fire, put it in the pot, light the fire, and that's it."

But the oldest one laughed and said, "Oh boy, don't believe that. There are people who've spent their whole lives making mezcal, and they still don't know a damn thing about it. To be a mezcalero, you need skill, love, passion, commitment and wisdom. Emotions and feelings are essential. They help you rise, to enjoy the spirit of the drink."

I really believe that. My whole life has been dedicated to understanding mezcal. It's my shelter. My life has been full of twists, like a hurricane, with critical moments that I've used to my advantage. At certain points, everything seemed to collapse, but I held on to my traditions.

I distil at night, when my emotions are most intense, under the shade of the night. The fire, the agave, and my feelings are all intertwined. Who hasn't tasted Macurichos jabalí or cuiche? At 55 degrees, those drinks are strong. But be careful when you drink them, because inside each sip lies all the sadness of my nights. It's a beautiful drink, but full of sorrow.

ABOVE Glass demijohns of mezcal sit patiently as they develop a complexity that only time can offer.

I swallow the mezcal and wipe a tear from my eye (strong drinks can do that to you) and feel a connection to the spirit that I'm drinking like I have never felt before. There's a connection to Gonzalo, but also to the plant and to the people that came before – the generations whose symbiotic relationship with the agave brought about mezcal. Not for money or for notoriety or even for flavour but simply because they were born to do it.

"Inside this distillate," says Gonzalo, raising his own glass. "Where they have had beautiful moments. Sad moments. Death, hunger. They have lived all the faces."

I wipe another tear away.

"El mezcal no te crea ni te destruye – solo te transforma," he says – "Mezcal cannot make or break you – it can only transform you."

EPILOGUE

At 32kg (70lbs) – the weight of a decent-sized agave piña – there really wasn't any way of avoiding the oversized luggage charge at Oaxaca airport. We had abandoned clothes, shoes, books, camera stands and other unnecessary items but the volume of mezcal and tequila was significant and non-negotiable. We paid the charges and headed through security into Oaxaca's tiny departure lounge.

Of the six stores in the lounge, three are selling mezcal. We have a couple of hours to spare so I take a look around. All of the brands are unknown to me – a reminder that this is a vast category of spirits. One of the stores has open bottles and sample cups and, with time to spare, I decide to try a few. The young man serving the mezcal doesn't speak English but by this point my Spanish is getting almost passable (particularly where matters of mezcal are concerned), so I listen and get the gist of what he is saying.

The first drink he gives me is a joven mezcal in a sturdy-looking bottle with a smart label. He pours me a sample and then tips the bottle to the side, pointing enthusiastically at the bottom corner and says *"tres gusano"*. Only then do I notice the three *gusano de maguey* ("agave worms") swimming around in the clear liquid. These creatures, which are not actually worms at all but a specific type of juvenile moth caterpillar, were once synonymous with mezcal.

The origins of worming mezcal are not entirely known. Some theories suggest it adds some flavour; others say it removes or purifies the flavour. One theory suggests that the gusano was added to prove the strength of the spirit, as a lower-proof alcohol would cause the larvae to rot. And, of course, there are those that believe that the gusano adds a psychotropic effect or somehow concentrates hallucinogenic properties into a neat package for those brave enough to indulge. In fact, the likely origin of the gusano goes back to the 1940s when Jacobo Lozano Paez, a former art student who turned into a mezcal producer, discovered that the gusano, which feeds on the maguey plant, altered the taste of the resulting spirit when it was made from agave roasted with worms inside. Inspired by this accidental discovery, Paez decided to incorporate the gusano directly into the finished bottles of mezcal.

It was a practice that stuck for a while and the worm wriggled its way so deeply into urban legend that it even cast a shadow over tequila, making it hard for anyone to think of Mexican spirits without imagining the infamous invertebrate lurking at the bottom of the bottle. In 1995, a group of mezcal producers launched a campaign to oust the worm from its bottle, citing concerns over authenticity and tradition. However, the move was met with resistance from other producers, who fretted that North American drinkers, having embraced the worm as a sign of the spirit's genuineness, would turn up their noses at wormless mezcal.

With the rise in premium mezcals from the early 2000s, the worm was slowly forgotten about and the fight to remove it became moot. Which is why I am surprised to see three worms in this bottle. Through all of our travels around Mexico, where we have tasted more than 500 products, I had not seen a gusano or given a second thought to one. And yet now, here I am, presented with three of them.

I sip the mezcal and I can hardly believe the taste. *It's insipid, watery, vodka-like and altogether devoid of character.* If the gusano were intended to improve the flavour of the mezcal, I would hate to have tried it before they were added. Moving on to the next bottle, which I am told is more premium as proven by the five gusano lurking around in the bottom. This also proves to be characterless and dull.

All of this comes as a bit of a wake-up call to me, spoiled as we have been.

I know that airports are not famous for sourcing the most artisanal products, but they do tend to stock a representative example of the local fare, albeit at an inflated cost. As travellers kill time in this departure lounge, these bottles of mezcal will be, for many, their last and maybe only encounter with agave spirits before they fly off to some other part of the world. They might tell their friends and family about them and draw conclusions about Mexican spirits based on them. They might even buy a bottle and take it with them, sharing the novelty of a bunch of worms in a bottle of mezcal.

But these products are awful.

I'm not saying they are awful merely because they taste bad (and they really do) or because they rely on perpetuating a nonsense practice of dropping insect larvae into the bottle as a misguided mark of quality (and they most certainly do) but because they fail to make any connection with the agave plant.

I have devoted a substantial amount of space in this book to addressing some of the challenges that mezcal, tequila and other regional agave spirits face. We have talked about ecology and the environment, sustainability and waste management, corporate interests and celebrity, community and cultural preservation, the economy and legislation. But this collection of sad gusano in their sterile tombs hit home to me the true scale of the challenge of identity that agave spirits face today.

How can a spirit so connected to its people and place but also racked by tired marketing tropes – and with budgets big enough to flaunt them in front of everyone who passes through the region – hope to resolve itself?

It begins with education.

If we are to support authentic producers, we have to start looking deeper into the production of these spirits and well beyond the classifications used by compromised certifying bodies. We need to be mindful of the plants that make these spirits, ensuring a sustainable future for farming and for the rich tapestry of agave species. We need to be respectful of the cultures that agave spirits originate from, acknowledging that making spirits for many of these people is not a process of manufacture or even craft, but rather an ancestral responsibility – a birthright – to the land and to the agave. And we need to ensure that farmers and producers are being paid fairly for their work.

While they may be diminutive in their proportions, the small tabernas, viñatas and palenques of Mexico remain large in number. Yet they represent a side of agave spirits' tradition that is absent from most books. History is written by the victor of course and "Big Tequila" has done an outstanding job of positioning wealthy Spanish families as the protagonists of this tale, neglecting to mention the ancestral stills and indigenous people that inspired production of mezcal in the Tequila valley in the first place.

On the contrary, these ancient sites of cultural tradition have suffered centuries of demonisation – for the claimed toxicity of their products, the primitive nature of their equipment and the low status of their craftspeople.

I am hopeful that we will see more regional agave spirits rising out of obscurity like vapours in a still and – to continue the analogy – become a potent representation of true Mexican spirit.

Regrettably we have not visited any *bacanora* producers on this trip, as the journey north to Sonora would no doubt have killed Pancho's car earlier than it did. *Bacanora*, named after a town whose Ópata name means "reed hillside", has become Sonora's most renowned distillate. With a 300-year history, it originally utilised various agave species but now exclusively uses *Agave angustifolia*, locally known as Pacifica or Yaquiana. In 2000, *bacanora* received a Denominación de Origen (DO), designating it as a uniquely Sonoran product from 35 municipalities. However, this DO, like all the rest, has faced criticism for potentially favouring commercialisation over traditional production methods.

Beyond tequila, mezcal, raicilla and bacanora, there is a hidden wealth of agave-spirit diversity here that neither this journey or this book – or perhaps any book – is long enough to address. Whether it's *bingarotte*, *chuchualco*, *comiteco*, *excomunión*, *huitzila*, *jarcia*, *sikua*, *tasequi*, *tauta*, *tlachuelompa*, *turicato*, *tuxca*, *zihiaquio* or *zotol*, all these spirits have their own unique stories and flavours. And who knows what other styles have been forgotten, erased or simply not yet discovered?

Fill your *copitas*, *jícaras* and *cuernos* to the brim and taste the spirit of culture, friends. Let's take the next step of the journey together, as to truly understand the range of possibility in the spirits that the world has conceived, you only really need to keep coming back to Mexico.

DRINKS

Besides sampling hundreds of neat spirits during our tour of Mexico, we drank more than our share of cocktails, too. The plethora of flavours summoned up during the production of agave spirits point to potential flavour pairings in mixed drinks that can amplify specific characteristics of the spirit and soften the burn of alcohol. We should not be precious about exploring and enjoying these drinks! The following pages include some classic tequila cocktails while also introducing new twists that we have enjoyed.

MARGARITA

Like most classic cocktails, the margarita has around half a dozen origin stories, none of which come with concrete evidence. In 1938, Carlos "Danny" Herrera, a bartender at Rancho La Gloria near Tijuana, is said to have created the Margarita for Marjorie King, a customer who could only drink tequila. In 1941, Don Carlos Orozco at Hussong's Cantina in Ensenada allegedly made the drink for Margarita Henkel, naming it after her. In 1948, Margarita Sames, a wealthy Dallas socialite, claimed she invented the cocktail at her Acapulco vacation home. Each story shares a common theme: tequila, lime and orange liqueur coming together in Mexican or border town settings to create a refreshing cocktail for a specific patron or occasion. One thing that seems clear is that the margarita evolved from the "Daisy" family of cocktails which go back well into the 19th century and comprised spirit, citrus and sweetener usually in the form of maraschino (cherry) liqueur, grenadine, or orange curaçao.

For preparation, the margarita is unique in its use of a salt rim. It isn't essential for the cocktail to work, but if you are using salt it is imperative to use flakes rather than fine table salt, as they tend to be softer in their delivery and more pleasing on the lips. A classic 2:1:1 ratio of tequila, curaçao and lime juice is a versatile template, adaptable to most brand combinations, but you can dial any of the components up or down.

40ML/1¹/₃ OZ RESERVA DE LOS GONZALEZ BLANCO
20ML/²/₃ OZ CURAÇAO
20ML/²/₃ OZ FRESH LIME JUICE

Shake all the ingredients with ice and strain into a chilled coupe glass. Salt rim optional.

BATANGA

The drink made famous by Don Javier at La Capilla might sound too simple to be true, but it delivers on every level and reminds us that tequila can perform well in long drinks as well as short.

Mexico loves Coca-Cola almost as much as tequila. The average Mexican drinks around 500ml (17 oz) of the stuff per day – the highest in the world – but in some regions, it's closer to two litres a day (half a gallon). Consumption is higher in poorer areas, ironically, because bottled sodas are considered the healthier choice over potentially contaminated municipal water. Coca-Cola has aggressively marketed in Mexico for years, many shop fronts have effectively becoming Coke billboards, the national football team is sponsored by Coke, their red trucks are a constant presence on the roads, and empty Coke bottles constitute a high percentage of the street litter. The overconsumption of Coke has contributed to the obesity and diabetes crisis that Mexico now faces.

All that said, I'd be lying if I said I'm not partial to a Coke myself.
But as with tequila, I try to enjoy it responsibly.

50ML/1¾ OZ EL TEQUILEÑO TEQUILA (the house pour at La Capilla)
20ML/⅔ OZ FRESH LIME JUICE
TOP UP WITH COCA-COLA

Salt the rim of a highball glass, add plenty of ice and all of the ingredients and stir. Serve with a lime wedge. If you can (and please accept my apologies because you probably can't), try to get hold of Mexican Coca-Cola. It's made using cane sugar instead of high-fructose corn syrup, and in blind tastings has been shown to be the tastiest cola variant.

TOMMY'S

The Tommy's margarita is a simple variation – and most agree, improvement – on the classic margarita, made famous by Julio Bermejo of Tommy's Bar in San Francisco. Julio began working at Tommy's in the 1980s and at that time the margarita on the menu had switched out triple sec for sugar syrup, probably because it was cheaper to make. Julio worked to elevate the quality of the drink, changing the mixto tequila for 100% agave in the form of Herradura and later introducing agave nectar in place of the sugar syrup. It didn't end there though. Most of the margaritas served at Tommy's in the 1980s were blended and made with cheap sour mix, but over the ten years that followed Julio's arrival he slowly instigated a shift towards serving them on the rocks and with no salt rim. By the end of the 1990s, all the pieces had come together to produce an on the rocks margarita made with 100% agave tequila, fresh lime and agave nectar – the ultimate expression of the drink.

The Tommy's is now a legitimate modern classic, and well know across the US, Europe and beyond. It's not so well known in Mexico, however. Which is why I was surprised to be served one in Morelia of all places at a tiny back-street bar, which you'd hesitate to take your mother too. No sooner had we entered than Pancho had befriended the bartender, howling with laughter at some joke we didn't catch while Addie took shots of the peeling turquoise walls and the dim light from the worn lampshade. The bartender, a young but weathered man with a wide grin, set a drink in front of me. "Margarita," he said. "Like Julio Bermejo makes it."

I distinctly remember the sound of Lola Beltrán's version of "Cucurrucucú Paloma" drifting softly from an old jukebox in the corner. It was one of those moments – where the simple combination of good company, a perfectly imperfect drink, and music rooted deep in Mexican culture makes everything feel right.

50ML/1¾ OZ BLANCO TEQUILA
25ML/¾ OZ FRESH LIME JUICE
12.5ML/½ OZ AGAVE NECTAR

Add all of the ingredients to a rocks glass and stir until the agave nectar is fully dissolved. Then add plenty of cubed ice and stir some more. Garnish with a wedge of lime or, if you have one, a little agave *penca*.

PALOMA

The magical transformation of the agave into a blanco tequila brings about many interesting flavours, but grapefruit has to be one of the most common. Sometimes it's a bitter, pithy note, other times it's like grapefruit candy, sherbet or salt. So we would be mad not to mix the spirit with grapefruit, which has the effect of taming the alcohol while maintaining the flavour of spirit.

When making a Paloma, my preference towards fresh grapefruit juice versus Squirt (in the UK the best alternative is Ting) is really one of circumstance. Real grapefruit juice makes this exceedingly light drink just a little heavier. It's less sweet too, and the bitterness it brings forces me to take my time a little. The ease with which Squirt can be consumed makes the grapefruit-soda version ultra-palatable and the ease with which it can be made is dangerous too. I do think a decent squeeze of lime is essential for the Squirt version of the drink, however, as it balances some of the sweetness.

Whichever version you opt for, very few cocktails can challenge the
Paloma for outdoor, summer sipping prowess.

40ML/1$\frac{1}{3}$ OZ DON ABRAHAM BLANCO
80ML/2$\frac{2}{3}$ OZ FRESH PINK GRAPEFRUIT JUICE
80ML/2$\frac{2}{3}$ OZ TOPO CHICO SODA WATER

Add all of the ingredients to a tall glass filled with ice cubes and briefly stir.
Finish with a grapefruit wedge.

SANGRITA

Originally the sangrita was made from the leftover juices from pico de gallo salsa, which varies from place to place, but is typically made using tomato, onion, lime, salt and chilli. The salt causes the juices to leach out of the ingredients and you end up with an intensely flavoured liquid at the bottom of the bowl. Rather than waste it, someone came up with the idea of sipping it alongside a tequila and the sangrita (the diminutive form of *sangre*, meaning "blood") was born.

A sangrita is therefore traditionally served in a small glass alongside a shot of tequila, with the two being sipped alternately. This combination allows the drinker to appreciate the contrasting yet somehow harmonious flavours of the tequila and the sangrita. To be honest, this is how I fell in love with drinking tequila in my twenties. I found that the sangrita refreshed the palate wonderfully between each sip and thus elevated the character of the agave in the spirit. Also, if your sangrita is especially spicy, the tequila can even serve as the antidote to the heat! There's also something to be said for a ceremony in drinking – something that demands an order or process to the imbibing – and this one beats any slammer or salt-and-lime ritual every time.

Because salsas vary so much in their preparation, the sangrita does too. I would say that chilli, lime and salt are essential but that basically anything else goes. Redness used to be a requirement, which was typically achieved via tomato juice, Clamato juice or, my preference, fresh pomegranate juice. Some people like to put orange juice in there too, and more recently we have started to see green sangritas, which can include cucumber, celery, apple, pineapple and fresh coriander (cilantro) in their recipes. The most important rule, however, is that the sangrita is fresh.

400ML/13½ OZ FRESH POMEGRANATE JUICE
200ML/6¾ OZ FRESH ORANGE JUICE
100ML/3⅓ OZ FRESH LIME JUICE
50ML/1¾ OZ AGAVE NECTAR
CHILLI POWDER, TO YOUR TASTE
LARGE PINCH OF SALT

MAKES 750ML/25 OZ

YERBA BUENA

This cocktail is one of the most popular drinks at Pancho's bar, Farmacia Rita Perez, in Guadalajara. The cocktail is along the same lines as a Mojito, except instead of using fresh mint in the glass, Mexicans make a mint syrup. To do this, they infuse mint and sugar into hot water for an hour, which makes a bright-green mint cordial. Pancho is vague on exactly how they do this, but my suggestion would be to put the ingredients in a Kilner-style jar and pop it in a hot pan for a couple of hours. In this case, I'm making it on the electric hob in the kitchen. You need a lot of mint, and the trick is not to cook it so hot or for so long that the water turns brown.

Once you have your mint syrup you then shake it with ice and the spirit of your choosing plus lime juice. They serve the drink in a Chabela goblet, which is just about the heaviest piece of glassware that I have ever encountered. Think Belgian beer glass but five times as thick. These are more popularly used for shrimp cocktail and serving desserts like ice cream, and anything else where the glass needs to withstand the impact of a metal spoon.

Once poured, the drink is topped up with soda water.

MEZCAL MARTINI

If the raw power of a Oaxacan mezcal sounds out of place to you in a drink renowned for its soft, botanical character, you're not alone in your thinking. I was also sceptical about whether mezcal belongs in a martini cocktail – that was until we visited Selva, a world-class bar in Oaxaca with a sort of Great Gatsby, Roaring Twenties feel about it. If that doesn't sound very Oaxaca, it isn't, but the bar team have Mexican charm in spades and know how to have a good time. We were fortunate to get seats at the bar and, after taking direction from the bartender, we watched him pour mezcal into a mixing glass, stirring it smoothly with dry vermouth. He strained the pale, almost clear liquid into a martini glass, finishing it with a twist of lime peel.

There's no denying the mezcal's smoky character in this cocktail, which hits immediately, but it's softened by the cool, herbal notes of the vermouth. It's clean and crisp, with just enough heat from the mezcal to remind me where we are. It's not as clean as a classic martini, but it has its own elegance, and a kind of wild sophistication.

60ML/2 OZ MEZCAL
20ML/2/3 OZ DRY VERMOUTH

Add the ingredients to a mixing beaker or shaker and stir with ice cubes for at least a minute. Strain into a chilled coupe or martini glass (preferably from the freezer) and then zest a small disc of lime peel over the top.

TEQUILA & TONIC

Tonic water is not just for gin and can be used to great effect to uncover fruit, herb and spice flavours in a spirit. Distillation does not typically carry any taste attributes over — sugar, acids and bitterness are left in the still — and tonic, with its unique combination of bitter, sweet and acid, steps in and reintroduces them. You could say it is reconstructing the taste and flavour of the base material.

For tequila, this usual means elevating notes of grapefruit and lime and other citrus characteristics that are inherent to the spirits. If you opt for a raicilla or mezcal you might find greener, bitter, vegetal flavours being emphasised and even notes of caramelised agave coming through.

You can switch the garnish based on the flavours that the combination emphasises, but grapefruit, lime, pineapple and sliced tamarind are all great options.

50ML/1¾ OZ OCHO TEQUILA
TOP UP WITH TONIC WATER

Fill a highball glass with ice, add the tequila and tonic water and stir.
Garnish with a strip of grapefruit peel.

COCONUT WATER

Coconut water is seen by most of us as a health drink, so perhaps not the obvious choice for mixing with agave spirits. That said, why not take the antidote and the poison at the same time?

You won't regret it, as coconut water has an almost supernatural ability to mix with spirits. There's something about that gentle salty sweetness, and of course the slightly fungal, slightly nutty, coconut flavour that seems to pair brilliantly with every spirit, but particularly whisky, rum and agave spirits. A squeeze of lime is all that's needed to really set it off. This combination is particularly effective with raicilla, where the cheesy character of mountain raicilla brings about a certain New York-cheesecake character when paired with the coconut and lime.

A LIME
50ML/1¾ OZ AYCYA ANCESTRAL RAICILLA
200ML/6¾ OZ COCONUT WATER

Cut the lime in half and squeeze one half into a glass filled with ice along with the raicilla and coconut water. Stir well and top up with more ice if needed. Garnish with the remaining half of the lime.

Take a sip and then start making more – you're going to want them.

MEZCAL CAFÉ

Espresso martini recipes often require a coffee liqueur as an ingredient. This makes little sense, however, as an espresso martini is effectively a homemade coffee liqueur: spirit + coffee + sugar. Adding the liqueur will increase the sweetness, alcohol content and coffee-ness of the drink, which can be done by simply adding a more concentrated form of sugar, alcohol or coffee to your recipe. This also makes the drink inherently customisable, as with fewer ingredients and fewer dials to turn, it's much easier to tune to your preferred ratio.

You can use any agave spirit for this cocktail, whether it be a nice, smoky mezcal, a herbal or floral raicilla, or a fresh and clean tequila. Aged products also work really well. For the sugar component, table sugar or sugar syrup will suffice, but why not use agave nectar if some is available. Couple that with some Mexican coffee and you have an entirely Mexican riff on what was originally a drink made with Swedish vodka and Italian coffee – invented in London.

Whatever coffee you use, you will need to brew it strong to get the necessary punch in the final drink (remember it is being diluted by the spirit and the melted ice). Espresso is ideal, but a strong brew in a mocha pot or cafetière also works. Aim for a brew ratio of five parts water to one part coffee. Brew it fresh if you can, or brew in advance and store in the fridge for up to 24 hours.

You can also premix the entire drink and store it in the fridge, then shake to serve. It will lose a little of its trademark foamy head (caused by dissolved CO_2 in the brewing process) if you do that, though.

50ML/1¾ OZ TESORO DEL OESTE RAICILLA
30ML/1 OZ STRONG COFFEE
15ML/½ OZ AGAVE NECTAR

Shake all of the ingredients with ice and strain into a clay cup.
Garnish with cinnamon and/or nutmeg.

CANTARITO

The Cantarito takes its name from the clay pots that are used to serve it, which are a mini version of the Spanish *cántaro* (pitcher). These terracotta pots hail from Jalisco and were originally used for collecting and storing water. Today they are used to serve up everything from tequila to pulque and micheladas and are usually stacked five high on the bar top. They are commonly sold at roadsides too, often with some tourist-attracting text or iconography emblazoned on the side. The clay cup is more than just a marketing gimmick, however – its thick walls actually help to keep the drink cooler for longer in Jalisco's warm climate. This isn't unique to Mexico; clay vessels are also used in Cuba for their oldest cocktail: the Canchánchara.

One of the interesting things about the Cantarito is that there is no universally accepted recipe for it. It's typically made with tequila, grapefruit, lime and orange juices, though some versions use other juices, like mandarin or hibiscus. Many are rimmed with the spicy–sour seasoning brand called Tajín, and some add chamoy, a pickled fruit and chilli sauce not a million miles from a chutney. Some Cantaritos even have beer in them, like this one.

50ML/1¾ OZ EL TEQUILEÑO BLANCO
50ML/1¾ OZ FRESH GRAPEFRUIT JUICE
50ML/1¾ OZ FRESH ORANGE JUICE
25ML/¾ OZ FRESH LIME JUICE
20ML/⅔ OZ AGAVE NECTAR
150ML/5 OZ COLD MEXICAN BEER

Add all of the ingredients to a clay cup (soak the clay cup in cold water for 10 minutes before mixing your drink to ensure it stays icy) or any large-handled mug, with plenty of ice. Stir, then garnish with citrus slices. This drink works very well as a punch too, where you can make it en masse and ladle it into mugs as needed.

DISTRITO FEDERAL

Not the catchiest of names, but the drink itself will grab you by the collar and pull you into a *lucho libre* grapple hold. As it is a twist on the classic Manhattan cocktail, the Distrito Federal is named after Mexico City's official designation. Like the Manhattan, it is best suited for late-night consumption in some dimly lit bar, where the low hum of conversation amid candlelight and the soft clink of glasses sets the mood. You can use blanco or reposado tequila if you wish, but this is one of the best uses for an añejo where, alongside the sweet vermouth and grapefruit bitters, you get a cocktail that exudes warmth but also energy. The Distrito Federal honours Mexico's traditions while embracing the cosmopolitan allure of a refined cocktail culture – ideal for those who appreciate the depth and richness that tequila brings to a classic.

50ML/1¾ OZ DON FULANO AÑEJO
25ML/¾ OZ ITALIAN VERMOUTH
1 DASH GRAPEFRUIT BITTERS

Stir all of the ingredients with ice for a minute and then strain into a chilled coupe glass. Garnish with a strip of orange or some dried pineapple.

MEZCALITA

A mezcalita is simply a margarita with tequila switched out for mezcal. It wasn't a drink that I was particularly fond of until our Mexican road trip, but now holds a special place in my heart after we polished off an entire bottle of mezcal in a little over an hour using this drink as the delivery mechanism. It was one of those days where, despite tasting mezcal all day, we were thirsty for more when we got back to our apartment in Oaxaca City. A couple of bottles are cracked open, the music turned up, and looking to hydrate with more than just Corona, our attention turns to cocktails.

Addie juices limes with an old Mexican elbow (a handy squeezer) we picked up at the market while Pancho belts out a ranchero song, his voice carrying out of the window and no doubt through other people's windows. Along with the lime juice and a quarter bottle of mezcal, we add a splash of Naranjo orange liqueur. The mezcal's aroma, robust and dusty, mixes with the bright citrus, and the kitchen smells like a palenque. I shake the cocktail with ice and give each of us each a generous serving. The liquid is cloudy and pale, promising that perfect balance of vegetal, sweet and citrus. The drink is bold and earthy, but then it softens into the fresh brightness of lime and the sweet orange notes from the liqueur. It's familiar, but with that distinctive edge mezcal brings – wilder than a regular margarita. Knowing where this was going, I mix the next round as Pancho raises his drink high, still singing, while wandering onto the terrace in his underwear and sunglasses to serenade the fading day.

50ML/1¾ OZ MEZCAL
25ML/¾ OZ NARANJO LIQUEUR OR TRIPLE SEC (COINTREAU)
20ML/⅔ OZ FRESH LIME JUICE

Take a piece of fresh lime and wipe it around the rim of a coupe glass. Dip the outside edge of the glass into a dish of sea-salt flakes. Then shake all of the ingredients with ice and strain into the glass.

MEZCAL NEGRONI

On one of our nights in Oaxaca, we spent half an hour walking around in circles in search of a mezcalería that Pancho has heard about. We eventually found it, hidden down an alley, the entrance unmarked except for a dimly lit red door. Inside, the air hums with low conversation; the scent of wood and smoke hang thick in the room. The only light comes from flickering candles on each table, casting long shadows that dance across the faces of the patrons. It was a place dedicated to the consumption of serious drinks, so we ordered a round of mezcal negronis.

The familiar deep crimson liquid of the drink conceals a different kind of cocktail to the original gin version of the drink. Campari hits, quickly followed by the earthy, smoky, vegetal warmth of the mezcal. Gin has a habit of getting lost in a Negroni, but you'll do well to misplace a large measure of mezcal in any cocktail. The sweet vermouth rounds it out, adding a hint of richness that lingers on the palate. If you like intensely flavoured cocktails such as a negroni, then this twist will take it to the next level. I'd love to tell you the name of the bar, but multiple rounds of Mezcal Negronis filed the memories amongst the boozy mists of forgotten things – where all the best nights are remembered. Here's my homage to what I can recall.

30ML/1 OZ MEZCAL
30ML/1 OZ CAMPARI
30ML/1 OZ SWEET VERMOUTH

Add all of the ingredients to a mixing beaker or shaker with plenty of ice and stir for a minute.
Strain into a rocks glass filled with ice and finish with a slice or orange or lime.

FAUSTINA

The origins of this cocktail date back more than 30 years to one Don Fausto de la Torre, who was the local distributor of Pepsi products in Tolimán in southern Jalisco. Back then, it was customary for businesses to close on Thursday and Saturday afternoons, when social gatherings would form among the merchants of the town. Don Fausto took the opportunity to conduct some product sampling and created a cocktail containing local red plum nectar, lemon, salt, agave spirit and lemonade. Soon he ended up doing guest shifts in canteens and bars in the region and the drink became a local hit. Now for almost 30 years, the San Gabriel Cultural Festival has included the Faustina cocktail competition, in which residents are given the chance to make their own spin on the drink.

This has caused all sorts of new variants to emerge, including ones that contain Pepsi, Squirt, Topo Chico, aloe vera juice, coconut and orange juice. The cocktail is effectively a local punch with the only necessary ingredients being agave spirit, citrus and plum. My version uses chopped dates in place of plum to add a sweet and earthy quality.

3 PITTED DATES, CHOPPED
50ML/1¾ OZ INDIO ALONSO TUXCA AGAVE SPIRIT
100ML/3⅓ OZ FRESH ORANGE JUICE
TOPO CHICO (OR OTHER SODA WATER)

Add the chopped dates to a wine glass and pour a splash of hot water over them. Let them infuse for a few minutes. Then add the Tuxca, orange juice and plenty of ice. Stir well and then top up with soda water.

BLOODY MARIA

The Bloody Maria is the bold, fiery cousin of the classic Bloody Mary, swapping vodka for tequila (or better still, mezcal) and infusing the drink with Mexican flair. When you consider that both tomatoes and chilli are native to Central America, using agave spirits as the base of this drink makes fare more sense than vodka. Brimming with flavour, the combination of earthy, smoky mezcal with tomato juice, lime, and a kick of spice from hot sauce, makes it a taste of Mexico in a glass. It's great for late-morning brunches or lazy weekends, when the sun is high and you crave something savoury with a bite.

This is traditionally served in a tall glass, such as a highball, and garnished with a salted rim, fresh lime wedge, and perhaps a fresh chilli wedged into the top of the glass. The drink's flavours also make it an ideal pairing with Mexican breakfast dishes like chilaquiles or huevos rancheros.

50ML/1¾ OZ DON MATEO MEZCAL (OR ANY SMOKY MEZCAL)
200ML/6¾ OZ TOMATO JUICE
30ML/1 OZ FRESH LIME JUICE
15ML/½ OZ AGAVE NECTAR
VALENTINA HOT SAUCE, TO TASTE
PINCH OF SEA SALT

Add all of the ingredients to a highball glass filled with ice and stir. Garnish with a fresh chilli, cucumber spear, heritage tomatoes and sprinkle some chilli powder over the top.

MEZCAL SERVE

We tasted hundreds of mezcals on our journey through Mexico, served in a variety of vessels from disposable coffee cups to sawn-in-half coke bottles, crystal tumblers and fruit shells. The important thing to note is that the serve should match the occasion, but also that mezcal should be enjoyed any way you like to enjoy it.

In Oaxaca, it's customary to serve it in small ceramic cups that come in sets so there is a nice ritualistic component to sharing a small serving with friends. Once again, that seems to play on the spiritual aspect of this incredible drink.

The thickness of the cups also provides the benefit of being resilient to being knocked about in the bottom of a backpack – an important feature, as portability of serviceware is crucial when you're visiting fields and remote palenques. Some of the cups even come with a travel case.

Personally, I drink my mezcal at the strength it was bottled at and neat, with no ice and never chilled. But that's just me. Agave spirits are not judgemental, and you are free to explore different approaches to enjoying mezcal in whatever way you please.

INDEX

ACKNOWLEDGEMENTS

This book is dedicated to Francisco "Pancho" Castillon, who not only organised and executed our crazy road trip, but who brought the passion and depth of Mexican culture to life on an hourly basis. I cannot imagine a better ambassador for the Mexican spirit than you, cabrón.

And my thanks, of course, to the third member of our party, Addie Chinn, whose keen eye has captured the magic of our time in Mexico perfectly.

Thanks, as always, the dream team at RPS and beyond: Nathan, who has now edited eight books in this series, Geoff who has designed all nine, and Julia and Leslie, who are really the linchpins that make all of this happen and have been from the start – it's great to have the old band back together!

I am grateful for the time and patience offered to us by the many people we met in Mexico. I appreciate every one of you, but would particularly like to thank Rolando Cortés, Sophie Decobecq, Esteban Morales, Sergio Mendoza, Jaime Orendain, the Partida family, Andres Cruz, Miguel Perez, Guillermo Sauza and Stefano Francavilla.

Thanks also to Steffin Oghene – for helping me to see that this was possible in the first place.

To the late Tomas Estes for his contribution to the tequila category and for personally inspiring me – I hope that some of your infectious spirit has found its way into this book.

Finally, to my family: Laura, Dexter and Robin, for tolerating me both at home and away and supporting the book with love.